MAKING ADMINISTRATIVE WORK VISIBLE

MAKING ADMINISTRATIVE WORK VISIBLE

Data-Driven Advocacy for Understanding the Labor of Writing Program Administration

EDITED BY
LEIGH GRAZIANO,
KAY HALASEK,
REMI HUDGINS,
SUSAN MILLER-COCHRAN,
FRANK NAPOLITANO,
AND NATALIE SZYMANSKI

UTAH STATE UNIVERSITY PRESS
Logan

© 2023 by University Press of Colorado

Published by Utah State University Press
An imprint of University Press of Colorado
245 Century Circle, Suite 202
Louisville, Colorado 80027

All rights reserved

 The University Press of Colorado is a proud member of the Association of University Presses.

The University Press of Colorado is a cooperative publishing enterprise supported, in part, by Adams State University, Colorado State University, Fort Lewis College, Metropolitan State University of Denver, University of Alaska Fairbanks, University of Colorado, University of Denver, University of Northern Colorado, University of Wyoming, Utah State University, and Western Colorado University.

ISBN: 978-1-64642-446-7 (hardcover)
ISBN: 978-1-64642-363-7 (paperback)
ISBN: 978-1-64642-364-4 (ebook)
https://doi.org/10.7330/9781646423644

Library of Congress Cataloging-in-Publication Data

Names: Graziano, Leigh, editor. | Halasek, Kay, editor. | Hudgins, Remi, editor. | Miller-Cochran, Susan K., editor. | Napolitano, Frank M., editor. | Szymanski, Natalie, editor.
Title: Making administrative work visible : data-driven advocacy for understanding the labor of writing program administration / edited by Leigh Graziano, Kay Halasek, Remi Hudgins, Susan Miller-Cochran, Frank Napolitano, and Natalie Szymanski.
Description: Logan : Utah State University Press, [2023] | Includes bibliographical references and index.
Identifiers: LCCN 2022061224 (print) | LCCN 2022061225 (ebook) | ISBN 9781646423637 (paperback) | ISBN 9781646424467 (hardcover) | ISBN 9781646423637 (ebook)
Subjects: LCSH: Writing centers—Administration. | Writing centers—Research. | Academic writing—Study and teaching (Higher) | College administrators—Vocational guidance. | College administrators—Workload.
Classification: LCC PE1404 .M354 2023 (print) | LCC PE1404 (ebook) | DDC 808.02071/1—dc23/eng/20230207
LC record available at https://lccn.loc.gov/2022061224
LC ebook record available at https://lccn.loc.gov/2022061225

The editors wish to acknowledge The Ohio State University College of Arts and Sciences, Division of Arts and Humanities Small Grants Program, and its award of a Publication Subvention Grant to support production of this volume.

Cover illustration: Cathedral Window Quilt by Viola Canady. From the Anacostia Community Museum Collection (https://www.si.edu/object/cathedral-window-quilt: acm_1995.5009.0003). Public domain image.

CONTENTS

Alternative Table of Contents   ix

Foreword
Seth Kahn   xiii

Introduction: Making Work Visible Work through Data-Informed Advocacy
   Leigh Graziano, Kay Halasek, Remi Hudgins, Susan Miller-Cochran, Frank Napolitano, and Natalie Szymanski   3

PART I: ADVOCATING THROUGH REPRESENTATIONS OF WPA LABOR

1. Nothing New: Systemic Invisibility, Epistemological Exclusion, and Faculty and Administrators of Color
   Sheila Carter-Tod   27

2. Teacher, Manager, Developer, Advocate: Representations of Work in WPA
   Kristine Johnson   39

3. Revising the Terminology and Frames around WPA Work to Uncover Networks of Sites of Writing Administration
   Jill Gladstein   58

4. The Value of Mentoring in Writing Program Administration
   Kimberly Emmons and Martha Wilson Schaffer   76

5. Naming What We Feel: Self-Dialogue as a Strategy for Negotiating Emotional Labor in WPA Work
   Kristi Murray Costello and Kate Navickas   91

PART 2: ADVOCATING BY ACCOUNTING FOR TIME AND LABOR

6. Trading Time: Communicating Grand Strategy to Stakeholders through Hour Tracking
   Ryan J. Dippre 109

7. Theorizing Programmatic Assessment as a Site of Visibility of WPA Intellectual Work
   Lilian W. Mina 120

8. Making Administration's Exchange Value Visible
   Heather M. Robinson 132

9. Invisible Labor: Tracking Email Practices in WPA Work
   Angela Mitchell and Jan Rieman 151

10. Opportunity Lost: Failing to Make Administrative Work Visible
    Brooke Anderson 162

11. Weighing down the Body: Quantifying the Nature of Antiracist Work
    Patti Poblete 175

PART 3: ADVOCATING IN AND THROUGH COMPLEX INSTITUTIONAL CONTEXTS

12. Institutional Matters: The (In)Visibility of Localized WPA Labor
    Michael Neal, Katelyn Stark, Amy Cicchino, Michael Healy, and Kamila Albert 185

13. Labor and Loneliness of the Multilingual WPA
    Greer Murphy and Troy Mikanovich 203

14. Conceptualizing Time in Hybrid and Online Writing Instruction and Program Administration
    Jennifer M. Cunningham, Natalie Stillman-Webb, Lyra Hilliard, and Mary K. Stewart 217

15. Community College WPAs Creating Change through Advocacy
    Lizbett Tinoco 230

16. Heavy Lifting: How WPAs Broker Knowledge Transfer for Faculty
    Lisa Tremain   240

17. Building an Antiracist WAC Program
    Genevieve García de Müeller and Ana Cortés Lagos   253

18. Making Research Methods Visible through the Alternative Table of Contents
    Caleb Lee González   264

Afterword
    Rita Malenczyk   277

Index   281
About the Authors   299

ALTERNATIVE TABLE OF CONTENTS

QUANTITATIVE DATA COLLECTION METHODS

Descriptive/Document Analysis
    Making Administration's Exchange Value Visible
        Heather M. Robinson   132

Big Data/Data Analytics
    Revising the Terminology and Frames around WPA Work to Uncover Networks of Sites of Writing Administration
        Jill Gladstein   58

Topic Modeling Algorithms
    Teacher, Manager, Developer, Advocate: Representations of Work in WPA
        Kristine Johnson   39

Corpus Analysis
    Teacher, Manager, Developer, Advocate: Representations of Work in WPA
        Kristine Johnson   39

Hour Tracking
    Trading Time: Communicating Grand Strategy to Stakeholders through Hour Tracking
        Ryan J. Dippre   109

QUALITATIVE DATA COLLECTION METHODS

Surveys
    Revising the Terminology and Frames around WPA Work to Uncover Networks of Sites of Writing Administration
        Jill Gladstein   58

Interviews
    Labor and Loneliness of the Multilingual WPA
        Greer Murphy and Troy Mikanovich   203

Theorizing Programmatic Assessment as a Site of Visibility of WPA Intellectual Work
Lilian W. Mina   120

Conceptualizing Time in Hybrid and Online Writing Instruction and Program Administration
Jennifer M. Cunningham, Natalie Stillman-Webb, Lyra Hilliard, and Mary K. Stewart   217

Literature Review
Nothing New: Systemic Invisibility, Epistemological Exclusion, and Faculty and Administrators of Color
Sheila Carter-Tod   27

Coding
Revising the Terminology and Frames around WPA Work to Uncover Networks of Sites of Writing Administration
Jill Gladstein   58

Trading Time: Communicating Grand Strategy to Stakeholders through Hour Tracking
Ryan J. Dippre   109

Opportunity Lost: Failing to Make Administrative Work Visible
Brooke Anderson   162

Ethnomethodology
Trading Time: Communicating Grand Strategy to Stakeholders through Hour Tracking
Ryan J. Dippre   109

Narrative/Storytelling/Self-Reflection
The Value of Mentoring in Writing Program Administration
Kimberly Emmons and Martha Wilson Schaffer   76

Naming What We Feel: Self-Dialogue as a Strategy for Negotiating Emotional Labor in WPA Work
Kristi Murray Costello and Kate Navickas   91

Building an Antiracist WAC Program
Genevieve García de Müeller and Ana Cortés Lagos   253

Case Study
Institutional Matters: The (In)Visibility of Localized WPA Labor
Michael Neal, Katelyn Stark, Amy Cicchino, Michael Healy, and Kamila Albert   185

MIXED METHOD APPROACHES

Explanatory Sequential Design
    Invisible Labor: Tracking Email Practices in WPA Work
        Angela Mitchell and Jan Rieman   151

Survey & Semi-Structured Interviews
    Community College WPAs Creating Change Through Advocacy
        Lizbett Tinoco   230

Open-Coding & Semi-Structured Interviews
    Heavy Lifting: How WPAs Broker Knowledge Transfer for Faculty
        Lisa Tremain   240

Research Methodological Scoping & Syllabi Review
    Making Research Methods Visible Through the Alternative Table of Contents
        Caleb Lee González   264

THEORETICAL FRAMEWORK METHODS

Antiracism
    Nothing New: Systemic Invisibility, Epistemological Exclusion, and Faculty and Administrators of Color
        Sheila Carter-Tod   27

    Weighing down the Body: Quantifying the Nature of Antiracist Work
        Patti Poblete   175

    Building an Antiracist WAC Program
        Genevieve García de Müeller and Ana Cortés Lagos   253

Thingification
    Trading Time: Communicating Grand Strategy to Stakeholders through Hour Tracking
        Ryan J. Dippre   109

Marxist Theory
    Making Administration's Exchange Value Visible
        Heather M. Robinson   132

FOREWORD

Seth Kahn

Historically, writing program administration (WPA) scholarship has focused largely (not exclusively, but largely) on how to do WPA work more effectively: solve problems more efficiently, engage the practices of the position more robustly, respond to macro- and micro-level politics more adroitly. In contrast, informal conversations on listservs and social media frame many of those problems as labor problems, and *Making Administrative Work Visible* is an important step in bridging the gap between those two lines of thinking—notice that the book's title uses both.

I see the terms *work* and *labor* differently, even if they describe the same activities. In simplest terms, work refers to behaviors or practices—observing TAs, writing assessment reports, scheduling, hiring, and more. Labor refers to those practices when compensation, evaluation, renewal, discipline, and termination are layered onto them. While many scholars and researchers use the terms more flexibly (including participants in this book), I think it's important to distinguish them at least as a heuristic because on the whole, while WPA research hasn't been inattentive to labor, I do think it's been much more focused on how to do the work well.

A skim of the *WPA: Writing Program Administration* journal since about 2010 shows a heavy emphasis on improving the practices of WPA work: placement programs/protocols, TA/teacher training and professional development, institutional advocacy, record keeping and program archives, implementing curriculum and pedagogy of various kinds, a special issue on ableism and updating/redesigning programs to account for varying abilities, evaluation regimens/practices, and more. More recently, increased and welcome attention has been given to identity (of WPAs and the students and instructors who populate our programs), as well as some attention to the macro-politics of higher education and how they influence WPA work/labor. Beyond the journal, we continue to publish books that address many of these same problems and are welcome additions to the research and scholarship on how to do better.

The chapters in this book will certainly help WPAs do the work better; the research presented here informs practices in rich and complex ways. Most important, it puts those practices and the people who do them unapologetically in the context of labor: analyses of working conditions, institutional authority, credit (toward tenure, promotions, reappointments) for the time and difficulty of what we do, evaluations of WPA work and its impacts on career trajectory, and more. By posing its central problems as labor problems, *Making Administrative Work Visible* provides usefully concrete data and models for other WPAs to document one's own labor; in doing so, it acts in its totality as a model for *making labor visible* to WPAs and other decision-makers outside one's informal networks.

This book responds to three calls—two of which are made frequently and the other of which didn't get made explicitly. In the way WPAs often do, the editors and contributors to this book took the third one up without having to wait for the invitation.

HELP!

If you follow the WPA-l list or are friends with WPAs on social media, you've seen this or something like it many times: "I need help! [For reasons I'll elaborate below] I need to be able to document my WPA labor in a way that [bean-counting dean/provost] will find convincing. Does anyone have a model for how you do that? Or a success story? Or a cautionary tale about something that didn't work? What kind of data can I show them to make my argument?"

Those "reasons" are often heavily loaded with professional consequences: tenure/promotion and, as more WPA positions become non-tenure-track reappointments, enough reassigned time to be able to do all the tasks in somebody's job description; requests for extra funding or extra hiring or changes in program practice to manage the workload. Put a different way, the requests are loaded with *labor* concerns, only sometimes referring to issues of programmatic quality or integrity and even then using them only as warrants for talking about the labor problems, as in, "Maybe I can argue that my program will struggle to meet assessment goals if the dean won't give me ___." That's not a knock on the people who make those arguments, by the way; I don't think they're doing anything wrong by prioritizing labor problems.

The problem with these requests, aside from the frequency with which they appear, is that historically, they have produced at best a House of WPA Lore (à la North 1987) next door to the House of Teacher Lore. I'm not especially concerned with the epistemological critiques of lore-as-knowledge, especially in serious situations where the most important thing is to win the argument, not to produce peer-reviewed publication-worthy scholarship to legitimize a discipline. Amy Ferdinandt Stolley's (2015) point in "Narratives, Administrative Identity, and the Early Career WPA" is more germane—that the substance of what we communicate in our lore isn't as "commonplace" (a term she borrows from Melissa Ianetta) as maybe we think it is. As a mid-level leader in my faculty union, for example, I've come to understand that the contract language under which 5,500 faculty on fourteen campuses work doesn't function the same way on all fourteen campuses; even though our entire state system's faculty is governed by the same contract and all the campuses are governed by a central body, the differences among the institutions are marked enough that even the simplest contract provisions don't work the same way everywhere. Keep in mind: that's collectively bargained, majority-ratified policy, not hallway conversations at conferences, listserv exchanges, or social media threads—the venues where so much lore gets created and propagated.

The other problem with depending only on WPA lore is that as more WPA work moves out of traditional WPA positions into non-tenure-track lines and, frighteningly, even into non-faculty positions where staff with no academic credentials make hiring/firing/curricular decisions, even the best lore loses its power because the people who need it may not know it exists. The WPA-l lost its primacy as the venue where people have these conversations because many of the conversations have moved to private social media accounts, while a handful of very public exchanges (e.g., WPA Feminist Revolution in late 2018, aka #FeministFightClubRhetComp; arguments about racism and free speech that led to the formation of Community Guidelines and a moderation process in 2019) revealed a site in which women and people of color expressed fear of participating on the list, even querying it, and noting the frequency with which senior white men (one of whom is me) often overrode diverse voices. In short, for many, the list was no longer—if it ever had been—a safe place to talk and learn. As a result, somebody who isn't socially networked with the WPAs who know the lore has almost no chance of finding it by accident.

By putting usable data and methods into circulation in venues less ephemeral and interpersonal than listservs and social media, *Making Administrative Work Visible* fulfills the charge of its title by putting data about that work and labor into print—in indexes and citations and databases—as the product of sustained, methodologically sound research.

WE NEED MORE RESEARCH BEFORE WE CAN DO THAT
You may have noticed that I haven't made the point that woven into the problem of WPA lore is the lack of "data" that convince upper administrators to make better decisions. I opted out of the epistemological debate about lore earlier, but such "anecdata" often fail to convince powerful decision-makers. As Anicca Cox, Timothy R. Dougherty, Michelle LaFrance, Amy Lynch-Biniek, and I (2016) have argued, not all demands for "research" are created equal. There are situations when recognizable research protocols and conventionally reliable data matter, and there are situations when the demand for such is primarily a way to delay decisions—either by simply slowing down the clock while we gather information or by implying that the request is unreasonable because the requestor hasn't done their homework. Discerning the differences between them can be tricky for sure, but the best way to handle it is not to wait until somebody demands data under duress before you produce them.

Making Administrative Work Visible responds to that call, like the call for something more systematic and less ephemeral than WPA lore, by reporting on concrete results many WPAs can use immediately. In addition, the book helps alleviate the difficulty of knowing in advance what questions you might have to answer under duress by already having asked and answered many of them: how to document the time you spend at various tasks; the value and costs of electronic communication; how different titles for WPAs inform relationships with upper administrators and other faculty; how to document the emotional labor of WPA work more systematically than simply observing and naming it; and more. Obviously, no book can ask, much less answer, all the questions, but the range of issues the contributors to this book raise is both extensive and generative; as such, it can help you respond to the delaying tactic of glibly demanding research by already having done it.

WE NEED MORE LABOR RESEARCH AS A FIELD
Along with the direct payoffs of specific studies and methods *Making Administrative Work Visible* documents, the book also contributes to a shift in the professional discourse of writing studies away from a long-standing resistance to talking explicitly about labor *as labor* and toward

using the word *labor* too expansively; a graduate school professor used the metaphor of *failing the elasticity test* to describe stretching the meaning of a term so far that it doesn't exclude anything. Those of us in the field who identify as labor activists have been trying for many years to bring labor into focus as a central issue. All too often, however, scholarship about WPA labor has tended to be largely theoretical/critical/historical, while calls for labor research have focused almost entirely on teaching and issues of professional status for faculty.

As an example: those of us involved in writing the Indianapolis Resolution spent more than a year (March 2014–July 2015) drafting, revising, and tweaking language, largely around the most contentious section (compliance with ethical labor practices). The section we settled on the quickest is the call for labor research support:

> We call on our disciplinary and professional organizations to support efforts to:
>
> 1. Offer more material and professional support and opportunity for the creation, publication, and dissemination of quantitative and qualitative research into the impacts of the labor system on the teaching and learning of writing.
> 2. Consider research into labor and its effects on teaching and learning with the same intellectual weight and scholarly respect as other subjects in our field. (Cox et al. 2016, 41)

Certainly, program administration is interwoven into everything on those lists, but the fact that those of us who worked on the resolution didn't explicitly name administration alongside teaching and learning is unfortunate. The invisibility of administrative labor is the primary exigency for this book, after all.

The better news, however, is that the six years since then have seen an uptick, if not the groundswell labor activists were hoping for, in labor research across composition studies and more broadly into English studies: articles aplenty in the major journals about labor conditions among faculty; attention to contingency, including work on contingent writing program administrators and writing center directors; edited collections; a book series I'm co-editing that's not focused on composition but is edited by two writing studies PhDs with WPA experience. The growing body of theory and methods of institutional ethnography is firmly (and explicitly) grounded in material labor conditions (e.g., LaFrance 2019). Obviously, we haven't solved the crises of labor exploitation and neoliberal hegemony, but as a field we've at least opened our eyes to labor problems of many kinds and are finding better ways to document and address them.

In some sense, then, *Making Administrative Work Visible* is both a response to a call that was at best tacit and at worst overlooked (much like WPA labor itself) to focus unapologetically on the material conditions of writing program administration. More expansively than any other text to date, this book insists that WPA labor belongs within that purview and, as I argued earlier, shows us what it looks like to add data-driven primary research about WPA labor to the historical/critical arguments we've been engaged in; to the primary research we've been doing for decades about the teaching and learning of writing; and to the growing body of primary research on contingent labor's effects on all of the above.

REFERENCES

Cox, Anicca, Timothy R. Dougherty, Seth Kahn, Michelle LaFrance, and Amy Lynch-Biniek. 2016. "The Indianapolis Resolution: Responding to Twenty-First-Century Exigencies/Political Economies of Composition Labor." *College Composition and Communication* 68 (1): 38–67.

LaFrance, Michelle. 2019. *Institutional Ethnography: A Theory of Practice for Writing Studies Researchers*. Logan: Utah State University Press.

North, Stephen. 1987. *The Making of Knowledge in Composition: Portrait of an Emerging Field*. Portsmouth, NH: Heinemann.

Stolley, Amy Ferdinandt. 2015. "Narratives, Administrative Identity, and the Early Career WPA." *Writing Program Administration* 39 (1): 18–31.

MAKING ADMINISTRATIVE WORK VISIBLE

Introduction
MAKING WORK VISIBLE
WORK THROUGH DATA-INFORMED ADVOCACY

Leigh Graziano, Kay Halasek, Remi Hudgins, Susan Miller-Cochran, Frank Napolitano, and Natalie Szymanski

Like writing itself, which Chris M. Anson (2011, 33) reminds us "takes place within social systems where particular practices evolve locally based on the purposes and goals of participants," writing program administration is situated within complex institutional systems that demand our attention to "goals, motivations, histories, actions, norms, hierarchies, and other elements of human interaction." That fact is not lost on the editors of this collection, which has its origins in 2016, when five of us—Leigh, Kay, Susan, Frank, and Natalie—happened to sit at the same table at the same session at the Council of Writing Program Administrators (CWPA) and began to chat about our work as writing program administrators (WPAs) at very different institutions and professional locations. Our collaboration began with a clear realization that the different institutional systems in which we serve as WPAs shape our experiences. Nonetheless, we also shared a common desire to make WPA work more visible to ourselves, our institutions, and our discipline by calling explicit attention to and examining WPAs' lived labor experiences. We began by tracking our own labor and reporting on our analysis of the data in "A Return to Portland: Making Work Visible through the Ecologies of Writing Program Administration" (Graziano et al. 2020). We learned through that process that the field needs to hear from a much broader range of voices using a much broader range of methodologies to truly understand the scope of lived WPA labor. This collection is a response to that need.

We write this introduction in a very different context from that CWPA conversation in Raleigh, North Carolina. In 2022, we are in a cultural and historical moment that has upended the way higher education operates, what spaces we work in, and how we plan for the future. The sudden outbreak of COVID-19 required every WPA and writing instructor to change course—for many, in the middle of a semester or term—and to reimagine what writing instruction might look like during a pandemic. Unexpected additional labor is not unique to writing programs, but it has impacted education at all levels on a global scale like nothing we've ever seen. Because they typically serve incoming students, writing programs tend to feel the impact of fluctuations in higher education enrollment trends first, and they always have to respond quickly. Because writing programs are often some of the largest programs on college or university campuses, the labor required to shift instructors and students to and maintain them in online environments is significant.

But is that surprising? Aren't WPAs always having to adjust and react? In writing studies scholarship, we often refer to writing programs as "ecologies," and never has the ecological scope of our work and disciplinary space been so evident. When one element of our work or context shifts, all others adjust and react in response. We are all adjusting and responding as we always do, but suddenly the pull of external ecologies is much greater than it has ever been, increasing the urgency and significance of what we must adjust to and how we do it. As is so often the case, the labor of writing programs and WPAs provides a model of response and often lightens the load for other units on campus. The burden writing programs carry in this context is great, and the support they provide to the campus as a whole extends far beyond support for student writing.

HOW THE COLLECTION IS ORGANIZED AND WHY IT'S FRAMED IN ADVOCACY

Much of our work as WPAs can be constituted as the work of advocacy. What is unique, however, is the appearance of that advocacy work across our different institutions and positionalities. Some WPAs are mired in the work of advocating for their own positions, responsibilities, compensation, or release time; others champion the colleagues (often tenure-free) who comprise our writing programs. The work we can do to fight for our programs, our peers, and ourselves is constrained by our positions, ecologies, and ability to find the right moment to embark on this important labor. Conceptualizing WPA work in this way is not captured in policy documents, like the Portland Resolution (Hult and the Portland Resolution Committee 1992), but it is examined in disciplinary scholarship (McLeod 1995; Adler-Kassner 2008). As Mark Blaauw-Hara and Cheri Lemieux Spiegel (2018, 253) explain, "We began to realize WPA could be a role of vision and activism, not just one of basic management." What we don't have as a field is a picture of what this advocacy work looks like and the spectrum across which that work is performed. The data-driven projects in this collection explore the different ways WPAs take up the work of advocacy to be "agents of change" (McLeod 1995).

We have elected to organize the collection across three themes—Advocating through Representations of WPA Labor, Advocating by Accounting for Time and Labor, and Advocating in and through Complex Institutional Contexts—each of which focuses attention on what we and the contributors to this collection identify as among not only the most confounding challenges facing WPAs but also the most compelling sites of their advocacy for and contributions to writing program administration, labor in higher education, and our collective obligation to forward the goals of antiracism and social justice. The contributions of our colleagues here, we believe, move us all toward a "more complete picture of the current state of the profession" (Graziano et al. 2020, 148). By taking up and answering questions about the range of WPA work (and the various forms of that work across institutional types, positions, and people) and the invisibility of much of that work—which is often unaccounted for and unrewarded—contributors create avenues forward that account for and acknowledge WPAs across the complex activity systems in which they lead the work of the university (Charlton, Charlton, and Graban 2011).

If we are honest, on some level we've known that our long-standing myths of WPA labor—the lone WPA protagonist-as-leader trope; the organized, internally consistent writing program truism; and the traditional tenure-driven checkboxes for labor—have provided us with tidy accountability narratives around which to build our field and our scholarship. However, these narratives do us a disservice as a field because they marginalize many of our colleagues and therefore obscure (or simply exclude) their important and potentially transformative and antiracist work. Reframing this work in terms of advocacy is a first step in revealing and including the diversity of labor performed by WPAs.

The authors in this collection bring important and challenging questions to the forefront:

- How can we use a variety of qualitative and quantitative research methods to uncover and thus expand our definitions of our labor, productivity, and value to ourselves and thus to others?

- How can those findings help us to not only avoid becoming anachronistic but also to emerge as advocates for ourselves—and by extension, and perhaps more important, for others and for our students (especially post-COVID and in light of calls for antiracism in our field)?
- How should/could "boss/canonical texts" (like our organization statements, journals, conferences, and more) work to align themselves with these lived realities? How does that alter the ways we build and conduct business in our professional executive boards and governing bodies?

PART 1: ADVOCATING THROUGH REPRESENTATIONS OF WPA LABOR

The chapters in this section highlight the interdependent nature of WPA work and narratives about it. Just as we often perform our duties in response to or in relationship with the needs of others, so too do we shape our narratives in response to the perceived expectations and unexplored assumptions of the community about and for which they are composed and in which they are situated—sometimes problematically so. This interdependence between individual and community even extends to our emotions, which are influenced, at least in part, by ongoing discussions among writing program administrators. These chapters account for WPA labor work through a range of critical lenses—including antiracism and white privilege—and analyze qualitative and quantitative data to help us understand the interconnected matrices in which administrators and writing programs exist.

Situated within the exigencies and challenges of our contemporary racial unrest and reckoning in the academy and across the nation, Sheila Carter-Tod calls for, in "Nothing New: Systemic Invisibility, Epistemological Exclusion, and Faculty and Administrators of Color," a disciplinary shift from epistemological exclusion to epistemological inclusion to redress the institutional practices and structures that disrupt and obstruct the personal and professional lives of faculty of color (FOC)—an abandonment of those "overt and covert systematic racialized structures that undervalue their labor and often discredit their scholarship." In reviewing a selection of the important but relatively few contributions to the scholarly conversation on race and writing program administration, Carter-Tod explores, among other topics, the intersectionality of racial hierarchies, discourse privileging, writing assessment, and curricular development as well as scholarship that illuminates the foundational whiteness of writing programs and the literal and figurative costs of the invisible labor of FOC. The time and emotional energy expended in supporting others within racist structures and institutions constructed to marginalize them is work they undertake to their own detriment and at their own expense, as such work goes unacknowledged in terms of reappointment, promotion, and tenure.

Despite its importance, Carter-Tod argues that this scholarship has done little to effect "true systemic, epistemological change," as such change requires "dismantling a structure that allows all other scholars to conduct and publish scholarship that reinforces existing racial hierarchies and only speaks to and for limited audiences"—a change the discipline and its predominantly white scholars have not yet made. Systemic change requires that the "invisible labor performed by FOC is recognized and rewarded for what it is—quantifiable work that sustains the university's reputation by helping the university meet larger strategic goals of 'diversification.' " Only then does the work of FOC "become not only visible but also rewarded accordingly." Such a shift, however, demands dismantling the hierarchies that inform what "counts" as scholarship, shifting the epistemology of the discipline from one of exclusion to one of inclusion in which definitions of "such concepts as knowledge, knowledge creation, research, and scholarship" are broadened to account for all labor—both visible and invisible.

In "Teacher, Manager, Developer, Advocate: Representations of Work in *WPA*," Kristine Johnson challenges Douglas D. Hesse's (2015) thesis that writing program administration as a field has replaced its initial emphases on teaching and management with a focus on programmatic development and, later, on advocacy. Using topic modeling of key terms in nearly forty years of *WPA: Writing Program Administration*, Johnson demonstrates that while the field has focused less on management in recent years, its attention to teaching has increased over time. Meanwhile, the disciplinary commitments to development and advocacy have remained steady—and in the case of the latter activity, low—throughout the decades. This dearth of advocacy-related scholarship appears despite Johnson and Hesse defining the term as labor that "focuses on the position of the writing programs on campus, within higher education, and in the minds of publics and policymakers" (Hesse 2015, 135; qtd. in Johnson, chapter 2, this volume). We suspect that if she were to use our more spirited definition—"fighting for our programs, our peers, and ourselves"—the footprint of advocacy would be even smaller. Despite a rise in work focusing on "ethical and rhetorical action and agency" since around 2010, topic modeling doesn't support the idea that our flagship publication has heeded Linda Adler-Kassner's (2008,

184) call for more "story-changing" advocacy to counter nonacademic narratives of student literacy. Instead, the narrative conveyed by the journal and foundational disciplinary documents, such as the Portland Resolution (Hult and the Portland Resolution Committee 1992) and the Council of Writing Program Administrators' (1996) "Evaluating the Intellectual Work of Writing Program Administration: A Draft," has sharpened its focus on development and "particularly its growth and improvement" (Johnson, chapter 2, this volume). While Johnson's study depicts a field dedicated to its pedagogical mission, it also reveals a discipline that is apparently slow to change narratives about composition outside writing programs.

Jill Gladstein's "Revising the Terminology and Frames around WPA Work to Uncover Networks of Sites of Writing Administration" acknowledges that the questions we ask about postsecondary writing administration and the terminology we use when asking those questions greatly affect the narrative of our field. Even more, our terminology frames what is and is not included, made visible, or deemed to have power/privilege within the landscape of writing program administration. Gladstein notes that we cannot understand writing at the university by simply asking who the WPA of a particular institution might be or even if the institution has a writing program. Instead, Gladstein advocates uncovering the "explicit and embedded sites" of writing in the academy. Using the expansive dataset of the National Census of Writing, Gladstein advocates expanding our terminology to be more inclusive and to better capture the complexity of administrative positions related to composition. By observing that writing at the university is often housed not in a writing program led by an individual WPA but instead in networked "sites of writing," Gladstein challenges our field to move past the conception of the WPA as a lone protagonist—noting that the term *WPA* has often led to exclusion and silos. By employing more inclusive terminology, our disciplinary conversations will allow many stakeholders to step forward and include themselves as participants in the ongoing discussion of writing program administration.

Kimberly Emmons and Martha Wilson Schaffer's "The Value of Mentoring in Writing Program Administration" highlights the importance of storytelling within and about writing programs. From data obtained—surveys, emails, calendars, and logs of daily interactions—Emmons and Schaffer assert that mentorship emerges through "dynamic, intellectual, and distributed moments" rather than through more discrete or formal interactions. All narrative relies on careful attention to the needs of its protagonists, and Emmons and

Schaffer reveal how mentoring, in its many forms, improves writing and teaching through communication, inclusion, and a dedication to instructors' professional development. Mentoring not only communicates program goals to its members and outside stakeholders but also develops individual instructors' professional identities, along with the identity of the program.

Kristi Murray Costello and Kate Navickas's "Naming What We Feel: Self-Dialogue as a Strategy for Negotiating Emotional Labor in WPA Work" shows that good storytelling requires both honesty and vulnerability. They demonstrate both qualities by introducing readers to their practice of a modified form of journaling that enables them to understand and process the emotional labors inherent in a WPA position. By illustrating how they journal about, organize, and engage with problematic emotions, Costello and Navickas demonstrate that their emotional labor arises from both their individual lived experiences and the ongoing narratives promulgated by our discipline and institutions. In contrast to traditional journaling or other purely expressive genres, their conception of "self-dialogue" includes formulating strategies to address the personal and programmatic effects of WPAs' emotional labor. In this way, self-dialogue also functions as a kind of self-advocacy, allowing WPAs to both make sense of their own representations of their labor and make more informed, self-aware choices. Self-dialogue also requires that practitioners reflect on what they have learned about themselves, their emotional labors, and the institutional or disciplinary narratives that contribute to them. The authors' commitment to candor shows their confidence in the process. For example, Costello shares how "staying with" her emotions surrounding the delegation of authority allowed her to see that she fears losing credit for her efforts in the writing program, and Navickas admits to sending "a defensive and presumptuous email" to a colleague over a misunderstanding. Their forthrightness about the process and its value to themselves and the field imbues with authenticity their call for more WPAs to share their individual stories of emotional labor. Doing so, they argue, will enable the field as a whole to recognize the power of emotions in WPA labor and the value of talking to each other about those emotions.

PART 2: ADVOCATING BY ACCOUNTING FOR TIME AND LABOR

Increasingly, institutions of higher education are contracting with corporations to implement time and labor platforms to track and manage workers' time and labor output—creating both implicit and explicit expectations for accountability. Platforms such as Workday, PrismHR, PeopleSoft, Interfolio's Faculty180, PeopleAdmin's Faculty Information System, and AltMetric clearly make legible the labor that results in measurable outcomes: number of clients served, number of grants awarded, number of hours in the office, number of students taught. However, these measures do not speak to the nature, scope, and invisible emotional labor of faculty or WPAs (Konkiel 2016). The authors in this section step boldly into this complex scene, providing critiques of institutional practices for measuring time and labor and tools for accounting (e.g., EmailAnalytics, Mailstrom, time-use diaries), methods of data collection (surveys, semi-structured interviews, discourse analysis), and theoretical frames (e.g., thingification and exchange value) for situating and analyzing the impact and consequences of that accounting. They also—in their theorizing—extend and complicate what "counts" *as* labor and how that labor might be more fully valued by writing instructors, institutional assessment coordinators, department chairs, promotion and tenure committees, and deans. Overall, authors' metaphors of valuing (Robinson), trading (Dippre), working "under the radar" (Mina), in/visibility (Mitchell and Rieman), failing (Anderson), and weighing down (Poblete) establish new grounds for advocacy and activism.

Deploying Harold Garfinkel's (1967) concept of "thingification," Ryan J. Dippre describes in "Trading Time: Communicating Grand Strategy to Stakeholders through Hour Tracking" how making WPA work into an object, or "thingifying" it, makes it more visible, more "palpable," to stakeholders. Working intentionally as he moved first into a role as associate director of college composition and then as director of the program, Dippre articulates principle-driven strategies from Adler-Kassner (2008) to guide his administrative calculus. Like Heather Robinson in chapter 8, Dippre speaks emphatically about the invisible, even nonexistent nature of much of his WPA work, a factor that contributes to his decision to situate his year-long record-keeping and timekeeping project within a set of five explicit "grand strategies" that enable visibility for and sustainability of his work through its connections to departmental and college initiatives and values. Dippre also challenges the Council of Writing Program Administrators' "Evaluating the Intellectual Work of Writing Program Administration" (1996). For Dippre, "Intellectual Work" complicates his accounting for how his reassigned time was "counted," "making things a little murky" and amplifying for him the necessity of continually *thingifying* all elements of his work. Dippre also speaks to the work of "keeping the lights on," of "program mechanics"—Robinson's "academic housework." Within his framework, "keeping the lights on" is situated on equal ground with such grand strategies as raising national awareness of the writing program or collaborating with K–20 schools, demonstrating that a decision to devote time to one strategy means devoting less time to another—and that pursuing the grand strategies is always accompanied by necessary attention to keeping the lights on.

Lilian W. Mina, in "Theorizing Programmatic Assessment as a Site of Visibility of WPA Intellectual Work," turns our attention to brokering alliances and enriching colleagues' professional learning—all while using program assessment as a vehicle for making WPA work more visible. Still attentive to the complexity and necessity of forging and sustaining relationships with institutional partners, Mina foregrounds a set of partners far different from the department chairs and deans we find in Dippre's and Robinson's studies. Here we are introduced to an assessment specialist from the Office of Institutional Effectiveness and the assistant director of and instructors in the writing program with whom Mina conducted semi-structured interviews about their engagements with and reflections on writing curricula, their own professional development, and program assessment as research. Although they are certainly critical stakeholders in the work of the writing program, these partners collaborate on the design, delivery, and evaluation of the program assessment—roles that then situate them for greater, deeper, firsthand understanding of the work of program assessment and its affordances for the writing program, its staff, and institutional assessment processes and practices. The powerful and substantive impact of the study leads Mina to argue that when undertaken as a site for professional development, program assessment can both broaden others' understanding of the value of qualitative approaches to assessment and increase the visibility of WPA work.

Heather M. Robinson continues this discussion of how institutions communicate what they value in "Making Administration's Exchange Value Visible," where she applies a Marxist theoretical analysis to make a sobering observation likely familiar to all WPAs: although our administrative work has "use value" (in that it serves meaningful institutional functions), it has little, if any, "exchange" value as a commodity that can be exchanged or rewarded with reappointment, tenure, or promotion. By analyzing the Council of Writing Program Administrators' "Evaluating the Intellectual Work of Writing Program Administration" (1996), she illustrates how disciplinary documents further obfuscate the value of administrative labor by separating intellectual work from emotional and "academic housework," those fundamental, named responsibilities of WPAs and other administrators. Consequently, the only administrative work granted exchange value is that which is singular, exceptional, and—above all—uncompensated. Through analysis of twenty-nine time-use diaries completed by English department faculty over a three-month period, institutional documents associated with promotion and tenure guidelines, and a thank you letter from her college president, Robinson advocates establishing formal, explicit metrics for evaluating administrative work. Such metrics would offer clarity to early-career administrators about which types of labor are valued in the reappointment, tenure, and promotion process and which are not, empowering administrators with the ability to focus and promote their efforts accordingly to those who would recognize and reward their labor. Analysis of the letter, for example, demonstrates that it was not her assigned responsibilities as chair but activities that lie outside those responsibilities that were lauded as "achievements." Such a calling out of the exceptional undervalues, dismisses, and makes invisible her departmental administrative work. Moreover, Robinson argues that attempts to commodify administrative labor and thereby assign it exchange value are complicated and even thwarted by the practice of granting release time or reassignment as compensation for administrative appointments, essentially releasing departments from an obligation to acknowledge, recognize, or reward the labor. As Robinson points out, release time is not compensation or reward but simply "a necessary allocation of time for this work to get done"; however, because it *is* considered compensated work, administrative labor is rendered "invisible in our rewards and recognition systems."

Angela Mitchell and Jan Rieman's "Invisible Labor: Tracking Email Practices in WPA Work" analyzes the email practices of WPAs in a large, urban, R1 institution. Like many contributors to this collection, Mitchell and Rieman combine quantitative and qualitative research methods to understand the defining influences of email (a ubiquitous medium) on WPAs' lives. They examine their own reflective journals, collect survey data from fellow WPAs, and employ automated email analytics systems with the hope of understanding their email practices. The qualitative data—in the form of stories about email we tell to each other and to ourselves—form the heart of this chapter. We witness and can empathize with a WPA's dismay when a single email upends an already crowded daily agenda. We nod in recognition when participants describe spending their time in response mode to the "miscellaneous" matters that arise throughout the day. And we identify with the emotional toll of keeping up with the informative but sometimes taxing interactions on the WPA Listserv. These affective factors, combined with the intellectual and time commitments that email imposes on us, Mitchell and Rieman argue, illustrate how this "visibly invisible mode of communication controls us" and defines our professional environments. For many, email forms not only a paper trail but also the repository for institutional and the WPA's professional memories. Although there is likely no way to entirely escape the demands of email, Mitchell and Rieman suggest steps to navigate its use more skillfully, including setting expectations among colleagues about when and how often they will respond to each other's emails and finding a way to include email work in annual reports.

Brooke Anderson's "Opportunity Lost: Failing to Make Administrative Work Visible" reports on her work spent advocating for the creation of the WPA and writing center director (WCD) positions, something that has further dramatized the importance of these positions and the need for other faculty to take up similar work on their campuses. Anderson makes use of autoethnographic methods (labor logs, internal documents, reflections) to capture her experience living through this change and applies Barbara Curry, Lillian M. Lowery, and Dennis Loftus's (2010) institutionalization framework to reflect on the data she collected to understand how and why she failed to get these positions created on her campus. Anderson reports on not succeeding in having these positions institutionalized on her campus; however, her efforts revealed important localized conditions that acted as barriers for her advocacy—namely, the perception of WPA work as managerial as well as other university conditions of salary and workload that demoralized faculty from engaging in the reorganization work necessary to create such positions. Although scholars like Curry, Lowery, and Loftus (2010) have already suggested a framework for engaging in the work of advocating for the creation of WPA-like positions, in her chapter Anderson rightly calls for data that can be used to both show that change is needed and document change as it is happening. Such data offer a possibility of combating localized pressures against institutionalizing these kinds of administration positions. However, Anderson picks up the call others make in this collection as well: the need for our governing organization to create more documents specifically focused on the needs of community colleges. Adding this disciplinary support to localized data would help community college faculty advocate for these positions.

Patti Poblete's "Weighing down the Body: Quantifying the Nature of Antiracist Work" notes that of the innumerable attempts to advocate for antiracist academic policies and environments, some have been heartfelt and some "purely cosmetic." For example, many commissions and task forces see the inclusion of Black, Indigenous, and people of color (BIPOC) faculty perspectives as a goal in and of itself rather than a starting point for informing or catalyzing meaningful change. Even worse, efforts to gain diverse perspectives often distill myriad backgrounds and experiences into reductive racial or ethnic categories that never encapsulate the trauma that institutional racism inflicts on individual people. Poblete contends that for antiracist efforts to be valued in the academy, they must be assessable and provide actionable data. However, she notes two problems attendant with such efforts. First, the pervasive nature of antiracist statements both dilutes the subject of its immediacy and lulls individual actors into complacency. Second, the emotional labor of antiracist advocacy is impossible to quantify. Poblete also contends that institutions of higher education are inherently racist and that the changes sought by antiracists would threaten the institutional structures of which they themselves are a part. She concludes by wondering if even the most intentional and goal-driven antiracist advocacy will achieve demonstrable reforms that would make visible the labors—and pains—of BIPOC scholars.

PART 3: ADVOCATING IN AND THROUGH COMPLEX INSTITUTIONAL CONTEXTS

The authors in this section highlight the myriad ways WPAs advocate within ever-changing institutional contexts and complex ecologies. In big and small ways, WPAs are always advocating and negotiating with changes to positions (Neal, Stark, Cicchino, Healy, and Albert; Murphy and Mikanovich), shifts in institutional culture that require programmatic changes (García de Müeller and Cortés Lagos), institutional constraints (Tinoco), needed professional development (Tremain), challenges to WPA identity itself (Cunningham, Stillman-Webb, Hilliard, and Stewart), and the methodologies that inform WPA research (González). Using both traditional and nontraditional data methods, these authors demonstrate that data can be used to advocate for change within our institutions at the same time that they acknowledge the limitations of data to reveal and sustain some labor, particularly as it relates to antiracist work. Together, these chapters provide a rich picture of the types of WPA advocacy work and ways we might explore additional avenues for activism in our programs.

As Michael Neal, Katelyn Stark, Amy Cicchino, Michael Healy, and Kamila Albert highlight in "Institutional Matters: The (In)Visibility of

Localized WPA Labor," no generalized curriculum can prepare graduate WPAs (gWPAs) to make the transition to the range of institutional contexts that await them and the complex transition from students to professionals. The difficulty of this transition is exacerbated by the homogeneity of the apprenticeship model research-focused institutions most often employ to prepare new WPAs. Using institutional profiles gathered from interviews of WPAs from across the institutional spectrum, the authors of this chapter—four of whom are graduate students—argue that preparing graduate students to transition into an administrative position requires an understanding of the way local writing contexts shape the nature of the position and the type of work encountered therein. Neal and colleagues' advocacy surfaces on two different fronts. First, gWPAs need to understand the types of labor that are not visible beyond the conditions of their graduate programs. By making this labor more visible, graduate programs will prepare gWPAs for the transition into new academic and administrative ecologies. Second, Neal and coauthors' work benefits the multiplicity of institutions that are often overlooked in both gWPA education and in scholarship. The chapter illustrates that advocacy for one party often results in benefits to all involved.

Greer Murphy and Troy Mikanovich also highlight the importance of institutional context and professional identity, especially for multilingual specialists-turned-administrators. In their chapter, "Labor and Loneliness of the Multilingual WPA," Murphy and Mikanovich explore the lived labor conditions of multilingual WPAs (mWPAs) embedded in writing programs. To further contextualize the material conditions that contribute to acknowledging or erasing their labor, the authors analyze position descriptions, mission statements, and other program materials. These data make visible the spaces mWPAs occupy at the intersection of the work they really do and the work others think they do. Much like Neal and coauthors' contribution to this collection, Murphy and Mikanovich's chapter advocates for marginalized institutions, as well as the WPAs working in them. The scholarship of our field, the authors note, neither adequately explores the pedagogical, material, and political realities of smaller, multilingual programs nor examines how institutional or emotional pressures make it difficult for mWPAs to move through the often precarious spaces they occupy.

Online writing instruction (OWI) offers instructors another kind of context, one that challenges their identities and teaching practices. In "Conceptualizing Time in Hybrid and Online Writing Instruction and Program Administration," Jennifer M. Cunningham, Natalie Stillman-Webb, Lyra Hilliard, and Mary K. Stewart share data from interviews with seventeen writing instructors of online and blended courses at four different institutions. Because OWI is not readily visible to other instructors, we don't have a clear conception of how OWI instructors spend their time. Applying content analysis and a grounded theory approach, the authors identify three key patterns: how instructors save/manage their time, the need for more time for training, and the time instructors spend designing/delivering the course. In gathering their own data to understand the time and challenges of OWI, a space often occupied by contingent faculty, the authors advocate for ways WPAs can consider both scheduling and issues of professional development and support.

Too often underrepresented and unaccounted for in disciplinary scholarship, the advocacy work of WPAs at two-year colleges is the focus of Lizbett Tinoco's "Community College WPAs Creating Change through Advocacy." Using a mixed-methods approach to gather both qualitative and quantitative data, Tinoco captures important demographic information about individual institutions and WPAs and contextualizes that information with open-ended survey questions and one-on-one interviews. Of notable interest in the data that emerged are the ways WPAs at two-year colleges described the rhetorical nature of advocacy, which Tinoco defines as the work of "engag[ing] with departmental and institutional constraints through the process of negotiation, mediation, and collaboration to affect change." This definition fits what many of the participants in her study describe when they engage in the work of creating positions, outlining job descriptions, negotiating compensation, or supporting adjunct faculty. She notes that the language used to describe this work can take many forms, including "championing," "building trust," and "fighting." Tinoco also emphasizes the complementary nature of two particular forms of advocacy that surfaced in her data: self-advocacy and peer advocacy. To gather and use data for one's own ends is to provide models that WPAs at other two-year colleges can use to advocate for their own work, positions, and professional authority. Our field will likely find it beneficial to examine the various categories of advocacy work we perform as WPAs, and room certainly exists for other studies to broaden these efforts.

In "Heavy Lifting: How WPAs Broker Knowledge Transfer for Faculty," Lisa Tremain explores a different facet of the advocacy work WPAs perform: how they strategically advocate for the learning and professional development of contingent and lecturer faculty. Tremain's qualitative approach includes data from three semi-structured interviews with WPAs. Using an open coding method to define the codes used in selective coding analysis, she focuses on language use in context, particularly around concepts such as leadership, teaching, and professional development. To understand these data, she uses the theoretical frames of *kairos* and David N. Perkins and Gavriel Salomon's (2012) transfer framework of detect-elect-connect to make sense of the ways WPAs find exigencies to advocate for their programs and their own knowledge development. One notable finding from her study is the different ways WPAs make use of micro- and macro-kairos. Micro-kairos might take the form of small conversations, sharing of interests, and finding ways to advocate for her collaboration. Macro-kairos, in contrast, involves examining and leveraging exigencies within our institutional contexts to make important curricular shifts. One WPA noted that a shift in her professional authority after earning tenure created an opportunity for her to take more risks and be bolder in her work and her calls for change. Similarly, for another WPA, employing this framework meant realizing her program's lack of readiness for change. This was not the moment to begin advocating for the work of uptaking knowledge from the field to make changes. "Detecting" these moments allows WPAs to be more strategic in their advocacy work. The contribution of these frameworks offers meaningful opportunities for the field to explore how WPAs make important changes in their programs. Similarly, as Tinoco notes in her conclusion, these frameworks can help us begin to paint a picture of how WPAs negotiate their work within complex ecological structures—material, labor, programmatic, institutional, cultural, and personal conditions—that shape the lived conditions of our positions and the work that we perform.

Advocacy work is always complex but perhaps more so when that work is grounded in antiracism. In their study, "Building an Antiracist WAC Program," authors Genevieve García de Müeller and Ana Cortés Lagos employ a method of reflective storytelling as a first attempt at understanding the effort and labor required to build and also sustain an antiracist WAC program at Syracuse University in light of institutional shifts (and a history of both racism and antiracism activism on their campus) and a national landscape under the Trump presidency. Building this program was not without substantial institutional challenges. They lacked a coordinated antiracist WAC initiative that spanned all parts of the department and had to convince the university that there was room for WAC in spite of a robust curriculum already in place while at the same time dismantling institutional assumptions that antiracist WAC is not an add-on or a quick fix to institutionalized racist practices. While the program they developed is grounded in practices of interrogating language conventions, analyzing values and conceptions of writing, genre-based pedagogies, and the need for antiracist assessment practices, their workshops with faculty revealed struggles with white guilt and discomfort in talking about racism and seeing connections between instructors' own pedagogical materials and antiracist practices. All of these institutional challenges required ongoing labor, adjustments to their program design, and constant advocacy and education. The value of their study, though, transcends their own institutional context and advocates for a shift needed in our field—perhaps presciently, given the 2021 conversation on and decline of the WPA-L. The authors argue that "antiracist WAC is an important and necessary step toward addressing the whiteness of writing studies" and take up Carmen Kynard's (2018, 523) call to "constantly name the structural violence of our institutions (our local settings, colleges, nation, and our field)."

In "Making Research Methods Visible through the Alternative Table of Contents," Caleb González extends the themes of advocacy, (in)visibility, institutional change, and complexity of ecologies by examining the ways WPA research methodologies reflect, refract, and challenge entrenched disciplinary practices. Working from his findings in an earlier project in which he "scoped" a randomized sample of the research methodologies informing the *WPA Journal* and two other writing studies journals, González analyzes the research methodologies deployed by the authors in *Making Administrative Work Visible* and designs an alternative table of contents for the collection. In framing that alternative table of contents, González creates a structure that makes those methodologies legible and accessible—especially for graduate students studying research methodologies. Through the alternative table of contents, González demonstrates the wide range of methodologies informing WPA research and the consequential activist work those methodologies do for writing program administrators and writing programs.

RECOGNIZING OUR HISTORIES AND THEIR (INHERENT) PARADOXES

Many of the authors in this collection highlight the invisible labor of WPAs: the many forms of mentoring WPAs do (Emmons and Schaffer), the constant emotional labor WPAs engage in (Costello and Navickas, Poblete), and the relentless need to be available, often through technology (Mitchell and Rieman). Cunningham and colleagues, Anderson, Tinoco, and Mina highlight some of the spaces where WPA labor is expected and ongoing but often ignored, under-compensated, or both (OWI, community colleges, and programmatic assessment, respectively).

But the authors of the chapters in this collection also offer solutions to these persistent challenges, and, most important, several of the authors describe tangible strategies that have made their work more visible. Dippre describes the importance of tracking time spent on WPA labor, and Mina describes pursuing collaborative relationships to make programmatic assessment more visible. Robinson highlights a core challenge for WPAs: the lack of clarity for how administrative labor translates into an exchange value for tangible rewards such as tenure and promotion. Both Johnson and Gladstein describe efforts to understand and learn from efforts to study, document, and catalog WPA labor in the *WPA Journal* and the National Census of Writing, respectively.

While we've been inspired to see the new scholarly avenues opened by these contributors, we've also been humbled. As with any scholarly endeavor, this one provides us with preliminary answers to our questions but also leaves us aware that much labor remains uncovered. Most conspicuous, this collection doesn't include data-driven projects focused on important institutional types such as historically Black colleges and universities (HBCUs) or Hispanic-serving institutions. While attempting to confront this, we realized that the limitations of our collection presented an unavoidable paradox: we wanted to amplify certain kinds of labor that historically have been devalued, marginalized, or "unseen"; yet our traditional ways of amplifying still privileged the kinds of participation many don't have access to *because* of the labor they are doing. The antiracist chapters in this collection reveal the difficulties of using traditionally defined data-driven methodologies to try to capture the complexity of this work. García de Müeller and Cortés Lagos deploy reflective storytelling as their method for understanding the labor involved in launching an antiracist WAC program; Poblete uses narrative as an argument to highlight the difficulty of even trying to quantify antiracist work using traditional measures; and Carter-Tod engages in a literature review of scholarship on issues of invisible labor to help explain why specific disciplinary efforts (to consider race and program administration) in isolation fall short of creating actual change. In short, traditional forms of data-driven research are themselves mired in inequity and therefore limited in their ability to make visible some of this work.

The visibility of the antiracism activism of the COVID-19 era presents us with a kairotic exigence of sorts (both in our culture at large and for our field). Once these inequities are unveiled more plainly to us (yet again), we must decide if we will continue to respond with apathy and negligence or take action. The authors in this collection and this moment inspire us to action, for it is our action now that will help create more equitable stability for our collective and disciplinary future. So the question(s) beg:

- How can we act?
- What can we do practically to ensure that the external representations of our writing programs and cultures of writing we articulate to others (and ourselves) catch up to our (already existing) realities?
- How can we pay more than lip service to the notion of creating an inclusive representation and thus understanding of writing program administration and those who do its labor?

FINDING A WAY FORWARD

Working on this collection has led us to believe that to move forward productively from this moment, we need to call into question, rethink, and (re)operationalize two major disciplinary assumptions: the *forms* of scholarship we value and the conceptions of *authorship* and *ownership* we prioritize.

Rethinking Forms of Scholarship in the Name of Equitable Representation

The traditional forms of scholarship that we (and our institutions) currently value most highly—single-author journal articles, chapters, book-length projects—require time-consuming research, both broad and deep knowledge of previous scholarship in the field, and lengthy processes of drafting, peer review, revision negotiations, editing, and document design. Completing these projects takes months of sustained attention, attention that many marginalized, non-, un-, or pre-tenured writing administrators simply cannot afford. The default preferred *form* of our scholarship and the processes inherent in its creation preclude those who most need to be represented and amplified in our future disciplinary narratives.

- What would it look like to rethink "acceptable" research methods and processes for WPA work? For example, one of our colleagues invited research participants to participate in a study and to be coauthors with him in all aspects of the work.
- What if our peer-review time lines moved more quickly and accelerated work so it reached an audience in a timely manner (e.g., Jordan Frith's 2020 Special Section COVID call for proposals [CFP] for the *Journal of Business and Technical Communication*)?
- What could we learn from models in other disciplines? For example, the Public Library of Science (PLOS) journal *PLOS ONE* publishes

research findings and data quickly, with an eye toward making data available to the scientific community.

Rethinking Authorship and Ownership in the Name of Equitable Representation
While much of our WPA scholarship is collaborative and we have persuasive arguments for the intellectual work of writing administration, we still largely exist—and are thus promoted and tenured—inside English departments with value systems that favor single-author, monolithic hierarchies of scholarship. Single-author researched pieces in national peer-reviewed journals or presses simply carry more weight. The default conceptions of *authorship* we are forced to operate within again preclude those who most need to be represented and amplified in our future disciplinary narratives.

What would it look like to reimagine publication, mentoring, and editorial relationships? How could we move toward feminist models of authorship and ownership in which empowered scholars empower other scholars? One of the authors of this conclusion had a graduate mentor who generously invited graduate students to coauthor nearly everything he published. These opportunities were valuable experiences for the students at the time and yielded tangible results the students could point to when interviewing for jobs.

At the same time, we feel it is important to note that already marginalized, non-, un-, or pre-tenured writing administrators and faculty members cannot advocate and enact these changes alone or for themselves. For both of these situations to realistically manifest, we need advocacy from (protected) senior scholars along the same lines of disciplinary collectives such as Tenure for the Common Good and New Faculty Majority, particularly in regard to external public relations–like messaging and internal negotiation/revision of tenure and promotion requirements in specific institutional contexts. The basic prerogatives of Tenure for the Common Good's (2021) mission align with ours here: "Let's transform our notion of tenure from being one associated principally with the professional achievements and privileges of the individual scholar into a concept associated, in addition, with the common good. . . . It may sound quixotic to try to get tenured professors together to fight for the common good, but we just don't have time to waste feeling powerless when we haven't exercised the power we have."

Those with protection and power need to advocate alongside their colleagues for these actions to take hold and for the field of writing program administration to build and support an equitable representation of its lived realities across institutional types (e.g., two year, four year, HBCU, HSI, Indigenous serving) and institution-specific administrative labels (e.g., WPA, writing across the curriculum, writing in the disciplines, writing center director, writing coordinator).

OPPORTUNITY > CRISES?

COVID-19 has been described as both a crisis and an opportunity for higher education. As Megan Zahneis (2020) highlights, "The pandemic doesn't pose new problems to academe as much as it magnifies existing ones. 'Everything was held together with gum and paper clips, and coronavirus came and just sort of knocked it all down at once,' [Tom] DePaola said. 'I think none of the crises that this virus is causing are new. They're just accelerated greatly. And the contradictions of the system are heightened all at once for people to see.'"

Other exigencies—antiracism and its calls to end institutional racism and the deep social, economic, and political inequities it breeds, for example—also magnify existing problems within higher education and writing program administration. We hope this moment inspires us to face the (lived) realities of administering writing, acknowledge the exclusionary shortcomings of our current disciplinary approaches, and come together to collectively determine and enact a solution. As Seth Kahn asserts in his foreword to this volume, the data-driven primary research in this collection nuances the historical/critical arguments we've been engaged in and begins to address a tacit or overlooked call for exploration of the varied material conditions of writing program administration. However, unless we actually rethink and then (re)operationalize the *forms* of scholarship we value and alter our assumptions of *authorship* and *ownership*, we will never truly be inclusive of the voices we need to productively move forward as a field. If we continue with business as usual, we can call on these voices all we want, but we will only hear our own echoes in response: marginalized, un-tenured, or pre-tenured voices will continue to be too busy to contribute; the same limited number of (protected, tenured) names and thus perspectives will (re)circulate in our scholarship; and we will continue to be complicit in the same exclusionary practices we claim to fight.

REFERENCES

Adler-Kassner, Linda. 2008. *The Activist WPA: Changing Stories about Writing and Writers.* Logan: Utah State University Press.

Anson, Chris M. 2011. "Fraudulent Practices: Academic Misrepresentations of Plagiarism in the Name of Good Pedagogy." *Composition Studies* 39 (2): 29–43.

Blaauw-Hara, Mark, and Cheri Lemieux Spiegel. 2018. "Connection, Community, and Identity: Writing Programs and WPAs at the Community College." In *WPAs in Transition: Navigating Educational Leadership Positions*, edited by Courtney Adams Wooten, Jacob Babb, and Brian Ray, 245–259. Logan: Utah State University Press.

Charlton, Colin, Jonikka Charlton, and Tarez Samra Graban. 2011. *GenAdmin: Theorizing WPA Identities in the Twenty-first Century*. Anderson, SC: Parlor Press.

Council of Writing Program Administrators. 1996. "Evaluating the Intellectual Work of Writing Program Administration: A Draft." *WPA: Writing Program Administration* 20 (1–2): 92–103.

Curry, Barbara, Lillian M. Lowery, and Dennis Loftus. 2010. "What a Community Will Bear: Leadership and the Change Process." *International Journal of Educational Management* 24 (5): 404–417.

Frith, Jordan. 2020. "Special Section CFP: Business and Technical Communication and COVID-19." *Journal of Business and Technical Communication*. https://www.jordanfrith.com/wp-content/uploads/2020/04/JBTC_CovidCFP.pdf.

Garfinkel, Harold. 1967. *Studies in Ethnomethodology*. Englewood Cliffs, NJ: Prentice-Hall.

Graziano, Leigh, Kay Halasek, Susan Miller-Cochran, Frank Napolitano, and Natalie Szymanski. 2020. "A Return to Portland: Making Work Visible through the Ecologies of Writing Program Administration." *WPA: Writing Program Administration* 43 (2): 131–151.

Hesse, Douglas D. 2015. "The WPA as Worker: What Would John Ruskin Say? What Would My Dad?" *WPA: Writing Program Administration* 38 (2): 129–140.

Hult, Christine, and the Portland Resolution Committee. 1992. "The Portland Resolution." *WPA: Writing Program Administration* 16 (1–2): 88–94.

Konkiel, Stacy. 2016. "How to Use Altmetrics to Showcase Engagement Efforts for Promotion and Tenure." https://www.altmetric.com/blog/how-to-use-altmetrics-to-showcase-engagement-efforts-for-promotion-and-tenure/.

Kynard, Carmen. 2018. "Stayin Woke: Race-Radical Literacies in the Makings of a Higher Education." *College Composition and Communication* 69 (3): 519–529.

McLeod, Susan H. 1995. "The Foreigner: WAC Directors as Agents of Change." In *Resituating Writing: Constructing and Administering Writing Programs*, edited by Joseph Janangelo and Kristine Hansen, 108–116. Portsmouth, NH: Boynton/Cook.

Perkins, David N., and Gavriel Salomon. 2012. "Knowledge to Go: A Motivational and Dispositional View of Transfer." *Educational Psychologist* 47 (3): 248–258.

Tenure for the Common Good. "About Us." 2021. https://tenureforthecommongood.org/about/.

Zahneis, Megan. 2020. "Faculty Members Fear Pandemic Will Weaken Their Ranks." *Chronicle of Higher Education*, April 9. https://www.chronicle.com/article/faculty-members-fear-pandemic-will-weaken-their-ranks/.

PART 1

Advocating through Representations of WPA Labor

1
NOTHING NEW
Systemic Invisibility, Epistemological Exclusion, and Faculty and Administrators of Color

Sheila Carter-Tod

It is difficult to consider invisible labor and race in relation to writing program administration without acknowledging that there are very few faculty of color in writing program administrative roles. This lack of administrative diversity is an issue that is not restricted to writing studies. A consideration of race in a data-driven approach to making visible the invisible labor associated with writing program directorship (or any academic administrative program directorship) must first make visible not only the statistics of faculty of color in higher education but also the invisible labor that often limits these faculty members' career trajectories—progress toward tenure and promotion and possible appointments to academic administrative positions. In addition, any exploration of race, invisible labor, and programmatic administration must be further examined in the current context of local and national racial unrest because such unrest expands expectations of labor (both visible and invisible) for faculty of color—expectations not placed on majority faculty.

In this chapter, I first examine the data on faculty of color in higher education, focusing on the statistics and percentages around tenure and promotion and appointments to administrative positions. In doing this, I account for the connections between invisible labor and academic career persistence. I then review the scholarship that explores the impact of invisible labor on faculty of color in higher education during local and national racial unrest. This exploration further makes visible an aspect of invisible labor that is not always understood or explored.

Finally, focusing specifically on writing program administration, I review the existing scholarship of race and writing program administration to consider why specific disciplinary efforts to consider race and program administration in isolation often fall short of creating actual change.

DATA ON FACULTY OF COLOR IN HIGHER EDUCATION: THE STATISTICS

While writing program administrators (WPAs) are appointed at various academic and professional ranks, the number of faculty of color (FOC) in academic positions significantly limits the pool of possible FOC in WPA positions. A 2020 National Center for Education Statistics study reports that in 2018, of the 163,677 earned doctoral degrees, 9.2 percent were earned by Black students, 8.4 percent by Hispanic students, and less than 0.4 percent by American Indian/Alaska Native students. This percentage is further reduced when considering students of color (SOC) who earned doctorates and went on to university faculty positions. A more recent National Center for Education Statistics (2022) report reveals that in the fall of 2020, of all full-time faculty in degree-granting postsecondary institutions, only 2 percent were Black males, Black females, Hispanic males, and Hispanic females. In addition, those who identified as American Indian/Alaska Native and those who were of two or more races made up only 1 percent or less of full-time faculty. For full-time assistant professors, Asian and Pacific Islander males and females made up 7 percent each, with African American females making up 5 percent and African American males and Hispanic males and females accounting for only 3 percent. American Indian/Alaska Native individuals and individuals of two or more races each comprised 1 percent or less of full-time assistant professors (National Center for Education Statistics 2022).

These statistics are even more problematic when examined in terms of persistence to associate and full professor—ranks most often targeted for administrative roles. A 2017 report (Bichsel and McChesney 2017) from the College and University Professional Association states that the gap in representation of minorities in higher education administrative positions is not narrowing but instead has been fairly consistent since 2010. And the 2019 Administrators in Higher Education Annual Report recorded racial/ethnic minority administrators as a mere 16 percent of the 50,880 administrators surveyed (Pritchard, Li, McChesney, and Bichsel 2019).

Beyond statistical underrepresentation, FOC have to negotiate additional, layered institutional obstructive and disruptive structures. FOC often encounter overt and covert systematic racialized structures that undervalue their labor and often discredit their scholarship. Research on and by FOC illustrates experiences of discrimination, hostile campus climates, social isolation, research censorship, ineffective mentoring, high service expectations, tokenism, invisibility/hyper-visibility, and professional and scholarly epistemological exclusion (Settles, Jones, Buchanan, and Dotson 2020). For FOC, understanding the issue of invisible labor is not a new concept. From terms such as *cultural taxation* (Padilla 1994) to the pressure of "double doubt" (Griffin, Bennett, and Harris 2013) to the cumulative effect of this invisible labor described as "racial battle fatigue,"[1] there is a well-researched body of knowledge documenting the burden of invisible labor (both physical and emotional) on FOC in institutions of higher education.

Recent scholarship documents the kairotic moments that have intensified this invisible labor—moments of local and national racial unrest (Haynes and Bazner 2019).[2] Such unprecedented upsurges in accounts and coverage of racial incidents, both on and off campuses, in the past five to seven years[3] compound the complexity of mental, physical, and emotional invisible labor associated with working within structures that enact, reflect, and react to local and national racial unrest. This invisible labor is further intensified for FOC who are expected to represent and support existing institutional structures, values, and practices (in order to experience professional success) while simultaneously personally and professionally responding and reacting to these structures' racist actions. T. Elon Dancy, Kirsten T. Edwards, and James Earl Davis (2018) characterize the double bind of this expectation as reinforcing existing university "settler colonialism and anti-Blackness." They state that "Black student, faculty, and staff experiences that have ignited these protests reflect higher education's investment in maintaining an institutional and social relationship of ownership with people of color and Black people in particular. Therefore, the experiences of Black people on historically White campuses are best understood as continuities of colonial preoccupations" (177).

Ruthanne Crapo Kim, Ann J. Cahill, and Melissa Jacquart (2020) characterize the personal toll of the invisible labor for FOC during racial unrest as ontological. For them, understanding ontological labor "begins with acknowledgement that being a member of a historically marginalized group comes with the burdens of managing the oppressive norms and behaviors expressed both individually and institutionally . . . [and] . . . comes with demands for labor that are utterly foreign to the experiences of members of historically dominant groups" (11). They go on to describe the demands of this ontological labor as taking "time and mental energy to navigate. [This labor] also demands that a person decide in what way they will engage the prevailing system . . . processes that are often beyond the scope of outlined duties. Additionally, all these choices have social and political implications for one's overall fitness to remain a worker at the university" (21).

Contextualizing the complexities of invisible labor for FOC in times of racial unrest, Claire Garcia (2017) explains the internalized stress of serving as the "voice of color on various committees or weighing in on diversity and inclusion issues outside of one's field" by stating that "we may feel vulnerable in the face of continuing police brutality, increasing numbers of apartheid schools, and stubborn disparities in all dimensions of life from health to employment. And one can't overlook the effects of the election of a president [Donald Trump] who is shameless in his bigotry on national and campus climates." Beyond being uncompensated, this labor benefits the university and not the FOC, thereby taking a cumulative professional toll. Patricia Matthew (2016) states that "chances are a faculty member of color is not going to get a sabbatical or a grant from her institution because she contributes to the diversity mission her university probably has posted somewhere on its website. She certainly isn't going to get tenure for it."

Across academic disciplines, the personal and professional cost of invisible labor inhibits promotion and advancement, thus contributing to the limited numbers of pre- and post-tenured[4] FOC in administrative appointments—both by consideration and personal choice. Natasha N. Croom (2017) reinforces the cost of invisible labor on persistence and promotion by stating that "when race and gender are accounted for, data show that there is less representation of womyn and FOC, and specifically womyn of color, beyond the Associate Professor rank. . . . These disparities then continue into institutional administrative positions (i.e., academic deans, provosts, presidents, etc.) where womyn of color are a rarity rather than a norm across institutional type."

General statistical representation of FOC and the invisible labor expected of them clearly contributes to the widening deficit of FOC in such administrative roles as writing program administration. While one solution may be to increase overall numbers, such continued efforts by professional organizations in writing studies has had limited effect. Yet as Genevieve García de Mueller (2016, 37) states, "The task to interrogate WPA work through the lens of race and ethnicity is daunting and requires more than a look at the lack of representation of minoritized groups."

RACE AND WRITING PROGRAM ADMINISTRATION

Unlike the wealth of scholarship exploring the intersections of race and invisible labor in institutions of higher education more broadly, a comprehensive search of race and invisible labor in writing studies (with a focus on writing program administration) yields limited results. What follows is a review of selected works by key scholars who have specifically addressed race and writing program administration.[5]

As far back as Asao B. Inoue (2010, 138), there were calls for writing program administrators to "engag[e] with the racialized, gendered, sexualized, and classed bodies in our classrooms in ethical ways, mean[ing] that we develop writing assessment technologies as critical processes that speak directly to the diverse subjectivities and linguistic diversity in our classrooms." Later, in his Council of Writing Program Administrators Conference Friday plenary address, Inoue (2016, 135) directly challenges the "well-meaning" racist practices of writing program administrators when he "make[s] the argument that how we judge language typically in writing classrooms and programs, and in all journals of the field, is racist because of the ways language and judgment work and because of the ways race is closely connected to language. . . . Our primary jobs as teachers, scholars, and administrators, our jobs as judges of language, is [*sic*] inherently a racist practice."

Other key scholarly voices that explore the intersection of race and writing program administration are Collin Lamont Craig and Staci Perryman-Clark (2011, 37), who, in an interview publicizing their book *Black Perspectives in Writing Program Administration*, describe the work as presenting a "framework for understanding . . . identity politics in WPA scholarship that is constructed along an axis of multiple intersecting identities."[6] This framework is further explored in the book (Craig and Perryman-Clark 2019, 1), in which they and the ten other contributors illustrate how "making race visible in our intersecting administrative and curricular practices creates opportunities to both explore and problematize writing program administration as a framework for institutional critique." In addition to providing evidence and analysis of the ways race and writing programs intersect, their book provides a "breadth of practical takeaway strategies that could address the complexities of structural racism and enact change" (2).

In addition, Genevieve García de Müeller and Iris Ruiz's (2017, 9) published findings directly address the challenges faced by FOC by "argu[ing] that scholars of color often work in isolation recognizing that programs lack effective strategies to systematically implement race-based pedagogy or examine specific institutional resources to help combat racism on campuses." Davila and Elder (2017) focus on the ideologies of whiteness inherent in the expectations of Standard English, which is often the foundation for many writing programs to challenge perspectives and attitudes in their programs at the intersectionality of race, language diversity, and program administration. In addition to these scholars' work, other published pieces in *WPA: Writing Program Administration* explore the intersection of race and writing program administration. The *WPA: Writing Program Administration* special issue (2016, 9), "Symposium: Challenging Whiteness and/in Writing Program Administration and Writing," provides "a variety of topics addressing race-based issues pertaining to WPA work such as supporting faculty and graduate students in writing studies, choosing textbooks, de-normalizing whiteness, and in general, becoming more thoughtful and attentive to issues of race as administrators."

But what changes has this scholarship made? Five or ten years from now, will there still be articles bemoaning the absence of FOC in writing program administration? Have the current racial unrest and protests against racist actions effected any real change beyond documenting the increased invisible labor of WPAs of color? Kimberly C. Harper (2020) raises similar questions in considering how current antiracist commitments will actually change practices in higher education. Noting the ease with which academics can "be anti-racist behind a computer screen," Harper asks a series of questions about the ability of those in higher education to have the courage to create real change: "Do we have the courage to forge a new path? Do we have the courage to be uncomfortable? Do we have the courage to be silent and let others walk into spaces that have been traditionally reserved for white men? Do we? Can we do this in real life—at our faculty meetings, in our classrooms" (n.p.). The same questions could be asked of existing writing program administrators as well as of the Council of Writing Program Administrators. Beyond courage, what would it take to make real change?

Because higher education was established to develop, support, and maintain existing racial hierarchies, smatterings of isolated attention will never be enough. As Pamela Quiroz (2020, 131) states, "We must look beyond individualistic approaches to solve the problems of racism in academia. . . . Racism is a systemic issue and therefore must be addressed systemically." Perryman-Clark and Craig (2019) also advocate for more systemic, institution-wide change: "We see WPA work, then, as a space to think about antiracist pedagogy to effect not simply classroom innovation, but also disciplinary and institutional transformation. . . .

In effect, for us, we believe that in order to move the field forward in our adoptions of antiracist pedagogy, we also need to advocate more strongly for institutional change beyond the work we do as WPAs in campus-wide writing programs."

In other words, true systemic change would mean acknowledging that expecting race-based scholarship to be solely the responsibility of FOC is isolated, ineffective, and invisible labor. Continuing to expect the research of scholars of color (and their allies) to be the only space for exploring race means allowing all other scholars to systematically conduct and publish scholarship that reinforces existing racial hierarchies and only speaks to and for limited audiences. Systemically, addressing invisible labor through quantification and reward begins to consider who is doing what work and for whom.

MAKING INVISIBLE LABOR VISIBLE THROUGH QUANTIFIED COMPENSATION

One possible data-driven disruption to addressing invisible labor and the battle fatigue associated with this labor would be operationalizing and ultimately compensating the invisible labor of FOC. According to the Social Sciences Feminist Network Research Interest Group (2017, 241), "Developing systems that link such labor with its economic value can validate faculty work and render this labor more visible." With the recent trend of university academic budget plans being based on business models, department heads and deans have sought ways for liberal arts and human sciences programs to survive in such performance-based models. If the retention of faculty; the mentoring, advising, and support of undergraduate and graduate students of color; the representation of "diversity" on committees; and the race-based insights around curriculum revision indeed constitute work that enhances the university, then it is the role of university leadership to devise some way "to quantify and analyze [that] work . . . [with] data being readily visible, in a manner that statistical metrics can accurately capture" (Cherry 2016, 1). When invisible labor performed by FOC is recognized and rewarded for what it is—quantifiable work that sustains the university's reputation by helping the university meet larger strategic goals of "diversification"—then that work becomes not only visible but also rewarded accordingly. However, for this work to be valued in the same ways existing university work is, there has to be a shift in existing epistemological hierarchies of what is and is not considered scholarship, teaching, and service. Quantification and reward alone do not necessarily resolve challenges to retention and promotion. While García de Müeller (2016, 37) makes the following statement about what is needed for students of color, the same could be said about the diverse logics and rhetorics often utilized in the scholarship of FOC—what is needed is a more systematic "critical analysis of how and why academia is embedded in white dominant discourses. Many WPAs of color have worked to add diversity to the canon, but rarely do writing programs have systems that value the diverse logics and rhetorics students employ or the diverse rhetorical and discursive skills students already possess."

MAKING INVISIBLE LABOR VISIBLE THROUGH EPISTEMOLOGICAL INCLUSION

For FOC and administrators of color (AOC), there is often a constant battle to have both scholarship on race and scholarship that utilizes nontraditional research methods, structures for reporting, and publication venues recognized as legitimate. This experience of having one's scholarship questioned, devalued, or even deemed illegitimate by members of the academy is known as "epistemic exclusion";[7] the work involved in defending one's credibility and scholarship is a form of invisible labor for FOC that is particularly pernicious. In "Epistemic Exclusion: Scholar(ly) Devaluation That Marginalizes Faculty of Color," a "study [that] investigates the multiple ways in which epistemic exclusion occurs, as well as identifies some of the ways in which it creates negative outcomes for faculty of color," Isis H. Settles, Martinque K. Jones, NiCole T. Buchanan, and Kristie Dotson (2021, 495) describe the foundations of epistemological exclusion as "racial prejudice toward faculty of color who are viewed as illegitimate and without credibility as scholars. This is based on stereotypes of Black, Latinx, and Native Americans as unintelligent, lazy, and getting unearned advantages" (494). The insidious nature of epistemological exclusion is that overcoming it becomes invisible/emotional labor not only in department-, college-, and university-based encounters but also in external scholarly efforts—conference proposals, grant applications, and publication. When FOCs' scholarship is not seen as "scholarly" or is not published in what are recognized as "prestigious" journals, their scholarship is often deemed pedagogical or service-based, relegating them to promotion to administrative positions that have heavy service- or pedagogical-based workloads—only furthering the expectations of invisible labor.

Making visible the invisible labor associated with epistemological exclusion means systemically recasting epistemological practices to be more inclusive. For many FOC, the choice of what to report, how to report it, and in what venues to disseminate scholarly work may be grounded in more than a need to adhere to existing structures for academic scholarly success. Epistemological inclusion means broadening definitions of such concepts as knowledge, knowledge creation, research, and scholarship. As suggested by Settles, Jones, Buchanan, and Dotson (2021), there is a two-part solution to epistemological inclusion. One part is to review disciplinary practices for bias and racialized practices. Next, with a great awareness of epistemic exclusionary practices, "institutions can then work to shift their disciplinary and institutional norms and values, and subsequently their policies and practices. Institutions can make explicit the value and contribution made by scholarship on marginalized groups, communities, and global populations and acknowledge how scholarship that addresses social problems is core to the mission of higher education. Doing so would then necessitate a shift in policies and practices, particularly those concerning performance reviews, tenure, and promotion" (505).

Epistemological inclusion goes beyond practices that acknowledge, reference, and legitimize the research done by and about scholars of color to courageously disrupt what is considered acceptable for all research done on and by WPAs and other scholars in writing studies. Because people of color are participants in all of the research done by WPAs and writing studies scholars, the failure to include or acknowledge race as a component of *all* research only reinforces the assumptions and institutionalized racist hierarchies that segregate (as separated and possibly different from) all research. In other words, until all scholars acknowledge that race (either implicitly or explicitly) is a component of all research practices and analysis, the research conducted and reported is incomplete. To borrow language used by Perryman-Clark and Craig (2019), any and all research conducted during times of racial unrest is race work.

CONCLUSION

An exploration of making invisible labor visible for FOC, particularly during times of local and national unrest, can seem daunting in light of making real change by disrupting racist educational hierarchies. However, failing to do so or continuing with strategies from the past is insanity—doing the same things over and over again and expecting different results. Instead, it is exactly in and through the current racial and social unrest that so much that had been invisible to the majority is now made visible. Armed with the multiple antiracist position statements that have been released by professional organizations affiliated with writing studies and writing program administration[8] and the untold numbers of antiracist position statements released by universities, writing program administrators now have the rhetorical power for accountability. For real, courageous change to occur moving forward, systematic, sustainable accountability plans will need to be created to disrupt assumptions, practices, behaviors, and expectations around the currently visible race and labor practices.

NOTES

1. *Racial battle fatigue* is a term coined by William A. Smith (2014) to describe the physical and psychological toll on racial minorities due to constant and unceasing discrimination, macro-aggressions, and stereotyped threats. *Racial Battle Fatigue in Higher Education* connects Smith's idea and extends it as a means of understanding how the "academy," or higher education, operates.
2. Documented dehumanizing, traumatizing, and even lethal injustices are recently represented by the deaths of Ahmaud Arbery, Rayshard Brooks, Tony McDade, Breonna Taylor, and George Floyd, along with the many, many other undocumented accounts, as well as the national and international responses to these events.
3. The *Journal of Blacks in Higher Education* (2020) has a running list of campus racial incidents from the present and dating back well before 2014 (https://www.jbhe.com/incidents/). See also *Recent Campus Racial Incidents in the News: A Bibliography* (2021).
4. Not all writing program administration positions are tenure or tenure-track positions, and not all of them are based in departments of English. For a broader understanding of the range of writing programs and administrative roles therein, the National Census of Writing (2013) provides a database landscape of writing instruction at two- and four-year public and not-for-profit institutions of higher education in the United States. https://writingcensus.ucsd.edu/.
5. For a broader examination of other writing studies journals and treatment of race, see García de Müeller and Ruiz (2017).
6. Some of the language in this review is taken from Carter-Tod (2019).
7. "Imported from Black feminist theorists to feminist philosophy, epistemic exclusion questions normative beliefs about what forms of knowledge (epistemology) are valued and which producers of knowledge are deemed legitimate" (Settles, Jones, Buchanan, and Dotson 2021, 494).
8. See WPA-GO Anti-Racist Assessment Task Force (2020) for the "WPA-GO Statement on Anti-Racist Assessment." See also Action Working Group of the Standing Committee against Racism and Bias in the Teaching of English (2017); Writing Spaces (2020), which includes "Racial Justice Resources"; and Conference on College Composition and Communication (2020).

REFERENCES

Action Working Group of the Standing Committee against Racism and Bias in the Teaching of English. 2017. "Racism Exists." National Council of Teachers of English. https://ncte.org/app/uploads/2017/06/NCTE-10008-AntiRascism-8.5x11-v3.pdf.

Bichsel, Jacqueline, and Jasper McChesney. 2017. *The Gender Pay Gap and the Representation of Women in Higher Education Administrative Positions: The Century So Far.* Research report. CUPA-HR. https://www.cupahr.org/surveys/research-briefs/2017-gender-pay-gap-and-representation-of-women-in-higher-education-administrative-positions/.

Carter-Tod, Sheila. 2019. "Reflecting, Expanding, and Challenging: A Bibliographic Exploration of Race, Gender, Ability, Language Diversity, and Sexual Orientation and Writing Program Administration." *WPA: Writing Program Administration* 42 (3): 97–105.

Cherry, Miriam A. 2016. "People Analytics and Invisible Labor." *Saint Louis University Law Journal* 61 (1): 1–16.

Conference on College Composition and Communication. 2020. "Black Technical and Professional Communication Position Statement with Resource Guide." Champaign, IL: National Council of Teachers of English. https://cccc.ncte.org/cccc/black-technical-professional-communication.

Council of Writing Program Administrators. 2016. "Symposium: Challenging Whiteness and/in Writing Program Administration and Writing." *WPA: Writing Program Administration* 39 (2): 9–52.

Craig, Collin Lamont, and Staci Perryman-Clark. 2011. "Troubling the Boundaries: (De)Constructing WPA Identities at the Intersections of Race and Gender." *WPA: Writing Program Administration* 34 (2): 37–57.

Crapo Kim, Ruthanne, Ann J. Cahill, and Melissa Jacquart. 2020. "Bearing the Brunt of Structural Inequality: Ontological Labor in the Academy." *Feminist Philosophy Quarterly* 6 (1). https://doi.org/10.5206/fpq/2020.1.7316.

Croom, Natasha N. 2017. "Promotion beyond Tenure: Unpacking Racism and Sexism in the Experiences of Black Women Professors." *Review of Higher Education* 40 (4): 557–583. Project MUSE, doi: 10.1353/rhe.2017.0022.

Dancy, T. Elon, Kirsten T. Edwards, and James Earl Davis. 2018. "Historically White Universities and Plantation Politics: Anti-Blackness and Higher Education in the Black Lives Matter Era." *Urban Education* 53 (2): 176–195. https://doi.org/10.1177/0042085918754328.

Davila, Bethany, and Cristyn L. Elder. 2017. "Welcoming Linguistic Diversity and Saying Adios to Remediation: Stretch and Studio Composition at a Hispanic-Serving Institution." *Composition Forum* 35. https://files.eric.ed.gov/fulltext/EJ1137852.pdf.

Garcia, Claire. 2017. "Self-Care and Black Intellectual Labor." *African American Intellectual History Society*, March 17. https://www.aaihs.org/self-care-and-black-intellectual-labor/.

García de Müeller, Genevieve. 2016. "WPA and the New Civil Rights Movement." *WPA: Writing Program Administration* 39 (2): 36–41.

García de Müeller, Genevieve, and Iris Ruiz. 2017. "Race, Silence, and Writing Program Administration: A Qualitative Study of US College Writing Programs." *WPA: Writing Program Administration* 40 (2): 19–39.

Griffin, Kimberly A., Jessica C. Bennett, and Jessica Harris. 2013. "Marginalizing Merit? Gender Differences in Black Faculty D/discourses on Tenure, Advancement, and Professional Success." *Review of Higher Education* 36 (4): 489–512.

Harper, Kimberly C. 2020. "Do White People Hate Us? A Year of Activism: Perspectives on the 2020 US Elections, Part 7." *Spark.* https://teacher-scholar-activist.org/2020/07/14/year-of-activism-part-7/.

Haynes, Chayla, and Kevin J. Bazner. 2019. "A Message for Faculty from the Present-day Movement for Black Lives." *International Journal of Qualitative Studies in Education* 32 (9): 1146–1161. doi: 10.1080/09518398.2019.1645909.

Inoue, Asao B. 2016. "Friday Plenary Address: Racism in Writing Programs and the CWPA." *WPA: Writing Program Administration* 40 (1): 134–154.

Inoue, Asao B. 2010. "Engaging with Assessment Technologies: Responding to Valuing Diversity as a WPA." "WPAs Respond to a Symposium on Diversity and the Intellectual Work of WPAs." *WPA: Writing Program Administration* 33 (3): 134–138.

Matthew, Patricia A. 2016. "What Is Faculty Diversity Worth to a University?" *The Atlantic*, November 23. https://www.theatlantic.com/education/archive/2016/11/what-is-faculty-diversity-worth-to-a-university/508334/.

National Census of Writing. 2013. University of San Diego. https://writingcensus.ucsd.edu/.

National Center for Education Statistics. 2022. "Characteristics of Postsecondary Faculty." *Condition of Education*. US Department of Education, Institute of Education Sciences. https://nces.ed.gov/programs/coe/indicator/csc.

National Center for Education Statistics. 2020. "Table 321.20." *Digest of Education Statistics*. US Department of Education, Institute of Education Sciences. https://nces.ed.gov/programs/digest/d20/tables/dt20_321.20.asp, https://nces.ed.gov/programs/digest/d20/tables/dt20_322.20.asp, https://nces.ed.gov/programs/digest/d20/tables/dt20_323.20.asp, and https://nces.ed.gov/programs/digest/d20/tables/dt20_324.20.asp.

Padilla, Amado. 1994. "Ethnic Minority Scholars, Research, and Mentoring: Current and Future Issues." *Educational Researcher* 23 (4): 24–27.

Perryman-Clark, Staci, and Collin Lamont Craig. 2019. *Black Perspectives in Writing Program Administration: From the Margins to the Center*. Carbondale, IL: National Council of Teachers of English.

Pritchard, Adam, Jingyun Li, Jasper McChesney, and Jacqueline Bichsel. 2019. "Administrators in Higher Education Annual Report: Key Findings, Trends, and Comprehensive Tables for the 2018–19 Academic Year." *Research Report CUPA-HR*, April. https://www.cupahr.org/surveys/results/.

Quiroz, Pamela. 2020. "At the Intersection of Gender and Race: Stories from the Academic Career of a Recovering Sociologist." In *Racial Battle Fatigue in Faculty: Perspectives and Lessons from Higher Education*, edited by Nicholas Hartep and Daisy Bell, 129–133. New York: Routledge.

Recent Campus Racial Incidents in the News: A Bibliography. 2021. PaperZZ. https://paperzz.com/doc/7520657/recent-campus-racial-incidents-bibliography.

Settles, Isis H., Martinque K. Jones, NiCole T. Buchanan, and Kristie Dotson. 2020. "Epistemic Exclusion: Scholar(ly) Devaluation That Marginalizes Faculty of Color." *Journal of Diversity in Higher Education* 14 (4): 493–507.

Smith, William A. 2014. *Racial Battle Fatigue in Higher Education: Exposing the Myth of Post-Racial America*. Lanham, MD: Rowman and Littlefield.

Social Sciences Feminist Network Research Interest Group. 2017. "The Burden of Invisible Work in Academia: Social Inequalities and Time Use in Five University Departments." *Humboldt Journal of Social Relations* 39: 228–245. *JSTOR*. www.jstor.org/stable/90007882.

"Symposium: Challenging Whiteness and/in Writing Program Administration and Writing." *WPA: Writing Program Administration* 39 (2): 42–46.

WPA-GO Anti-Racist Assessment Task Force. 2020. "WPA-GO Statement on Anti-Racist Assessment." Council of Writing Program Administrators. http://wpacouncil.org/aws/CWPA/pt/sd/news_article/313021/_PARENT/layout_details/false.

Writing Spaces. 2020. *Anti-Racist Commitment*. Anderson, SC: Parlor Press. https://writingspaces.org/?page_id=69.

2
TEACHER, MANAGER, DEVELOPER, ADVOCATE
Representations of Work in WPA

Kristine Johnson

With responsibilities ranging from grade arbiter and scheduler to teaching mentor and researcher, writing program administrators (WPAs) are multifunctional workers. Writing program administration is not one thing but many things, and this diversity of labor has been formalized in documents such as the "Portland Resolution" (Council of Writing Program Administrators 1992) and "Evaluating the Intellectual Work of Writing Administration" (Council of Writing Program Administrators 1998), which outline areas of responsibility including program creation, curricular design, faculty development, assessment, registration and scheduling, counseling and advising, and scholarly production. Perhaps because these responsibilities are numerous, varied, and conflicting, WPAs have often turned to the *WPA as* _____ trope to conceptualize both their own work and writing program administration as a field. Across decades of scholarship, they have called themselves researchers, archivists, and theorists (Rose and Weiser 1999, 2002); unappreciated wives, scholars, politicians, change agents, and managers (McLeod 2007); activists (Adler-Kassner 2008); heroes, victims, technologists, and politicos (Charlton et al. 2011); and kitchen cooks, plate twirlers, and troubadours (George 1999), among other roles and identities.

Writing program administration encompasses pedagogical, intellectual, managerial, emotional, and physical labor. Yet not all work is equally visible and valued, and each *WPA as* _____ trope carries assumptions about the work that should characterize writing program administration as a field. In his inaugural *WPA Newsletter* editorial, Kenneth Bruffee (1978, 11–12) argues that the work of writing program administration is fundamentally educational: "Writing program administrators in their administrative capacity *are* writing teachers. Writing program administrators in fact teach students how to write in almost exactly the same sense—although not, of course, in the same ways—that we classroom teachers teach students how to write, because both of us are actively undertaking *to create conditions in which learning can occur*" (emphasis in original). Bruffee identifies teaching as the primary function (and identity) of a WPA as well as the work that distinguishes WPAs from other university administrators. Forty-five years later, however, this argument about teaching fails to resonate in the field. Critics such as Marc Bousquet (2004) contend that WPAs are distinct from other faculty precisely because they have abandoned the work of teaching—teaching composition specifically. And in writing program administration, the commonplace holds that WPAs are distinct from other administrators because our work requires disciplinary expertise. Claims about the nature, scope, and ethos of writing program administration are claims about work, and the work we make visible—and thus the work to which we assign value—shapes our professional community and the working lives of its members.

Douglas D. Hesse (2015) argues that the work of writing program administration has undergone significant change in the four-and-a-half decades since Bruffee characterized the field as educational and WPAs as teachers. Hesse notes that WPA work once fulfilled two functions: *teaching* and *management*. Early WPAs were writing teachers called upon to perform managerial tasks such as "staffing and scheduling, handling placement and transfers, [and] maintaining basic course goals and features" (135). When the *development* function later emerged, Hesse explains, WPAs began to prioritize entire writing programs—particularly their growth and improvement—over students, teaching, and writing. Development work envisions entire programs as the primary "unit for transmuting theory and research into pedagogy," and it asks WPAs to represent the discipline of composition studies by educating the teachers they manage (135). The most recent function of WPA work is *advocacy*, which focuses on "the position of the writing programs on campuses, within higher education, and in the minds of publics and policymakers" (135). Advocacy work intervenes in public and institutional narratives about writing, extending beyond local, individual academic writing programs.

The trajectory from *teaching* and *management* to *development* to *advocacy* produced at least two effects on the work WPAs perform and on the field of writing program administration itself. First, because each function has been added to the others, Hesse (2015, 135) explains, there is now "more work for WPAs as well as different kinds." He offers this expanded scope of work as evidence that writing program administration has drifted from its foundational—and more purposeful—allegiance to teaching and writing. Second, because the *development* and *advocacy* functions create a self-perpetuating need for further administration, WPAs have become increasingly interested in their own administrative identities. Writing program administration today "is centrally concerned with writing program administration," a focus that "defines and reifies the nature of WPA work" (135–136). As the presence of this collection illustrates, writing program administration exists today as an activity and an object of scholarly inquiry.

Hesse tells the story of a scholarly community that has drifted from its fundamental allegiances, but he also tells a story about work—a story about the different functions of WPA work and the extent to which our professional community values them. In this chapter, I offer a computational, data-driven perspective on this story. Working with a corpus of *WPA: Writing Program Administration* articles, I use topic modeling to describe how frequently the four functions of WPA work have been represented in the journal and how those representations have changed (or not) over time. Maureen Daly Goggin (1997, 324) argues that academic journals "authorize intellectual and institutional pursuits" and "serve as an important locus of disciplinary power, shaping a discipline even as they are shaped by it." Work represented in academic journals is not simply visible but also authorized. For forty-five years, *WPA* has shaped the field of writing program administration by representing—and thus authorizing and privileging—particular kinds of work and the intellectual and institutional pursuits that work makes possible.

TOPIC MODELING METHODS

Topic modeling is a computational method for indexing the contents of large language corpora, producing reliable results far more efficiently than could human readers.[1] Search engines use topic modeling algorithms to analyze website content and assign optimal keywords, and scholars across the disciplines have employed topic modeling to analyze scholarly journals and primary texts. Literature scholars, for example, have analyzed historical trends in *PLMA* and conducted "distant readings" (Moretti 2013) of thousands of fictional texts. The primary methodological benefit of topic modeling is its objectivity and thus its ability to identify themes in a corpus that human readers—particularly those familiar with the corpus—may not define through their own analysis. Yet topic modeling provides only one perspective on the information contained in a corpus, based on a highly decontextualized approach to language. The algorithms view each document as simply a "bag of words" (Blei 2012, 82), and any findings must be contextualized and interpreted. Modeling a scholarly journal provides one kind of answer to questions about intellectual scope and historical change: which topics are addressed, which ones are not, and does the model confirm our intuitions about the field? Modeling *WPA* answers questions about work because the journal reports on and theorizes the labor of writing program administration: which kinds of work are represented in the journal, which ones are not, and is the historical progression from *teaching* and *management* to *development* to *advocacy* reflected in a topic model?

Underlying all topic modeling algorithms are three assumptions: first, writers generate texts by drawing preexisting conceptual topics; second, every text is a mixture of topics in varying proportions; and third, every topic is a mixture of words in varying proportions. Topic modeling aims to reverse engineer this generative process by identifying the topics from which writers generate texts. It does so by statistically analyzing how frequently words appear and co-occur in a given document. The corpus for this project includes all *WPA* articles published from 1978 through 2017, excluding book reviews, interviews, and conference speeches. Because the algorithm most accurately identifies co-occurring words in shorter documents, I split the 2.3-million-word corpus into 10,766 documents, each associated with a publication year. Using R, I asked a Latent Dirichlet Allocation (LDA) algorithm to identify seventy-five topics, identify the most prominent topic in each document, produce a list of the words in each topic, and rank the words within each topic by probability. Although each word in the corpus is assigned to each topic in varying proportions, fewer than fifteen words typically constitute 97 percent of the topic.[2]

The LDA defines topics without syntactical or semantic information, and its results require both researcher judgment and interpretation. I first assigned each topic a name that captures its overall meaning. As illustrated in figure 2.1, the most prominent words in the topic *Portfolios*—*portfolio, portfolios, scoring*, and *readers*—suggest that the topic addresses portfolio assessment. The ten most prominent words are strong collocates with one another, further suggesting that the topic is coherent.[3] Sixteen topics could not be named because they contained random words; fourteen topics represented neither an activity WPAs perform nor writing program administration itself. One such topic contained these words: *two, years, one, five, three, number, four, six, percent,* and *twenty*. The topic is coherent to the extent that it contains dates and measures, but it does not represent work. I finally assigned the remaining

Figure 2.1. Word probability distribution for portfolios

forty-five topics either to one of the four functions Hesse outlines or to a fifth category addressing writing program administration as an object of scholarly inquiry.

Just as administrative work resists being neatly categorized into institutional metrics, the work represented in *WPA* challenges the boundaries among teaching, management, development, and advocacy. However, these categories serve as heuristics for understanding which kinds of work have been promoted in our scholarly production. Topics representing *teaching* met two criteria: the scope of work could be reasonably limited to one teacher and one classroom, and the work—such as giving feedback or having a class discussion—is regularly performed by writing teachers. For work representing *teaching*, the presence of a program or a program administrator is not necessary. Hesse (2015) describes the *management* function as "minimal management," contrasting it with intellectual and pedagogical work. Bruffee (1978, 12) similarly notes that "the managerial tasks of making up schedules, assigning classes, hiring and firing" do not characterize the educational work of writing program administration. Topics representing *management* met one or more of these criteria: either Hesse or Bruffee explicitly names it as managerial, the scope of the work extends to multiple classes rather than to a program, or the work simply keeps courses running without prompting further programmatic activity.

Development work improves, expands, and refines entire writing programs; as Hesse (2015) argues, it perpetuates the need for further development and more administration. Topics representing *development* require the presence of a program and a professional administrator, and they meet one of two criteria: first, the work is explicitly named in "Evaluating the Intellectual Work of Writing Administration" (Council of Writing Program Administrators 1998) as an element of program creation, curricular design, faculty development, program assessment, or textual production. Second, the work represents the disciplinary work of rhetoric and composition. Hesse (2015, 135) argues that developmental WPAs bring "the religion of composition studies" to the program, work that depends on knowledge about rhetoric and writing. Finally, when WPA work extends across campus or beyond the university, it fulfills the *advocacy* function. Bruffee (1979, 8) outlined topics for *WPA* to address, many of which extended beyond academic writing programs: "relations with government bureaus and legislatures; grant sources and strategies; uses of public relations techniques; techniques of organization and leadership." Hesse (2015, 135) argues that WPAs become advocates when they undertake this external work, promoting writing beyond and across campus. Topics representing *advocacy* were categorized based on scope: the work either exists beyond the writing program itself or intends effects beyond the writing program.

THE TEACHING FUNCTION

Although Bruffee (1985, 6) and subsequent *WPA* editors emphasized that the "*WPA* does not publish articles on classroom practice" unless the topic is directly related to program administration, the work of classroom teaching is nonetheless represented in the journal. Twelve topics represent the teaching function; they include the work of literacy instruction (*Information Use, Reading, Students: Skills*, and *Process: Reflection*), enacting specific pedagogical approaches (*Community Learning* and *Knowledge Transfer*), interacting with students in the classroom and through written feedback (*Papers, Instructor Feedback, ESL Writers, Students: Classrooms*, and *Online Learning*), and translating theory into pedagogical practice (*Theory and Practice*). Table 2.1 and all subsequent tables list these topics in decreasing order of overall frequency, and they list the most prominent words (in decreasing order of probability) within each topic.

Across time, the teaching function has been consistently represented, and its overall prominence has increased (see figure 2.2).[4] Individual topics vary in frequency, often tracking with shifts in the field; for example, *Papers* (which includes *grammar* and *sentences*) was most prominent in the 1980s, and *Knowledge Transfer* emerged as a topic around 2006.

Table 2.1. Teaching topics

Papers	paper, grammar, writer(s), write, audience, sentence, example
Information Use	information, use, computer, technology, web, computers, literacy
Instructor Feedback	instructor(s), students, papers, assignments, peer, feedback, review
Reading	reading, text(s), rhetorical, argument(s), analysis, sources, critical
Process: Reflection	process(es), writing, reflection, writers, reflective, composing
ESL Writers	language, students, esl, writers, second, english, international, native
Students: Skills	students, skills, write, academic, learn, help, prepare
Community Learning	learning, community, service, project(s), engagement, work, engaged
Theory and Practice	theory, practice(s), pedagogy, pedagogical, theoretical, approach(es)
Students: Classrooms	student(s), class, classes, classroom, discussions, learning
Knowledge Transfer	knowledge, fyc, transfer, strategies, learned, writing, genre(s)
Online Learning	design, online, space, learning, principles, needs, practices

The twelve topics representing teaching accounted for 8.5–28.0 percent of total topics each year, and they account for 25.0 percent of the forty-five topics in this project. Despite some editorial policies that locate teaching on the margins of writing program administration, the work of teaching—the intellectual, physical, and relational labor of teaching college writing—has been frequently represented in its scholarship.

THE MANAGEMENT FUNCTION

Writing program administration established itself as an intellectual project by defining its work as more than management, and Donna Strickland (2011, 90–96) highlights the way the field has actively suppressed or disguised managerial work. Only six topics represent the management function, the majority of which represent work either Bruffee or Hesse explicitly labels as merely managerial (see table 2.2). *Testing* and *Placement* represent the work of assigning students to courses; although *Placement* could be understood as development work that prompts programmatic research, it could also be understood as the work of simply assigning students to courses. *Staff, Course Offerings*, and *Course Sections* represent the work of scheduling and staffing; the infrequent *Problems* represents the work of *addressing problems, issues*, and *concerns*. *Problems* perhaps typifies minimal management because it is reactive work that resolves problems rather than proactive work that prompts programmatic improvement, refinement, and more administration.

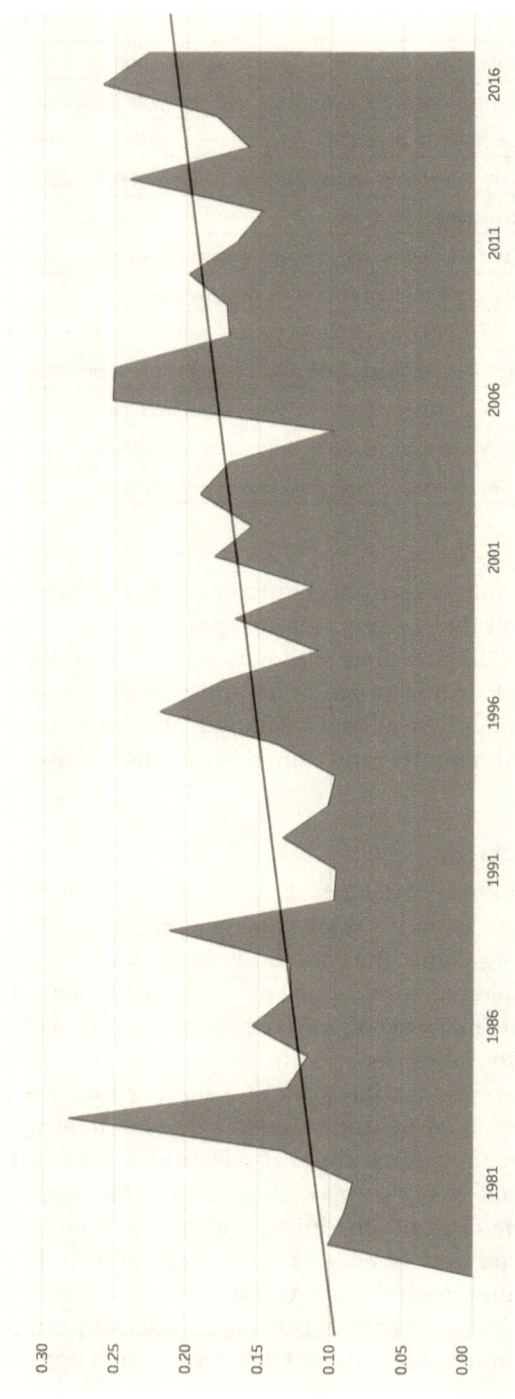

Figure 2.2. Teaching function, 1978–2017

Table 2.2. Management topics

Testing	test(s), essay(s), writing, exam, testing, students, ability
Course Offerings	course(s), writing, general, level, required, requirement, level
Staff	time, part, full, hours, teach, spend, pay, timers
Placement	placement, student(s), placed, basic, course, make, decisions, self
Course Sections	course, semester, sections, students, classes, fall
Problems	problem(s), issue(s), case, address, concern(s)

The management function accounts for 2 percent to 19 percent of topics over time and 13 percent of topics in this project (see figure 2.3). Across time, the function has become less frequent, with *Staff* and *Testing* almost imperceptible during the last decade. The topics *Course Offerings* and *Course Sections* have remained stable at low levels, accounting for 4 percent of topics across time. Management work continues to be represented, perhaps because topics such as *Course Offerings* and *Course Schedules* are inescapable and implicated in other types of work. Yet managerial labor has been overshadowed by the emotionally preferred work of teaching and the intellectual work of development.

THE DEVELOPMENT FUNCTION

Fifteen topics represent the *development* function, and most represent work named in "Evaluating the Intellectual Work of Writing Administration" (Council of Writing Program Administrators 1998). Outlined in table 2.3, four topics represent teacher and/or faculty development: *Graduate TAs, Writing Instruction, Teachers: Training*, and *Workshops*. Writing Instruction represents *writing instruction* and *teaching*, but it also includes the work of *improving instruction* and *curriculum*. Three topics—*Assessment, Portfolios*, and *Scores*—represent program assessment, work that often prompts *Survey Research, Program Evaluation*, and *Research*. When viewed together, these topics are clearly developmental; findings from *interviews* and *focus groups* and the work of *reviewing* and *evaluating* programs effect change and prompt further administrative work. Two topics represent curricular design: *Outcomes Statement* and *New Curriculum*. The work of *curricular change* and *new program* creation is developmental, as is the work of articulating *outcomes* and aligning programs with national *requirements* and *standards*. Although the work is not described in "Evaluating the Intellectual Work of Writing Administration" (Council of Writing Program Administrators 1998), *Writing Tutors* and *Writing Centers* represent the distinctive work

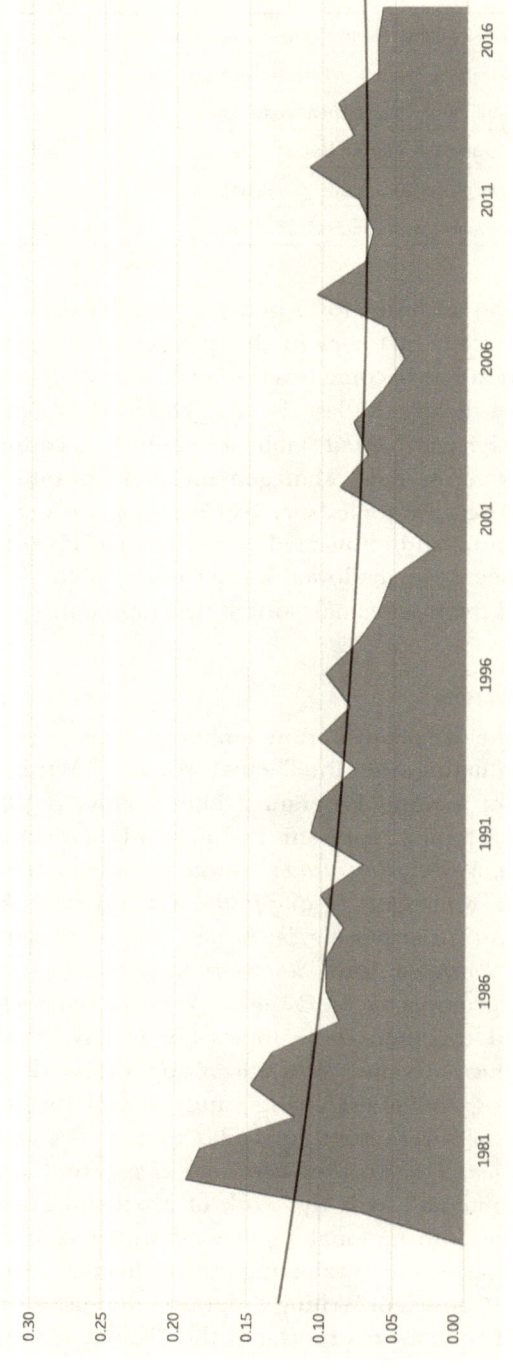

Figure 2.3. Management function, 1978–2017

Table 2.3. Development topics

Graduate TAs	teaching, graduate, TAs, training, new, assistants, teach, preparation
Portfolios	portfolio(s), scoring, readers, rater(s), read, essays, holistic, rubric
Survey Research	survey, respondent(s), response(s), asked, reported, indicated
Writing Instruction	writing, instruction, curriculum, across, classes, teach, improve
Teachers: Training	teacher(s), teaching, classroom, training, observation, experience
Workshops	group(s), participants, workshop(s), discussion(s), meeting(s)
Program Evaluation	evaluation(s), outside, review, evaluate(ing), criteria, procedures
Scores	scores, data, differences, higher, low, average, significant, sample
Writing Tutors	writing, student(s), tutor(s), peer, lab, tutoring, reports
Assessment	assessment(s), writing, local, values, outcomes, context, assessing
Research	research, stud(ies), data, findings, results, interview(s), focus, methods
Writing Centers	writing, center(s), director(s), academic, support, services
New Curriculum	new, curriculum, change(s), changing, program, curricular
Disciplinary Expertise	knowledge, disciplinary, expertise, discipline(s), academic, research
Outcomes Statement	statement(s), outcomes, goals, document, standards, requirements

of writing center administration—work represented frequently enough in *WPA* to produce two topics. Finally, *Disciplinary Expertise* meets the second criterion for the development function, representing the intellectual work of deploying *disciplinary knowledge* and *expertise* in the service of program development.

Development is the most prominent function represented, with its fifteen topics accounting for 20 percent to 71 percent of topics in each year and 35 percent of topics overall (see figure 2.4). It has remained consistently frequent over time, with its overall frequency only slightly decreasing in the late 1990s and increasing during the last decade. Although some topics (*Outcomes Statement* and *Disciplinary Expertise*) were nearly imperceptible before the early twenty-first century and others (*Writing Tutors* and *New Curriculum*) have functionally disappeared, each broad category of development work—faculty development and teacher training, curriculum, and assessment—has been represented in the journal.

THE ADVOCACY FUNCTION

Six topics represent the advocacy function (see table 2.4), yet none explicitly addresses public or governmental policy. Three topics represent the contexts in which WPAs work beyond the program: *Higher Education*,

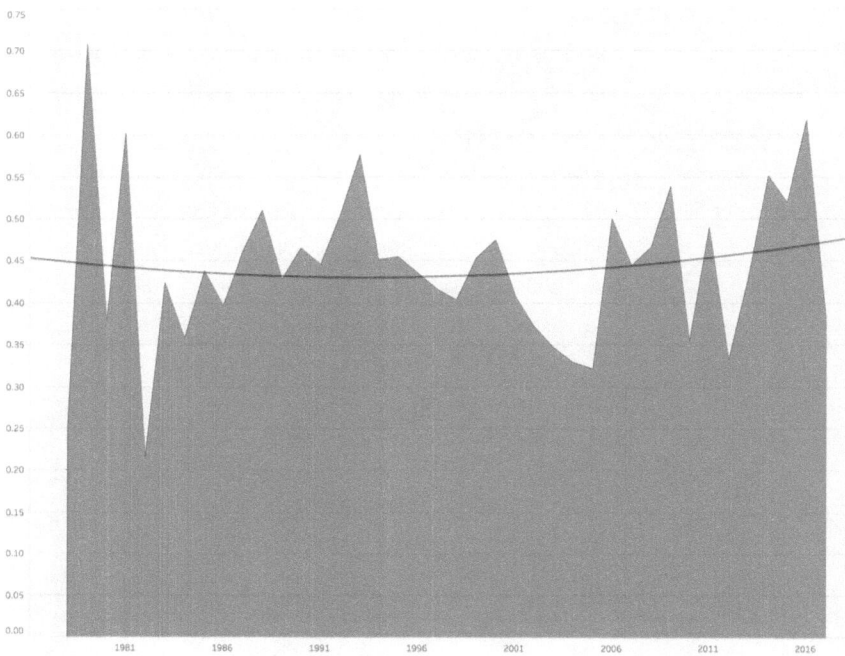

Figure 2.4. Development function, 1978–201

University, and *Institutional.* Two topics represent work with stakeholders beyond the writing program or the university: *Dual Credit* and *WAC* represent work that intends effects for *high school students* and for writing instruction *across the curriculum.* Finally, *Action* represents *ethical and rhetorical action* and *agency*—the agency Adler-Kassner (2008) calls on activist WPAs to exert beyond writing programs and into the public sphere.

The advocacy function was represented in *WPA* only slightly more frequently than *management*, and its overall frequency did not vary across time (see figure 2.5). The six topics representing advocacy accounted for 3 percent to 19 percent of topics in individual years and 14 percent of topics in the project. *WAC* and *Higher Education* are the most frequent topics representing the advocacy function, but *WAC* has become less frequent since around 2010. *Action* and *Institutional* were infrequent before the late 1990s and became increasingly frequent after 2010. Although Bruffee (1979) suggested that advocacy should be within the province of administrative work and scholarship and Adler-Kassner (2008) renewed these calls with the *WPA as activist* trope, representations of advocacy work have been consistently infrequent.

Table 2.4. Advocacy topics

WAC	faculty, wac, program(s), across, teaching, curriculum, development
Higher Education	education, institutions, college(s), programs, higher, universities, schools
Dual Credit	college, high, school(s), students, credit, courses, dual, enrollment
Action	action(s), agency, ethical, rhetorical, making, others, wpas
University	university, campus, state, place, institution, new, large
Institutional	institutional, programs, policy, local, change, practices, within, policies

WRITING PROGRAM ADMINISTRATION AS AN OBJECT OF INQUIRY

The four functions of writing program administration encompass various forms of work, and each function is represented in *WPA*. In his historical narrative of the field, Hesse (2015) argues that WPAs have recently become interested not in work but in themselves. As WPAs turned their attention outward to development and advocacy, they also turned inward to administration itself (136–137). Of the forty-five topics analyzed in this project, six represent discussions of writing program administration as a professional identity, an activity, or an object of scholarly inquiry (see table 2.5). It is arguable that these topics represent work—the work of scholarly production and storytelling and sustaining a professional community—but this work is less materially related to students, classrooms, and individual writing programs. These topics represent the work of sustaining writing program administration as a professional community. *WPA Work* and *Intellectual Work* refer to discussions of *WPA* and *administrative work*, including *job responsibilities* and the intellectual work of *research* and *scholarship*. *WPA Professional* represents the activities of the *profession* itself, specifically the *conferences* and *development opportunities* offered by the *CPWA organization*. And *WPA Narratives* represents the *experience* of being a WPA, recounted through published *stories* and *narratives* about the intersection of *life* and administrative work.

Two topics represent broader issues surrounding administrative work: *Leadership* and *Power*. Although power refers to conventional ideas about *authority, influence,* and *control,* leadership has strong connotations of *collaboration* and includes discussions of *feminist administrative* strategies. The frequency of these two topics characterizes writing program administration topics overall: they were most frequent from 1991 through 2006 and subsequently decreased (see figure 2.6). Discussions of writing program administration as an object of inquiry accounted for 0 percent to 15 percent of topics in each year and for 12 percent of topics in this

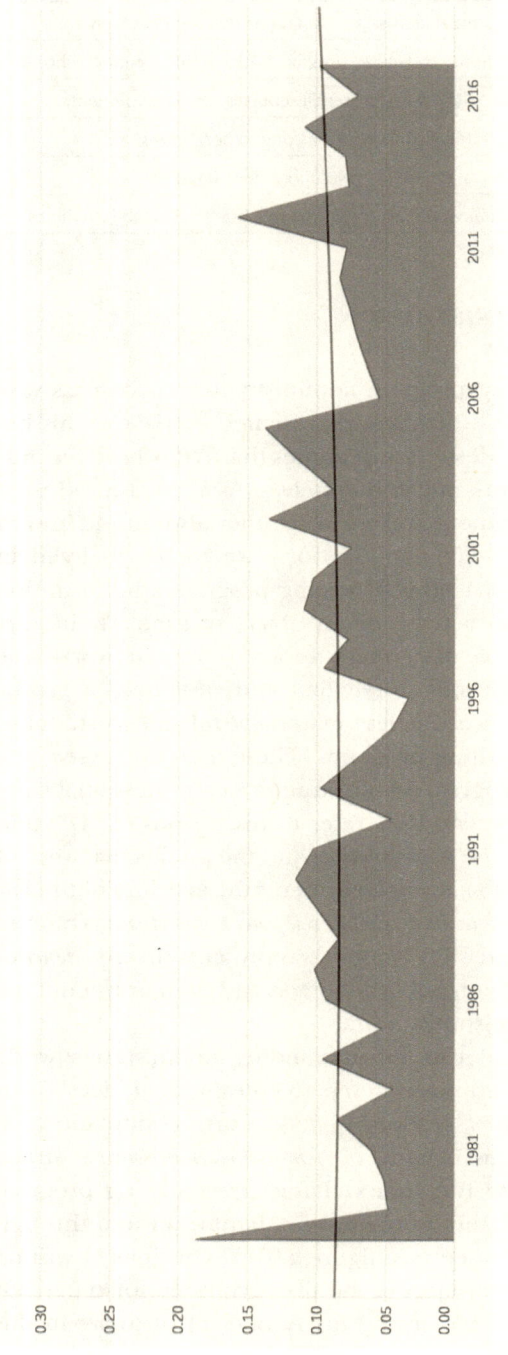

Figure 2.5. Advocacy function, 1978–2017

Table 2.5. Writing program administration topics

WPA Work	WPA(s), work, administrative, position(s), graduate, job, responsibilities
Leadership	collaborative, collaboration, leadership, shared, administration, feminist
WPA Narratives	experience(s), story(ies), narrative(s), tell, anxiety, life
Power	power, authority, influence, status, position, control, institution, others
Intellectual Work	work, intellectual, scholarship, research, scholarly, administration, value
WPA Professional	profession(al), conference, development, members, CWPA, opportunities, organization, national

project—slightly less than both management and advocacy. The decade in which these topics were most frequent also saw the publication of the "Portland Resolution" (Council of Writing Program Administrators 1992) and "Evaluating the Intellectual Work" (1998), documents that fostered the ideas that writing program administration itself can be theorized and that WPA work is intellectual work. Although writing program administration topics became less frequent overall, this decrease does not apply to *WPA Work* and *WPA Professional*, which have increased over time, with *WPA Work* accounting for 4–5 percent of topics after 2010.

CONCLUSION: AUTHORIZED PURSUITS

Scholarly journals reveal the "social, cognitive, and rhetorical dimensions" of a discipline, authorizing particular "intellectual and institutional pursuits" (Goggin 1997, 324). In writing program administration, *WPA* fulfills this role by authorizing intellectual pursuits, but it also authorizes labor by adjudicating the work most worthy of scholarly representation. Forty-five years after the *WPA* was established as a scholarly journal, it seems that writing program administration has moved beyond its founding ethos, and certainly the field has developed in countless ways. My study of the journal, which begins with the distant perspective afforded by topic modeling, suggests that the four functions of WPA work—*teaching, management, development,* and *advocacy*—have been represented contemporaneously. Although writing program administration itself has been represented as an object of scholarly inquiry, these discussions have been overshadowed by representations of work.

The topic model offers some evidence that the earliest functions of WPA work were *teaching* and *management.* Both functions were prominent in the early 1980s, accounting for nearly 50 percent of topics in some years. Yet while *management* decreased over time, *teaching* increased, and five of the ten most frequent topics from 2010 through 2017 represent

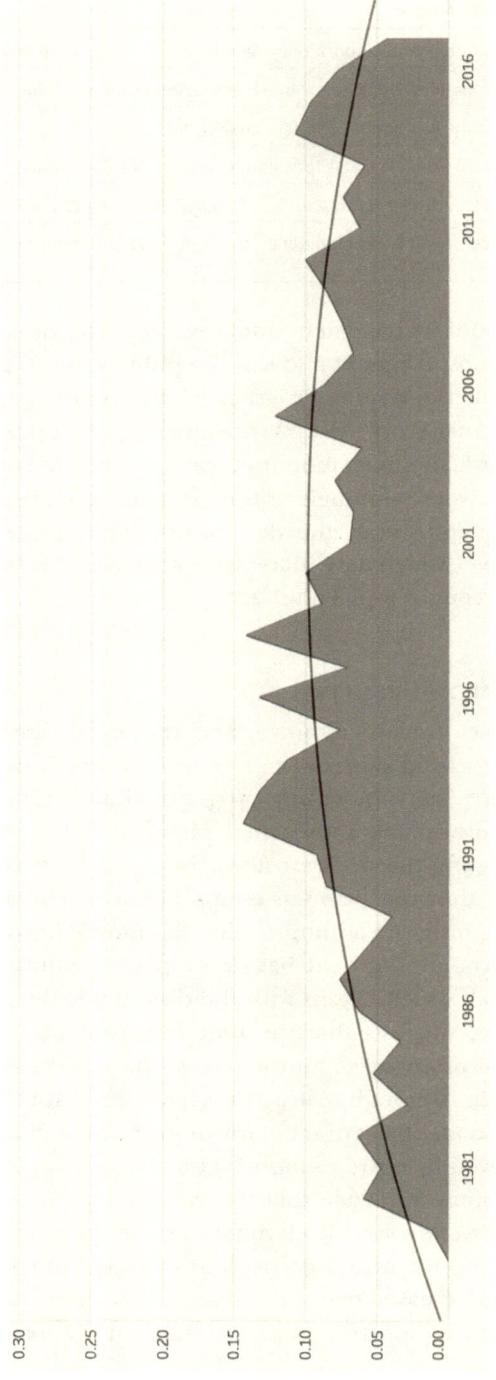

Figure 2.6. Writing program administration, 1978–2017

teaching: ESL students, online learning, instructor feedback, community learning, and reading. If the identity of *teacher* has become less significant, representations of the work of *teaching* have increased. The model further does not offer good evidence that *development* and *advocacy* emerged later than *teaching* and *management*; it also does not offer evidence that *advocacy* has been increasingly represented. It is certainly arguable that *WPA* did not fulfill its founding vision for public advocacy, but it did not replace this external vision with an inward focus on administration and administrative identities. Topics representing writing program administration as an object of scholarly inquiry emerged later than those representing *teaching* and *development*, but they were most frequent in the late 1990s and early 2000s.

Across the history of the journal, the *development* function has been represented most frequently and consistently. Development work produced both the greatest number of topics—the widest range of conceptual categories from which writers generate texts—and the greatest number of documents in which those topics were most prominent. The fact that we have granted development work such visibility suggests two conclusions about the way our community represents, authorizes, and values work. First, the prominence of the development function highlights the relationship between work made visible, measurable, and even tenurable by the Council of Writing Program Administrators (CWPA) and work authorized in *WPA*. The "Portland Resolution" (Council of Writing Program Administrators 1992) and "Evaluating the Intellectual Work of Writing Administration" (Council of Writing Program Administrators 1998) are two public, significant moments when the CWPA made the work of teacher training and development, curricular development, program assessment, and program-based research especially visible. Perhaps because WPA work is multifaceted and historically undervalued, these documents give clarity to the kinds of work WPAs should perform and how that work should be evaluated. Goggin (1997) explores the dialectical relationship between disciplinary pursuits and scholarly journals; in writing program administration, that dialectical relationship encompasses policy statements from the CWPA. The work our professional organization makes visible shapes our scholarly agenda, yet it also shapes the way we individually and collectively value different kinds of work.

Second and finally, the most frequently represented forms of WPA labor have in common not only the development function but also the form of agency the function seems to require. Laura R. Micciche (2011) calls attention to the presence of "big agency" in writing program administration. Big agency intends structural, material, and developmental effects such as establishing programs, developing teachers, leading initiatives, assessing programs, and advocating for writing; the products of big agency are visible, measurable, and tenurable. Micciche argues that WPA agency exists on a "continuum that includes action and change as well as less measurable but no less important forms of action like thinking, being still, and processing" (74). However, she notes that these smaller and slower forms of agency and the work they effect are not equally valued in the field. My study of *WPA* provides some evidence for this argument; these slower, smaller forms of agency have not been represented in *WPA* frequently enough to constitute topics. The work *WPA* authorizes intends structural, material effects on students, teachers, programs, and institutions. Understanding how our community has historically authorized work ultimately asks us to consider what kinds of work and what forms of agency we intend to make visible in the future. As this collection illustrates, making the full range of WPA work and agency visible holds the potential to (re)shape the nature, scope, and ethos of our professional community.

NOTES

1. For an accessible, more comprehensive introduction to topic modeling, see Blei (2012).
2. Andrew Goldstone and Ted Underwood (2014, 365) explain that topic modeling often produces "largely coherent topics with 'intrusive' words . . . and there is the omnipresent low-level froth of randomness, assigning small parts of each document to each topic in an arbitrary way."
3. To further validate the coherence of each topic, I used AntConc (Anthony 2021) to determine if the most prominent words within a topic were collocates—if they co-occur within four words of one another more often than they would by chance. As suggested by Susan Hunston (2002), I define collocate as two words with a Mutual Information Score above three and a T-score above two.
4. The data in all figures have been normalized. The most prominent topic in each document was counted as *one*, and I calculated the percentage distribution of topics each year (with the average number of topics/documents each year around 270).

REFERENCES

Adler-Kassner, Linda. 2008. *The Activist WPA: Changing Stories about Writing and Writers*. Logan: Utah State University Press.
Anthony, Laurence. 2021. *AntConc* (Version 3.5.9). Tokyo: Waseda University. http://www.laurenceanthony.net.
Blei, David. 2012. "Probabilistic Topic Models." *Communications of the ACM* 55 (4): 77–84.
Bousquet, Marc. 2004. "Composition as Management Science." In *Tenured Bosses and Disposable Teachers: Writing Instruction in the Managed University*, edited by Marc Bousquet, Tony Scott, and Leo Parascondola, 11–35. Carbondale: Southern Illinois University Press.

Bruffee, Kenneth. 1985. "The WPA as (Journal) Writer: What the Record Reveals." *WPA: Writing Program Administration* 9 (1–2): 5–10.
Bruffee, Kenneth. 1979. "Editorial." *WPA: Writing Program Administration* 3 (1): 7–8.
Bruffee, Kenneth. 1978. "Editorial." *WPA Newsletter* 1 (3): 6–12.
Charlton, Colin, Jonikka Charlton, Tarez Samra Graban, Kathleen J. Ryan, and Amy Ferdinant Stolley. 2011. *GenAdmin: Theorizing WPA Identities in the Twenty-First Century*. Anderson, SC: Parlor Press.
Council of Writing Program Administrators. 1998. "Evaluating the Intellectual Work of Writing Administration." https://wpacouncil.org/aws/CWPA/pt/sp/statements.
Council of Writing Program Administrators. 1992. "The Portland Resolution: Guidelines for Writing Program Administrator Positions." *WPA: Writing Program Administration* 16 (1–2): 88–94.
George, Diana, ed. 1999. *Kitchen Cooks, Plate Twirlers, and Troubadours: Writing Program Administrators Tell Their Stories*. Portsmouth, NH: Heinemann.
Goggin, Maureen Daly. 1997. "Composing a Discipline: The Role of Scholarly Journals in the Disciplinary Emergence of Rhetoric and Composition since 1950." *Rhetoric Review* 15 (2): 322–348.
Goldstone, Andrew, and Ted Underwood. 2014. "The Quiet Transformations of Literary Studies: What Thirteen Thousand Scholars Could Tell Us." *New Literary History* 45 (3): 359–384.
Hesse, Douglas D. 2015. "The WPA as Worker: What Would John Ruskin Say? What Would My Dad?" *WPA: Writing Program Administration* 38 (2): 129–140.
Hunston, Susan. 2002. *Corpora in Applied Linguistics*. Cambridge: Cambridge University Press.
McLeod, Susan. 2007. *Writing Program Administration*. West Lafayette, IN: Parlor Press.
Micciche, Laura R. 2011. "For Slow Agency." *WPA: Writing Program Administration* 35 (1): 73–90.
Moretti, Franco. 2013. *Distant Reading*. London: Verso.
Rose, Shirley K., and Irwin Weiser, eds. 2002. *The Writing Program Administrator as Theorist: Making Knowledge Work*. Portsmouth, NH: Heinemann.
Rose, Shirley K., and Irwin Weiser, eds. 1999. *The Writing Program Administrator as Researcher: Inquiry in Action and Reflection*. Portsmouth, NH: Heinemann.
Strickland, Donna. 2011. *The Managerial Unconscious in the History of Composition Studies*. Carbondale: Southern Illinois University Press.

3
REVISING THE TERMINOLOGY AND FRAMES AROUND WPA WORK TO UNCOVER NETWORKS OF SITES OF WRITING ADMINISTRATION

Jill Gladstein

Discourse communities use terminology to show shared understanding. These terms and their implied meaning signal who may be an insider or an outsider to the discourse community. In an academic discipline such as writing studies, we use terminology to define the work of the field, how that work is discussed, and who identifies with that work. Terms such as WPA, FYW, and WAC are bantered around in the conversations of our publications, conferences, and practice as if most participants in these conversations already agree on their definition. But when we look more closely, questions arise. Does WPA refer to a particular person or the work that person performs? Is FYW used synonymously with FYC, first-year composition taught out of a writing or English department, or does it also represent WAC-based first-year writing? If an institution says it has WAC, is it making a statement about where writing is taught, or does this statement imply deeper meaning as to the values or culture of writing at that institution? This lack of clarity around key terms in the field begs the question of why more has not been done to increase the precision and transparency of this terminology.

The field of writing studies, in particular writing program administration, lacks an agreed-upon definition for the term *WPA*. We have not looked to find where this work exists beyond what some assume is the norm of a definitive writing program. We rationalize the lack of a definition by stating that it depends on local context. We often skip over the definition and ask who the WPA is and what work they do. We argue that this work should be considered both intellectual and emotional labor. We examine how different identities and roles interact with and inform the work of writing program administration. Even when attempts are made to

https://doi.org/10.7330/9781646423644.c003

look at the big picture, the perspective of the individual performing this work or the position the work embodies becomes the focus.[1]

We use this singular term, *WPA*, in an attempt to maintain inclusivity within the field of writing program administration by inviting people to self-identify as WPAs; however, this line of reasoning can lead to more exclusion than desired as people operate off an assumed norm they derive from the field or from a siloed position. People may look at the type of positions discussed in the literature and at conferences and make their own decision as to whether to self-identify as a WPA. They may be disconnected from the discourse community of writing program administrators and therefore not classify their work with this term. The current approach to defining this work allows some of it to go unrecognized because the people embodying the work do not self-identify or engage with the field; therefore, their site of writing lacks discussion and research. To better understand the work of writing program administration, we need to look beyond the term *WPA* and terms closely associated with it, such as FYW, because people engage with the existing terminology in a variety of ways and in some cases this terminology does not speak to those who do this work.

The National Census of Writing (NCW), a collaborative project, asks participants to document the networks of sites of writing at their institutions.[2] Through the use of a large dataset, the NCW creates a space to document the locations and positions where the labor of administration takes place across different types of institutions. It provides a space to observe and analyze how a large group of individuals responds to the stated terminology. Because the NCW recurs every four years, it allows for revision of terminology and further analysis of how respondents engage with an expanded set of terms. This revision process creates opportunities for better self-identification and locates patterns across institutions while at the same time identifying the unique and dissimilar positions that exist at different institutions.

This chapter introduces the NCW and the processes employed to locate the work of writing program administration. Using a large dataset, grounded theory, and networks of explicit and embedded sites of writing, this chapter looks at two questions:

- How can the terminology used around writing program administration be more inclusive so a diverse set of schools better identifies with this work?
- How does the revised terminology of the NCW better articulate this work?

This chapter shows how the NCW, through its different iterations, reframes the question of who is a WPA by revising and expanding the terminology used to characterize this work and applying this new terminology to the various sites of writing. It reveals a multi-step process in which survey respondents identify the network of sites of writing that exists at an institution and then self-identify the administrative structures of the network (Mueller 2017). These networks allow us to see not only the individual positions within each site but also the relationship between them. They allow us to uncover the collaborative nature of this work and help us better ascertain the intellectual and emotional labor associated with the work of administering the different sites of writing.

THE NATIONAL CENSUS OF WRITING

The National Census of Writing contains a 275-question set of surveys designed to locate and document the curricular, support, and administrative structures around the writing produced for and in classrooms at public and not-for-profit private colleges and universities in the United States. Administered every four years, the NCW covers eight broad areas: institutional goals, first-year writing and beyond, labor conditions of those teaching first-year writing, writing across the curriculum, writing centers, writing majors and minors, identifying and supporting a diverse set of writers, and the demographics of those completing the survey.[3] Much as the US Census does not set out to find the best people, the NCW does not make judgments about best practices or programs. Instead, it aims to uncover and count the different sites of writing on a given campus. If an institution identifies that a particular site of writing exists on its campus, the survey asks follow-up questions to learn more about that site. For example, once someone identifies that their institution has a writing center or a learning center with writing tutors, the survey asks questions about the location of the center; services and events offered; staffing, including training and professional development; and traffic trends.

Participants

After searching the website of individual institutions and requesting information using e-lists, invitations to complete the NCW were sent to one or more people at each participating institution. Table 3.1 shows the number of schools invited to complete the NCW and the number who participated.[4] The response rate in 2013 for four-year institutions was 42 percent and for two-year institutions, 24 percent. In 2017, the

Table 3.1. NCW participation rates for 2013 and 2017

	Invited to Participate in 2013	Participated in 2013	Invited to Participate in 2017	Participated in 2017
Four-year Institutions	1,621	680	1,316	622
Two-year Institutions	924	220	829	104

Table 3.2. Participation in 2017 NCW by institutional type at four-year institutions

Type of School	Number of Schools	Percentage of Participating Schools
Doctoral universities	202	33
Master's degree colleges and universities	220	35
Baccalaureate colleges	174	28
Baccalaureate/associate's colleges	7	1
Other	18	3
Minority-serving institutions	67	11
Small liberal arts colleges	96	15

response rate increased to 47 percent for four-year institutions but decreased to 13 percent for two-year institutions.

The responses to the NCW presented in this chapter represent a diverse set of four-year institutions (see table 3.2). This diversity of responses highlights where the labor of administration takes place at different types of institutions, identifies similarities across institutional type, and gives voice to underrepresented structures in the literature.

Survey Design

The NCW sets out to locate the different sites of writing at a variety of institutions, a task that sounds easier in theory than it proved to be in implementation. The survey instrument needs to utilize language that allows and encourages respondents to self-identify with the options presented. When trying to uncover similarities across institutions, the goal is to limit the number of schools that mark "other" because they do not believe their institution fits the question posed or the options presented. Using a large dataset and analysis of responses to it, we began to learn which language or terminology spoke to the largest group of individual respondents.[5]

We learned early on that language mattered when we made the decision to change the name of the survey from *WPA Census* to *National Census of Writing*. We began the project with the initial name because of its genesis at the 2012 Council of Writing Program Administrators (CWPA) conference. During the business meeting, then vice president Rita Malenczyk introduced a project she had conducted on the institutional diversity of membership with the question of how we invite underrepresented institutions into the organization's conversations. Several of us thought a first step would be to locate and count the number of people doing the work of writing program administration. We knew who was attending the CWPA conference, but we did not have awareness of who was not doing so. We could not answer the simple question of whether each school had a writing requirement or a person who administered that requirement.

The initial *WPA Census* title spoke to those at the conference, but we soon discovered that these three words in combination—writing, program, administration—either did not resonate with others or produced a negative response. In particular, when we first asked for participation in the survey, people shared that their institution did not have a writing program. An institution may have had a writing requirement or a set of elective writing courses, but nothing on the campus had the label "program" or the resources associated with such an entity. In addition, several people who worked in a writing center responded negatively to the project because they assumed we only wanted to inquire about curricular-based sites of writing, which they associated with the term *WPA*. Follow-up messages explaining our goal to look at all sites of writing and the fact that I myself directed a writing center at the time did not assuage some participants. An invitation to self-identify with the term *WPA* was understandably unacceptable to some because this invitation implied that "you are one of us" when they wanted to be seen on their own terms. Individuals may respond to the terminology differently depending on how they see the relationship between the curricular sites of writing, which some associate with the term *program*, and the support sites of writing, which others associate with the term *center*. Their reaction to the terminology may have to do with how the different sites of writing function on their campus. For example, does each site maintain the same status? What kind of working relationship exists between the different sites? If a writing center director has a different status than the first-year writing director, then they might be dismissive of the term *WPA* in relation to their own professional identity.

With the questions asked in each iteration of the NCW, we focus more on sites of writing than on definitive programs or centers. This focus eliminates the distinction between program and center, which Melissa Ianetta and her coauthors (2006) problematize when they question whether writing center administrators are WPAs.[6] This sites of writing approach uses the lens of explicit and embedded sites. Explicit sites are those that can be easily identifiable on websites and in college catalogs—first-year composition or the writing center. In contrast, embedded sites are those that are embedded in other institutional units whose primary function does not connect with writing. For example, a school might not have a separate writing center; rather, it has a learning center that employs writing tutors. With embedded sites, the institution embeds the site of writing in another institutional unit.[7]

After locating the embedded and explicit sites of writing and the administrative structures at each site, the NCW attempts to locate the work associated with these administrative structures. The survey asks people to identify who has primary responsibility for a particular site of writing such as first-year writing, WAC, or a writing center and then to identify the responsibilities associated with that position from the following list:

- Develop curriculum
- Create program or center documents
- Write grants
- Conduct assessment
- Consult with faculty and departments
- Oversee budget
- Hire (tutors, professional staff, faculty)
- Supervise (tutors, professional staff, faculty)
- Mentor (tutors, professional staff, faculty)
- Schedule writing courses or center appointments
- Place students in courses
- Facilitate placement exam
- Oversee exemption/transfer credit
- Advertise program or center
- Plan events
- Maintain website
- Serve on committees
- Serve as academic adviser
- Other[8]

This list of responsibilities allows for comparison between different administrative structures to better articulate who performs this work and in what manner. It speaks to questions about whether this work should be classified as intellectual work and whether it needs to be performed by an academic leader or a department manager. It unpacks the work of administration and has the potential to decouple the work from the position or person. For example, someone may facilitate a placement test and assign students to courses. If a registrar conducts this work by using the same metric year after year and places students based on machine-graded test results or preexisting data, we probably would not consider this person a WPA or an academic leader; however, if a first-year writing director performed this same work, they may self-identify as a WPA because of the title of their position. On the other hand, if the registrar attends conferences on assessment and works with writing faculty to properly place students based on a variety of criteria including test results, would we now consider the registrar a WPA or co-leader? Is the term *WPA* about the work, how the person performs that work, or how the person identifies with that work that enables them to assume the WPA designation? No matter the answer, we need to first locate the work before we can move on to these important questions. We can begin this process by shifting away from a focus on program to sites and assume the umbrella term *site of writing administrator* instead of WPA. Once we make this change, we then need to look at the terminology used to label these sites, such as first-year writing, to see if the current terminology allows us to locate all of these sites or if an expansion or revision of terminology allows us to locate and better understand additional sites of writing.

First-Year Writing Comes in Several Flavors

The trajectory of the first-year writing survey through the different iterations of the NCW illustrates how we used what we observed and analyzed from each survey to expand the terminology to include a variety of approaches to the first-year writing requirement (table 3.3). The goal of this revision process was twofold: to provide enough options for respondents to self-identify the structure of first-year writing that best represents their institution and to eliminate the number of schools marking "other" so we could begin to see patterns across institutions.

In *Writing Program Administration at Small Liberal Arts Colleges* (SLAC) (Gladstein and Regaignon 2012), the terminology around requirements and positions utilized in that survey derived from what we knew from our experiences on our own campuses and in the field. We knew to ask about first-year composition (writing taught in the English or writing department) and first-year writing seminar (FYWS), writing taught by faculty across the curriculum; however, as we processed the data used in

Table 3.3. Evolution of terminology used in first-year writing

Survey	Options Available to Describe First-Year Writing Requirement
Gladstein and Regaignon (2012)	**First-year composition (FYC)** predominantly taught by English or writing faculty **First-year writing seminar (FYWS)** taught by faculty across the curriculum
National Census of Writing (2013)	**FYC** **FYWS** **First-year seminar (FYS)**—a first-year course where writing is an embedded goal for a course not considered a writing requirement **Core**—part of a core curriculum **Writing-intensive**—part of a writing-intensive (W) course program **Other**—followed by a text box
National Census of Writing (2017)	**FYC** **FYWS** **FYS** **Other**—If you believe your institution's first-year requirement does not fit into one of the other three categories, feel free to explain as much as you want about your first-year writing requirement.
National Census of Writing (2022)	**FYWS** **FYC** **FYS** **Elective FYW** **Other**

the book, we uncovered another category—a first-year seminar (FYS). In spaces where respondents could "explain more," several people commented that even though their institution did not have a writing requirement, it had an FYS requirement where writing existed as one of the embedded learning goals.

In addition to FYS, people in the SLAC survey described additional approaches to first-year writing that we included in the first iteration of the NCW. We wanted to see if these different approaches existed beyond the SLAC context. Unfortunately, these additional codes (core, W courses) and the manner in which we presented them in the first iteration of the NCW confused some respondents who had been accustomed to the singular term *FYC*. Some schools became confused if they had an FYC requirement that they called Core but it was a different Core than we stated on the survey. This confusion led people to leave the survey incomplete or provide explanations in the "other" text box. In the second iteration of the NCW, we simplified the responses available to describe the institution's first-year writing requirement. With these revised categories, of the 420 schools that responded to the question that asked them to describe the type of first-year writing requirement at their institution, only five had a unique structure that warrants the code "other."

While processing the 2017 data, I looked more closely at those schools who stated that they do not have a first-year writing requirement. My own

Table 3.4. Percentage of four-year institutions in the 2017 NCW that have a particular site of first-year writing (n = 433)

FYC	FYWS	FYS	Elective	Other
79%	14%	12%	3%	1%

institution at the time fit into this category, so I was interested to see if schools took up Sharon Crowley's (1998) argument to make first-year writing elective. All but one of the 13 schools has an elective first-year writing (EFYW) course. Table 3.4 illustrates the distribution of the 433 schools across the five categories of first-year writing, both required and elective.

Some schools have more than one site of first-year writing represented in these data, which is why the total amount adds to more than 100 percent; however, by expanding the terminology beyond FYC, the NCW captures many more schools whose approach to first-year writing differs from the norm. This expansion of the terminology led us to look more closely at who administers these different sites of first-year writing and how the administrative labor compares between sites.

Administration of First-Year Writing

The current iteration of the NCW asks who has primary responsibility for administering FYW, WAC, the writing center, and basic or developmental writing. We assumed that most of the explicit administrative positions resided in these sites more so than with majors or writing fellows, where we assumed in most cases that these sites were embedded in the responsibilities of other positions. Within these sites, we asked several questions about the work of the six most explicit structures: writing program director or chair of writing department (WPD), first-year writing director (FYWD), writing center director (WCD), WAC director (WACD), learning center director (LCD), and solo writing administrator (Solo).[9] We did ask whether the responsibilities of these sites are embedded in positions such as chair of the English department or the chief academic officer, but we did not ask for details for either position.

Figure 3.1 illustrates the data for the expanded sites of first-year writing in combination with the specific categories of administrative positions. Over 40 percent of the schools that have an FYC requirement have an FYWD administering it, which may be why some see this structure as representative of what a WPA is. The requirement tends to reside in one department where perhaps just one person takes primary responsibility for the administrative tasks associated with it; however, the inclusion of other sites of first-year writing uncover additional administrative

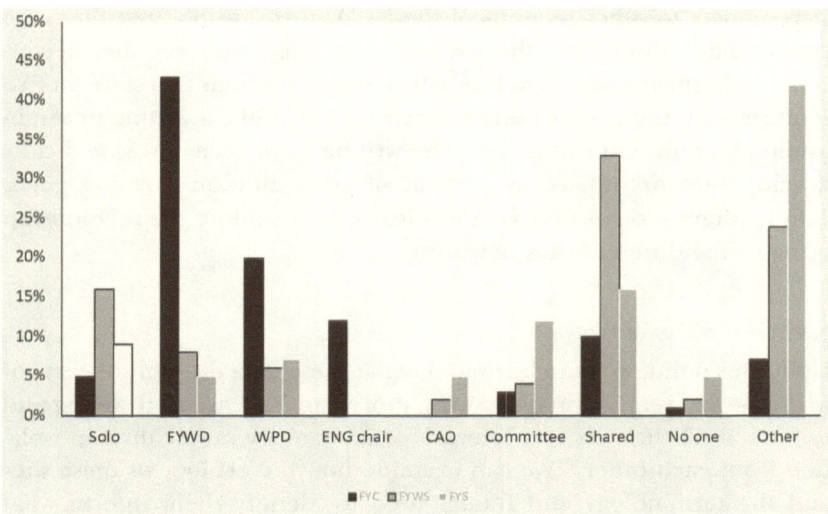

Figure 3.1. Percentage of positions that have primary responsibility for administering a site of first-year writing

structures. When an institution takes a more WAC-based approach to first-year writing, the administrative labor or leadership may be more collaborative. Over 30 percent of schools with an FYWS requirement report a shared responsibility structure. In the next iteration of the NCW, we will ask a follow-up question to those who choose "responsibilities shared" to find out more about this structure. In some cases, this structure may represent two or more people sharing responsibilities as co-directors, or it could be multiple people who have individual responsibilities with no one having the title of director.

The data show that explicit administrative positions perform work in embedded sites (an FYWD administering FYS) and vice versa (chair administering FYC). Questions remain as to what can be learned when we look at both explicit and embedded positions within embedded sites. If we unpack the "other" category of FYS, we find many schools stating that a director of first-year seminar or a comparable position oversees the administration of this site. This construct raises the question of whether an FYS director carries out comparable work or serves as an academic leader in regard to writing, similar to that of an FYC director. Now that the NCW has identified these positions, more research is needed to assess the intellectual and emotional labor of these different positions.

The latest iteration of the NCW did not ask about the administrative structures for the elective site of first-year writing, but by looking at responses to other sections of the NCW, it is possible that the same person who administers the writing center also oversees the elective courses. In these cases, as well as with some institutions that have an FYS requirement, the writing center functions much like a writing program would at a different institution. The writing center may provide faculty development or oversee assessment of an institution's writing goals. This configuration as well as others leads us to explore the relationship between the different sites of writing.

Networks of Sites of Writing

Up to this point, we have been looking at these data through one site of writing—first-year writing; however, more can be learned if we expand to look at all the sites as a network or an ecology rather than in isolation from each other.[10] We can examine how the ecology of these sites and the terminology and frames used to identify them inform what we know about the administrative structures at institutions. Figure 3.2 represents the network of sites of writing at College X—an institution whose administrative structure would not come into full view if we look only at explicit writing requirements, support structures, and administrative positions.[11] This institution subscribes to an elective model for the teaching of writing in which students choose where they will pay explicit attention to their development as writers. This elective model means College X does not have a first-year writing requirement but rather takes a WAC approach to its writing requirement that seems to be in the hands of disciplinary faculty. Through the lens of explicit requirements and structures, a WCD position shows up as the only explicit administrative position at College X.

If we add the sites of elective first-year writing and writing fellows programs and then ask about the administrative structures of each site, we discover that College X employs a writing program director who administers the elective FYW courses and the writing fellows program. Figure 3.3 illustrates the one-to-one correspondence of each site of writing to each administrative structure. However, as we saw earlier with the response "responsibilities shared," we need to uncover whether the work for administering these sites is done individually or collaboratively.

In the 2017 NCW survey, we added a question that asked, who else has administrative responsibilities for a particular site of writing? We made this addition at the suggestion of a colleague who wanted to know more about the resources assigned to a particular site.[12] In addition to learning about the resources assigned, this question allows us to see the spaces

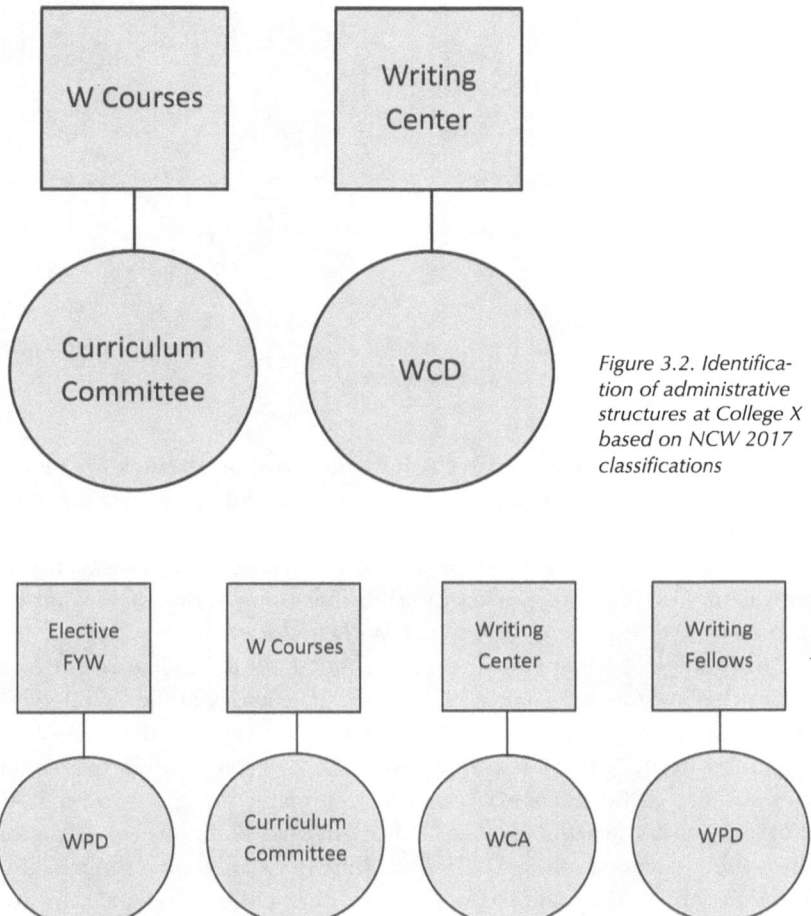

Figure 3.2. Identification of administrative structures at College X based on NCW 2017 classifications

Figure 3.3. Identification of administrative structures at College X after revision of NCW classifications

where sites of writing administrators collaborate within and across sites. Figure 3.4 shows the networks around the sites of writing at College X. The addition of the question about who else has administrative responsibilities for a particular site and an examination of position titles reveal that the WPD is the director of a writing program that includes a suite of elective writing courses, a writing center, and course-based writing tutors (writing fellows) where the WCA serves as assistant director of the writing program. There is a W-course requirement in which the Curriculum Committee approves W courses. From looking at other questions in

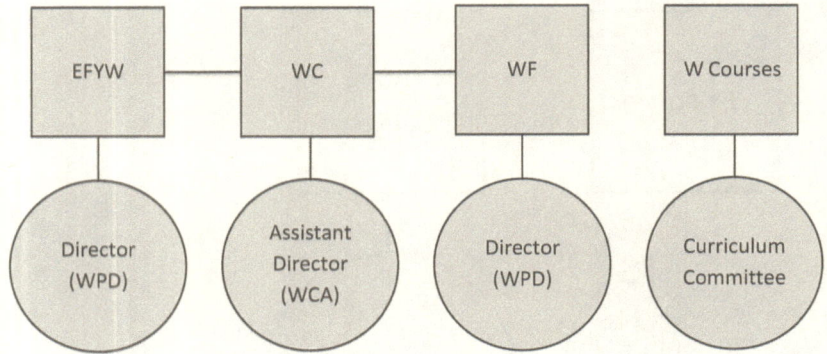

Figure 3.4. Network of sites of writing at College X

the NCW, we know that the WCA has some responsibilities for faculty development, and we might assume that they collaborate with the WPD on these initiatives. Because we did not ask about elective FYW or about the administration of that site or the site of writing fellows, we can only infer from looking at responses to other questions in the NCW what the administrative responsibilities of the WPD include.

This analysis leads us to question if and how the WPD would have responded to the original WPA census. If asked whether College X has a writing program, the WPD may have said yes, but they may have explained in an "other" text box how their program differs from what they suspect is the norm—a required first-year writing course, a WAC program, and a writing center. Although this qualitative explanation has value because it allows the respondent to express how their institution does not fit the assumed norm, it does not allow College X to find schools that may have similar sites of writing. However, adding elective first-year writing as an option turns an "other" into an identifiable response, allowing the WPD to self-identify with a stated category. Due to the NCW's large dataset, the addition of this category also adds a response with which other respondents can self-identify and creates a space for better representation of how different institutions approach first-year writing and additional sites of writing.

SHIFTING FROM WRITING PROGRAM ADMINISTRATION TO SITES OF WRITING ADMINISTRATION

Uncovering who performs the work of administering the different sites of writing cannot be accomplished by simply asking, who is the WPA—a term that implies that we should look at this work through the lens of a program. The revision of the National Census of Writing over time and analysis associated with these revisions illustrate how the use of sites of writing serves as a better frame than does program. This move allows for the consideration of local context while questioning the perceived commonplaces for this work. A sites of writing frame allows schools without definitive writing programs, schools with multiple writing programs, and those with many varieties in between to better articulate the structures in place around the teaching and administering of writing. This reframing allows for increased inclusivity and shared conversation between sites, which allows for a more substantive exploration of questions already being discussed about who performs this work and how the identity of the work engages with the identities of the individual.

A reframing with an expansion of terminology allows for increased inclusivity because it increases the number of positions or people counted. At many institutions, the teaching of writing no longer resides in one course, one department, or one requirement. This expansion requires an extensive examination of the administrative positions associated with the change. For example, some institutions for a variety of reasons take a WAC-based or interdisciplinary approach to their sites of writing. They create a curriculum with courses placed vertically throughout the curriculum and located outside any one department. The positions responsible for providing intellectual leadership to these sites may not have "writing" as part of their title, and yet the work performed mirrors that of a first-year or writing across the curriculum administrator. The revised terminology created through inclusion of both explicit and embedded sites invites the positions and the people occupying these sites to bring their different experiences into conversations about the field. These new sites may challenge current pedagogical approaches, as they provide a perspective on writing beyond the traditional first-semester course.

The term *WPA* places more value on the single position and individual program and, in turn, minimizes a collaborative leadership configuration, whereas a sites of writing frame allows for the recognition of more diverse spaces for individual or shared leadership. This reframing around sites and expanded terminology meet the aspirations of organizations such as the Council of Writing Program Administrators (CWPA) to increase belonging and decrease othering among their memberships. If people interpret WPA as the person who directs first-year writing, it may send a message that administrators of other sites of writing are not leaders in the culture, network, or ecology of writing on their campuses or in the field. Future research needs to look at the leadership configurations around and within the different sites of writing at institutions to learn what it means when leadership emerges not only from first-year writing but from a writing center, WAC initiatives, or an FYS.

The embedded and explicit distinction helps us see the positioning of the work of administering sites, but it does not tell us how the person who occupies these positions approaches this work. The reframing and revised terminology does not necessarily help us better understand whether the site of writing administrator serves as a leader or a manager. We need more research to examine what determines whether a site of writing administrator perceives their role as one of leadership, which connects to previous arguments around this work being considered intellectual work.

With the NCW, we set out to look at all sites of writing because we wanted to encourage conversation between sites and highlight spaces of collaboration between and within the different sites. By using a sites of writing lens instead of a program lens, we eliminate imposed binaries such as those between center and program or between first-year writing and WAC. There may be institutional or personal constraints as to why sites work in isolation from each other on a given campus, but our terminology does not need to enforce these divisions in discussions in the field. An FYWD and a WCD may still work in parallel to each other at some institutions, but an expansion of terminology and reframing allows different configurations of leadership to be recognized and studied. Institutions need to decide the costs and benefits of how to institutionally locate these different sites in regard to their goals and values, but as a field we need to look past these boundaries to better understand how the different sites function in relation both to each other and to the goals and culture of an institution.

The shift from WPA to a more inclusive set of terms based on a sites of writing framework will not be easy. An organization, a journal, and an entire sub-field center their work around the term *WPA*; however, the data collected through the NCW begin to show us why this shift remains necessary. Through this realignment, the WPD at College X will be able to locate other schools with a similar leadership configuration, and the registrar who works on placement and attends conferences to stay informed of best practices should be counted as part of a collaborative leadership configuration. This reframing does not mean to suggest elimination of the term *writing program*; instead, it is an invitation to better define what we mean by this term both on our own campuses and in the field. Close examination of the terminology of the field of writing studies in general and the administration of different sites of writing in particular provides a new lens for looking at topics such as roles, identities, labor, and power. Instead of looking past or accepting the terminology as it is, we should begin to interrogate it to examine its limitations and benefits. The reframing allows us to better answer the question of where this work takes place and who is performing this work. This shift will invite more people into the discussion and add a richer understanding of this work.

APPENDIX 3.A: GLOSSARY OF SITE OF WRITING ADMINISTRATOR POSITIONS

Developmental Writing Administrator (DWA) is a person or persons who administer or direct developmental or basic writing.

First-Year Writing Administrator (FYWA) is a person or persons who administers an aspect of or directs the first-year writing requirement. This does not include a department chair, chief academic officer (CAO), or chair of a writing program or department.

Learning Center Administrator (LCA) is a person or persons who administer or direct a learning center with writing tutors, which may or may not include a designated writing center.

Solo Sites of Writing Administrator (Solo) is the only writing professional at an institution and often directs all sites of writing. This classification was not utilized when a chair or CAO oversaw the administrative tasks of a particular site of writing such as WAC or FYW.

Writing Across the Curriculum Administrator (WACA) is a person or persons who administers or directs writing across the curriculum initiatives or program.

Writing Center Administrator (WCA) is a person or persons who administers or directs a writing center.

Writing Program Administrator or Chair of Writing Department (WPA) provides leadership for most or all of the sites of writing at the institution and supervises and mentors the other sites of writing administrators within the program or department. For example, a WPA may have an FYWA and WCA report to them or with an assistant director they oversee all sites of writing at the institution with the assistant director managing the day-to-day operations of a particular site, most likely a writing center.

NOTES

1. Writing program administration is a field of study with many publications. The following list is just a sample and is not meant to be exhaustive: Malenczyk (2016);

McLeod (2007); Jackson, McKinney, and Caswell (2016); Council of Writing Program Administrators (1998); Horner (2007); Perryman-Clark and Craig (2019); Vidali (2015); Balester and McDonald (2001); Charlton and Rose (2009); Gladstein and Regaignon (2012).

2. The National Census of Writing is a collaborative project. Brandon Fralix and I serve as co-principal investigators. We each take primary responsibility for different sections and conduct our own analyses but often in consultation with each other. I would like to acknowledge and thank Brandon for his assistance with this chapter.
3. Results from the NCW are available on a publicly accessible website, writingcensus.swarthmore.edu.
4. The number of invitations decreased between 2013 and 2017, both because of school closings and because of better discernment as to whether a school had any undergraduate education. The NCW does not include medical schools, law schools, or other institutions that cater only to graduate students.
5. The terminology used in the NCW evolved from work presented in Gladstein, Lebduska, and Regaignon (2009) and Gladstein and Regaignon (2012).
6. Kelly Ritter and Melissa Ianetta (2019, 4) revisit this conversation in the introduction to *Landmark Essays in Writing Program Administration*.
7. More extensive discussion of these terms can be found in Gladstein and Regaignon (2012, 38).
8. Even with this exhaustive list, we unwittingly omitted three responsibilities that we will include in the next iteration. We already include questions around the teaching responsibilities connected with these positions, but we failed to ask about research. This omission became most apparent when many respondents to the writing center survey wrote in research as an "other" responsibility. Someone having the responsibility to conduct research signals a level of engagement with the field. We also need to add whether someone needs to participate in professional development activities, such as attending conferences or reading the field's publications, as additional measures for whether they have the responsibility to engage with the field. In the next iteration of the NCW, we also need to add the responsibility of advocacy. Many individuals in these positions advocate for space, class size, and labor conditions, to name a few. This responsibility may not show up on a job description but becomes apparent when observing the daily practice of someone administering a writing site.
9. To further revise the terminology, in the next iteration of the NCW we will change the "D" in FYWD, WACD, WCD, and LCD to an "A" to represent that administrators may go by director, coordinator, or some other related title. Definitions of each term are found in appendix 3.A.
10. In Reiff, Bawarshi, Ballif, and Weisser (2015), the editors build on the notion of the individual writer as part of an ecology to argue that writing programs function within ecologies. They maintain the construct of "program" by labeling a writing center as a third space, whereas I argue that all sites of writing form the ecology of writing at an institution.
11. Although not inspired by Sharon McGee's (2005) use of postmodern mapping, the visual representation of the different sites of writing used in this chapter speaks to her idea of sites of writing administrators locating their place within a larger institutional structure.
12. Thank you to Laurie Pinkert for making this suggestion. She was interested in better articulating the labor resources afforded to a particular site of writing, but we have found that this line of questions provides data beyond this initial inquiry.

REFERENCES

Balester, Valerie, and James C. McDonald. 2001. "A View of Status and Working Conditions: Relations between Writing Program and Writing Center Directors." *WPA: Writing Program Administration* 24 (3): 59–82.

Charlton, Jonikka, and Shirley K. Rose. 2009. "Twenty More Years in the WPA's Progress." *WPA: Writing Program Administration* 22 (1–2): 114–145.

Council of Writing Program Administrators. 1998. "Evaluating the Intellectual Work of Writing Program Administrators." WPAcouncil.org.

Crowley, Sharon. 1998. *Composition in the University: Historical and Polemical Essays*. Pittsburgh, PA: University of Pittsburgh Press.

Gladstein, Jill, and Dara Rossman Regaignon. 2012. *Writing Program Administration at Small Liberal Arts Colleges*. Anderson, SC: Parlor Press.

Gladstein, Lisa Lebduska, and Dara Rossman Regaignon. 2009. "Consortia as Sites of Inquiry: Steps toward a National Portrait of Writing Program Administration." *WPA: Writing Program Administration* 32 (3): 13–36.

Horner, Bruce. 2007. "Redefining Work and Value for Writing Program Administration." *JAC* 27 (1–2): 163–184.

Ianetta, Melissa, Linda Bergmann, Lauren Fitzgerald, Carol Peterson Haviland, Lisa Lebduska, and Mary Wislocki. 2006. "Polylog: Are Writing Center Directors Writing Program Administrators?" *Composition Studies* 34 (2): 12–42.

Jackson, Rebecca, Jackie Grutsch McKinney, and Nicole Caswell. 2016. "Writing Center Administration and/as Emotional Labor." *Composition Forum* 34. http://composition forum.com/issue/34/writing-center.php.

Malenczyk, Rita. 2016. *A Rhetoric for Writing Program Administrators*, 2nd ed. Anderson, SC: Parlor Press.

McGee, Sharon. 2005. "Overcoming Disappointment: Constructing Writing Program Identity through Postmodern Mapping." In *Discord and Direction: The Postmodern Writing Program Administrator*, edited by Sharon McGee and Carolyn Handa, 59–71. Logan: Utah State University Press.

McLeod, Susan. 2007. *Writing Program Administration*. Anderson, SC: Parlor Press.

Mueller, Derek. 2017. *Network Sense: Methods for Visualizing a Discipline*. Louisville: WAC Clearinghouse and University Press of Colorado. https://wac.colostate.edu/books/wri ting/network/.

Perryman-Clark, Staci M., and Collin Lamont Craig. 2019. *Black Perspectives in Writing Program Administration: From the Margins to the Center*. Urbana, IL: Conference on College Composition and Communication and National Council of Teachers of English.

Reiff, Mary Jo, Anis Bawarshi, Michelle Ballif, and Christian Weisser, eds. 2015. *Ecologies of Writing Programs: Program Profiles in Context*. Anderson, SC: Parlor Press.

Ritter, Kelly, and Melissa Ianetta, eds. 2019. *Landmark Essays in Writing Program Administration*. New York: Routledge.

Vidali, Amy. 2015. "Disabling Writing Program Administration." *WPA: Writing Program Administration* 38 (2): 32–55.

4
THE VALUE OF MENTORING IN WRITING PROGRAM ADMINISTRATION

Kimberly Emmons and Martha Wilson Schaffer

Mentoring as a collaborative learning process is a widely recognized professional practice, and its value is usually understood within the realm of personal and professional development. Indeed, the Council of Writing Program Administrators (CWPA) facilitates mentoring relationships among its members, who come from a wide variety of institutional, structural, and disciplinary locations. As Lois J. Zachary (2011, 3) describes it, mentoring is "a mutual discovery process" in which two parties "work together to achieve specific, mutually defined goals that focus on developing the mentee's skills, abilities, knowledge, and thinking." The benefits of mentoring are not one-sided, however, as the CWPA Mentoring Project makes clear: "All mentoring becomes co-mentoring in that . . . those who come together to exchange ideas leave the experience mutually enriched" (Walcher, Janangelo, and Roen 2010, 89). This type of mentoring—a collaborative learning partnership—has been adopted and studied extensively in writing studies scholarship in the context of writing (Curry 2016), teaching writing (Restaino 2010), dissertation advising (Casanave 2008), and writing program administration (WPA) work (Phillips, Shovlin, and Titus 2016). The tendency in this scholarship has been to describe the interpersonal, situated work of mentoring, what Lynn Bloom (2007, 87) describes as a "mosaic" of personal making that guides and supports an individual in their professional pursuits.

While exploring personal relationships in mentoring is extremely important, we believe it can reinforce an individual ethos and occlude a broader, more significant contribution that mentorship makes to program administration. Indeed, a focus on co-mentoring dyads fails to make legible the cumulative and collective effects of mentoring on programs and institutions. In our own WPA work, we wondered what

https://doi.org/10.7330/9781646423644.c004

mentorship looked like at the community level, asking ourselves and our colleagues how mentoring might contribute not just to the individual professional development of our faculty and ourselves but also to the inner workings of the writing program itself. In this chapter, we seek to explore mentoring activities as essential not just as job training for individuals but also as socialization and sharing ways of doing work within particular institutions, not just as individual professional development but also as systematic development of writing programs themselves. By examining the invisible work of mentoring as an aspect of program development, we hope to emphasize the value of multidirectional relations and the interaction of the personal and professional in ways that advance our thinking about how programs are built and sustained.

In Michelle F. Eble and Lynée Lewis Gaillet's (2008) collection, *Stories of Mentoring: Theory and Praxis*, the authors use narration to explore what mentorship is and what it does as an interpersonal experience. As an example of this narrative approach to mentorship study, Shari Stenberg and Debbie Minter (2018, 642) interviewed veteran WPAs about weathering shifting economic pressures and examined their "'shadow' stories" to explore resilience in the face of frustration. The interviewees reported that "the act of forging connection [is] a deliberate and intentional part of their work" (648). Such connections are both built and discovered through storytelling and narrative investigation. We find that the use of "story" as a practice and as a research method has resulted in a deeper consideration of mentorship as "a mutual discovery process" (Zachary 2011). We wondered what this method might reveal about mentorship if we took a programmatic perspective, a perspective that imagines mentorship as a collection of dynamic relationships and interactions intertwined with and embedded in administrative practices. We began with our own lived experience, which suggested that mentoring was a significant and ubiquitous part of our administrative duties, even when we looked beyond any specific mentoring partnerships. To make mentoring more visible and valuable, however, we needed a more concrete taxonomy of mentoring activities and a means of quantifying, documenting, and analyzing their effects. To investigate these issues, we began with two simple research questions:

- What activities constitute mentorship in a writing program?
- How do mentorship activities contribute to the work (and success) of a writing program?

As we performed our research, we discovered again a disconnect between individualized mentoring *relationships* and collective programmatic *activities*. Despite the fact that traditional definitions of mentoring focus on individual, interpersonal relationships, we kept identifying instances where mentoring appeared to be collective—in pre-meeting greetings and in acknowledging our own positionalities within our larger department and university. We observed significant fluidity in the roles of mentor and mentee, and we identified mentoring moments that were embedded in the daily, administrative work of running our program. As we came to see the program itself as the product of effective mentorship activities, we began to reframe otherwise mundane programmatic development activities as essential plot points in our collective narrative.

This study expands on the interpersonal definition of mentoring—mentoring as collaborative work aimed at enhancing careers—to highlight the value of effective mentorship not just for individuals but also for programs. We believe that using the metaphor of storytelling—or more precisely, perhaps, collaborative authorship—responds to the need to make mentorship work identifiable, quantifiable, and visible. The "storying" of a writing program requires collective alignment with the program's values and purposes, and such alignment develops, in part, through mentoring activities that engage multiple members of the program community simultaneously. Examining mentorship in this way reveals how it unifies the disparate members of the program through the articulation of the program's purposes and values—preserving the program's history, moving the program forward, and clarifying the program to the communities in which it exists. Storytelling also captures the ways programs are developed through personal and social interactions simultaneously. More than acts of individual professional development and different from the traditional methods of creating cohesion around practices and outcomes in program development, storytelling empowers the members of the program as agents in multi-directional relationships.

In the end, we argue that mentoring should be intentional, not only in the practice of sustaining interpersonal mentoring relationships but also in the process of creating membership and cohesion around program values. Thus, mentorship becomes essential to program administration because it encourages program members to become storytellers themselves, invested in and empowered to tell the program's story in ways that thoughtfully build the connections that preserve and advance the work of the program.

BRIEF CONTEXT FOR OUR STUDY

We work at a midwestern research university, with an undergraduate population of approximately 5,000. Our writing program is distributed and decentralized; it operates partially within a seminar-based, writing-intensive general education curriculum, which is administered by an associate dean in the College of Arts and Sciences. This program is comprised of five seminars across four years of undergraduate study, from First Seminars to Senior Capstones. Our writing program interacts most closely with the first two years' courses, including First Seminars for non-native speakers of English and college writers who are less prepared or less confident in their writing processes and various topical seminars for first- and second-year students. In addition, our program includes a campus-wide writing center, a traditional expository writing sequence (operated for the benefit of our partner, the Institute of Music), a professional communication for the engineers' program, and a few writing-intensive English literature courses.

Kim, our writing program director, has pedagogical responsibility for the writing program overall. Martha, our program associate director, has responsibility for the English Department graduate student pedagogical development, the Foundations of College Writing program, and our Directed self-placement process. We are supported by three additional faculty administrators in the English Department—a director of the Writing Center, an ESL coordinator, and an instructional coordinator—as well as by a fourth administrator who holds both staff and adjunct faculty appointments in the general education program. The writing program overall includes more than fifty instructional personnel in a variety of positions: undergraduate peer tutors, graduate student teaching assistants, and part- and full-time lecturers.

Our interest in mentorship has been heightened over the last few years, as our campus has been embroiled in ongoing deliberations over general education reform. As new structures for general education began to be discussed, we were confronted by the human cost of uncertainty and narrative incoherence. Rumors circulated and recirculated: about how quickly a new general education program would be implemented, about how ruthless it would be toward current writing courses and personnel, and, fundamentally, about how writing and communication were understood and valued by the campus community. Our writing faculty were distrustful and anxious about their own and their students' futures, and we found ourselves consistently engaged in both interpersonal and programmatic storytelling and mentoring.

Non-writing faculty members across campus were skeptical of both the structural and the conceptual practices of the writing program. Many failed to understand or accept commonplaces of writing pedagogy: that classes should be small, that revision is necessary, that writing instruction (as opposed to assigning writing) is vital to students' development. Kim spent much of her time trying to articulate the values and knowledge of the writing program to colleagues *outside* the program, while she and Martha simultaneously tried to assuage fears and lead discussions about the role of writing for the university with our writing faculty staff *inside* the program. General education reform made visceral the dual responsibilities of WPA work: to the people (faculty and students) who work and learn in the program and to the program itself, which must be meaningfully articulated to the larger university community. As we reflected on our work over this critical year, we found that mentoring was a central aspect of leading not just people but also programs; we realized that mentorship's characteristic storytelling could benefit not simply individuals but also programs themselves.

RESEARCH METHODS

We began the project with the intention of being able to bring to light work that deserved to be acknowledged by identifying and defining mentorship activities and tasks. To do that, we sought out concrete, countable evidence of mentoring in our email logs, calendars, meeting agendas, and daily routines as recorded over the course of the year. First, we searched and logged all of our emails related to writing program activities from May 2018 to May 2019. Then, we reviewed our calendars for the same period and logged all of our writing program meetings. We examined available meeting agendas and minutes to fill in the details. Finally, we each took one week (April 24–April 30, 2019) and tracked our intended schedules and how we actually spent our days (in fifteen-minute increments). We made use of the search tools available in our Google Mail and Calendar accounts, as well as our note-taking and file folder systems (Google Drive, Microsoft Word, and Evernote), and we built spreadsheets of events and their documented content from both of our accounts. In addition, we consulted with the group of administrators with whom we work closely in order to define mentoring. We used a short survey to ask them to identify activities they understood to be part of mentorship, both as mentees themselves and as mentors (see appendix 4.A).

The survey results provided a constellation of interactions, including faculty workshops and orientations, development of training materials, consultations about course proposals and teaching, annual performance reviews, university-wide committee meetings, collaboration on writing research, giving advice on student concerns, assisting new instructors and those playing new, temporary roles in the program, and weekly meetings with other administrators in the program. Much of what the program leaders described as mentorship activity fell beyond the traditional, visible interpersonal goal-oriented relationships between two individuals, yet it still bore key qualities of mutual professional development and discovery. Alongside these survey responses, our own quantitative inquiry also made processes of mentorship visible in a way that expanded how we understood mentorship in relation to our writing program. In an effort to explore this more fully, we began a process of qualitative coding of our collected data, according to type of interaction and time spent. From these data, we developed a taxonomy of mentoring activities, categorizing mentoring moments according to two characteristics: level of formality and number of participants.

FINDINGS

Despite a lengthy list of regular activities that co-administrators identified as mentoring, they estimated spending only an average of 2.4 hours per week on those activities—only 6 percent of a 40-hour work week. What this constellation of activities and time revealed to us was not entirely unexpected: mentoring felt ubiquitous, occurring through a variety of social and professional interactions with each other, writing program faculty, and university officials; yet much of the work of mentoring took place in the performance of job duties that had explicit purposes other than mentoring. Similar patterns were revealed in our own data. Turning to our documentation of email exchanges, meeting agendas, and calendared time, we discovered that, added together, we engaged in 281 hours of activities that could be explicitly labeled as mentoring between May 2018 and May 2019. In other words, only 18 percent of our combined time was devoted to mentoring activities, far less than we had expected.

A further analysis of that time revealed that we had recorded specific activities that constituted mentoring along two axes: from informal to formal and from one-on-one to large groups. Table 4.1 describes our findings along these two dimensions and gives us a basic taxonomy for considering the kinds of activities that include mentorship in our writing program. Kim's experience as director found her more often mentoring in the formal/structural category, doing less individual mentoring and more collective mentoring in an effort to address the

Table 4.1. Where mentoring happens in our programs

	Formal/Structural	Implicit/Inherent	Informal/Unplanned
Individual professional development	Faculty mentoring for GTAs Scheduled "check-in" meetings with administrators	Emails (tone and content) Structure of workshops and individual meetings	Hallway conversations Occasional social gatherings
Small-group professional development	Team staff meetings Specific workshops on targeted issues	Teaching schedules, policies, and assignments Reports and subcommittee responses to reports	Impromptu meetings to address issues shared by multiple individuals
Collective professional development	Orientations Email announcements All-staff meetings	Modeling behaviors and values in community settings Representing program to outsiders Rubrics and official program documents	All-staff emails and meetings in response to emergent issues

concerns of a large and disparate writing faculty. Martha, by comparison, found her mentoring (as mentor and mentee) happening in the middle ground: implicit/inherent mentoring in small groups gathered for training and development. While we both recalled instances of informal/unplanned mentoring, these activities often did not appear in the easily documented records. Hallway conversations are not recorded; small-group discussions develop spontaneously (and are therefore often not put on the calendar); emergent issues are lost in email threads that are not always addressed to administrative aliases.

In addition to giving us a means of identifying, describing, and categorizing our data, this taxonomy allowed us to see connections among the discrete activities, the arcs of our social interactions, and the intellectual and emotional labor that occurred invisibly to create coherence around our program's goals and values. Mentoring was not just occurring in traditional, formal/structural ways, such as through official mentoring relationships established by the department for graduate teaching assistants (GTAs); it was also occurring in the context of the events and activities that constituted the business of the writing program: conversations before and after meetings, email exchanges about announcements and updates, processes of planning schedules and teaching assignments. Wherever we were interacting with our colleagues in the writing program, we were also saying and doing the things that helped individuals grow as professional writing instructors and administrators—and wherever we were helping individuals grow as professionals, we were co-creating the story of the writing program.

By way of example, Martha was surprised to find that her academic calendar revealed 156 hours of events (only 10% of her recorded time) that fit a traditional definition of mentoring. Of interest to her was the fact that the largest majority of those events (34 out of 80) were designated as "staff meetings": small groups of faculty and graduate students that organized around various topics at regular intervals. In reviewing her agendas and notes, Martha saw that these meetings served multiple purposes but that they were always conducted with an eye toward the professional development of the individuals present *and* the engagement of those individuals in the larger work of the writing program. She might talk with her graduate students and faculty about teaching a particular lesson on writing, but that was always embedded in a conversation about how this served the program's outcomes, demonstrated the program's values, or both. Often, those meetings shaped Martha's own conception of both outcomes and goals for her own work as associate director.

Similarly, Martha was surprised to discover that in the year studied, her third most frequently calendared event (after meeting with co-administrators and meeting with mentees) was a research project she worked on with the associate director of the general education program. The project, a writing analytics approach to reading students' reflective essays (a document in students' cumulative Writing Portfolio), arose from questions that grew out of our programmatic portfolio assessment process but quickly developed into a more involved scholarly endeavor that put Martha and the associate director on the path to two conference presentations, a digital scholarship fellowship, and plans for an article. While the work had an obvious individual mentoring component—both Martha and her collaborator developed professional skills as scholars—it also put these two colleagues into a new relationship with each other and with the program. Their project engendered conversations about student writing as well as about the program's terminology and assessment practices. Drawing on their different professional roles and positions, they mentored each other as they learned new methods for research and shared their knowledge domains and perspectives—writing assessment and general education administration. Their work on the project contributed to the program's narrative around its assessment practices, which became part of the response to larger university debates about general education reform, the importance of writing across the curriculum, portfolio development, and students' written reflections. Thus, a scholarly project—in itself a mentoring opportunity—served also as a means of co-constructing programmatic leadership and of shaping the stories told by and about the writing program.

Against the backdrop of general education reform, Kim found herself narrating program goals for colleagues outside the program, as well as managing her own and her colleagues' expectations within the program. Over the course of the year, she identified 1,498 email conversations that she associated with her WPA work, addressed to various groups: writing program faculty (using a number of administrative lists), writing program administrators, and university administrators. A review of these conversations revealed that the majority of her emails could be characterized as managing "sideways" and "up": more than half of the email conversations were addressed to co-administrators in the program (51%), and nearly as many addressed her department chair and the associate deans who oversee various parts of the curriculum (43%). These interactions comprised the "daily work" of program administration—setting meetings, monitoring enrollments, responding to concerns and queries—but they also provided opportunities to build trust, reiterate programmatic priorities, and establish working relationships. When she reviewed her calendared events, Kim was struck by the low percentage of appointments that appeared to be direct mentoring activities: classroom observations (3%) and pedagogy sessions (10%). A much larger percentage of her appointments were staff meetings (21%) and individual/small-group meetings (40%), which, as they did for Martha, served multiple purposes. Kim's email conversations and calendared events revealed a pattern of communicative activities that while sometimes indicating interpersonal mentoring work, most often focused on the story of the program in the larger context of the university.

This story became visible as an iterative process in her time log, where Kim recorded two instances of "thinking about" teaching assignments for GTAs (something she had never consciously tracked before). Such reflection time would eventually inform conversations she would have with GTAs about how teaching assignments meet program needs and suit each teacher's development. In addition, those conversations invite collaboration in the narrative development of the program, as the GTAs respond to the "plot" of the story Kim has constructed and offer their own interests as supporting or refuting evidence for particular teaching assignments. During the week she was recording her time, Kim also logged two serendipitous encounters with colleagues that touched lightly on writing program and general education matters; each of these was an occasion to practice the developing narrative about the writing program. Such moments of contemplation or hallway conversation are important opportunities for "storying" the program; they are informed by and become part of the collaborative, narrative work of program mentorship.

Table 4.2. How we manage our programs through mentoring

Social/Interpersonal Development	Intellectual/Programmatic Development
Stories about people	Stories about program
Emphasis on acquisition of skills/practices	Emphasis on learning outcomes/assessment
Professionalism	Programmatic vision/mission
Collaborations and consultations	Program reports and presentations

Our quantification processes taught us that each countable instance gains greater meaning when it is understood as part of the development of *narrative coherence* for the program overall. This ultimately led us to propose a third axis of mentorship: from social/interpersonal to intellectual/programmatic development. As table 4.2 suggests, this third axis of mentorship cuts across our original formal/informal and individual/collective axes. In addition to our original taxonomy, mentorship can be understood to include the stories created by/with individuals and the stories told within/beyond programs. This third axis connects all the individual instances of mentoring (whether formal and documented or informal and ephemeral) and helps tie mentorship to more visible artifacts, which, in turn, makes it more valuable to the university community.

This research project ultimately led us to revise the material for our traditional fall semester orientation activities to tell the story of the writing program as intentionally connected to the university's ongoing educational reform and its strategic planning processes. In addition to highlighting the work of the writing program faculty in the semesterly *Celebration of Student Writing and Research*, we identified how this activity connected to the university's description of an academic "marketplace" where knowledge is shared beyond the boundaries of the classroom. This example demonstrates the value of understanding mentorship as *both* individual/dyadic *and* collective/programmatic; it suggests that one concrete result of productive mentoring at all levels is the ongoing *storying* of a writing program.

IMPLICATIONS FOR WRITING PROGRAMS

Grappling with definitions of mentorship and its hierarchical attachments, composition and rhetoric scholars have forged a notion of mentorship that emphasizes the dynamic interaction of WPAs through collegiality (Fishman and Lunsford 2008), "interdependence" (Ratcliffe and Schuster 2008), and "mutuality of respect" (Mullin and Braun 2008).

Based largely on individual experience and the process of storytelling, writing scholars such as Bloom (2007) and Eble and Gaillet (2008) have demonstrated the value of mentorship as a function of reciprocal and productive relationships that occur within writing programs and that create mutually co-constructed leadership. Storytelling has been a powerful means and metaphor for documenting *individual* mentorship experiences, but it has not been fully engaged as a means of examining the *programmatic* experience of mentorship. We believe it is important to identify and quantify mentorship tasks in ways that demonstrate its value as real labor, material and time-consuming, to those outside of a writing program. What our study demonstrates is the value in becoming aware of the data we are all inadvertently collecting—in sites such as email archives and online calendars—and becoming more purposeful about using the data we are collecting to inform our mentoring and our programmatic storytelling. Data alone cannot tell the whole story of a writing program; but collecting, reviewing, and presenting them can encourage more connected mentorship (of both people and the program itself) and more deliberate planning (for both people and the program).

Mentoring occurs beyond the interpersonal interactions of mentor and mentee; it includes the thinking, worrying, and planning around our quantifiable instances of professional development, which makes those instances connect and build into professional and programmatic growth. But lest it simply be subsumed into "program development," the idea of mentorship that we advance here reveals an opportunity to see the growth of individuals and programs as a multidirectional process that engages whole persons as creators of their personal and collective evolution. Mentorship is what links individuals to the creation and evolution of the writing program itself; it is how we "story" the program by interweaving our own labors as mentors and mentees into the living narrative that is the program. The social aspects are the recognizable "doing" of mentorship, the plot points and the characters, but the intellectual and emotional aspects are the rhetorical moves: the instructions, the connections, the flourishes that engage the audience and construct the narrative in a way that empowers the storyteller and engages the audience to hear the story as intended. Mentoring, especially during this year of uncertainty around the general education program, was crucial to having our faculty co-construct the narrative that represents the program to the university community.

In our attempt to quantify and make visible our administrative labor, we discovered that in between the countable events, activities, and social interactions that are the hallmarks of mentorship, mentoring is dynamic and multidirectional. It is happening perpetually through the intellectual and emotional work of being aware of people's needs as professionals working and developing within an institutional structure. It has, or should have, a meta-cognitive element that involves taking stock of our interactions and intentionally using those interactions to improve conditions both for individuals and for the program itself.

Quantifying revealed that despite the complications, there is another way to make the work visible than through telling our own individual stories of mentorship. Storying the program—collectively articulating the program's purposes, processes, and outcomes—is an activity that grows out of individual, daily mentoring and administrative tasks; but it is also an activity that changes the way the program operates and is perceived by the larger institution. Thus, there is another data site we can access for evidence of mentoring: program and administrative statements, reviews, and reports. These are the data WPAs present to the world, the figures and counts that describe the work of the writing program and its members. Being able to articulate the work of the writing program is essential to how the university perceives it, how it functions, how it evolves (or doesn't)—especially in significant moments such as general education reform, where people's jobs are at risk and where we should play a role in defining what is valued. These moments call for a rich and multidirectional conception of mentoring, one that is negotiated and enacted across the spectra: formal/informal, individual/programmatic, and social/intellectual.

This work has taught us that it is worth taking stock of our time using the electronic data we are inadvertently gathering as administrators: calendar, email, and daily logs. It would be even more valuable to keep those data more intentionally, to see them as data that tell the story of the work a writing program does. The story, in return, gives shape and purpose to our daily work and allows us to reflect and look forward as we plan and extend work over the long term, not just during one semester. It promotes a sense of continuity and facilitates individual and institutional memory.

It is not easy to quantify mentorship: it is multidirectional and much of it is invisible, not just because we are not intentionally documenting it but also because it is the kind of labor that defies visibility. It is thought, worry, care, momentum toward goals, instilling of values, identity creation. It is also difficult to quantify things that are not formally structured into our job descriptions, performance reviews, and institutional practices. Nevertheless, even in the absence of formal documentation, our program has a variety of disparate moments in which we mentor each other, not across hierarchical lines but in collaboration on research and development of programmatic guidelines. As Martha's observations reveal, this is a rich and generous space for developing personally and professionally, but it is also a significant piece of how the writing program itself moves forward toward its vision and larger goals, as Kim's observations suggest. We need to think more purposefully about the role mentoring plays in the lives of our individual administrators who have professional goals and aspirations but also in the lives of our writing programs. Mentoring is essential to programmatic storytelling, and programmatic storytelling is an essential and visible product of the labor of WPA mentorship.

APPENDIX 4.A: PROGRAM ADMINISTRATORS' REFLECTIONS ON MENTORING

What activities in your regular work do you consider to be "mentoring" of faculty and administrators?
- Aspects of faculty development workshops and orientations. Consultations about classroom instruction. Annual performance reviews. Committee meetings. Assessment committees/research.
- Answering questions about curriculum and program policies; giving suggestions and advice about how to deal with different student cases; reading research drafts and providing feedback.
- Ad hoc and formal meetings to discuss topics related to working with students and colleagues; providing financial resources.
- Weekly pedagogy sessions; working with new portfolio coordinator every year (helping them respond well to student issues).

What mentoring do you receive from others?
- Collaborating with colleagues; solicited/unsolicited advice from other administrators.
- Advice about policies and procedures; feedback to administrative decisions and planning; feedback to and advice about research; feedback to teaching methods and approaches.
- I always feel comfortable asking other administrators and colleagues questions.

Estimate how much time you spend per week doing mentoring activities.
- Less than 1 hour per week = 0%
- 1–3 hours per week = 60%
- 3–5 hours per week = 40%
- 5 or more hours per week = 0%

How would you describe the value of mentoring?
- Much of the mentoring I have received has been passive . . . I learn by watching how others do their jobs.
- Mentoring is valuable in that it provides somebody else's viewpoint on important decisions or day-to-day aspects of one's professional development.
- It's important to have someone to talk to who has done what you're trying to do and to get their help with troubleshooting but also to learn how to be productive and to work well with others in a particular context.

How would you describe the role mentoring plays in our writing program?
- Mentoring is very important . . . to create and maintain consistency.
- I personally have experienced very little *intentional* mentoring . . . I attribute my growth . . . to collaborations with my colleagues.
- I think there is a lot of informal, one-off mentoring among the writing instructors who often touch base with each other.
- I do think of . . . one-on-one meetings . . . as a sort of mentoring, but I might be past needing mentoring.

REFERENCES

Bloom, Lynn. 2007. "Mentoring as Mosaic: Life in Guerilla Theater." *Composition Studies* 35 (2): 87–99.

Casanave, Christine P. 2008. "Learning Participatory Practices in Graduate School: Some Perspective-Taking by a Mainstream Educator." In *Learning the Literacy Practices of Graduate School: Insiders' Reflections on Academic Enculturation*, edited by Christine P. Casanave and Xiamonimg Li, 14–31. Ann Arbor: University of Michigan Press.

Curry, Mary. 2016. "More than Language: Graduate Student Writing as 'Disciplinary Becoming.'" In *Supporting Graduate Student Writers: Research, Curriculum, and Program Design*, edited by Steve Simpson, Nigel Caplan, Michelle Cox, and Talinn Phillips, 78–96. Ann Arbor: University of Michigan Press.

Eble, Michelle F., and Lynée Lewis Gaillet. 2008. *Stories of Mentoring: Theory and Praxis*. West Lafayette, IN: Parlor Press.

Fishman, Jenn, and Andrea Lunsford. 2008. "Educating Jane." In *Stories of Mentoring: Theory and Praxis*, edited by Michelle F. Eble and Lynée Lewis Gaillet, 262–275. West Lafayette, IN: Parlor Press.

Mullin, Joan, and Paula Braun. 2008. "The Reciprocal Nature of Successful Mentoring Relationships: Changing the Academic Culture." In *Stories of Mentoring: Theory and Praxis*, edited by Michelle F. Eble and Lynée Lewis Gaillet, 262–275. West Lafayette, IN: Parlor Press.

Phillips, Talinn, Paul Shovlin, and Megan Titus. 2016. "(Re)Identifying the gWPA Experience." *WPA: Writing Program Administration* 40 (1): 67–89.

Ratcliffe, Krista, and Donna Decker Schuster. 2008. "Mentoring toward Interdependency: 'Keeping It Real.'" In *Stories of Mentoring: Theory and Praxis*, edited by Michelle F. Eble and Lynée Lewis Gaillet, 248–261. West Lafayette, IN: Parlor Press.

Restaino, Jessica R. 2010. *First Semester: Graduate Students, Teaching Writing, and the Challenge of the Middle Ground*. Carbondale: Southern Illinois University Press.

Stenberg, Shari, and Debbie Minter. 2018. "Always up Against: A Study of Veteran WPAs and Social Resilience." *College Composition and Communication* 69 (4): 642–668.

Walcher, Sheldon, Joseph Janangelo, and Duen Roen. 2010. "Introducing 'The CWPA Mentoring Project' and Survey Report." *WPA: Writing Program Administration* 34 (1): 84–116.

Zachary, Lois J. 2011. *The Mentor's Guide: Facilitating Effective Learning Relationships*, 2nd ed. San Francisco: Jossey-Bass.

5
NAMING WHAT WE FEEL
Self-Dialogue as a Strategy for Negotiating Emotional Labor in WPA Work

Kristi Murray Costello and Kate Navickas

In a recent review essay, Erin J. Rand (2015, 161) describes a contemporary "affective turn" in academic discourse. And she's right. There have been some recent and notable advances in scholarship pertaining to the relationship between work and emotion from scholars like Laura R. Micciche (2002, 2007, 2016), Sara Ahmed (2004), and others. In fact, in summer 2016, *Composition Forum* offered a special issue on emotion in which Micciche (2016) advocated that we as a field need to "stay with emotion." But what does it mean to "stay with emotion," especially in the context of understanding the emotional labor of WPA work? And once we've done the vulnerable work of acknowledging emotional labor, what's next?

Despite Sara Ahmed's (2004, 117) argument that emotions are not private matters and that they do not simply belong to individuals or come from within and then move outward toward others, many of us have been socially conditioned to understand emotions as highly individual and personal; thus, "staying with emotions" might itself feel like an act of indulgence, of navel gazing, and certainly not worthy of serious academic study. When we each took on our own individual studies of our emotional labor at our very different institutions, we both assumed that our emotions and emotional labors would be situational; however, through critically studying our own "personal" emotional labor—in Kristi's role as an early-career WPA at a midsize state university in the Delta and in Kate's first year as a non-tenure-track writing center director at an Ivy League school—we found that emotional labor is concurrently individual *and* shared and that it stems from a negotiation between larger disciplinary and/or institutional narratives that we've adopted as a result of our specific institutional contexts and histories.

We further and perhaps more importantly discovered that "staying with" our emotions helped us better understand and negotiate them.

Thus, in this chapter, we offer an analytical, methods-based strategy we're calling self-dialogue that individual writing program administrators (WPAs) can use, alone or collectively, to understand and negotiate emotional labor. We define self-dialogue as a self-reflective action-research method that serves as an analytical approach to journaling. Next, in following Micciche's (2016) call for "staying with emotion," building on existing heuristics of emotional labor (Glomb and Tews 2004; Hochschild 2012; Mastracci, Newman, and Guy 2011), and using Ahmed's (2004) definition of emotions as an analytical frame, we foreground the method in theory and then illustrate it in practice. Ultimately, we argue that "staying with" our experiences, emotions, and emotional labor through self-dialogue can help WPAs recognize the ways we're haunted by narratives of the past and help us minimize the extent to which they impact our presents and futures.

THE RHETORIC AND (EMOTIONAL) REALITY OF WRITING PROGRAM ADMINISTRATION

Affect and emotion have long been staples of WPA, writing center, and field stories and lore. In fact, Diana George's (1999) iconic collection, *Kitchen Cooks, Plate Twirlers, and Troubadours: Writing Program Administrators Tell Their Stories*, includes several chapters dedicated to the emotional labor of the WPA. Undoubtedly, both of us have found expertise and comfort in this text and the stories of our field. However, we also agree with Richard Bullock (2000) that many of these stories are just that—stories—and they often present a WPA at their wit's end or at the mercy of their emotions (Bullock 2000, 674). While such stories can help normalize our emotions and emotional labor, they do little to help us effectively navigate them.

More recently, Micciche (2002, 2016), Ahmed (2004), Nicole Caswell (2011), Caswell, Jackie Grutsch McKinney, and Rebecca Jackson (2016b), and Kelly Ritter (2011) have illustrated how the "relationship between work and emotion" can "provid[e] context" for further examination (Micciche 2002, 437). In addition, in their *Composition Forum* article, Caswell, McKinney, and Jackson (2016b, n.p.) explain how their study of nine writing center directors showed "that it was a shame or problematic not that the directors have to devote so much time to emotional labor, but rather that they hadn't been prepared to expect and negotiate it." Combined, these works offer an understanding of how emotional labor develops, in part, through disciplinary histories and narratives and how data regarding emotions and emotional labor can illustrate trends.

Like much of the research discussed above, we use Ahmed's (2004) definition of emotions as an analytical frame to illustrate how they function, circulate, and hold power. Ahmed offers an economic model of emotions. While arguing that "emotions do not positively reside in a subject or figure," she suggests—similar to findings of Caswell, Grutsch McKinney, and Jackson (2016b)—that "they still work to bind subjects together" (Ahmed 2004, 119). Ahmed uses the word *sticky* to describe the ways emotions get bound to subjects, discourses, and objects as they circulate. Her work helps us locate emotions externally and thus identify the sources (disciplinary or institutional narratives, for instance) of our individual emotions as a way of critically understanding their origin, power, and relationship to the personal. This is especially important for WPAs because, as Micciche (2002, 446) points out, "the unique situation of WPAs in the academy involves a form of emotion management that enhances and affirms the emotional and professional well-being of others, often to the neglect of the WPA's own emotional stability."

In following Micciche's (2016) call for "staying with emotion," a concept she adapted from Frankie Condon (2012), in this chapter we each engage in self-dialogue—which we see as a form of "staying with"—to pay attention to our individual and collective (through disciplinary and institutional discourses) emotions and emotional labor. To be clear, though, we're not advocating here for emotion management, which can perpetuate what Ian Craib (1994, 17; quoted in Micciche 2002, 444) calls "the myth of self-control and of the all-powerful self that can control itself"; nor are we advocating for a neoliberal approach to self-care in the interest of efficiency. Instead, we're arguing for the value of creating space and time for emotional awareness and emotionally informed thinking and calling on the field to make a commitment to continue reducing the stigma of honestly addressing emotions and emotional labor in WPA scholarship.

SELF-DIALOGUE DEFINED

We have developed our method, self-dialogue, from one of the self-care movement's oft-touted methods—journaling. We see self-dialogue as an analytical strategy related to and supported by composition theories, including Peter Elbow's freewriting, the process movement, and more recent work on reflection on writing in transfer research (Taczak 2016; Yancey, Robertson, and Taczak 2014).[1] Elbow (1985, 1) points out that "too much audience awareness may be injurious to the health of

[our] writing." Given the emotional labor and frequent performativity of WPA work, we argue that our filtering and hyper-attention to audience without recognition of the emotional labor that accompanies such expression or lack thereof can be, as Elbow says, *injurious* (1). While we are not going so far as to suggest that our method will resolve trauma, stress, or emotional labor and certainly not on its own (though studies have shown that such methods can alleviate stress and reduce the effects of trauma),[2] we are suggesting that self-dialogue as a method functions in a structured and sustained way to help individuals better understand and process their experiences and emotional labor.

Effective self-dialogue is a form of storytelling; in line with feminist and cultural rhetorics methodologies, we evoke storytelling as a method of theory making (Ahmed 2004; Cultural Rhetorics Theory Lab 2014; Martinez 2014; Royster and Kirsch 2012). More specifically, two of Jacqueline Jones Royster and Gesa Kirsch's (2012) methodological practices inform self-dialogue: strategic contemplation and critical imagination. Although they're writing about studying women in the archives, these methodological strategies, like Micciche's (2016) advice to "stay with emotions," help us to understand what this work involves. Royster and Kirsch explain that strategic contemplation is coupled with critical imagination because researchers must meditate and spend time on the research subject and contexts in order to imagine them. Beyond critically imagining the research subjects, though, strategic contemplation focuses on the embodied experiences and emotional journey of the researcher.

We call this method self-dialogue rather than journaling, precisely because we are using it to "stay with emotions," to dwell in, but then to study from a distance. More than simply helping us to understand and validate our own emotions, this strategy enabled us to acknowledge the influence of institutional and disciplinary narratives in the everyday emotional labor of WPAs and to more productively manage our emotional labor. Self-dialogue includes five steps: 1. Journaling; 2. Sorting; 3. Staying with; 4. Making plans; and 5. Reflecting on the process. We'll briefly elaborate on each of these steps before exploring them in practice.

Journaling

Journaling, in a freewriting-like mode, is useful before, during, or after emotional labor; however, we've both found that journaling while facing emotional labor—especially more challenging work-related emotions such as stress, anxiety, fear, or anger—is perhaps most useful for isolating the roots of the emotions and negotiating that emotional labor. We suggest writing nonstop for roughly twenty to twenty-five minutes about specific work-related feelings and anxieties. As you write, allow the writing to wander and oscillate from broad to specific and back. We further suggest that upon getting stuck, write whatever comes next to your mind, even if you have already written it, being open to the possibility that the concerns considered more frequently may be of more note. We suggest keeping the entries in a folder or a streaming document to better facilitate the next step.

Sorting

Sorting involves taking a step back and studying journal entries—preferably multiple entries—as texts. Methodologically, this step involves what Royster and Kirsch (2012, 72), drawing from Clifford Geertz, have called "tacking out," which is similar to "the technologically enhanced ability to view the Earth from satellites in outer space in order to gain the capacity to see." Sorting ideally involves using basic open and axial coding strategies to categorize themes. The sorting step is a form of studying and close reading of journal entries and thus also potentially helps foster distance from the events and emotional labor.

Staying With

More than just coding the journals, we also advocate for "staying with" them—that is, spending time re-reading the journal entries and considering the significance of the categories created. This step should be a meditation on your sense of self, what you wrote, and the larger context of the situation. We recommend "staying with" the journals for a few weeks—re-reading and thinking about them once a week for twenty to thirty minutes or so and writing down reactions and thoughts during each session. This step is similar to the work involved with writing memos when using grounded theory as a research method. Robert Thornberg and Kathy Charmaz (2014) collate a number of relevant explanations of memo writing in grounded theory: "According to Glaser (1978, 83), memos are 'the theorizing write-up of ideas about codes and their relationships as they strike the analyst while coding.' Other definitions of memos are: 'the narrated records of a theorist's analytical conversations with him/herself about the research data' (Lempert 2007, 247); and 'documentation of the researcher's thinking process and theorizing from data' (Thornberg 2012, 254). By memo writing, grounded theorists step back and ask, 'What is going on here?' and 'How can I make sense of it?'" (Thornberg and Charmaz 2014, 10).

For us, "staying with" involves focusing on one category at a time, creating a self-dialogue with yourself through re-reading and further writing, and considering Thornberg and Charmaz's (2014) final questions.

Making Plans

This step, making plans, is about thoughtfully responding to emotions and emotional labor and using your study of your journaling to be conscious in your future actions. We recommend taking about ten minutes to review your coding, memos, and journals and then developing a plan about what can be done in the future to prevent less desirable situations, be better emotionally prepared for situations that may arise, and alleviate difficult emotional labor. The point here is, again, not to alleviate *feeling* but rather to understand the emotions' roots, recognize what you do and don't have control over, and find ways to improve (or celebrate) your approaches of negotiating emotional labor. Further, this step is flexible—making plans can be as abstract as developing a mantra to remind yourself of certain values or goals to as concrete as setting up a meeting with university administrators to discuss an ongoing issue.

Reflecting on the Process

This last step, reflecting on the process, involves a final read-through of everything you've written and done so far, along with a consideration of what you've learned about yourself through the process of self-dialogue. Kara Taczak (2016, 78) has described reflection as "a mode of inquiry: a deliberate way of systematically recalling writing experiences to reframe the current writing situation." When applied to self-dialogue as a method of negotiating emotional labor, reflection allows us to consider both the emotional labor of our work and what we've learned about ourselves.

As a method, self-dialogue is complicated and not without limitations. This work requires a commitment to vulnerable, honest self-reflection and a willingness to engage with raw and potentially traumatic experiences, which will vary in severity depending on both context and a WPA's identities and histories. This type of processing will always benefit from and might even necessitate further mental health support from professionals (e.g., counseling, therapy). Self-dialogue is also a time-consuming endeavor, which can make it difficult for WPAs—many of us already facing demanding pressures and time constraints. Finally, beyond research method limitations, we recognize that advocating for self-care work as institutionally valuable risks it becoming a free and too-easy solution for improving workplace efficiency and deficiencies in ways that replace resource-based support and necessary funding.

SELF-DIALOGUE IN PRACTICE

We came to self-dialogue as a method through a shared interest in analyzing and being transparent about the emotional labor of transitioning into and out of administrative positions. As a creative writer and an advocate of freewriting, journaling was intuitive for Kristi. Rather serendipitously, Kate had been journaling about her own emotional labor as preparation for an interview focused on the emotional labor of her predecessor (see Adams Wooten et al. 2020 for more on the interview). That is, for this study, our data come from previous intentional journaling both of us did on the subject of our emotional labor as administrators.

These two applications dig into and study administrative emotional labor we previously might have been ashamed of and discussed only with close friends. Through this work, both of us have come to a more complex understanding of the sources of our emotional labor, understanding their relationship to institutional context, disciplinary narratives, and others. As a result, we have both let go of some specific anxiety, stress, shame, and guilt—in part because we can now see this emotional labor as less personal. Further, these self-studies have also fostered concrete plans for self-care, better programs, and institutional relations.

Application 1: Pick up a Pen, Start Writing

Kristi: I was listening to the *Hamilton* soundtrack after a particularly rough day—I woke up late because I'd been up late the night before grading. In a rush to make it to a scheduled graduate teaching assistant (GTA) observation, I hadn't put on eye makeup, which led to three people telling me I looked tired before lunchtime—which was interrupted by a student in the writing center who was in tears because her economics professor had written "Drop this class. Come back after you learn English" across the top of her paper. I was then late to a shared governance committee meeting where I planned to speak against a problematic proposal for a new plagiarism policy. Finally, I returned to my office to find a frantic note on my office door from my secretary asking me to submit a rationale for my course releases to the dean's office by the end of the day. I was assured the latter was just a formality, but it was still disheartening since I served as the director of first-year writing, the writing center, writing studies, *and* writing across the curriculum/writing in the disciplines (WAC/WID). As I drove home that night, exhausted and frustrated, I heard "One Last Time," the song from the hip-hop musical *Hamilton* that imagines George Washington's decision to step down from the presidency; for the first time since I'd entered the field, I found myself able to imagine a world in which I wasn't a WPA. Yes, that's how overwhelmed I felt; I was unintentionally (and unironically) comparing my situation to that of our first president. This may be in part because I am not what Jeannette Harris and others have called an "accidental" administrator (paraphrased from George 1999, xiiii). I haven't imagined doing anything different with my life since my first day as an MA student. In the beginning of "One Last Time," Washington says to Alexander Hamilton, "Pick up a pen, start writing," so I did just that and began journaling about my experiences (Jackson and Miranda 2015).

To be honest, some of the concerns I wrote about in my original journal entries were not ones I consciously knew I had. For example, while I love having awards, I've never liked receiving them. Standing onstage while someone says nice things about me has always left me blushing and wondering what best to do with my hands. So, when I realized that one of my concerns with delegating leadership of the Campus Writing Program to others was a fear that I would lose both attachment to the program and credit for my previous work, I was surprised.

Next, I read the journal entries and sorted them—using basic open and axial coding strategies—into broad categories, such as quality control, outside perception, and tenure. In the end, I found that every concern I had fell under one of nine categories: program growth, the view from outside (or perception of others), labor issues, too many cooks, quality control, loss of credit or legacy, tenure, asking for help, and work-life balance. In the two weeks that followed, I considered each category, one per day, and read through the concerns in that day's category—"staying with" each one for about twenty to thirty minutes; ruminating and writing about the anxieties and feelings and when, where, and why I felt them; tracing their roots; and examining the sources of their power.

As I was "staying with" my emotions, I realized in the kind of moment that pierces one's abdomen like a severe menstrual cramp that I sometimes feel embarrassed, maybe even ashamed, asking for additional help because of all the people who have had this WPA position, I have been the most supported. Worse, I started to unknowingly conflate one colleague's opinion of my "cushy" job with others who had never expressed such an opinion. As Ahmed (2004, 171) argues, what we "feel might be dependent on past interpretations that are not necessarily made by us, but that come before us." Thus, by recognizing and naming the root of this anxiety, it began to lose its momentum.

Application 2: Dialing down Defensiveness

Kate: It was early December, after my first semester postgraduate school as a new, non-tenure-track writing center director (WCD) at an Ivy League school. I had committed to interviewing the previous WCD about her emotional labor in the position for my Conference on College Composition and Communication (CCCC) presentation. I was hoping to honor her legacy, understand the parts of the work she was proud of, and figure out how to grow and evolve the program in respectful ways. I didn't really want to be thinking about *my emotional labor* because I thought it was obvious and self-indulgent. Of course, during my first year as a new administrator in an entirely new context, I'd had missteps, bad email exchanges, fear, anxiety, and stress. I struggled with institutional context and knowledge, working with graduate students, establishing authority, and cross-campus relationships, among other things. I expected this stress and these feelings, and if it weren't for the interview and a presentation I had to write, I probably wouldn't have thought much about any of these early struggles. Indeed, a previous graduate faculty member once commented in response to a string of complaints about being stressed, "We're all stressed out. We just don't talk about it." However, I started writing and reflecting on my own experiences out of a desire for some sense of reciprocity in the interview. I knew I'd be asking the previous WCD to reflect on her emotions and emotional labor, perhaps getting into potentially personal and vulnerable stories; thus, I wanted to be prepared to share a little bit of my own experiences and sense of the emotional labor of the job after one semester.

My journal entries thus explored several experiences from my first semester as a new WCD. I wrote about the committee meeting during which one of my colleagues with a background in literature coolly noted, "Well, it seems relevant that none of us chose this work." He meant teaching writing. I wrote about the defensive and presumptuous email I wrote to the new director of the entire writing program in which I noted that full conference funding was one of the expectations I had been promised, regardless of budget cuts. He was new to the position and simply didn't know. I journaled about the ongoing battle of being a stressed-out introvert in a closed suite of offices, in which everyone is perky, friendly, and seemingly full of expendable time to chat. Closing my door felt offensive, but I was struggling to do anything with the door open. I wrote about the meeting during which I forgot to contain the horror and shock on my face as a writing teacher colleague demanded that consistent assessment measures were pedagogically unsound. Perhaps most present in my journals were the *ongoing* internal conversations I was having with past peers and mentors about my decision to take a non-tenure-track job.

In sorting the journal entries summarized above, I discovered three broad themes: status, writing center narratives, and administrative agency. I was surprised at the number of times I had referenced feelings of shame, inferiority, or worry over having taken a non-tenure-track job; although I knew I had been defensive, I didn't realize the extent to which those feelings were affecting me. In regard to writing center narratives, in my journaling I found several references to what I had imagined writing center work to be and the ways my new writing center was different from that imagined center. Finally, sorting led me to see that several of my journal entries named struggles to have agency and authority as a new administrator—moments in which I was trying to figure out who to be in this role.

Similar to Kristi, I decided to "stay with" the most vulnerable of my emotions—feeling defensive and hurt about my non-tenure-track status. I stayed with this emotional labor in a few ways—I journaled more about it; I read scholarship about status and writing center positions; and I shared and discussed my emotional labor openly in the interview with the previous WCD. I started to realize that my feelings about my status—hurt, anger, sadness, shame, guilt—were the result of a discrepancy between disciplinary narratives about what a "good job" for a new PhD student is and the realities of the actual "good job" I had. That is, coming into this position, I had come to believe that a tenure-track job was the gold standard and anything else was a failure to meet that standard. Naturally, I saw this failure as a personal one. However, the more I stayed with these painful feelings and experiences, the clearer it became that I was placing more value in a disciplinary narrative than I was in my reality—in which I was, in fact, very happy.

A CALL FOR SELF-REFLECTIVE ACTION RESEARCH AND COLLABORATION

Through the final steps of our method—making plans and reflecting on the process—we both found that engaging in self-dialogue produces more than just data. It is self-reflective action research and a form of processing and self-care. Specifically, Kristi's future-directed tangible plans included asking for an additional course release; developing proposals for additional administrative faculty to oversee different program components; instituting a one-in, one-out policy for service assignments; creating organizational structures to make collaboration, delegation, and communication with first-year composition faculty more feasible; and creating an interactive time line of progress, major decisions, and traditions to celebrate people and decisions that have shaped the writing program (to name a few). Similarly, Kate identified strategies to foster greater understanding about her transitional struggles over status and disciplinarity. She identified the aspects of the position that are truly enjoyable and reflected on why; asked "why does this institutional version of X (e.g., tutors, writing center space, first-year composition program) seem wrong to me"; and talked to colleagues about how they navigate being in non-tenure-track positions. Then, reflection (step 5) enabled us to let go of some of the anxieties and stresses we were carrying, particularly those that were unproductive and unreasonable (i.e., fear of asking for reasonable institutional support, shame over wanting to be recognized, shame and hurt over institutional status and writing center context). Our reflections also helped us recognize the role of others, institutional contexts, disciplinary narratives, and other outside forces on our emotional labors and actions. For both of us, engaging in the five steps of self-dialogue was meaningful and in stark contrast to the censoring, suppression, and performativity that often occur as a result of and alongside WPA work.

Although we come from very different institutions and have very different jobs, we found similarities in our experiences and how they were affecting us, as well as a reminder that our emotional labor is neither isolated nor solely individual—which is why we want to advocate for this type of self-reflective action research. These activities offered us a wealth of knowledge, specifically by:

- Providing more institutional history and context
- Offering a new perspective on the emotional labor of a position—creating understanding about where work emotions come from and why
- Lessening work-related anxieties
- Creating an understanding of emotional labor as constructed from larger disciplinary and institutional narratives rather than as individual and situational
- Fostering empathy and sensitivity toward colleagues
- Affording the opportunity to reflect on what administrative agency means.

Of course, these insights not only help us enjoy our work more, but they also benefit our programs, universities, and discipline (Murray Costello, Navickas, and Simpson-Farrow in press). Given the limitations of our individual studies, we hope others might broaden and extend the disciplinary insights of this research through a sustained study of a semester's worth of journaling from multiple WPAs. The larger project of studying the emotional labor of WPAs through this method would help us to better prepare graduate students for the demands of administrative work, create administrative positions that name and support new hires in all dimensions of the work, and develop richer understandings of the ways emotional labor contributes to WPA work in our disciplinary documents to better advocate for greater resources and support for individual WPAs. As our above overview of the literature suggests, as a field we are neglecting the significant ways affect and emotional labor are central to the work we do. Research that prioritizes emotional labor, especially on a broader scale, may significantly contribute to basic understandings of WPA labor and, as a result, to more equitable working conditions, more resources and support, and less "disappointment" in the work (Micciche 2002).

As we share our stories with you, then, we want to emphasize that self-dialogue is the first but not the last step for negotiating and supporting emotional labor. Recognizing the transformative value of this method, we invite you, the reader and our colleague, to test and revise this practice to meet your own needs. While sharing our vulnerabilities requires energy and bravery, we have found that doing so forges connections with other WPAs over shared experiences. As Elizabeth Saur and Jason Palmeri (2017, 152) explain, "It is through dialogue with other [WPAs] that we can come to name, share, and reflectively act upon the emotions that permeate our [work] lives." As we have been engaging in this work more broadly, with Jacob Babb and Courtney Adams Wooten through a 2019 CWPA interactive table that asked conference-goers to share their emotional labor stories,[3] we've also seen the wider exigence and desire for more disciplinary acknowledgment of and research on emotional labor. That is, we've come to believe that studying emotional labor is more than just self-care; it's fostering the well-being and longevity of our larger disciplinary community.

NOTES

1. The benefits of journaling have also been discussed in relation to the composition classroom (Levine 2004; Elbow 1985; Elbow and Clarke 1987), professional development (Yinger and Clark 1981), and pedagogy (Flinchbaugh, Moore, Chang, and May 2012).

2. Journaling is seen as a therapeutic method for mental health in clinical settings (Utley and Garza 2011). In a 2002 study published in the *Annals of Behavioral Medicine*, Philip Ullrich and Susan Lutgendorf (2002, 248) found that journaling about trauma that includes both emotional reflections and cognitive processing can produce "positive growth from trauma over time," findings also supported by social psychologist James W. Pennebaker (1988), who argues that journaling "improves our immune system and our moods; we go to work feeling refreshed, perform better and socialize more" (quoted in Phelan 2018).

3. The project, Make It Matter: Contribute Your WPA Emotional Labor Story, invited participants to publicly or anonymously respond to three overarching questions—the what, the how, and the why of emotional labor. We are hoping to develop this space into a larger conversation for a WPA statement on emotional labor. You can contribute by sending your emotional labor story to emotionallaborwpa@gmail.com. Stories and the project can be viewed here: https://bit.ly/2m3gXP6.

REFERENCES

Adams Wooten, Courtney, Jacob Babb, Kristi Murray Costello, and Kate Navickas. 2020. *The Things We Carry: Strategies for Recognizing and Negotiating Emotional Labor in Writing Program Administration*. Logan: Utah State University Press.

Ahmed, Sara. 2004. *The Cultural Politics of Emotion*. New York: Routledge; Edinburgh: Edinburgh University Press.

Bullock, Richard. 2000. "*Kitchen Cooks, Plate Twirlers, and Troubadours: Writing Program Administrators Tell Their Stories* (Review)." *College Composition and Communication* 51 (4): 672–676.

Caswell, Nicole. 2011. "Writing Assessment: Emotion, Feelings, and Teachers." *CEA Forum* 4 (1): 57–70.

Caswell, Nicole, Jackie Grutsch McKinney, and Rebecca Jackson. 2016a. *The Working Lives of New Writing Center Directors*. Logan: Utah State University Press.

Caswell, Nicole, Jackie Grutsch McKinney, and Rebecca Jackson. 2016b. "Writing Center Administration and/as Emotional Labor." *Composition Forum* 34 (Summer). http://compositionforum.com/issue/34/writing-center.php.

Condon, Frankie. 2012. *I Hope I Join the Band: Narrative, Affiliation, and Antiracist Rhetoric*. Logan: Utah State University Press.

Craib, Ian. 1994. *The Importance of Disappointment*. New York: Routledge.

Cultural Rhetorics Theory Lab (Malea Powell, Daisy Levy, Andrea Riley-Mukavetz, Marilee Brooks-Gillies, Maria Novotny, and Jennifer Fisch-Ferguson). 2014. "Our Story Begins Here: Constellating Cultural Rhetorics Practices." *Enculturation: A Journal of Rhetoric, Writing, and Culture* 18. http://enculturation.net/our-story-begins-here.

Elbow, Peter. 1985. "Closing My Eyes as I Talk: An Argument against Audience Awareness." Paper presented at the Conference on College Composition and Communication, Minneapolis, MN. https://files-eric-ed-gov.proxy.library.cornell.edu/fulltext/ED261408.pdf.

Elbow, Peter, and Jennifer Clarke. 1987. "Desert Island Discourse: The Benefits of Ignoring Audience." In *The Journal Book*, edited by Toby Fulwiler, 19–32. Portsmouth, NH: Boynton/Cook.

Flinchbaugh, Carol L., E. Whitney, G. Moore, Young K. Chang, and Douglas R. May. 2012. "Student Well-Being Interventions: The Effects of Stress Management Techniques and Gratitude Journaling in the Management Education Classroom." *Journal of Management Education* 36 (2): 191–219.

George, Diana. 1999. *Kitchen Cooks, Plate Twirlers, and Troubadours: Writing Program Administrators Tell Their Stories*. Portsmouth, NH: Heinemann.

Glaser, Barney G. 1978. *Theoretical Sensitivity.* Mill Valley, CA: Sociological Press.

Glomb, Theresa M., and Michael J. Tews. 2004. "Emotional Labor: A Conceptualization and Scale Development." *Journal of Vocational Behavior* 64 (1): 1–23.

Hochschild, Arlie Russell. 2012. *The Managed Heart: Commercialization of Human Feeling.* Berkeley: University of California Press.

Jackson, Christopher, and Lin-Manuel Miranda. 2015. "One Last Time." *Hamilton: An American Musical.* New York: Avatar Studios.

Lempert, Lora B. 2007. "Asking Questions of the Data: Memo Writing in the Grounded Theory Tradition." In *The SAGE Handbook of Grounded Theory,* edited by Bryant Antony and Kathy Charmaz, 245–264. Los Angeles: Sage.

Levine, John. 2004. "Writing in the Wilderness without a Guide: How Not to Use Journals in the College Composition Classroom." *The Quarterly* 26 (2). https://archive.nwp.org/cs/public/print/resource/1791.

Martinez, Aja Y. 2014. "A Plea for Critical Race Theory Counterstory: Dialogues Concerning Alejandra's 'Fit' in the Academy." *Composition Studies* 42 (2): 33–55.

Mastracci, Sharon H., Meredith A. Newman, and Mary E. Guy. 2011. *Emotional Labor and Crisis Response: Working on the Razor's Edge.* New York: Routledge.

Micciche, Laura R. 2016. "Staying with Emotion." *Composition Forum* 34 (Summer). https://compositionforum.com/issue/34/micciche-retrospective.php.

Micciche, Laura R. 2007. *Doing Emotion.* Portsmouth, NH: Boynton/Cook.

Micciche, Laura R. 2002. "More than a Feeling: Disappointment and WPA Work." *College English* 64 (4): 432–458.

Murray Costello, Kristi, Kate Navickas, and Tabatha Simpson-Farrow. In press. "Tales of Becoming and Letting Go: The Emotional Labor of Writing Center Directors." In *Affect and Emotion in the Writing Center,* edited by Janine Morris and Kelly Concannon. Anderson, SC: Parlor Press.

Pennebaker, James W. 1988. *Opening Up: The Healing Power of Expressing Emotion.* New York: Guilford.

Phelan, Hayley. 2018. "What's All This about Journaling?" *New York Times,* October 25. https://www.nytimes.com/2018/10/25/style/journaling-benefits.html.

Rand, Erin J. 2015. "Bad Feelings in Public: Rhetoric, Affect, and Emotion." *Rhetoric and Public Affairs* 18 (1): 161–176.

Ritter, Kelly. 2011. "'What Would Happen if Everybody Behaved as I Do': May Bush, Randall Jarrell, and the Historical 'Disappointment' of Women WPAs." *Composition Studies* 39 (1): 13–39.

Royster, Jacqueline Jones, and Gesa Kirsch. 2012. *Feminist Rhetorical Practices: New Horizons for Rhetoric, Composition, and Literacy Studies.* Carbondale: Southern Illinois University Press.

Saur, Elizabeth, and Jason Palmeri. 2017. "Letter to a New TA: Affect Addendum." *WPA: Writing Program Administration* 40 (2): 146–153.

Taczak, Kara. 2016. "Reflection Is Critical for Writers' Development." In *Naming What We Know: Threshold Concepts of Writing Studies, Classroom Edition,* edited by Linda Adler-Kassner and Elizabeth Wardle, 78–81. Logan: Utah State University Press.

Thornberg, Robert. 2012. "Informed Grounded Theory." *Scandinavian Journal of Educational Research* 56 (3): 243–259.

Thornberg, Robert, and Kathy Charmaz. 2014. "Grounded Theory and Theoretical Coding." In *The Sage Handbook of Qualitative Data Analysis,* edited by Uwe Flick, 1–15. Los Angeles: Sage. https://dx.doi.org/10.4135/9781446282243.n11.

Ullrich, Philip, and Susan Lutgendorf. 2002. "Journaling about Stressful Events: Processing and Emotional Expression." *Annals of Behavioral Medicine* 24 (3): 244–250.

Utley, Allison, and Yvonne Garza. 2011. "The Therapeutic Use of Journaling with Adolescents." *Journal of Creativity in Mental Health* 6 (1): 29–41. http://web.b.ebscohost.com.proxy.library.cornell.edu/ehost/detail/detail?vid=0&sid=f08dda6b-3568-4c66-9d44

-e9a1e36487a3%40sessionmgr103&bdata=JnNpdGU9ZWhvc3QtbGl2ZQ%3d%3d#AN=59330171&db=sxi.

Yancey, Kathleen Blake, Liane Robertson, and Kara Taczak. 2014. *Writing across Contexts: Transfer, Composition, and Sites of Writing.* Logan: Utah State University Press.

Yinger, Robert J., and Christopher M. Clark. 1981. "Reflective Journal Writing: Theory and Practice." IRT Occasional Paper 50. East Lansing: Institute for Research on Teaching, Michigan State University.

PART 2

Advocating by Accounting for Time and Labor

6
TRADING TIME
Communicating Grand Strategy to Stakeholders through Hour Tracking

Ryan J. Dippre

Time is a scarce resource at the university in general (Kinman and Jones 2003) and for writing program administrators in particular. Writing program administrators (WPAs) and particularly junior WPAs (jWPAs) (Schell 1998; Phillips, Shovlin, and Titus 2014) struggle with pressing and sometimes conflicting demands on their time (Dew 2007) as well as perhaps unsympathetic audiences to listen to their needs and time constraints (Charlton et al. 2011). The tensions that arise through discussions of time, however, may also serve as an opportunity for promoting program principles and strategies (Adler-Kassner 2008) to upper-level administrators. Discussions about time and what WPAs trade their time for can be a productive avenue to change the stories of writing (and writing programs) our administrators tell.

In this chapter, I present an approach to thinking through time, accounting for it, and communicating about it through an ethnomethodologically informed (Garfinkel 1967) lens. Drawing on Harold Garfinkel's early work on what became ethnomethodology (a sub-field of sociology), I make the case that time is something that must be constructed, talked into being—"thingified"—and that this thingification needs to both take advantage of and transform the communicative avenues we work through as WPAs. I will use my own work on hour tracking, which I completed for the 2018–2019 academic year, to build out this framework and explore its uses in promoting an administrative vision. I close by suggesting next steps for WPAs interested in trading time for administrative vision.

DEVELOPING GRAND STRATEGIES

In fall 2015, I was hired as the associate director of college composition at the University of Maine. The then-director, Pat Burnes, was on a phased retirement plan, and the aim was for me to step in as director of college composition when she retired in May 2017. This process went according to plan and, in the process, allowed me to learn a great deal about the ebb and flow of activity in the program throughout the academic year before I was sitting in the director's chair. Having this experience proved important, as by the start of my second year as director, I felt prepared to begin accounting for my time regularly, with the expectation that my time commitments were only minimally hampered by the fact that I had no idea what I was doing.

This prior experience also allowed me to identify principle-driven strategies (Adler-Kassner 2008) for the work I do. That is, it allowed me the time and the space to define the values I saw enacted in the program, the values I brought to the program myself, and the ways I could enact those values to develop the program further. Throughout my two years as associate director, I identified what I came to understand as *grand strategies* for developing and promoting the program:

- Raise awareness of the University of Maine in the writing studies community
- Continue to develop the reputation of the college composition program across campus
- Enhance the quality of the college composition program through the continued development of teachers
- Collaborate with K–12 schools to discuss and support writing instruction and assessment across the state of Maine.

These grand strategies emerged before I turned to time tracking. I used these strategies as guides for thinking about how I could commit time and resources to various projects. When I began to see the possibilities of using time tracking to communicate program goals and values, I turned to these grand strategies to organize my time commitments.

I refer to these strategies as *grand* because of their long-running nature. Although Linda Adler-Kassner (2008) frames strategies as a way to think across a longer chunk of time than *tactics* (which focus more on the day-to-day enactment of strategies), I envisioned them as decade-long themes in developing the program, something I could attend to through a range of shorter-term strategies (which, in turn, would be enacted by tactics).

By the second year of my term as WPA, these grand strategies were only beginning to be taken up in particular ways, but I saw them as

Table 6.1. Categories for tracking time commitments

#	Category
1	Raise awareness of the University of Maine in the writing studies community
2	Continue to develop the reputation of the college composition program across campus
3	Enhance the quality of the college composition program through the continued development of instructors
4	Collaborate with K–20 schools to discuss and support writing instruction and assessment across the state of Maine
5	Writing program maintenance
6	Lifespan writing research
7	Teaching
8	Advising
9	Service

something that could be folded into my communication with my chair when we discussed my time commitments as a WPA. In other words, I saw these two separate aspects of my work as WPA as areas that could be thingified together, sustained through communication with stakeholders across campus. As I thought about communicating with my chair, I considered how the hours I committed could be organized according to these grand strategies.

My hour tracking throughout the year involved all aspects of my job. But when communicating with my chair, I focused on the aspects of my work that were related to my course reassignment (categories 1–5 in table 6.1). I broke these aspects down by the grand strategies addressed above, with one additional category, which I titled "program mechanics." This category gave me a way to separate the broader vision of the program (i.e., the grand strategies) from its "keeping the lights on" aspects. Interviewing and hiring contingent faculty, for instance, would fall under "program mechanics." While the work was important and hiring high-quality instructors was an integral component of the strategies I hoped to enact, the time I had to commit to these hiring time lines sprang from inequitable hiring practices. The label "program mechanics" allowed me to highlight the cost of these practices on the time I had available to commit to pursuing the grand strategies of program development.

The coding of my hours provided me with a way to make my hourly commitments more palpable to the stakeholders I was interested in communicating with. As things stood before I began this work, the idea of a "course reassignment" summed up the time I used for WPA work according to many stakeholders. But this way of understanding my time commitments obfuscated what the course reassignments purchased for my department chair, my dean, and the wider department and college. In other words, my coding provided the framework through which my time commitment could become a *thing*, an object to think with, about, and through. With this *thing* to help me communicate with administrators in my department and college, I could make a stronger case for program initiatives, needed resources, and so on.

NONEXISTENT TIME AND HOW TO THINGIFY IT

The challenge, as I've come to understand it in my work as a WPA, is that bureaucratically, much of my time is treated as nonexistent. The invisible work of program administration—finding sites for portfolio review, meeting with transfer students looking for 101 credit in their past coursework, interviewing new contingent instructors, and so on—is both a significant time commitment and an insignificant addition to one's tenure and promotion materials. In fact, it might be more accurate to refer to such time not as invisible but as institutionally nonexistent. The problem is not that the time cannot be seen by various institutional stakeholders; the problem is that such time does not exist. Time, the time WPAs dedicate to their work, needs to be made real, structurally present, and accountable for new understandings about the work WPAs do to arise.

To make sense of the work I need to do to make my time commitments "existent," then, I turned to Harold Garfinkel and his early work leading up to what he would term *ethnomethodology*. The word *ethnomethodology* means, literally, the study of members' methods (Garfinkel 1967). "Members" in this case refers to people involved in a social situation. What Garfinkel and the other ethnomethodologists wanted to understand was how people came together and constituted social order in a given situation. How do turns at talk, gestures, intonation, objects, and other elements get put together by people-in-interaction in ways that produce mutually recognizable activity? Ethnomethodologists frequently turn to what they refer to as *perspicuous settings* (Garfinkel 2002) to study this work: for example, people navigating busy intersections and people forming lines in a retail store.

This everyday (and perspicuous) setting is a useful starting point for considering how an intersection or a queue is thingified—transformed into something we all recognize and act in relation to in a given situation—through interaction. In *Toward a Sociological Theory of Information*, Garfinkel (2008) invokes the term *thingify* to describe how information comes to be rendered useful to the parties working with it—that is, how the information becomes a *thing* that can be worked with. Throughout his text, Garfinkel is less concerned with what happens to the thing than with the act that renders it a thing—that is, the thingification process.

At the heart of Garfinkel's understanding of thingification is interaction. We act in concert with others to recognize objects and events in certain ways. My dining room table, for instance, can be recognized through interaction with my family members as a place to eat food, a workspace, a place to have a conversation, a fort for my child to play in, and so on. We talk the object into being through our interactive work with it—we make it a *thing* we can work with.

Considering objects not as preexisting but as *thingified* through interaction can help us wrap our heads around more abstract concepts, such as time commitments at work. Our administrative superiors cannot bump into a time commitment like they can a table, but we can attend to the ways we *make* those time commitments *into* something like the table: a thing produced with and through our interactions with colleagues, administrators, and other stakeholders. This work begins with our understanding of interaction as historical and interconnected.

We arrive at any given situation from somewhere else. This is true not only of us but of the objects we render into things through our interaction. These assemblages (Prior 2018) of objects are pulled together in any given situation, but the act of pulling those objects and people together also brings with it the histories those objects and people have. This is true for both individuals and objects.

But the histories of people and objects do not extend only across similar assemblages; the essay assignment I write and revise across multiple sections of a writing course over the years, for instance, shapes more than just the day I assign the paper in class. It shapes my preparation for the class, the schedule I keep of responding to student writing, and the broader arc of the semester; it may even be caught up in being "thingified" in situations far from the classroom walls. This interconnected and historical nature of thingification is important for considering how we thingify time. When we try to talk our time into being, to render it a *thing* through interaction, we have to do more than simply accomplish it once. The thingification has to become something that transforms the history, that engages with the interconnected nature of a wide range of assemblages in order to be sustained.

THE MECHANICS OF THINGIFICATION: AN EXPERIENCE WITH HOUR TRACKING

If we think about the building and sustaining of objects as a process, something that is ongoing, then we can turn our attention to the ways this process occurs. How can we make sure that such work interferes with the past history of nonexistent time and sustains itself in future interactions—not just interactions with WPAs but those among other stakeholders throughout our institutions?

I can turn to my own time tracking to make sense of this work. Throughout the 2018–2019 academic year, I accounted for the hours I committed to my work on a daily basis. This record of my hours served as the basis for a report to my department chair, which could be used to discuss how I was committing the hours given to my course reassignment. My time, in other words, was rendered into a number on a spreadsheet, incorporated into a report, and *thingified* through both the reading of that report by my chair and subsequent discussion with him about the work I was doing. Below, I articulate *how* I did this work—the specific decisions I made in thingifying my time—and attach that thingifying work to the broader aims of my role as a writing program administrator.

Table 6.1 provides an overview of the nine categories I drew on to track the time I was committing to various projects. My work as WPA involved the first five categories: each of my grand strategies and any "writing program mechanics" I engaged with. As each day unfolded, I kept my time-tracking notebook on my desk, and I checked in regularly throughout the day to miss as little data as possible. At the end of each week, these hours were added up and placed in an Excel spreadsheet on my laptop. Essentially, the notebook depicted in figure 6.1 allowed me to thingify a time commitment in the flow of my daily routine. I could respond to a batch of emails, then write up how long it took me to do this work. Then, I could move on to the next task and track that as well. The accounting of time became an ordinary part of my day,[1] which set the stage for further thingification when talking with my department chair.

The movement of my hours into an Excel file at the end of each week allowed me another opportunity to thingify my hours, this time more directly in the service of speaking with campus stakeholders. In the movement, the material presence of my time commitments congealed into totals and percentages, which I was able to use to build a broader image—a shareable *thing*—of the kinds of work my course reassignment "purchases." Note the simplicity of figure 6.2. The specifics of each time commitment—what it was that drew me to commit 13.25 hours of my

Trading Time   115

Date	Time	Description	Hours	Category
2/20/19	4:00p - 5:00p	402 work	1	7
2/20/19	8:30p - 10:30p	Teaching Prep	2	7
2/20/19	10:30p - 11:00p	Lifespan Book	1.5	6
2/21/19	9:00a - 1:00p	Teaching	5	7
2/21/19	1:00p - 2:00p	E-mails, etc.	1	5
2/21/19	2:00p - 3:30p	Calibration /	1.5	4
3/21/19	8:00p - 10:00p	UMass-B Conf. Proposal	2	1
2/21/19	10:00p - 12:00a	Lifespan Book	2	6
2/22/19	11:00a - 12:00p	Lifespan Book	1	6
2/22/19	12:00p - 1:00p	E-mails, etc.	1	5
2/22/19	1:00p - 2:00p	Teaching Prep	1	7

Figure 6.1. Notebook of time tracking

	October 15-1	October 22-2	October 29 - Novembe
Strategy 1: Raise Av	4.25	4.5	5.5
Strategy 2: Continu	13.25	0	0
Strategy 3: Develop	0	0	0
Strategy 4: Enhance	3	4.25	5.75
Program Mechanics	2.75	2.5	2.75

Figure 6.2. Excel file of time tracking

time on grand strategy 2, for instance—are deliberately absent, providing me with a broad overview I could use to orient campus stakeholders to the general outline of my time commitments. From here, I could draw general conclusions (such as the percentage of time I am committing to program mechanics in this stretch, which suggests that the support structure we have for WPA work is sufficient, at least in this block of weeks) or use this as a guide to dive deeper into my notebook of hourly commitments so I can develop a more detailed image.

CATEGORIES IN ACTION

The categories I developed allowed me to do more than simply thingify my time; I was able to thingify them in a sustainable manner, one that invited further thingification across a range of situations regarding not only college composition but the missions of the department and the college as well. Consider, for instance, the connections among grand strategies, shorter-term strategies, and the daily tactics to support both.

The grand strategies were a sense-making mechanism; they provided a lens through which other people could make sense of my time commitments and, through that sense-making activity, talk further about the expectations they have for both the program and my position. At the heart of thingifying these categories, in other words, was sustainability, the durability of the categories from one situation to the next, from one stakeholder to the next.

Consider, for instance, the position in which my department chair finds himself. He is charged with not just the mission of first-year writing but the multiple missions of entire departments. He needs to be able to communicate these missions to other stakeholders (and, in years of tight budgets, he needs to do so persuasively). My thingification of time needs to, among other things, enable him to use that thingification—to render my time into a thing "for another first time" (Garfinkel 1967, 9) in these communications. The grand strategies, sub-strategies, and day-to-day tactics I deploy allow him to thingify my time in a way that can link with that communication so he may know, for instance, that I participated in my state's recent rewrite of the English language arts standards. This, in and of itself, may seem like a valuable service to the state and good visibility for both the department and the university. But without the time commitment being connected to the broader vision I have for the program, my chair may struggle to see the place of this commitment in the forward movement of college composition.

One of my grand strategies is to "collaborate with K–20 schools to discuss and support writing instruction and assessment." In pursuit of this grand strategy, the standards revision is not simply a service to the state; it is an opportunity to discuss the values our program holds about writing and how it works with other stakeholders and to lay the groundwork for further partnerships, workshops, presentations, and information sharing in the future. Articulating a single decision—to participate in a revision of the state standards—is now connected to the broader vision of what the college composition program does and what it should do in terms of supporting writing instruction throughout the state.

Let us bring this back to the issue of time—something that has been floating in the background through the above example. My department chair, by attending to my report and the strategy breakdown, is now in a position to talk to other stakeholders about the work I do in the broader context of the college composition program's ongoing development. It is in this context that time can be enacted as a thing. The decision that such a strategy is worth pursuing means that some other strategy is *not* going to be pursued due to time constraints, and my chair can now have discussions with other stakeholders about such a cost. The thingification of my time has now been brought into stakeholders' understandings of the broader missions of the department and the university.

The thingification of time also allows my chair and me to discuss the priorities of the program. If I am going to commit to rolling out a program of professional development for adjunct teachers, it will certainly further my grand strategy of enhancing the quality of the program through the continued development of instructors. But that would mean that some other strategy—grand or otherwise—might fall off the table, unable to be pursued. Given the structure of the time commitment my chair can see in my report, is this worth it? Would it line up with the other missions of the department, of the university, to emphasize a different strategy for the moment and backburner this one? This can lead to very grounded discussions of what certain programmatic decisions will cost the department.

MAKING TIME MATTER

In the above sections, I applied this concept of thingification to my own work to account for my hours as a WPA and to communicate that with my chair. What was the impact of this thingification of time throughout the academic year? Currently, minimal; a busy departmental schedule even before the COVID-19 outbreak slowed the rate of communication of these grand strategies, and they have been slow to gain staying power, to filter into everyday discussions about the college composition program both in the department and with other stakeholders on campus. Furthermore, the history this thingifying is intended to disrupt is not easily disrupted, even with the best intent. Consider, for instance, the work I have done for this chapter and other, similar publications. I would frame this under the first grand strategy: it is a way to communicate the work of college composition at the University of Maine to a broader audience. Because of this writing, awareness of the program and its work will be, if only slightly, raised.

As I was discussing this work with my department chair, however, he mentioned that this might actually be time committed to research, following the Council of Writing Program Administrator (CWPA) guidelines for Evaluating the Intellectual Work of Writing Program Administrators. I agreed that it was indeed intellectual work, but it also seemed that this is the kind of thing that should fall under a course reassignment (since it was, in fact, the result of accounting for reassigned time) and should count toward that time. We realized, in the process of this discussion, that my reassigned time had been directly taken from my teaching time in my contract, making things murkier still. The converging historical threads that worked their way into the CWPA guidelines, the details of my contract, and the grand strategies I developed for the program created this murkiness; and it will require continued work—continued thingifying—of my time to clear the muddied waters.

I raise this example not to suggest its irregularity but rather to suggest that this is only one of what will be recurring issues in the thingification of time: there is constant work to be done across the bureaucratic nooks and crannies of university life to render WPA time fully and completely a *thing* that is countable, even by people committed to the idea. My department chair is fully supportive of WPA work and has expressed a sincere desire to make sure the duties assigned are proportional to the time allotted. But even with two people working to make sense of time in a dedicated way, the complex threads of history interfered with such thingification. I can only imagine how easily such interference would multiply if the situation were not as conducive to the thingification of time as mine is.

In future work, I can imagine how the thingification of time might be able to render more visible the complex ways we decide what to prioritize in our programs. What time are we committing to issues of social justice? How are antiracist approaches to teaching integrated into the grand strategies that move our programs? How do we commit time to equitable hiring and evaluation practices? Thingifying time does not just help us communicate with higher administration; it also allows us to see how we live our values, how we manage to make time for what, and when.

Thingification—that is, sustained thingification that leads to institutional transformation—does not come quickly. The work I have done to track hours has served to transform time *into* a thing, and the categories the hours were organized through can allow *other people* to continue to thingify time as they move away from the work of considering our program and on to separate but related tasks. The framing of thingification and the mechanism of hour tracking and strategy-related categories serve as effective tools for bringing WPA time to life, for making it an active agent in the ongoing discussions about the work of writing programs within universities.

NOTE

1. The tracking of my hours became a labor of its own, one with particular time commitments. However, I was able to, for the most part, integrate it unproblematically with my workday, although unexpected events proved a challenge to track.

REFERENCES

Adler-Kassner, Linda. 2008. *The Activist WPA: Changing Stories about Writers and Writing.* Logan: Utah State University Press.

Charlton, Colin, Jonikka Charlton, Tarez Samra Graban, Kathleen J. Ryan, and Amy Ferdinandt Stolley. 2011. *GenAdmin: Theorizing WPA Identities in the Twenty-First Century.* Fort Collins, CO: Parlor Press.

Dew, Deborah Frank. 2007. "Labor Relations: Collaring the WPA Desire." In *Untenured Faculty as Writing Program Administrators,* edited by Deborah Frank Dew and Alice Horning, 110–136. West Lafayette, IN: Parlor Press.

Garfinkel, Harold. 2008. *Toward a Sociological Theory of Information.* Boulder, CO: Paradigm.

Garfinkel, Harold. 2002. *Ethnomethodology's Program: Working Out Durkheim's Aphorism.* Lanham, MD: Rowman and Littlefield.

Garfinkel, Harold. 1967. *Studies in Ethnomethodology.* Englewood Cliffs, NJ: Prentice-Hall.

Kinman, Gail, and Fiona Jones. 2003. "'Running up the down Escalator': Stressors and Strains in UK Academics." *Quality in Higher Education* 9 (1): 21–38.

Phillips, Talinn, Paul Shovlin, and Megan Titus. 2014. "Thinking Liminally: Exploring the (Com)Promising Positions of the Liminal WPA." *WPA: Writing Program Administration* 38 (1): 42–64.

Prior, Paul. 2018. "How Do Moments Add up to Lives: Trajectories of Semiotic Becoming vs. Tales of School Learning in Four Modes." *Making Future Matters.* Computers and Composition Digital Press. https://ccdigitalpress.org/book/makingfuturematters/prior-intro.html.

Schell, Eileen E. 1998. "Who's the Boss: The Possibilities and Pitfalls of Collaborative Administration for Untenured WPAs." *WPA: Writing Program Administration* 21: 65–80.

7
THEORIZING PROGRAMMATIC ASSESSMENT AS A SITE OF VISIBILITY OF WPA INTELLECTUAL WORK

Lilian W. Mina

The writing program administration literature is full of calls for writing program administrators (WPAs) to collaborate with local and external partners on programmatic assessment. Linda Adler-Kassner (2008) encourages WPAs to build local bridges with personnel in their programs, departments, and campuses to communicate program assessment goals and their relevance to campus conversations about assessment. Adler-Kassner advises WPAs to find those individuals or units that are most invested in assessment to initiate these conversations and to reach some form of consensus on the meaning and purposes of writing programmatic assessment. Similarly, Sonya Lancaster, Heather Bastian, Justin Ross Sevenker, and E. A. Williams (2015, 95) encourage WPAs to identify, navigate, and use possible networks for assessment projects because moving and communicating within these networks allows WPAs to claim their role as "spokespersons for their assessment projects," or as Chris W. Gallagher (2009) asserts, allows WPAs to claim their authority and leadership roles in the assessment process. WPA scholars name portfolio and writing sample readers (Knievel and Baalen-Wood 2017) and various administrators (Gallagher 2009) as potential partners in program assessment.

In her 2015 Council of Writing Program Administrators (CWPA) plenary address, Melissa Ianetta (2015) calls WPAs to create and make public our story as a means of making our work visible to counter the frustrating invisibility of that work, especially at the local institutional level. Addressing assessment work in particular, Gallagher (2009, 41) also notes that WPAs need to "make visible" the extensive and intensive labor involved in a writing program assessment. However, Ianetta (2015), Gallagher (2009), and other WPA scholars don't tell WPAs how to make their work visible. More important, we don't know how collaboration in programmatic assessment initiatives can make WPA work visible or to whom.

As I was planning the first writing programmatic assessment at my institution, I wanted to use the assessment process as a site to respond to Ianetta's (2015) and Gallagher's (2009) calls to make WPA work visible. My purpose was to examine whether claiming my leadership role in designing and implementing writing programmatic assessment through forging collaborative partnerships would make my work as a WPA visible while achieving our programmatic and institutional assessment goals and what that visibility may look like. I articulated these research questions to guide my qualitative case study research: How does collaboration in programmatic assessment endeavors make WPA work visible? And which part of WPA work is made visible through this collaboration?

Findings of six interviews with various partners reveal that the programmatic assessment process became a site for professional development, and these collaborative partners demonstrated better understanding of the curriculum and its goals, articulated plans to change some pedagogical practices to achieve these goals, and acknowledged assessment as a robust research informed by the rich theories of writing studies. In the following sections, I introduce the context of the study, present and discuss findings of my interviews, and build on these findings for future work in WPA scholarship.

CONTEXT OF THE STUDY

In fall 2018, our writing program started using an adapted version of the Teaching-for-Transfer (TFT) curriculum that included three components: key composition terms, reiterative reflective writing, and student theory of writing (Yancey, Robertson, and Taczak 2014). Two student learning outcomes (SLOs) addressed transfer in each of our two first-year writing courses, and I aimed to assess these SLOs in summer 2019, after the first year of implementing the TFT curriculum. My goal was to assess the effectiveness of the TFT curriculum, identify any potential problems, and determine intervention to remedy those problems.

With that goal in mind, I designed a programmatic assessment plan that would allow me to collect two types of data: quantitative data (scores of students' portfolio cover letters) and qualitative data (written and verbal comments from cover letter readers and student responses to an anonymous survey about their learning of the different components of TFT). My next step was to identify the institutional partners with whom I'd collaborate to implement this assessment plan. My partners were Phil, our assessment specialist from the Office of Institutional Effectiveness (OIE); Liz, then–assistant director of the composition program; and writing instructors participating in the two-day portfolio-reading assessment.

SITES OF COLLABORATION

Collaboration with assessment partners happened at various times and took many shapes,[1] but I focus here on two main collaboration sites: my planning meetings with Phil and conversations with Liz and the instructors during the two-day assessment. The conversations that happened at these two sites centered mostly around the program goals, the curriculum, and the assessment process design and goals and thus are more relevant to the scope of this study.

Site #1

I first met with OIE staff to discuss my programmatic assessment plan. This was the first time OIE had to deal with writing programmatic assessment, so I wanted to explain my plan in detail: the objectives, the process, and data-gathering methods. At first, Phil wasn't sure why I wanted to collect qualitative data, especially readers' comments and thoughts on the cover letters. Adler-Kassner and Peggy O'Neill (2010) discuss the tension regarding the assessment data type different parties are interested in: writing instructors and program directors care about qualitative data that reveal more of what's happening in the writing classroom and how to improve it, while administrators want to see quantitative data about the same phenomenon. They suggest that one way to reframe the conversation on assessment is to reconcile both sides rather than choosing one side over the other, and that is exactly what I did.

I used Phil's questions about our data types to explain that the purpose of the assessment process was not simply to collect numbers that we would report back to OIE; my more important purpose was to gain insight into the pedagogical practices and the coherence of teaching and learning our TFT curriculum. My interest in collecting qualitative data intrigued Phil, and he was able to acknowledge that while we would collect the quantitative data both the program and the university needed, there was a need to collect the data I would use to improve teaching and learning in the composition classes. This long conversation facilitated our agreement that there was no contradiction between our goals, and we were, in fact, able to see them as two perspectives of the same issue. By the end of the meeting, we had agreed to collect both types of data, and Phil further suggested some minor changes in my plan to streamline the collection of qualitative data. We hence reconciled our data types to satisfy our relatively different but complementary assessment purposes.

Site #2

Prior to the two-day assessment session, Liz and I selected and scored sample cover letters to use for norming and calibration purposes. We met and discussed our scores and how we used the assessment rubric to make our decisions before we planned for the norming sessions. The rubric used to assess the portfolio cover letter was constructed collaboratively in one of the program professional development sessions at the beginning of the fall 2018 semester. Thus, the creation of that rubric was a bottom-up process that involved instructors of all ranks in the program. After that professional development meeting, I had a draft of the rubric that I revised, streamlining its language based on my assessment knowledge and training. I then shared it with the full-time lecturers in the program for feedback before we finalized it and shared it with all instructors to use in their evaluation of the portfolio at the end of the semester. We used the same rubric in the programmatic assessment process.

At the very beginning of the two-day assessment, Liz and I led a one-hour norming and calibration session in which we used those pre-scored cover letters to engage instructors in an active discussion of the assessment rubric. Instructors had time to read through each sample letter, ask questions, verify their scoring, discuss discrepancy in scores, and reach a consensus. They took notes on the rubric to guide them as they started reading and scoring cover letters. We had a shorter norming and calibration session at the beginning of the second day as a refresher.

Throughout the assessment process, instructors took written notes and made verbal comments on what they were seeing in the cover letters and their interpretation of these issues. Similar to one case in Adler-Kassner and O'Neill's (2010, 118) study, our assessment time became "both an opportunity to see, across our program, what students do well and what we feel isn't being taught as consistently as we'd like."

After obtaining an Institutional Review Board (IRB) approval, I conducted semi-structured interviews with six collaborators in the assessment process.[2] Table 7.1 displays the roles these collaborators played. The interviews were conducted and transcribed in the three weeks following the two-day assessment. Due to the absence of theories that

Table 7.1. Assessment partners and their roles

Name	Position	Role in Assessment
Phil	Assessment specialist	Advising on my plan and coordinating the process with OIE
Liz	FT lecturer and assistant director of the composition program	Collecting, coding, reading, and scoring cover letters
Amanda	PT adjunct	Reading and scoring cover letters
Eleanor	PT adjunct	Reading and scoring cover letters
Juanita	PT adjunct	Reading and scoring cover letters
Tye	Graduate teaching assistant (GTA)	Reading and scoring cover letters

explain how collaboration in writing programmatic assessment may contribute to the visibility of WPA work, I used inductive analysis and active codes to identify emerging themes.

PROGRAMMATIC ASSESSMENT AS A SITE FOR PROFESSIONAL DEVELOPMENT

As I engaged in active coding of interview data, several themes emerged, one of which became the core category around which all others can be organized and related: assessment as a site for professional development that can increase visibility of key aspects of WPA work. Around this central category, other sub-themes emerged and clustered: demonstration of better understanding of the curriculum and its goals, reflecting on and articulating decisions about teaching the curriculum, and acknowledging the rigor of programmatic assessment as research.

Visibility of Curriculum Goals

When asked about the benefits gained from participating in the programmatic assessment process, Amanda emphasized that she found her participation informative of "not just how to teach it [the TFT curriculum] but where the department [writing program] is going . . . what we're trying to accomplish." Eleanor echoed the same sentiment: "It was 'specially helpful to me in understanding and getting a better hold on what we're doing with the reflective writing." She explained her answer: "Being involved in the department activities, no matter what they are, helps you have a better understanding of the goals of the program. So since assessment is a huge part of that . . . having more experience and gaining more knowledge in that area helps me to help the department achieve that goal . . . their goals . . . our goals." Eleanor's comments point to how collaboration in programmatic assessment can facilitate building a common vision of the program and its goals and the best ways to achieve those goals, making them "our goals" rather than "that goal" or "their goals." Not only do these answers demonstrate a better and more profound understanding of the TFT curriculum goals, but instructors showed their willingness to adopt them as their own goals and to help achieve them.

Interestingly and despite his initial uncertainty about my assessment plan, Phil seems to have formed a deeper understanding of the TFT curriculum from our conversations around the curriculum components, SLOs pertaining to TFT, and the assessment plan. When asked how he thinks our assessment results may be useful for his unit and for the institution, he said that first-year composition, as an integral part of the core curriculum that every student is required to complete, means that "any improvement[s] that we make here are improvements for the entire student body and then how that goes into affecting how those students perform in their majors . . . if they're in a writing-intensive major, that would certainly go a long way."

Without reading the scholarship on writing transfer, Phil captured the essence of our curriculum goals in his statement: to help students transfer their writing knowledge learned in first-year writing courses to writing in other courses. This comment shows how collaboration and communication with partners on campus can build understanding of and support for the writing program curriculum and goals, making them more visible and appreciated. The visibility of the curriculum goals is likely to result in more instructors' buy-in and willingness to change teaching practices to better achieve those goals.

Reflection and Change
Participating in the programmatic assessment appeared to have worked as time for reflection on dispositions and pedagogical practices. Liz captures the spirit of programmatic assessment facilitating self-assessment as a springboard for professional development and change: "Program assessment is a way for you to really evaluate not just how the students are doing in the program but how you're doing . . . where are you and what you need to do to be better." Further, Amanda reflects on how she structures assignments: "I know I need to space it [the cover letter assignment] out more so they [students] have time to reflect, which is something I really didn't think about until I started reading their essays and the other essays, thinking . . . maybe if they had more time to actually sit back and think, they would do better."

I first attributed Liz's and Amanda's responses to their relatively long teaching experience (ten and eight years, respectively), which would make them reflective, but Tye (a GTA with less than a year of teaching experience at the time of the interview) talked about a similar moment of reflection on how to make the key terms clearer to students "even though I thought personally I was making it clear."

This combination of conscious and intuitive reflection and self-assessment made it possible for these instructors to reconceptualize reflective writing and to think of adopting different pedagogical practices to teach the elements of our TFT curriculum. The three instructors' thoughts indicate how their involvement in the programmatic assessment process and engagement in the conversations during the norming sessions and cover letter scoring served as time for professional development that may have contributed to what appears to be an increased awareness of their teaching practices that may need to change. They talked about (re)structuring assignments and modifying their approaches to teaching certain elements of the curriculum, namely, teaching reflective writing and contextualizing the e-portfolio and cover letter to students. Amanda, for instance, said, "When I was looking through some of the rubric questions in the essays, I started to realize . . . here are some things I can tweak, here are some things that I can change and explain better." Similarly, Juanita seemed to have thought about scaffolding the e-portfolio: "It [assessment] helped me with the steps going into the portfolio." Liz had already implemented some changes in her summer courses: "I've changed the way that I approach talking to my students about the reflection and the cover letter based on what I saw during program assessment."

In contrast, Phil articulated his conception of assessment as "the basis of learning and improving." He saw assessment as reflection aimed at improvement at the individual and programmatic levels, thus expounding the instructors' reflection and perspective: "If you don't take the time to really look into these things and all you're doing is just letting the days go by doing the same things over and over again . . . hell knows if you're really getting anything to improve the students [who] are coming through every year."

Phil's expertise-driven conception of assessment as a vehicle for improvement in learning and teaching echoes the core goal of assessment: revealing what's happening in the writing class and improving it (Adler-Kassner and O'Neill 2010).

Visibility of Assessment as Research

A significant theme I identified in the data was the visibility of the rigorous intellectual work that goes into programmatic assessment as well as the visibility of writing studies as a robust discipline with rich theories. Three of six participants referred to the assessment process as research, although I never described it as such in my communication, especially with instructors. Amanda refers to e-portfolio cover letters as "data" several times and says, "it was hard to separate the idea that you're looking at data, not student work." She says that thinking about assessment as research helped her overcome that emotional mind-set and focus on the assessment goal: "When you step back and think I'm just doing this for data . . . then you can kind of distance yourself from that emotional feeling."

Eleanor, in contrast, acknowledges the labor and time that go into designing and implementing assessment research: "It's very different moving parts that you have to put together to do research like this, especially to not only research [but] then also use the results in your immediate program . . . like, that is not just interesting but really exciting." Eleanor's statement reveals a profound understanding of programmatic assessment, not only as a research project that requires careful design and managing "moving parts" but also as a project with implications and using assessment results in the program.

Not surprisingly, as an assessment specialist, Phil frames assessment as research and describes our assessment plan as research with a thoughtful design, particular goals, and appropriate data collection and analysis methods. He compares our model to others and says that it was different from traditional assessment driven by accreditation purposes and institutional need for data: "This is how assessment should be done across every program in the sense that it shouldn't be my template." Further, he expresses his hope to encourage more programs to think of their programmatic assessment as research and to use a similar design in their assessment processes that would allow them to "have an actual impact and something that's measurable for [their] program."

Phil's comments support writing assessment scholars' position that assessment is research. Adler-Kassner and O'Neill (2010) argue strongly that framing assessment as empirical research is essential to us as program directors because it influences how our departments and institutions define our field. My assessment partners' responses provide evidence of how meaningful collaboration in the assessment process initiated by a WPA can help institutional partners—within and outside the program—understand more about assessment in our field, which reflects more positively on the perception of writing studies as a robust field with strong theories. This was another dimension of visibility to WPA work that I didn't expect when I started this study.

PROGRAMMATIC ASSESSMENT AND THE VISIBILITY OF WPA INTELLECTUAL WORK

The purpose of this study was to elucidate whether and how collaboration in writing programmatic assessment may make WPA work visible. Findings from interview data answer my research questions, indicating that collaboration in programmatic assessment can transform the assessment process to a site of professional development that substantially enhances the visibility of WPA work at three intersecting tiers: visibility as better understanding of the curriculum goals, visibility as making pedagogical changes to achieve those goals, and visibility as conceptualizing assessment as research.

My local partners, or the writing instructors who participated in the assessment, expressed more awareness of and support for the curriculum and its goals, and they discussed their plans to change their teaching and to find more ways to support student learning. This significant level of visibility verifies the anecdotal observation Tim McCormack and Mark McBeth (2017, 192) make that portfolio reading and the discussion that follows become a form of faculty professional development, as instructors can see how students in other classes have engaged with the curriculum and develop new perspective and ideas for their teaching the following semester.

Moreover, my institutional partner Phil has developed a new understanding of programmatic assessment and the value of the writing studies model that uses assessment to improve teaching and learning. At the interview, Phil expressed his interest in using our assessment model to perhaps begin enticing other stakeholders to try to work with it: "Hey, if we really make this a really strong and sound assessment tool and we can use the results to make interventions, you could talk about publications and presentations . . . if you really put the time and effort into doing something."

In a campus-wide presentation on programmatic assessment success stories, Phil presented our assessment process as a model for other programs to follow. As displayed in figure 7.1,[3] he specifically emphasized how assessment can be approached as empirical research to yield results that can be used to create meaningful interventions not only in the

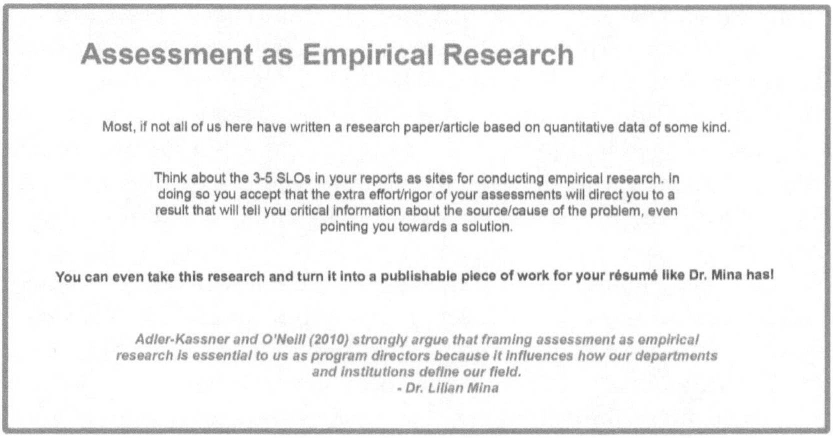

> **Assessment as Empirical Research**
>
> Most, if not all of us here have written a research paper/article based on quantitative data of some kind.
>
> Think about the 3-5 SLOs in your reports as sites for conducting empirical research. In doing so you accept that the extra effort/rigor of your assessments will direct you to a result that will tell you critical information about the source/cause of the problem, even pointing you towards a solution.
>
> You can even take this research and turn it into a publishable piece of work for your résumé like Dr. Mina has!
>
> *Adler-Kassner and O'Neill (2010) strongly argue that framing assessment as empirical research is essential to us as program directors because it influences how our departments and institutions define our field.*
> *- Dr. Lilian Mina*

Figure 7.1. Slide from Phil's presentation

program but also in academic publications and presentations (Brodeur 2019). Not only did his statement reveal a deeper understanding of the value of our assessment process, but it is also a testament to our field's theories that have always regarded assessment highly and conceptualized assessment as a means to improve teaching and learning.

These findings substantiate Gallagher's (2009, 36) proposition that WPAs may use assessment as a site for the professional development of writing teachers by engaging them in conversations on learning and teaching and that these conversations are a form of collaboration. In our experience, the norming sessions, discussion of the assessment rubric in detail and in-depth, and conversations about our observations in the cover letters served as an opportunity for teacher professional development, albeit unintentional. William Condon, Ellen R. Iverson, Cathryn A. Manduca, Carol Rutz, and Gudrun Willett (2016, 5) define professional development as "intentional, in-service activities overtly planned to improve various aspects of teaching performance." Although some conversations were planned (e.g., the norming sessions), they were nuanced and extended during the process, and instructors' statements reveal a change in attitudes (conceptualization of the TFT curriculum) and behaviors (planned pedagogical changes) that are likely to lead to better teaching and learning in first-year composition classes taught be these instructors.

Gallagher (2009, 36) also asserts that WPA knowledge of "classroom assessment theory and practice" opens the door for productive collaboration with teachers to achieve better and more effective assessment of student writing. In her interview and in reference to using the rubric in her classes, Juanita talked about how the rubric can be confusing and admitted that she "probably never really read the rubric intensely" or knew how to apply it to the cover letter. She juxtaposed that confusion to the clarity she gained about the rubric as we discussed it in-depth during the norming sessions: "Talking about it [the rubric] and then doing it and then talking about it again connected all the dots." Juanita's "aha" moment made the rubric, the cover letter assignment, and more broadly the TFT curriculum more meaningful and their core benefits more visible and tangible. This visibility wouldn't have been possible without the productive collaboration in the assessment process.

Further, these findings support Adler-Kassner and O'Neill's (2010, 143) argument that program directors should use assessment as "opportunities to build alliances with others and to communicate messages about writing instruction based on their own values as well as values articulated in the field of composition and rhetoric." The multiple conversations I had with Phil in which I explained the goals of our TFT curriculum and the foundation of our assessment practices seem to have delivered a clear message that improving the teaching and learning of writing is the ultimate goal of programmatic assessment.

Collectively, these three tiers of visibility—better understanding of the curriculum goals, making pedagogical changes to achieve those goals, and conceptualizing assessment as research—shine more light on WPA intellectual work, work that is based on rigorous research and rich theories and that aims to improve the teaching and learning in the writing classroom. When WPAs claim leadership roles in orchestrating meaningful and productive collaboration in programmatic assessment with institutional partners, their intellectual work becomes more visible to those partners on the teaching and research levels—the two wings of intellectual work highly regarded by academic colleagues. Forming what John R. Hollenbeck, Bianca Beersma, and Maartje E. Schouten (2012, 86) describe as a "cross-functional project team," I claimed my leadership role in planning this collaboration toward achieving a common goal: assessing transfer-focused SLOs using "appropriate assessment methods" that "match the purpose" of our assessment (Gallagher 2009, 37). In the process, I also created a space in which multiple aspects of my WPA work became visible to assessment partners.

NOTES

1. In addition to these partners, I talked to the department chair, the associate provost for undergraduate studies, and the director of OIE to discuss various aspects of our assessment plan and processes.
2. All participants opted for using their real first names in interview transcripts and academic presentations and publications resulting from the study.
3. The quote on the slide comes from this chapter draft that was shared with all interview participants to check whether I had correctly interpreted their statements and fairly represented them.

REFERENCES

Adler-Kassner, Linda. 2008. *The Activist WPA: Changing Stories about Writing and Writers.* Logan: Utah State University Press.

Adler-Kassner, Linda, and Peggy O'Neill. 2010. *Reframing Writing Assessment to Improve Teaching and Learning.* Logan: Utah State University Press.

Brodeur, Philip. 2019. "Beyond Bureaucracy: Case Studies of Success in Annual Assessment." Auburn University at Montgomery: Office of Institutional Effectiveness. Presentation to Faculty Development Institute.

Condon, William, Ellen R. Iverson, Cathryn A. Manduca, Carol Rutz, and Gudrun Willett. 2016. *Faculty Development and Student Learning: Assessing the Connections.* Bloomington: Indiana University Press.

Gallagher, Chris W. 2009. "What Do WPAs Need to Know about Writing Assessment? An Immodest Proposal." *WPA: Writing Program Administration* 33 (1–2): 29–45.

Hollenbeck, John R., Bianca Beersma, and Maartje E. Schouten. 2012. "Beyond Team Types and Taxonomies: A Dimensional Scaling Conceptualization for Team Description." *Academy of Management Review* 37 (1): 82–106.

Ianetta, Melissa. 2015. "Absence and Action: Making Visible WPA Work." *WPA: Writing Program Administration* 38 (2): 141–158.

Knievel, Michael, and Meg Van Baalen-Wood. 2017. "University of Wyoming Professional Writing Minor." In *Writing Program Architecture: Thirty Cases for Reference and Research*, edited by Bryna Siegel-Finer and Jamie White-Farnham, 101–117. Logan: Utah State University Press.

Lancaster, Sonya, Heather Bastian, Justin Ross Sevenker, and E. A. Williams. 2015. "Making the Most of Networked Communication in Writing Program Assessment." *WPA: Writing Program Administration* 38 (2): 93–112.

McCormack, Tim, and Mark McBeth. 2017. "John Jay College of Criminal Justice First-Year Writing Program." In *Writing Program Architecture: Thirty Cases for Reference and Research*, edited by Bryna Siegel Finer and Jamie White-Farnham, 184–201. Logan: Utah State University Press.

Yancey, Kathleen Blake, Liane Robertson, and Kara Taczak. 2014. *Writing across Contexts: Transfer, Composition, and Sites of Writing.* Logan: Utah State University Press.

8
MAKING ADMINISTRATION'S EXCHANGE VALUE VISIBLE

Heather M. Robinson

The scholarship of writing program administration (WPA) has already taken a valuable turn toward making visible the labor that is writing program administration, through time-use diaries and other descriptive and quantitative measures (for example, Graziano et al. 2020; Ianetta 2015). In broader academic contexts, several authors have examined the time use of academic workers (e.g., Barrett and Barrett 2010; Link, Swann, and Bozeman 2008; Misra, Lundquist, Holmes, and Agiomavritis 2011; Winslow 2010; Ziker 2014), as well as how faculty describe their time allocations in official reports (e.g., O'Meara, Kuvaeva, and Nyunt 2017). However, what remains elusive is a measure of the value of this work in our institutional contexts. That is, which elements of this labor "count" a lot, and which "count" a little? This gap in our research and institutional discourses means it is often difficult to answer these questions: What should faculty be spending their time on? What do we do with the imbalances between what takes up our time as WPAs and what is recognized and rewarded at our institutions? In my proposed answer to these questions, I frame WPA labor using the Marxist concept of "exchange value," which describes the commodification of labor. Karl Marx and Friedrich Engels (2001, 55), in *Capital*, define exchange value as "a quantitative relation, as the proportion in which values in use of one sort are exchanged for those of another sort, a relation constantly changing with time and place." The term highlights the degree to which labor and its products are *recognized* as having value within a particular market, not just in terms of how the products of that labor are used but in terms of how they might be exchanged for other commodities within that market. Exchange value, then, is an abstraction away from how useful a thing actually is and the labor that went into its production. In the context of this chapter, the "market" is the market of academic labor and rewards systems. I apply the term *exchange value* to the value of administrative labor as a commodity that can be exchanged for some kind of reward, following the definition in Dale M. Bauer (2002, 256; quoted in Bird, Litt, and Wang 2004, 201), who describes academic exchange value as "value formally recognized as worthy of formal rewards like salaries, promotions, and special benefits."

While the application of Marx and Engels's (2001) concept of exchange value to WPAs, a group that is effectively a managerial class (see, for instance, Strickland 2011), shifts the original concept's application, in doing so I follow a number of authors who have productively applied the term *exchange value* in the context of academic labor—including the labor of writing program administrators—to better understand how academic administrators function as workers and how their labor as such is and is not valued.[1] For instance, Sharon Bird, Jacquelyn S. Litt, and Yong Wang (2004) use the concept of exchange value in the context of women's service labor in academic institutions. Using the definition from Bauer (2002) cited above, they discuss how little exchange value service work in universities has, particularly for women and faculty of color as they undertake it.

The lack of exchange value for the service labor of faculty, especially those who are minoritized, has also been discussed by, for instance, Ana Martinez Alemán (2014), Katie J. Hogan (2010), and Bruce Horner (2007). Horner (2007, 168) suggests that WPA and other academic administrative work must be considered "social" labor and thus subject to being rendered invisible because it cannot be as readily commodified as individualized "intellectual" labor. Furthermore, the term *exchange value* is used in the Council of Writing Program Administrators' (1998) statement "Evaluating the Intellectual Work of Writing Program Administration" in its consideration of how WPA work might or might not "count" in the academic rewards system. The statement describes academic work, if it is to be rewardable with tenure and promotion, as needing to be recognizable as "the production of specific commodities—albeit scholarly commodities—with a clear exchange value, perhaps not on the general market but certainly in academic institutions" (1998). The statement goes on to explain that academic work is rewarded when it features "recognizable and conventional forms to which value can be readily assigned and [whose] valuations are likely to be recognized and accepted by most colleagues and academic departments" (1998). Finally, it acknowledges that service and administration are rarely accorded exchange value in our institutions, "no matter how highly they might be valued on an individual basis by fellow faculty, by administrators, or society" (1998). The statement connects the exchange value of WPA work with that of intellectual work, which is well recognized and understood in our systems of academic rewards.

Important for this discussion, exchange value must be considered in contradistinction to use value, the use to which people may put a commodity, and the value of that use to an individual or community. As our academic institutions demonstrate through their continued inclusion of "service" in criteria for reappointment, tenure, and promotion and their continued reliance on faculty administrative labor in the running of essential programs, the use value of faculty administrative work is well understood. The issue I explore, then, is the extent to which such labor is accorded exchange value in the reappointment, tenure, and promotion marketplace: how is the labor of academic administration valued? While this study draws on data and documents taken from a specific institutional context—my own—the literature indicates that the problem of how to value service and administration is a common one, especially for members of minoritized communities (for example, Bird, Litt, and Wang 2004; Gutiérrez y Muhs, Flores Niemann, González, and Harris 2012; Heijstra, Steinþórsdóttir, and Einarsdóttir 2017; Ianetta 2015; Horner 2007; Kynard 2019; Massé and Hogan 2010; Misra, Lundquist, Holmes, and Agiomavritis 2011; O'Meara, Kuvaeva, and Nyunt 2017; Perryman-Clark and Craig 2019).

While the articulation of the meaning of exchange value in the context of WPA labor in the Council of Writing Program Administrators' (1998) statement "Evaluating the Intellectual Work of Writing Administration" is very useful for this project, my goal here differs from the one articulated in that statement. In the statement, the authors make an argument for treating WPA work as equivalent to scholarship because these "service activities" are "tied directly to [WPAs'] special field of knowledge and relate to, and flow directly out of, this professional activity" (Council of Writing Program Administrators 1998, citing Boyer 1990, 22). As Alice Gillam (2003, 123) writes, "Despite the invaluable contribution of the WPA position statement on 'Evaluating the Intellectual Work of Writing Administration' in validating WPA work, it reifies the distinction between intellectual and emotional labor and ignores the less visible and commodifiable aspects of our work," a point also taken up by Bruce Horner (2007). Rather, my goal is to take steps toward valuing administrative work as its own entity, connected with service, using my own local campus experience to consider how institutions might create explicit local discourses of administrative "exchange value." I leave to the side, at least at the outset, the question of intrinsic motivation (Ryan and Deci 2000), whereby people do things because doing so brings them personal satisfaction and fulfillment. Such motivations have been shown to be exploited by institutions to extract uncompensated labor from faculty who are people of color and white women (e.g., Hogan 2010; Schell 1992; Tokomitsu 2014), even as they may be valuable for individuals from minoritized groups on a personal level. In this chapter, rather, I focus on the realm of extrinsic motivation, where labor is motivated by the promise of rewards from external actors. In most academic institutions, rewards take the form of reappointment, tenure, and promotion; some institutions may also have systems of merit pay or some type of institutional award system. However, alongside the invisibility of administrative labor in systems of workload accounting, the connection between administrative work and institutional rewards is complicated by the fact that administrative work is often "compensated" with time reassigned from teaching duties, which is often the only part of a faculty member's workload that is routinely quantified.

To make the argument here, I present data and documents from my own institution and department, of which I was chairperson from 2016 through 2019 and at which I served as the writing program director from 2011 through 2016. At the City University of New York (CUNY), department chairs do not only chair department-level reappointment, tenure, and promotion (RTP) committees; all chairs, alongside other academic leaders in the institution, also comprise the college-wide RTP committee. From this vantage point, I saw firsthand the mismatch among the time faculty were spending on administration, their perceptions of what they could claim as notable labor, and the labor for which they would actually be rewarded or recognized. In particular, I saw the lack of clarity among newer faculty at the college about what administrative and service activities they should put forward as activities with exchange value in the RTP process. On the level of my department and as an academic chairperson, I worked with colleagues to put in place various documents and structures that articulated the value of administration and service. I believe it is in its administrative documents—more than in its vision and mission statements and formal articulations of institutional values, institutional learning objectives, and collective bargaining agreements—that an institution lays out its values, particularly as they relate to employees.

To develop the discussion here, I examine time-use diaries completed by faculty in the English department in 2016 to find out what people were doing with their time. I also discuss documents faculty at my institution use to argue for, or commodify, their service and administrative work's exchange value as part of the RTP process and the response to these documents written by department chairs in the 2018–2019 academic year.[2] Finally, I consider the document in which my own service as English department chair from 2016 through 2019 is valued by my college president in the form of a "thank you" letter (Keizs 2019). Together, these documents and data highlight the "institutional housekeeping" (Bird, Litt, and Wang 2004, 194) or "academic housework" (Heijstra, Steinþórsdóttir, and Einarsdóttir 2016, 765) that is at the heart of success in administrative work in higher education. In particular, my thank you letter affirms one of the contentions I develop in this chapter, whereby I suggest that administrative work has little to no exchange value in the RTP market because the "institutional housekeeping"—which, as Leigh Graziano, Kay Halasek, Frank Napolitano, Susan Miller-Cochran, and Natalie Syzmanski (2020) show, makes up so much of the labor of administrative jobs—is already "compensated" by reassigned time and so does not need to be rewarded. Instead, what is rewarded and recognized is service labor that somehow individuates the faculty member within established systems of "legible" (Ianetta 2015) faculty work.

TIME-USE DIARIES

In fall 2017, following an Academic Program Review in the Department of English in which we established that the faculty in that department perceived a high degree of gendered and racial imbalance in the amount of service, administration, advising, and mentoring work undertaken by full-time faculty,[3] I asked faculty to record their administrative, service, and mentoring labor for three months. Participation was voluntary, and the logs were collected in September, October, and November of 2017. The survey asked faculty to describe their non-teaching, non-research work and to estimate how much time they were spending on each area in a month. The goal was to develop an impressionistic rather than a scientifically valid accounting; to be more valid in this way, I would have followed methods such as those used by John Ziker (2014), where faculty recorded their activities in small increments over shorter time spans, or something like the Toggl timer tracking used in Graziano, Halasek, Napolitano, Miller-Cochran, and Syzamanski (2020). This method is, however, more fine-grained than the one in KerryAnn O'Meara, Alexandra Kuvaeva, and Gudrun Nyunt (2017), which uses an annual institutional reporting system to examine faculty self-reports of administrative and service labor.

In table 8.1, I present average hours per week and month that Department of English faculty spent on administrative, service, and mentoring tasks during the fall 2017 semester, based on the time-use diaries I collected. I received twenty-nine reporting forms in total—twelve

Table 8.1. Average hours of service, administration, and mentoring labor spent by faculty

	Committee or Other Meeting	Planning and Logistics for Service and Mentoring Work	Student Advising	Other Student Mentoring (fieldwork/independent study students; student clubs)	Mentoring Other Faculty	Other Emotional Labor	Service to the Profession	Other (e.g., email, recommendation letters, supervising staff)	Total
Average hours **per month** for faculty with AdRT	16.5	12.3	3.9	6.0	6.7	5.6	4.1	18.5	73.6
Average hours **per week** for faculty with AdRT	3.7	2.7	0.9	1.3	1.5	1.2	0.9	4.1	16.3
Average hours **per month** for faculty without AdRT	3.64	2.15	0.85	0.18	2.30	0.15	6.25	2.30	17.8
Average hours **per week** for faculty without AdRT	0.81	0.48	0.19	0.04	0.51	0.03	1.39	0.51	4.0

from September, eleven from October, and six from November—at which point reporting fatigue had set in, especially among those faculty who were not in designated reassigned time-bearing roles. Ten reports came from faculty who were not receiving administrative reassigned time (AdRT), and nineteen came from those receiving AdRT. Since the sample was so small, the results I present are not statistically valid, and so I present findings based on impressions drawn from the data. The reporting form provided the categories that are included in the top row of the table. The full form is available in appendix 8.A.

Most faculty received either three or four hours of administrative reassigned time per week, equivalent to one course; the fact that these faculty were involved in meetings, meeting planning, and faculty mentoring reflects, I believe, the work they were doing in these reassigned time positions. Certainly, the data suggest that these are the primary areas in which faculty administration takes place. However, these data also show that they were doing significantly more of the department's "pastoral care" (Barrett and Barrett 2010, 143) than those faculty whose workload hours were only counted by teaching. The disproportionate amount of advising of students in the major, student mentoring, and other "emotional labor" (Hochschild 2012) reported by the faculty members receiving AdRT can only partially be accounted for by their administrative roles; for instance, advising students in the major is written into the job description of every faculty member, and yet the faculty with AdRT were doing four times as much of this work as faculty not receiving AdRT.

Furthermore, these data are skewed in several ways. For instance, one of the faculty members who was not receiving AdRT was receiving reassigned time for their editorial work on a journal and organization of conferences in their discipline; hence, their service to the profession numbers were much higher than anyone else's in the sample. Eliminating this response from the sample creates a still greater disparity between the mentoring and service load borne by faculty who were receiving AdRT compared with those who were not. Faculty receiving AdRT were also more likely to count time spent attending department meetings than were those not receiving AdRT. These data may also be exhibiting some bias in the sense that during this particular semester, faculty doing administrative work in the Department of English were those who had shown themselves to be more engaged with service, advising, and mentoring than those who did not receive reassigned time. Certainly, because reassigned time has been seen as a reward, those who perform well in service and mentoring roles tend to be offered administrative positions that come with reassigned time because they have indicated interest in and demonstrated the skills necessary for succeeding in those roles.

The time-use diaries also highlighted for the faculty exactly how much time their reassigned time "costs" faculty administrators, in terms of time that is not being spent on areas that have well-established exchange value in the university. The time-use diaries revealed the large amount of pastoral care and academic housekeeping that form an important-to-see part of the labor our institutions value but do not reward—that is, labor with use value but little exchange value. However, the reality of this low exchange value is not necessarily understood or accepted at my institution. In the next section, I develop this contention through examination of a list of "Routine Responsibilities" developed by York College department chairpersons, which we developed after reviewing the ways faculty attempt to commodify routine academic work in their reappointment applications.

ROUTINE RESPONSIBILITIES AND ACADEMIC HOUSEWORK

O'Meara, Kuvaeva, and Nyunt (2017) analyzed annual faculty reports of service to examine issues of inequality in campus service activities in order to review faculty articulations of their non-teaching, non-research labor in official institutional documents. At CUNY, tenure-track faculty are reappointed annually; they must apply to be reappointed and then achieve a positive vote from two committees (department and college level), as well as the college president's recommendation to the Board of Trustees. Reappointment letters, addressed to the college president, form part of a reappointment packet that also includes an online curriculum vitae (CV) and the department chairperson's Memorandum of Evaluation (MOE); candidates for a third reappointment and tenure and promotion (separate decisions in the CUNY system) prepare a portfolio of scholarly or creative works. Candidates respond, in a Candidate's Letter, to a "prompt" published in the college's Faculty Handbook, which instructs candidates to address "the nature and value/scope of the teaching, scholarship/creative work, and service during the year under review" and to outline plans for activity and "improvement" over the coming years (York College Faculty Handbook 2018). Notable about the prompt to which faculty respond is that administrative work is completely elided; faculty who do administrative work must create a fourth category if they wish to describe initiatives and successes in that area. In the candidates' letters, faculty generally devote one paragraph each in the two-page letter to discussion of administrative and service contributions to the college. The necessity of educating colleagues and RTP committees about what administration entails and how it can or should be counted is well-known; the Council of Writing Program Administrators' (1998) document, as well as essays such as E. Shelley Reid (2008), speak directly to that necessity. However, the necessity of educating junior faculty about what service is tends not to be explicitly discussed.

In our examination of reappointment applications from the 2018–2019 cohort as part of our service on the college's RTP committee, another chairperson and I noted that many of the letters made claims to "service" that seemed to misinterpret what "service" is. We extended this conversation to include all department chairs at my college; from that conversation, we set out to create a document that describes both what might "count" and the activities we consider to be the foundations for service but that don't "count" as service itself. The list we created indicates what counts as "service" in specific contradistinction to the routine "academic housework" of a faculty member at the college. That is, this document, shown in its entirety in appendix 8.B, is an attempt to indicate explicitly the labor that has significant use value but no exchange value in reappointment, tenure, and promotion decisions. We included as routine the following activities:

- Attending on-campus events

- Attending department meetings
- Advising students
- Conducting teaching observations
- Proctoring exams (makeup or other)
- Staffing tables/making presentations at open houses and accepted students' receptions
- Holding office hours
- Assessing programs and courses
- Writing recommendation letters

The routine activities listed above certainly reflect what faculty spend the bulk of their time doing on the job, as the time-use diaries discussed in the previous section attest. So in that sense, if we consider that service is the non-teaching, non-research labor that makes the institution function, then the work these colleagues describe absolutely falls into that category. However, our institutions also foster a tacit understanding that there is a difference between "service" that counts and the routine responsibilities I will name "academic housework," following the definition offered in Thamar M. Heijstra, Finnborg S. Steinþórsdóttir, and Þorgerður Einarsdóttir (2016, 765): "All the academic service work within the institution [that] is performed by all academic staff, both women and men, but that receives little recognition within the process of academic career making or within the definition of academic excellence." Heijstra, Einarsdóttir, Gyða M. Pétursdóttir, and Steinþórsdóttir (2017, 203) go on to include "tasks relating to giving back to the community, administrative and committee work, gender equality initiatives and various teaching and research-related activities such as student interactions and the organization of conferences" as examples of academic housework. Bruce Horner (2007, 172) writes that "exchange value is conferred through recognition, and hence is ideological." The fact that on our campus this academic housework cannot be recognized within the RTP system—that is, it cannot have exchange value conferred on it—reveals the ideology of service as something that individuates a faculty member, an entirely appropriate commodification in academic capitalism.

The fact that these faculty members were offering examples of academic housework as evidence to support a claim of adequate and meaningful service highlights the problem I am discussing in this chapter: that our institutions do a poor job of articulating the types of service that "count" for RTP, thus leading to situations where early-career faculty in particular are claiming routine faculty work as service, perhaps because that work takes up so much time. Furthermore, it sets up a situation where doing administration well—that is, attending to academic housework such as staffing courses, evaluating instructors, evaluating course equivalences, and more—is also not visible because it does not individuate the faculty members who undertake it. Hence, the only service and administration that is recognized is that which few or no other people on campus do: its exchange value emerges from relative scarcity and, more troubling for administrative work, because the work is otherwise "uncompensated."

Important for my purposes in this chapter, the Routine Responsibilities document also reveals slippage in two areas: when routine responsibilities might become service, and when routine responsibilities may never become service. In the letter, we identified three "gray areas," described as follows:

- Advising students in the major and conducting teaching observations are notable as service if the advising load is particularly high (>50?) or the number of teaching observations is particularly high (>5?) and is not accompanied by administrative reassigned time in a coordinator position.
- While mentoring research students or providing professional mentoring to students does count toward our teaching workload, the amount to which it counts is very minimal. Therefore, we consider such mentoring as a hybrid of teaching and service that could be mentioned in either category.
- We have also drawn a line between administrative work that is compensated with reassigned time and administrative work that is not. So, faculty members contributing to assessment efforts and who are receiving reassigned time would describe this as administration rather than service.

In these areas of slippage, the chairs' Routine Responsibilities document reveals deep confusion and tension between compensation and reward for administrative labor. This confusion and tension means that administrative labor has little to no exchange value in reappointment, tenure, and promotion processes because there is often no category in which it can be considered *and* because the release time from teaching that faculty often receive for conducting administrative work is seen as compensation for that work rather than a necessary allocation of time for the work to get done. Viewing reassigned time as compensation rather than as an appropriate allocation of workload time also has the consequence, I suggest, of rendering administrative work invisible in our recognition systems, whereas service, which shares many functional similarities with administration, is "uncompensated" labor and therefore can be considered to have exchange value.

CAN ADMINISTRATION BE VALUED?

So, how can administration be valued? Are the routine responsibilities of a WPA different enough from the routine responsibilities of faculty members listed above that they can individuate the WPA who does them? These responsibilities include "managing programmatic budgets, designing and implementing transfer equivalency policies, hiring, developing, and firing contingent faculty, or advocating for the writing program at institution- or leadership-level meetings" (Napolitano 2019), as well as participating in the architecture of academic capitalism described by John Trimbur (2008, xi): "strategic planning, performance reviews, focus groups, benchmarking exercises, outcomes assessment, high-stakes testing, or total-quality management of one sort or another." Scholarly discussions such as those included in Theresa Enos and Shane Borrowman (2008) do not suggest much reason for hope. For instance, as Reid (2008) discusses, excellence in administration is not easily (or, indeed, willingly) evaluated as equivalent to excellence in teaching; and the problems of evaluating administration as equivalent to research, as suggested by the Council of Writing Program Administrators (1998), are well-known (e.g., Snyder 2009). Assessing and counting excellence in administration requires, as Reid (2008) suggests, an extensive education campaign for evaluators, something untenured and otherwise vulnerable faculty do not necessarily have the institutional stature or networks to do. Reid (2008, 209, emphasis added) writes, "Despite my good fortune and the optimism of the WPA Statement—the Council of Writing Program Administrators is convinced that WPAs *can be* evaluated on the basis of their administrative work—translation of possibility into a local institutional reality remains a significant, time-consuming, unmapped challenge." Furthermore, Kathleen Blake Yancey's (Roen, Yancey, and Schwalm 2008) response to Reid's (2008) essay and others in Enos and Borrowman (2008) does not provide much optimism; she suggests that successful WPAs might well be those who keep their WPA work "invisible, . . . with classes staffed, budgets small, and initiatives as insubstantial as possible" (Roen, Yancey, and Schwalm 2008, 214).

Melissa Ianetta's (2015) proposal for the articulation of administrative labor as part of a faculty administrator's curriculum vitae suggests that to assign exchange value to administrative work, there must be an independent process of recognition and reward that is nonetheless tied to the RTP system—which is the only value system that "counts" in institutions of higher education. Such a system would require an agreed-upon job description that is understood at all levels of evaluation and against which success is measured. In this way, the work of an administrator can be individualized. However, such an approach still runs the risk of eliding and devaluing the academic housework, which, as Graziano, Halasek, Napolitano, Miller-Cochran, and Syzmanski (2020) describe, can take up the bulk of a WPA's time and which should, I suggest, be not only grounds for evaluation but also the basis for reward. In considering this point further, I now turn to an examination of my own "thank you for your service" letter, which I received at the end of my term as department chairperson. This letter highlights the problem of the mismatch between the realities of administrative work and the activities for which administrators may receive recognition, in particular, the disjunction between administrative job descriptions and our academic reward and recognition structures.

"THANK YOU FOR YOUR SERVICE"

The responsibilities of department chairpersons are articulated in the CUNY bylaws and include such tasks as running department meetings, creating the class schedule, keeping departmental records, evaluating faculty, and "generally supervis[ing] and administer[ing] the department" (Board of Trustees Bylaws n.d., section 9.3. I include the bylaws in full in appendix 8.C.). In addition to these responsibilities, informal internal documents—shared among chairs and by deans—outline what needs to be done. There is also an unofficial "chair evaluation" process that includes self-evaluation on a number of metrics, accompanied by a brief narrative from the school dean and the provost. However, this evaluation has no place in the broader RTP process, should a chair put themselves forward as a candidate for promotion.

My time-use diaries from fall 2017 show that the bulk of my time in September to November 2017 was spent prepping for and attending meetings, creating and staffing schedules, mentoring faculty and supervising staff, writing curriculum grants, and responding to emails—in other words, "generally supervising and administering the department" (Board of Trustee Bylaws n.d., Section 9.3.12(a)). However, at the end of my term as department chairperson from 2016 through 2019, I received a letter from the college president as a thank you for my service. The letter specifically thanks me for two accomplishments:

- Your leadership on the College's LGBTQ [lesbian, gay, bisexual, transgender, queer] Committee that successfully launched compliance protocols, as well as expanded the culture of acceptance in and out of the classroom; and
- Serving actively on the Personnel and Budget Committee that reshaped the guidelines for promotion and tenure. (Keizs 2019)

The letter concludes: "I am sure that others will have their own highlights, but for me, these are some of the identifiable achievements; and I thank you for them" (Keizs 2019). This "thank you" letter suggests that the responsibilities outlined in the CUNY bylaws are invisible in terms of exchange value: the administrative labor that differentiates a good chair from a mediocre or poor one cannot be commodified. Instead, the only labor that has exchange value, in terms of recognition or reward, is labor that goes beyond the duties that are articulated in the bylaws. And the role of department chairperson is much more institutionally visible and well-articulated than that of the WPA. Nonetheless, this thank you letter demonstrates that the issues that prevail in trying to establish the visibility of WPA work are also true of chair work. As Ianetta (2015, 153) puts it, "When I frame my work in terms of my colleagues['] previously-held values, the system of representation based on their work, not mine, all the things that make me awesome—things on which I spend most of my time—disappear." We see this disappearance in full force in my thank you letter. Horner (2007, 168) writes, "In practice . . . WPA work is virtually impossible to identify as a set of individual accomplishments." In this letter, the college president chose two items that can be seen as individual accomplishments but which have little to nothing to do with my effectiveness as a department chairperson or, indeed, my fulfillment of the stated responsibilities associated with the position. The accomplishments the president notes are ones of which I am proud, but I am probably less proud of them than I am of the thank you letter and half-pound of beef jerky given to me by an adjunct faculty member who, in her own letter, said I had made the adjuncts in my department feel respected and safe.

CONCLUSION

In this chapter, I do not challenge prevailing models of the value placed on academic administration and labor; I do, however, offer such a challenge in Heather M. Robinson (2021). Rather, here I suggest that within the strictures of academic capitalism under which faculty work across the globe, our institutions must do a better job of articulating what they value in terms of faculty administration and service and thus guide faculty who are seeking "rewards" within that system on how to spend their time. Making administration visible is important and establishing its exchange value in our reward systems is important because otherwise we require people to do this work for "love" or other intangible "rewards" that have little to do with ensuring their professional success. It is not enough to make administration visible. Our institutions and our RTP committees need to establish metrics for success in administration and contextualize administrative work within a specific institutional context and broader discourses of success. To adapt an idea from Bird, Litt, and Wang (2004), it is necessary for administration to assign exchange value to administrative labor in our institutional reward and recognition systems.

The argument I have presented here focuses on ways our institutions fail to establish explicit exchange value for administrative labor, but accompanying this argument is a challenge to the low exchange value of certain administrative and service labors I have shown in this chapter. When the exchange value of administrative work is visible, faculty can make better choices about what to do and when to embrace failure as an alternative—because our rewards and recognition structures do not have any way to value our administrative success and yet continue to ask this labor of us because it is what makes the university run.

APPENDIX 8.A: SERVICE AND ADMINISTRATION LABOR REPORTING SHEET

Name _____ OR Race _____ and Gender _____ Month/Year ___ ___

What was the task?	How long did you spend?	Do you receive reassigned time for doing this work?	How much/week?	Was this task voluntary, requested, or assigned/appointed?
Committee or other meeting				
Planning and logistics for service and mentoring work				
Student advising				
Other student mentoring (including, but not limited to, independent studies/fieldwork supervision)				
Mentoring other faculty				
Other emotional labor				
Service to the profession				
Something else				

APPENDIX 8.B: ROUTINE RESPONSIBILITIES DOCUMENT

Routine Responsibilities of Faculty Work

October 15, 2018

These are duties that everyone is expected to fulfill as part of their faculty appointments at York College. Since all faculty are expected to fulfill these responsibilities, they are not useful inclusions in reappointment, tenure, and promotion materials. In general, these items should only occur in reappointment documents if the candidate is not fulfilling them, and then they should be part of the chair's narrative.

- Attending on-campus events
- Attending department meetings
- Student advising*
- Conducting teaching observations*
- Proctoring exams (makeup or other)
- Staff tables/make presentations at open houses and accepted students receptions
- Hold office hours
- Program and course assessment
- Writing recommendation letters

*These are notable as service if the advising load is particularly high (>50?) or the number of teaching observations is particularly high (>5?) and is not accompanied by administrative reassigned time in a coordinator position.

There are, of course, some gray areas in the category that we define as "service." For instance, while mentoring research students or providing professional mentoring to students does count toward our teaching workload, the amount to which it counts is very minimal. Therefore, we consider such mentoring as a hybrid of teaching and service, and it could be mentioned in either category.

Clear examples of institutional service include:

- Faculty adviser for student clubs
- Standing or ad hoc committees of the senate
- Departmental committee work (e.g., Personnel and Budget, assessment)
- Search committee work
- Doing presentations at various other college meetings

For each of these, candidates should explain specifically what their role in each item is. It is not very useful to list membership of a committee if the committee never meets or if the candidate attends meetings when called but does no work for the committee outside attending these meetings.

Furthermore, we also have a category for service to the field. In this category is included such things as:

- Reviewing articles and books for journals and publishers
- Serving as an officer in professional organizations

We have also drawn a line between administrative work that is compensated with reassigned time and administrative work that is not. So, faculty members contributing to assessment efforts and who are receiving reassigned time would describe this as "administration" rather than service.

APPENDIX 8.C: CUNY BOARD OF TRUSTEES BYLAWS, DUTIES OF DEPARTMENT CHAIRPERSON

SECTION 9.3. DUTIES OF DEPARTMENT CHAIRPERSON.

a. The department chairperson shall be the executive officer of his/her department and shall carry on the department's policies, as well as those of the faculty and the board which are related to it. He/she shall:
   1. Be responsible for departmental records.
   2. Assign courses to and arrange programs of instructional staff members of the department.
   3. Initiate policy and action concerning the recruitment of faculty and other departmental affairs subject to the powers delegated by these bylaws to the staff of the department in regard to educational policy, and to the appropriate departmental committees in the matter of promotions and appointments.
   4. Represent the department before the faculty council or faculty senate, the faculty, and the board.
   5. Preside at meetings of the department.
   6. Be responsible for the work of the department's committee on appointments or the department's committee on personnel and budget which he/she chairs.
   7. Prepare the tentative departmental budget, subject to the approval by the department's committee on appointments or the department's committee on personnel and budget.
   8. Transmit the tentative departmental budget with his/her own recommendations to the president or the dean or provost as the president may designate.
   9. Arrange for careful observation and guidance of the department's instructional staff members.
   10. Make a full report to the president and to the college committee on faculty personnel and budget of the action taken by the department committee on personnel and budget or department committee on appointments when recommending an appointee for tenure on the following, as well as any other criteria set forth in university policies:
      a. Teaching qualifications and classroom work.

b. Relationship of the appointee with his/her students and colleagues.
   c. Appointee's professional and creative work.
   11. Hold an annual evaluation conference with every member of the department after observation and prepare a memorandum thereof.
   12. Generally supervise and administer the department.
b. Each library, where size makes it practicable, shall constitute an instructional department of the college. The chairperson thereof shall be designated by the president. Such chairperson, in addition to the duties of department chairperson as enumerated in paragraph "a" of this section, shall be charged with the administration of the library facilities of his/her college and shall perform such other duties as the president may assign. Such chairperson is hereby authorized to use the additional title of "chief librarian."
c. Where student personnel services are constituted an instructional department of the college, the dean of students shall be the department chairperson.

NOTES

1. Thanks to Kay Halasek and one anonymous reviewer for helping me work out this framing.
2. This document is, as far as the author knows, still under review at CUNY Central's Office of the General Counsel and so cannot yet be distributed.
3. The survey was closely modeled on the instrument used in the MLA's Committee on the Status of Women in the Profession report titled "Standing Still," which examined roadblocks to advancement for women at the associate professor level.

REFERENCES

Barrett, Lucinda, and Peter Barrett. 2010. "Women and Academic Workloads: Career Slow Lane or Cul-de-sac?" *Higher Education* 61: 141–155. doi: 10.1007/s10734-010-9329-3.
Bauer, Dale M. 2002. "Academic Housework: Women's Studies and Second Shifting." In *Women's Studies on Its Own: A Next Wave Reader in Institutional Change*, edited by Robyn Wiegman, 245–257. Durham, NC: Duke University Press.
Bird, Sharon, Jacquelyn S. Litt, and Yong Wang. 2004. "Creating Status of Women Reports: Institutional Housekeeping as 'Women's Work.'" *NWSA Journal* 16 (1): 194–206.
Board of Trustees Bylaws. n.d. City University of New York. https://policy.cuny.edu/bylaws/article-ix/#section_9.3.
Boyer, Ernest. 1990. *Scholarship Reconsidered: Priorities of the Professoriate*. Carnegie Foundation for the Advancement of Teaching. San Francisco: Jossey-Bass.
Council of Writing Program Administrators. 1998. "Evaluating the Intellectual Work of Writing Administration." wpacouncil.org/positions/intellectualwork.html.
Enos, Theresa, and Shane Borrowman. 2008. *The Problems and Perils of Writing Program Administration*. Anderson, SC: Parlor Press.
Gillam, Alice. 2003. "Collaboration, Ethics, and the Emotional Labor of WPAs." In *A Way to Move: Rhetorics of Emotion and Composition Studies*, edited by Dale Jacobs and Laura R. Micciche, 113–123. Portsmouth, NH: Boynton/Cook.

Graziano, Leigh, Kay Halasek, Frank Napolitano, Susan Miller-Cochran, and Natalie Szymanski. 2020. "A Return to Portland: Making Work Visible through the Ecologies of Writing Program Administration." *Writing Program Administration* 43 (2): 131–151.
Gutiérrez y Muhs, Gabriella, Yolanda Flores Niemann, Carmen G. González, and Angela P. Harris. 2012. *Presumed Incompetent: The Intersections of Race and Class for Women in Academia*. Logan: Utah State University Press.
Heijstra, Thamar M., Þorgerður Einarsdóttir, Gyða M. Pétursdóttir, and Finnborg S. Steinþórsdóttir. 2017. "Testing the Concept of Academic Housework in a European Setting: Part of Academic Career-Making or Gendered Barrier to the Top?" *European Education Research Journal* 16 (2–3): 200–214.
Heijstra, Thamar M., Finnborg S. Steinþórsdóttir, and Þorgerður Einarsdóttir. 2017. "Academic Career Making and the Double-Edged Role of Academic Housework." *Gender and Education* 29 (6): 764–780. doi: http://dx.doi.org/10.1080/09540253.2016.
Hochschild, Arlie Russell. 2012. *The Managed Heart: The Commercialization of Human Feeling*, 3rd ed. Berkeley: University of California Press.
Hogan, Katie J. 2010. "Superserviceable Feminism." In *Over Ten Million Served: Gendered Service in Language and Literature Workplaces*, edited by Michelle Massé and Katie J. Hogan, 55–72. Albany: State University of New York Press.
Horner, Bruce. 2007. "Redefining Work and Value for Writing Program Administration." *JAC* 27 (1–2): 163–184.
Ianetta, Melissa. 2015. "Absence and Action: Making Visible WPA Work." *WPA: Writing Program Administration* 38 (2): 141–158.
Keizs, Marcia V. 2019. "Dr. Heather Robinson No Longer Chair June 30 2019." June 6.
Kynard, Carmen. 2019. "Administering While Black: Black Women's Labor in the Academy and the 'Position of the Unthought.'" In *Black Perspectives in Writing Program Administration: From the Margins to the Center*, edited by Staci Perriman-Clark and Collin Craig, 28–50. Urbana, IL: Conference on College Composition and Communication/National Council of Teachers of English.
Link, Albert N., Christopher A. Swann, and Barry Bozeman. 2008. "A Time Allocation Study of University Faculty." *Economics of Education Review* (27): 363–374. doi: 10.1016/j.econedurev.2007.04.002.
Martinez Alemán, Ana. 2014. "Managerialism as the 'New' Discursive Masculinity in the University." *Feminist Formations* (26) 2: 107–134.
Marx, Karl, and Friedrich Engels. 2001. *Capital: A Critique of Political Economy*. Vol. I, Book One, of *The Process of Production of Capital*. Trans. Edward B. Aveling and Samuel. Moore. London: Electric Book Co.
Massé, Michelle A., and Katie J. Hogan, eds. 2010. *Over Ten Million Served: Gendered Service in Language and Literature Workplaces*. Albany: State University of New York Press.
Misra, Joya, Jennifer Hickes Lundquist, Elissa Holmes, and Stephanie Agiomavritis. 2011. "The Ivory Ceiling of Service Work." *Academe* 97: 2–6.
Napolitano, Frank. 2019. "Making WPA Work Visible." Email message to author. August 5.
O'Meara, KerryAnn, Alexandra Kuvaeva, and Gudrun Nyunt. 2017. "Constrained Choices: A View of Campus Service Inequality from Annual Faculty Reports." *Journal of Higher Education* 88 (5): 672–700.
Perryman-Clark, Staci, and Collin Craig. 2019. "Introduction: Black Matters: Writing Program Administration in Twenty-First Century Higher Education." In *Black Perspectives in Writing Program Administration: From the Margins to the Center*, edited by Staci Perriman-Clark and Collin Craig, 1–27. Urbana, IL: Conference on College Composition and Communication/National Council of Teachers of English.
Reid, E. Shelley. 2008. "Will Administrate for Tenure, or, Be Careful What You Ask For." In *The Promise and Perils of Writing Program Administration*, edited by Theresa Enos and Shane Borrowman, 203–211. West Lafayette, IN: Parlor Press.

Robinson, Heather M. 2021. "Time, Care, and Faculty Working Conditions." In *Transformations: Change Work across Writing Programs, Pedagogies, and Practices*, edited by Kirsti Cole and Holly Hassel, 87–104. Logan: Utah State University Press.

Roen, Duane, Kathleen Blake Yancey, and David Schwalm. 2008. "A Prologue and Three Responses." In *The Promise and Perils of Writing Program Administration*, edited by Theresa Enos and Shane Borrowman, 212–224. West Lafayette, IN: Parlor Press.

Ryan, Richard M., and Edward L. Deci. 2000. "Self-Determination Theory and the Facilitation of Intrinsic Motivation, Social Development, and Well-Being." *American Psychologist* 55 (1): 68–78.

Schell, Eileen E. 1992. "The Feminization of Composition: Questioning the Metaphors That Bind Women Teachers." *Composition Studies* 20 (1): 55–61.

Snyder, Laura Bartlett. 2009. "Feminisms and the Problem of Complicity in Writing Program Administrator Work." In *The Writing Program Interrupted: Making Space for Critical Discourse*, edited by Donna Strickland and Jeanne Gunner, 28–40. Portsmouth, NH: Boynton-Cook.

Strickland, Donna. 2011. *The Managerial Unconscious in the History of Composition Studies*. Carbondale: Southern Illinois University Press.

Tokumitsu, Miya. 2014. "In the Name of Love." *Slate*. January 16. www.slate.com/articles/technology/technology/2014/01/do_what_you_love_love_what_you_do_an_omnipresent_mantra_that_s_bad_for_work.html.

Trimbur, John. 2008. "Foreword." In *The Promise and Perils of Writing Program Administration*, edited by Theresa Enos and Shane Borrowman, ix–xiv. West Lafayette, IN: Parlor Press.

Winslow, Sarah. 2010. "Gender Inequity and Time Allocations among Academic Faculty." *Gender and Society* 24 (6): 769–793. doi: 10.1177/0891243210386728.

York College Faculty Handbook. 2018. www.york.cuny.edu/academics/academic-affairs/faculty-resources/York_FacultyHandbook-2008.pdf.

Ziker, John. 2014. "The Long, Lonely Job of Homo Academicus: Focusing the Research Lens on the Professor's Own Schedule." *Blue Review*. March 13. thebluereview.org/faculty-time-allocation/.

9
INVISIBLE LABOR
Tracking Email Practices in WPA Work

Angela Mitchell and Jan Rieman

John Freeman's book *The Tyranny of e-Mail* (2009) detailed much of what we know is still true today, claiming that "email is our electronic fidget" (5), that email "has made us a workforce of reactors" (5), and that "in the past, only a few professions—doctors, plumbers perhaps, emergency service technicians, prime ministers—required this kind of state of being constantly on call. Now almost all of us live this way" (7). In higher education and specifically as writing program administrators (WPAs), we are subject to the expectations that email use in a university context requires.

As ubiquitous as email may be in higher education, it has the odd effect of rendering much administrative work invisible. As Randy Malamud (2020, 18) explains, "There are so many emails that they may be invisible. They are so necessary that they are worthless." Does constantly working in email make our work also seem "necessary and worthless?" Ensuring that our email work is visible is one issue; making it be seen as valuable work is another.

Any WPA knows that the amount of time and emotional labor we spend working through email is significant. Often, the conversations and decisions we are making for our writing programs and departments are high stakes, and we are often working across institutional lines—with the registrar's office, advisers, writing faculty, and individual students. What we hope to show in this chapter is that WPAs *can* and *should* find ways to make this work both visible and valued, and that begins with reframing the work we do in email for ourselves so we can translate that labor into the formal documents we are required to complete for annual review and promotion.

We began our research on our email patterns and practices at the beginning of the spring semester in 2019. As we finalize the work on this chapter after enduring the effects of COVID-19 during the spring and summer semester of 2020, email has become even *more* significant to our daily work. At the beginning of the pandemic in the United States, the number of emails we received in March 2020 alone—more than 2,000—from the university, our department, students, various entities on campus offering training, support, resources, and the like required an enormous level of discernment to figure out which needed to be tended to first. Working from home during the spring and summer of 2020 increased administrative emails dramatically, with significant decision-making happening through email threads that demanded constant time and attention.

Our study of a typical semester seems even more urgent to us now as we realize the power and complexity of the medium. An essential part of any WPA's job during typical times is to do the daily work of not only managing our inboxes (figuring out what is urgent and requires immediate responses versus what can wait) but also to smartly and strategically use our outboxes—to solicit information, gather responses, share knowledge, and more. Our qualitative and quantitative data from spring 2019 invite analysis of WPAs' email work and, we hope, contribute to a wider understanding of effective practices for WPAs to consider when using email.

OUR STUDY

As WPAs at a large, urban research university in an independent writing program, we were interested in and frustrated with our own email practices. We knew we did important work in that space; we knew we spent *a lot* of time there (as if email land were a place); and we also knew that much of what we *do* through email goes largely unaccounted for when we are asked to quantify our workload. In an effort to uncover the work we were doing through email, we spent spring semester 2019 tracking our use of email, analyzing it, and thinking about it in relation to a survey we did that semester with other past and current WPAs.

Methods

To make email work visible, our approach to collecting data on email practices required a combination of qualitative and quantitative measures. We analyzed all of the emails we received and sent from our university email addresses over spring semester 2019, which represents a typical one for us.

We gathered our qualitative data by using our work Gmail suite and two analytical tools available by subscription—Mailstrom and

EmailAnalytics. Mailstrom is an email management system that allows users to see email in batches and provides at-a-glance analytics about the number of emails sent and received, time spent with email, and most frequent senders and receivers of emails. It also allows users to block or unsubscribe from unwanted email, making it an effective triage tool for managing email volume. EmailAnalytics gives users specific data, such as average response times per day/week/month/year, but it does not help clean up an inbox, as Mailstrom does. We both used Mailstrom to track our email while Angela also employed EmailAnalytics. Using these tools allowed us to track the amount of emails by day, week, or month, as well as to sort them easily into categories for further quantitative or qualitative analysis.

To collect our qualitative data, we each kept a reflective journal to capture the responses—intellectual, analytical, visceral, emotional—we had while working with email that week. We met weekly to talk through what we were thinking, observing, and finding with research and to share and discuss what Mailstrom and EmailAnalytics were revealing to us. The reflective journaling method was a way to think through not only what we *do* with email but why and when we choose that medium of communication over others. Scholars have done this sort of reflective work with their own email labor previously (Roberts 2014; Sinclair 2017), and it proved rich fodder for our weekly discussions. During our meetings we would identify themes we were seeing in our email work—issues around exigency, time (when we sent emails and how much time we spent in email, for example), and the content of our emails. What we discussed during these weekly reviews shaped the focus of our attention the following week.

In addition to tracking and analyzing our own email work, in February 2019 we surveyed a group of current and former writing program administrators and writing studies scholars during a regional Carolinas WPA conference. We coded the survey responses by keywords such as "time" and "documentation" and categorized the responses by code. These survey responses serve to represent regional patterns of email use among current and former WPAs.

Content/Quality

Although we use email every day and it has taken on a kind of *tiresome* familiarity, in its mix of formality and informality, its apparent urgency, and user response expectations, email represents the most dangerous medium for the workplace. It can lead you into conversations that don't move anything forward and waste your time. In turn, the expectation for an immediate reply makes it ripe for anxiety-producing typos and tonal mistakes. We all hit the reply button both too soon and too late.

While kairotic moments in email may require immediate responses and delay other, more intellectual work for the WPA, they may also be at the heart of some WPA work. For example, Angela's email content as first-year writing (FYW) director falls into categories aligned with her administrative duties: assessment, registration tracking, scheduling, research studies/grants, student concerns, scholarship, part-time faculty, textbook orders. Any one of these categories often includes emails that require problem solving, last-minute fires to put out, and, inevitably, conflict. Whether it is emailing a refusal to the dean about increasing class sizes or quickly needing to work up numbers for last-minute budget changes or managing a disgruntled student for faculty members, any one of our common administrative emails has the power to burden us with stress and anxiety. These examples also illustrate how emails are not equivalent to one another. A high-stakes response often requires time-consuming research, consultation with the department chair, and careful writing and revision before sending; a low-stakes email takes only three minutes to craft and send a response.

In every way, emailing represents more high-stakes work for the WPA than for a non-administrator faculty member. Not only are many of our administrative duties carried on through email, we are also working to create and maintain various relationships and alliances across campus. Tone, patience, and clarity can be difficult to achieve when a WPA has lots of emails to return. Conflict stemming from email exchanges inevitably arrives in our inboxes; long after our emailing is done for the day, we can be left with the weight of these conversations on our consciences. Many of the negative associations about email from our survey are damning and imply both the emotional and physical ramifications of the work: "exhausting," "stress," "addicted," "overwhelmed," "drowning" (survey). For our survey respondents, the quantity of emails could be just as stressful as the content.

Amount/Quantity

Tracing the number of emails we received was key to making visible to us what our email load and practices really were, but the number of emails alone tells only part of the story. One email can be a quick thirty-second "thank you" or "got it"; another can be a fairly easy five-minute response to a colleague you know well; yet another can be a high-stakes response to multiple audiences that requires a day's worth of research, consultation with others, and careful composing before being able to hit send. A WPA's inbox is also usually full of surprises—an unanticipated scheduling conflict for an instructor in the program that requires immediate attention, a significant enrollment number change that also requires immediate attention, an unexpected administrative change that requires quick action, a request from one's chair or dean for information you need to provide quickly.

During this project, Angela was the current director of first-year writing, a position Jan had held the previous six years. Jan was serving as the interim associate executive director of our independent writing program, charged primarily with launching our new minor in writing, rhetoric, and digital studies.

Angela began the second semester of her tenure as a first-year writing director without an associate FYW director to share the workload—and the email. The email increase from teaching full-time to becoming a WPA was staggering. Overall, during the course of the spring semester, 7,673 emails went to or from Angela's inbox, averaging 1,534.6 a month. In comparison, Jan's monthly average of incoming and outgoing emails was 984 that semester. The most email Angela received in the semester was from the WPA-L at a whopping 1,504, with 616 alone coming in March—related to the Conference on College Composition and Communication's (CCCC's) Chair Address and resulting listserv implosion. Meanwhile, Jan had unsubscribed from the WPA-L at the beginning of the semester in favor of the WPA announcements through Google Groups. This change resulted in a significant decrease in email volume for Jan. The busiest month for email for Angela was easily February, with 1,751 emails moving to or from her inbox, reinforcing a long-held belief that February is the cruelest month for WPAs.

On average, we both received the most emails (not surprisingly) from the executive director, the Writing Resources Center directors, and each other. Every month, the most emails we each sent were to the executive director, though many were as ccs to make her aware of the work we were doing. Angela received the most email during the week on Wednesday and Thursday, while she averaged the most sent emails on Thursdays. February 13 and 14 saw Angela sending the most emails of the semester; in fact, that was the only week she sent more emails than she received. Our fall schedule building deadline was February 15, accounting for the many emails Angela sent to various administrators, staff, and faculty (228). As of July 24, 2019, a little over a year as the new FYW director, Angela's inbox had grown so large that Mailstrom noted it was larger than 70 percent of the inboxes of all Mailstrom users. By contrast, according to Mailstrom, Jan's inbox was consistently at least 84 percent smaller than those of other Mailstrom users after she moved out of the FYW director position.

We are not alone in taking the time to calculate the number of emails we send and receive. Scholar Leena Rao (2015) revealed that she had 584,341 unread emails in her inbox; Taylor Lorenz (2019) discussed her 2,700 unread emails accumulated over a month. Laura Roberts (2014) at Stanford Medical School stated: "In a 48-h period this past week, on my primary email account (I have six), I received 235 messages. . . . Thirty emails were 'high stakes,' pertaining to a major negotiation, faculty matter, or patient concern, and none of this subset of more than 100 emails was trivial." Why should WPAs bother to tabulate their email volume? Because the first step in being able to make this work visible is to quantify it in exact ways. Typically, we describe email in terms similar to those our survey respondents used, exclaiming that email is "difficult to keep up with" and that it resembles a "snowdrift." It's also helpful to differentiate what percentage of our email is received by us versus initiated by us.

Angela received three times as many emails as she sent, reinforcing one survey participant's claim that there's "too much email, mostly useless." The mental energy it takes to filter out irrelevant emails is immense. Email tracking through Mailstrom or EmailAnalytics can aid WPAs in seeing patterns in email use that would allow for filtering the most important senders or content and strategizing when and how to respond, whether through email or face to face. These platforms allow WPAs to see what their email labor actually looks like—the first step in seeing what is productive about their email use and what is, using Malamud's (2020) word, "worthless."

Time

During this semester of email analysis, Angela and Jan learned that like other WPAs in our survey, we often respond to emails quickly and usually take time outside traditional work hours to do so. According to EmailAnalytics, Angela usually replied immediately or within an hour or two and never later than twenty-four hours. Her hourly email traffic started around 6:00–7:00 a.m. and peaked at 11:00 a.m. for received emails. She sent the most emails from 1:15 to 2:15 p.m. This pattern revealed how much email structured her days and took advantage of prime thinking time. Our survey respondents were both WPAs and former WPAs, and, surprisingly, the breakdown in self-reported time spent on email per day was marginal. WPAs spent an average of 2.4 hours per day on email versus 1.8 hours for non-WPAs. Despite this thirty-six-minute difference, a non-WPA respondent said, "it's too much emotional labor for me no matter what the email is" (survey). Sixty-five percent of survey respondents indicate that they spend about a quarter of their workday on email. Since email often brings unexpected and urgent work, WPAs may feel tension when they lose control of their day when an email shows up in their inbox. With the user expectation that emails will be returned promptly, a few morning emails can derail the day and keep you from focusing on less immediate but no less important projects.

When we asked about email habits that might help WPAs manage the volume of emails received, responses ranged from very clear boundaries around email work—"morning," "morning and afternoon," "first and last thing"—to the other end of constant engagement with the medium: "check immediately and leave open all day." By using EmailAnalytics, Jan and Angela were able to see that they both tended to open their email first thing and dip in and out of it all day long. This awareness led both to seek more mindful ways of structuring their day by making visible what their email workload really looks like on a daily basis.

Email Culture

Identifying the email culture at an institution can be helpful in understanding the email system one is working in and perhaps seeing if it can be shifted in any way. Although email culture can vary across institutions, most survey respondents indicated that email is the "main means of communication—inquiries, complaints, announcements, reminders, soliciting volunteers, documentation"—and that "across the university [email use is] high—yet so high that a number of all faculty emails (I imagine) are deleted without reading." Another respondent indicated that the email culture is "uncontrolled. Excessive."

We have noted an increasing number of taglines in WPA colleagues' email messages that remind us that there are small steps we can take to help shape the culture of email expectations. One such tagline is "*Please note: Much of my work involves face-to-face interaction: teaching, meetings, workshops, and conversations. I am unable to access my computer during these times, and some of them extend the entire workday. Please be patient if I am unable to immediately answer email." Another is "NOTE: I am learning to control my workflow, which means I respond to email twice a day: 8:00 am–9:00 am and again in the afternoons, usually around 2:00 pm." In part, these taglines remind us to make moves that support a "responsive workplace" instead of a "reactive one." Participating in creating a department's email culture allows WPAs to use email more efficiently, giving them more time and energy to focus on other WPA duties and obligations. Most important, by focusing on email culture, a WPA may be able to ask, as Malamud (2020, 20) does, "How can we attain a high caliber of performance within this medium—smarter content, more thoughtful interaction; less mechanical and more humanistic . . . less confusing, sloppy, and random."

Documentation/Organization

Like many WPAs who participated in our survey, we use email as a repository. It acts as institutional memory, serves as a means of official documentation, and is used to track decisions we have made. "Accountability" and "documentation" were repeated purposes of email work noted by the survey respondents. On average, according to Mailstrom, Angela kept 60 percent of her email in her inbox while 40 percent generally went to folders. She kept the most relevant emails in folders, as backup to administrative folders on Google Drive. This allowed Angela not only to easily keep documents for extra documentation but also to track her email use for accountability and to measure workload on various projects. Jan worked similarly in email, keeping folders as a way to organize documentation of work and to be able to pull up important information when it's needed. The WPA survey revealed, however, that some WPAs do not use folders or other email organizational tools and that they "keep a full inbox." One respondent even noted that they had to "request more inbox space from IT" because their inbox was so full. Many of those in the survey recognized that they "seriously need to organize in files" and "prioritize" emails in their inbox.

WPAs typically do not have the luxury of living with an email box that doesn't have intentional order. Documentation for accountability for annual reports, promotion, and tenure requires that WPAs know how to document and show their work. Since so much invisible work happens in email, WPAs who don't track and document their work in email may find they are missing key components needed for professional review. If, as Laura R. Micciche (2002, 446) argues, "emotional management is an important part [of a WPA's] job," then email management—where so much of writing program administration's work happens—becomes a means to survive.

The number of emails in our inboxes or folders or whatever system we use may be less important than how we work with and within an email service. Claire Lauer and Eva Brumberger (2019, 635) argue that "the delivery of writing—by which we mean the channels through which it is distributed and consumed—has been evolving so rapidly in the past decade that our fundamental assumptions about writing in the workplace must evolve." Lauer and Brumberger (635) call this newly emergent workplace "responsive," which means that "writers must adapt to making meaning not just through writing, but across a range of modes, technologies, channels, and constraints." To avoid losing the day to chains of reactive emails, WPAs who recognize the real complexity of a medium used so widely for so long can deliberately track patterns and cycles of email use and learn ways to be more responsive than reactive in their email use. In doing so, they can learn to use the medium instead of being used by it, focusing on its strengths to organize and document and make visible administrative work.

RESPONSIVE INSTEAD OF REACTIVE STRATEGIES

1. Take the time to track your email labor so you know what and how much you are dealing with.
2. Ask if there is any work you typically do in email that can be done another way. For example, will a phone call be more efficient than four email exchanges? Can a walk down the hall to a colleague's office replace an email?
3. Prioritize emails using favorites or flags or folders. Often, our priorities are determined for us, but you can create a general idea about what is most important to your work to handle first.
4. Use taglines on your email signature to establish email response expectations.
5. Document all your work outside email—email, at its best, is simply the medium to communicate the work.
6. Set up platforms or internal documentation where faculty can find answers to common curricular and pedagogical and policy-related issues; remind them of where this documentation is and how to find it.
7. Respond to students first.
8. Create an email culture that is, following Malamud (2020), "less mechanical," "more human," "more thoughtful."

CONCLUSION

Our research has left us with insights about how WPAs can make the labor of email work more visible and perhaps manage it with more attention and awareness. While email makes our work visible in many ways to the people we correspond with, the time spent on routine emails rarely shows up on work reports and is invisible to most other faculty and department chairs. When annual reports are due or when asked to classify and quantify WPA work (as we were recently required to do for upper administration), we need to find ways to include email labor in those accounts. As an institutional delivery system, email works to establish our ethos within the university, operating as a simultaneous opportunity and risk for review and promotion, and it often leads to the heavy weight of email conversations that linger in a WPA's mind. In Christine Sinclair's (2017, 59) study of email use in higher education using Cultural Historical Activity Theory, she clearly articulates some of the changes in the way email mediates what we do in a university context, specifically in regard to workload:

> It is interesting that the division of labour that once separated out the more administrative functions in a university began to change in the 1980s and 1990s when practitioners began to do their own typing and document keeping. Copies of memos would once have been filed by administrators and [been] available for consultation. This ancient history does not excuse my poor email filing, but the distance from my own major motives and goals offers an explanation. Combined with the time required to learn how to do it properly, the result is two time-consuming sets of actions that distract me from what I see as more pressing ones. In other words, the work I am doing now might once have been done by two or more people. There is no time in our workload model for the extensive filing exercise I intended to do.

Sinclair (2017, 49) advocates that we need to "detach from a personal response to email and recognize its contribution to collective practices and their implications, including resistance and solidarity in the face of excessive and hidden workloads." The visible yet "hidden" work of email for WPAs lies not only in the time we spend creating, responding, and deleting email but also in how we use this medium. As WPAs, through local analysis of our own email patterns, we may develop strategies to detach from the weight of email so we can use the medium to manage, document, and make our work both visible and valued for ourselves and for others.

REFERENCES

Freeman, John. 2009. *The Tyranny of e-Mail: The Four-Thousand-Year Journey to Your Inbox.* New York: Scribner.

Lauer, Claire, and Eva Brumberger. 2019. "Redefining Writing for the Responsive Workplace." *College Composition and Communication* 70 (4): 634–660.

Lorenz, Taylor. 2019. "Don't Reply to Your Emails: The Case for Inbox Infinity." *The Atlantic*, January 8. https://www.theatlantic.com/technology/archive/2019/01/case-inbox-infinity/579673/.

Malamud, Randy. 2020. *Email (Object Lessons)*. New York: Bloomsbury Academic.

Micciche, Laura R. 2002. "More than a Feeling: Disappointment and WPA Work." *College English* 64 (4): 432–448. doi: 10.2307/3250746.

Rao, Leena. 2015. "Email: Unloved, Unbreakable." *Fortune* 171 (6): 54–56. https://uncc.primo.exlibrisgroup.com/discovery/fulldisplay?docid=proquest1678625008&context=PC&vid=01UNCC_INST:01UNCC_INST&search_scope=CentralIndex&tab=CentralIndex&lang=en.

Roberts, Laura. 2014. "My Email—48 Hours." *Academic Psychiatry* 38 (3): 373–375. doi: 10.1007/s40596-014-0117-8.

Sinclair, Christine. 2017. "You've Got Mail: Tracking and Framing Academic Lives." *Knowledge Cultures* 5 (2): 49–64. https://librarylink.uncc.edu/login?url=https://search-proquest-com.librarylink.uncc.edu/docview/1936099815?accountid=14605.

10
OPPORTUNITY LOST
Failing to Make Administrative Work Visible

Brooke Anderson

Faculty administrative work is visible when institutions recognize and reward it. Praise for working hard is not meaningful recognition and reward; meaningful recognition and reward comes in the form of titled, compensated jobs with authority. In his introduction to the collection *Tenured Bosses and Disposable Teachers*, Marc Bousquet (2004, 1–8) reminds us that working hard to serve our institutions does not guarantee that we will be rewarded. He calls working conditions for most non-tenure-track faculty who teach composition an unacceptable consequence of the managed university. A neoliberal value at work in the managed university is to do more with less, which should remind faculty that we are managed professionals (Rhoades 1998). For faculty, this value can manifest in administrative responsibilities being categorized as service work. Donna Strickland (2010) distinguishes between the two by defining administrative work as compensated and done on company time and service work as uncompensated and done on one's own time, which results in what Katie Hogan (2005) calls an insidious and invisible economy of service and Strickland (2010) expresses as the invisible work of the not-quite-administrator. Faculty work that should be compensated and done on company time is writing tutor training and mentoring; yet all too frequently, this administrative work is categorized as service and therefore frustratingly invisible. Service work is how faculty involvement in the training and mentoring of writing tutors is categorized at my institution. However, in 2016, I saw an opportunity to change this. At first, my efforts resulted in success, but it did not take long for them to fail.

METHODOLOGY

This chapter is an autoethnographic account of my experience of trying and failing to institutionalize a writing center director (WCD) position

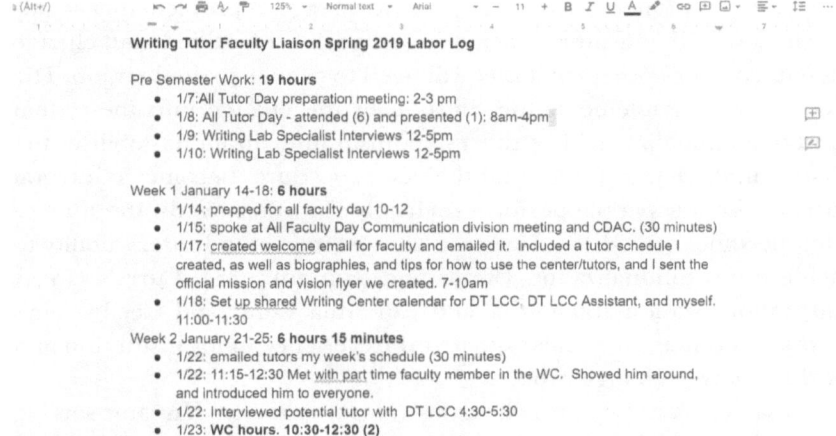

Figure 10.1. Spring 2019 labor log

while my institution reorganized. The data I discuss in this chapter were not collected for external research purposes but for pragmatic, internal reasons: to create a position, assess its effectiveness, and continually improve the role. Here, I use autoethnographic methods to capture my experience of living through this change as well as Barbara Curry's (1992) institutionalization framework to reflect on the pragmatic data I collected while in the role of writing center discipline coordinator.

While serving, I collected quantitative and descriptive data about my labor in the form of Google Form surveys, a labor log, and other internal documents. The surveys gathered data on faculty, tutor, and staff supervisor perspectives on their needs and the effectiveness of my work. In the labor log (figure 10.1), I tracked the time I spent doing the labor of the position. The job description gave me categories to record, and every day for a full academic year, in a Google document, I noted the time and duration for when I tutored, mentored tutors, prepared and led tutor trainings, planned events, attended meetings, developed professionally, collected data, marketed services, and reached out to faculty. Several times a semester, I created a weekly summary of the log for meetings with my dean. At the end of the year, I used NVivo coding (Saldana 2016) to discover the amount of time I spent laboring in each category (figure 10.1).

THEORETICAL FRAMEWORK

Curry (1992) provides a three-step framework for understanding how and why sustained change either does or does not happen. The first step, mobilization, prepares the system to change. A problem that stands in the way of the institution achieving its goals is identified, and change agents convince others that they will need to change to do their job. The second step, implementation, introduces the change into the system and operationalizes it. The third step, institutionalization, stabilizes the system in its changed state, and the new procedures become an integral part of the way people perform their jobs. In other words, the innovation becomes valued (8). However, context impacts a leader's ability to achieve institutionalization (Kezar and Sam 2013, 58). Curry's (1992) institutionalization framework and Adrianna Kezar and Cecile Sam's (2013) emphasis on context situate my experience in my institution and within a larger change process.

Gina Ann Garcia and colleagues' (2019) work on Hispanic-serving institutions' (HSIs') organizational identities emphasizes that a unified identity is needed for institutions to improve Latinx students' success. The authors connect organizational identity to other organizational phenomena—such as commitment, change, culture, and competition—and claim that all of them are important, especially because of the rapidly changing demographics in postsecondary institutions. This is the ideal; however, what happens internally reveals that who institutions say they are can run counter to how they function. Spoken values do not always align with actions, which can render problems—like administrative work labeled as service work—invisible.

INSTITUTIONAL CONTEXT

Pima Community College (PCC) is the only comprehensive community college and HSI in Tucson, Arizona. It is one district with five campuses. In fall 2011, it served approximately 35,000 students. By fall 2017, that number had dropped to roughly 22,000 (Institutional Research 2018). Not only is the institution dealing with declining enrollment, it has also lost state funding and was placed on probation in 2013 by its accrediting agency, the Higher Learning Commission (HLC). One reason for the sanctions was that PCC lacked a governance and administrative structure that promoted effective leadership and supported collaboration (Higher Learning Commission 2013); in other words, the organization lacked unity.

In an effort to maintain HLC accreditation, PCC began to reorganize. The five separate campuses started operating as one college, which meant top administrative positions were cut. This reduction in staff continued down the chain of command. For faculty, these reductions

Opportunity Lost 165

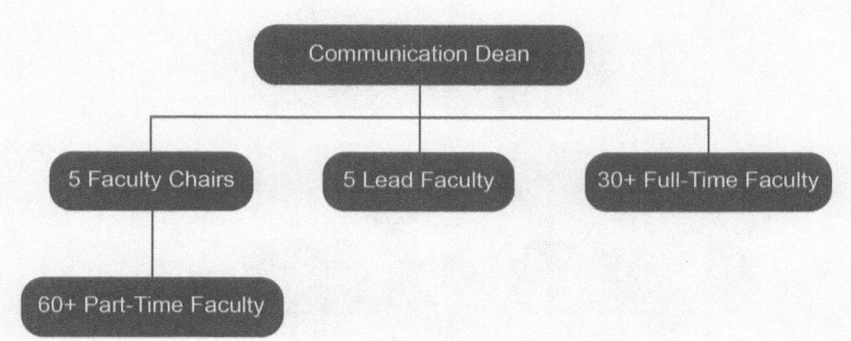

Figure 10.2. English Department organization before reorganization

came in the form of changes to leadership roles. We had been functioning as campus-based departments but were reorganized to operate as a single, college-wide department (figure 10.2). This was communicated to faculty through the creation of a new faculty leadership handbook (Handbook 2017) that included organization charts for each division, descriptions of faculty administrative jobs, and compensation information. Some of these new leadership positions would become responsible for supervising full-time faculty, which had previously been the responsibility of the deans. In addition, some faculty administrators would become responsible for leading student learning outcome data collection and reporting. Deans gave faculty budget information and a draft of the handbook that included new job titles and corresponding job descriptions and compensation formulas, and they asked departments to submit reorganization recommendations. The changes were made in the name of promoting effective leadership and supporting collaboration, but in reality, they were designed to decrease personnel costs and increase employee workloads.

The English Department worked with these new limitations by adopting the recommended job titles and compensation formulas and resisting moving to a college-wide department model. We went along with the recommendation to use the title head instead of chair, but we did not support changing leadership responsibilities from campus-based to college-wide ones. While we grumbled about adding supervisory responsibility to the jobs, we did not formally protest that change. We did not resist shifting to the college-wide department model when it came to eliminating campus-based faculty administrator positions—titled lead—and adopting new college-wide discipline coordinators (DC). Lead faculty had been working collaboratively with their campus chairs to complete important campus-based administrative work. In the new

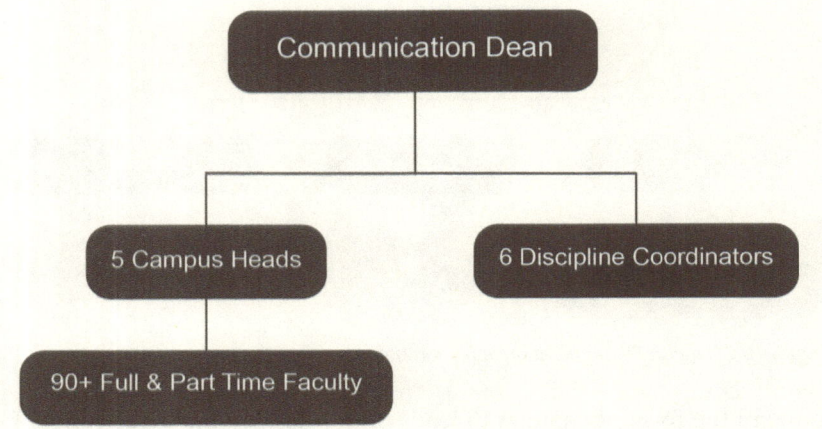

Figure 10.3. English Department organization after reorganization

model, heads would be responsible for all campus-based matters, and discipline coordinators would have no supervisory power but would oversee other important areas, such as tutoring and student learning outcome assessment practices (figure 10.3).

INITIAL SUCCESS

During this process, I managed to mobilize faculty to support creating a writing center faculty administrator job. Prior to the reorganization, I was compensated as a lead faculty member responsible for running a series of self-paced composition classes in one of PAA's campus learning centers. Because of my background in writing center theory and practice (Bruffee 1984; North 1984, 1994; Grimm 1999; Greenfield 2019) and my daily proximity to tutors, I often served unofficially as a writing tutor faculty mentor and trainer. While I was known across the college for this work, I was not officially recognized or compensated for it. One faculty member on another campus was compensated for mentoring and training writing tutors on their campus. However, this person had no faculty administrator title or authority. The other three campuses had no institutionalized connection between composition faculty and writing tutors. Faculty, learning center staff, and administrators all agreed that this was a problem that needed to be solved. The college needed stronger connections between the composition faculty and the writing tutors.

I set out to solve this problem by recommending that we create a compensated and titled faculty administrator position responsible for training and mentoring writing tutors across the college. Composition faculty, learning center staff, and my division's dean agreed with my recommendation, and the position was created and added to the faculty leadership handbook (Handbook 2017). Administration had made the title discipline coordinator available to us but not director, so we created a position titled writing center discipline coordinator (WCDC). I was hired to serve in this role for a three-year term.

To my dismay, at the end of the term, the dean cut the position. In the end, the institution's values failed to align with its actions. Faculty, staff, and administrators all said they supported the idea of faculty providing leadership for writing tutors. They even went so far as to meaningfully back those words by creating a titled, compensated faculty administrative position. However, because the position included no authority, my implementation efforts were met with unexpected resistance from all three groups.

ADMINISTRATIVE RESISTANCE

I didn't realize that the administrative resistance I experienced would set me up to fail. Administrators claimed they wanted faculty to make reorganization decisions for their departments, but the administration did not give faculty the authority to write the job descriptions included in the faculty leadership handbook. When the handbook was sent to faculty, the WCDC job description included no duties related to the training or mentoring of writing tutors across the college. Instead, it described the role as responsible for the self-paced writing courses on a single campus. At the time, these classes were being phased out, so the college needed a faculty member to oversee this process. I was willing to serve in this role even though the job description was not what I had hoped for. During my first year as WCDC, I fulfilled my self-paced administrative responsibilities, and I continued my writing tutoring service work. Because my title made it look as though I worked with writing tutors and because the job was compensated, I believed I had the institutional power to change my responsibilities in the handbook for my second year of service. What I didn't realize was that the misalignment between what administrators were saying and what they were doing was a form of resistance Sarah Ahmed (2012) calls non-performative speech acts. Ahmed uses this term to describe public speech that expresses a commitment to diversity and a rejection of racism that are not followed by actions. What I experienced was not about racism or diversity, but it was about statements that expressed an appreciation for faculty input and an intent to include it that was not followed by action—in other words, lip service.

By the end of that first year, the self-paced classes were no longer offered. I had submitted a job description revision to my dean that had been approved by my faculty and learning center staff colleagues, and I was looking forward to a second year in which my job description would align with my title. I had faith that I would be able to implement this change because I had the verbal support of everyone directly involved. I was wrong. By the start of my second year, administration had not released a revised handbook to faculty; in fact, the dean continued to reference the first version throughout all three years of my term. In April 2020, while I was serving in this role for a final semester, a new version of the handbook (Handbook 2020) was published on the college website that did not include a WCDC role. This left me serving in a nonexistent faculty administrator role in the last semester of my three-year term.

In the first and second years of my term, I did not realize that the support I was receiving was non-performative. I thought I was serving in a new, innovative role at the college and that my work would establish an important foundation for future WCDCs. Because I was the first, and I believed my job description now matched my job title, that second year I recorded all of my writing tutor–oriented work in a labor log. In the classroom, I had my students keep labor logs (Inoue and Open Textbook Library 2015). I liked the way the students documented the time they were spending on their homework, so I started keeping a log to track how I was spending my time. I thought I could use my log to make all my work visible to the dean. I thought that if he saw what I was doing and how hard I was working, my position would be more highly valued and funding would continue. I was not sure how time-consuming the role would be; nor was I sure exactly what I would be doing. While far from a perfect way to record my labor, the log made my work more visible to me. At the end of the year, I used in vivo coding to discover the amount of time I spent laboring in different categories, and I shared what I learned with my dean.

LABOR LOG DATA FINDINGS

While the dean did not count my labor log as valid evidence of success, it did end up being personally valuable (figure 10.4). My data showed me that I spent the majority of my time (37.5 hours/semester, or 24.8% of my time) participating in professional development and networking activities. This revealed that I relied on a great deal of support from

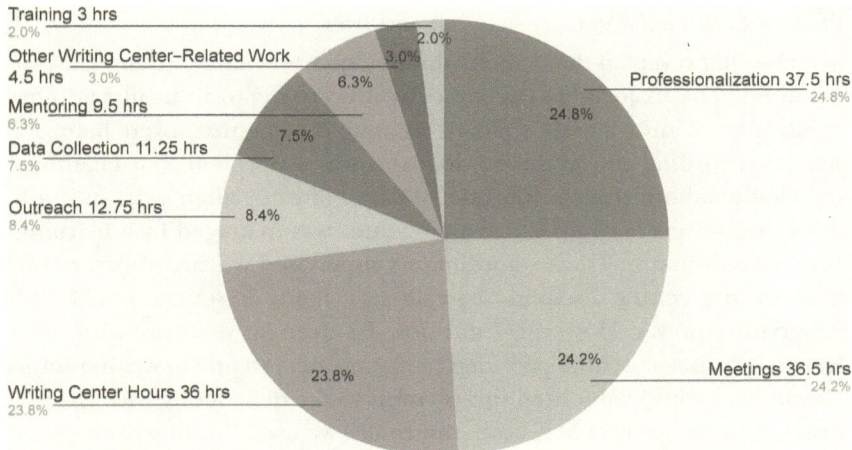

Figure 10.4. Pie chart of writing tutor discipline coordinator spring 2019 activities

outside my institution to do this work, especially since a faculty leadership position with tutors was new for us but not new to the field. Second to professional development activities was time in meetings (36.5 hours/semester, or 24.2% of my time). At first, I was surprised by this, but then I started thinking about how meetings are another form of networking. In the moment, this work felt like wasted time, but I realized that by attending meetings, I was building trusting, collegial relationships and influencing decision-making. Time in the learning center tutoring and interacting with tutors came in third (36 hours/semester, or 23.8% of my time). My fourth most common activty was reaching out to faculty (12.75 hours/semester, or 8% of my time), and fifth was collecting data (11.25 hours/semester, or 7.5% of my time). Finally, I spent the least amount of time mentoring (9.5 hours/semester, or 6.3% of my time) and training tutors (3 hours/semester, or 2% of my time). In the end, I was surprised to discover that I spent very little of my time working directly with tutors. Had I not kept this log, I may not have noticed how much time I spent seeking outside support and professional development and that the job was less about training tutors and more about attending meetings and networking. How I spent my time would have been largely invisible to me without the log, and it would have definitely been invisible to my dean. This data collection system may not have been enough to persuade him to keep the position, but at least it gave me a way to make my work more visible to both of us. Also, this tool helped me see where my labor was met with resistance and the ways I struggled to overcome these obstacles.

Chain-of-Command Resistance and Consequences

My labor log revealed that I spent almost a quarter (24.2%) of my time in meetings. The majority of that time involved trying to fit faculty administrative work into a staff chain-of-command structure. Even before I started recording my labor in a log, this was a problem. For example, my faculty administrative job title, WCDC, did not align with staff job titles. Almost every campus learning center was managed by a learning center coordinator. These coordinators supervised writing tutors, so my title, writing center discipline coordinator, made it appear as if I had supervisory power. However, I did not. To clear up this confusion, the learning center staff and I decided to change my job title to writing tutor liaison lead, and I submitted this revision to the dean along with the job description revision in May 2018. Internally, we used this title for most of my three-year term, but the change never made it into the official faculty leadership handbook.

I interpreted this first conflict with my job title as an understandable part of negotiating a new faculty role in a space run by staff. I took it in good faith that administration was listening, that the staff wanted me working with writing tutors in the centers, and that our recommendations were being institutionalized through their inclusion in the college handbooks. While all of this was in the works, I continued laboring with the understanding that I was responsible for training and mentoring tutors across the college. However, another common topic in the many meetings I attended was that I could only fulfill my responsibilities if the tutors' supervisors permitted me to do so. I could not make decisions about paying tutors for their time, and I could not require them to attend meetings, trainings, or mentoring sessions. I had no authority. I didn't even have the power to hire or fire tutors. I could only make recommendations to the tutor supervisors, and they did not have to include me in writing tutoring decisions. In fact, the tutors' supervisors could outright ignore and exclude me if they wished. My lack of authority over the tutors explains in part why my log shows that I spent less than 2 percent of my time on training tutors and only 6 percent on mentoring. I would have loved to do more, but doing so was not within my power.

As my second year progressed, it became more and more apparent that my lack of institutionalized authority was making it impossible for me to implement even the simplest solutions, such as uniting writing tutors across the college through a college-wide listserv. Because coordinators hired and supervised tutors, they were the only ones who could identify all the writing tutors across the college. When I expressed my desire to create a listserv, the learning center coordinators promised to send me their tutors' emails, but most of them never did. Without a listserv, I was unable to send a single introduction email to all writing tutors across the college. Instead, each campus kept functioning as it always had, with the learning center supervisors making the decisions for their campuses' writing tutors. This one small act of resistance communicated to me that some of the learning center supervisors' verbal support for my role was, in fact, non-performative—lip service. They were unwilling to back their supportive words with supportive actions.

Advocacy Resistance and Consequences

My labor log documents that even though I encountered resistance from some learning center supervisors, my work positively impacted my campus and the larger college community. When I add up the time I spent in the writing center (36 hours/semester), mentoring (9.5 hours), training (3 hours), and doing outreach (12.75 hours), it equates to 61.25 hours (or 38.7% of my time) directly working with tutors, faculty, and students. Because I had a good working relationship with the learning center coordinator and faculty on my campus, I provided campus-specific tutor trainings and mentorship and improved the connections and communication between campus composition faculty and writing tutors. My time in meetings (36.5 hours/semester total) made a difference college-wide because I was at the table during learning center meetings and involved in learning center reorganization discussions with top administrators. I organized a series of regular college-wide writing tutoring meetings between interested faculty and staff, and we produced a writing tutoring mission statement and the first ever college-wide writing tutoring flyer. Many of the professional development hours (37.5 hours total) were spent attending and presenting at conferences (both alone and with colleagues), which began the building of a supportive professional network that extended beyond PCC.

Sadly, even this positive, community-building work was met with resistance from two of the learning center coordinators. In meetings, they questioned the value of the products and statements we produced and tried to use existing work groups, policy, and bureaucratic processes to de-legitimize my mobilization and implementation efforts. Had administration backed my work with more than verbal praise and given me more institutional authority and financial support, I could have continued uniting tutors and faculty across the college and strengthening our bonds with other institutions and professionals across the nation.

Instead, I spent my last year in a series of meetings trying to convince my dean and faculty colleagues that the position was worth their continued support without having the authority to collect the necessary data to make a convincing case.

Continuing the pattern of non-performative acts and a lack of authority, my dean praised my work and its value but failed to advocate for my position when, in year three, the department faced budget cuts. My role was the only faculty administrative position in the department with no supervisory authority, direct connection to courses, or student learning outcomes data collection responsibilities; yet my impact was college-wide and indirectly affected all courses that included writing assessment. Nonetheless, I spent 11.25 hours (7.5% of my time per semester) doing what I could to collect and assess data. I diligently created and distributed a number of survey assessments to faculty, staff, and tutors; few responded. When I shared the results from the limited data resources available to me—including my labor log—they showed that I was very productive and that I invested many hours per week, and all groups expressed overwhelming support for my work. My dean praised me for my hard work and accomplishments and awarded me with certificates of appreciation. However, he also asked me for data I did not have—data that would prove that my work increased student success and retention, data I could not access.

Data Collection Resistance and Consequences

I saw no way to fulfill the dean's request. Because I mainly worked with staff, faculty, and tutors, I could not prove that my writing center hours, constant meeting attendance, tutor mentoring, college-wide tutoring conversations, tutor training, faculty outreach, professional development, or data collection and assessment efforts were directly improving student success and retention. I have no doubt that they were, but how do you prove with student data that all your labor is effective when you don't have the authority to directly collect those data? Because I failed to produce this evidence and because of continually increasing budgetary limitations, the dean stopped funding the writing center DC role. My faculty colleagues did not protest, and the position was gone.

CONCLUSION

I tried to make faculty writing center service work visible by turning it into faculty-administrative work, but all my laboring did not lead to the institutionalization of the writing center discipline coordinator position. Barbara Curry, Lillian M. Lowery, and Dennis Loftus (2010, 404) state that working hard on initiatives that are not institutionalized can make change efforts feel like an exercise in futility. Their statement comforts me and helps me accept the failure of my laboring. Institutional cultures can change only if those with solutions can make the problem visible to others and motivate them to implement the solutions. To make the problem visible, visionaries need to articulate the problem that stands in the way of the institution achieving its goals and convince others that change will make it easier for everyone to do their jobs effectively (406–407). While I did manage to mobilize faculty, staff, and administrators to support creating a writing center faculty-administrator role, my implementation efforts did not result in continued support. Instead of making people's jobs easier, my solutions cost money, disrupted existing college processes, and failed to produce quantifiable student success results.

Now that I have experienced this failure, I can see how making different choices could have resulted in different outcomes. Had I recognized that the job description that ended up in the handbook (Handbook 2017) indicated that administration was not empowering me to work officially with tutors, I would have served differently. I could have written a formal proposal for the position that used accessible student data to prove there was a disciplinary problem that faculty-administrative writing center work could solve. That proposal could have included a specific action plan that addressed the problem, a budget request, a time line, and a plan for how I would use student data to assess my effectiveness. I should not have interpreted a title and words of support or encouragement as evidence that I should spend my time doing writing center work. If verbal praise is the main reward for administrative work, then faculty should exercise their right to say no. When we do administrative work that is not recognized and rewarded with titles, compensation, and authority, we enable our institutions to continue to exploit our labor and disguise the administrative work that must then get done as invisible service work.

REFERENCES

Ahmed, Sara. 2012. *On Being Included: Racism and Diversity in Institutional Life*. Durham, NC: Duke University Press.

Bousquet, Marc. 2004. "Introduction." In *Tenured Bosses and Disposable Teachers: Writing Instruction in the Managed University*, edited by Marc Bousquet, Tony Scott, and Leo Parascondola, 1–8. Carbondale: Southern Illinois University Press.

Bruffee, Kenneth A. 1984. "Collaborative Learning and the Conversation of Mankind." *College English* 46 (7): 635–652. National Council of Teachers of English. http://www.jstor.org/stable/376924.

Curry, Barbara K. 1992. *Instituting Enduring Innovations: Achieving Continuity of Change in Higher Education.* ASHE-ERIC Higher Education Report no. 7. Washington, DC: George Washington University, School of Education and Human Development.

Curry, Barbara K., Lillian M. Lowery, and Dennis Loftus. 2010. "What a Community Will Bear: Leadership and the Change Process." *International Journal of Educational Management* 24 (5): 404–417. doi: http://dx.doi.org.ezproxy2.library.arizona.edu/10.1108/09513541011055974.

Garcia, Gina Ann, Jenesis J. Ramirez, Oscar E. Patrón, and Nik L. Cristobal. 2019. "Constructing an HSI Organizational Identity at Three Hispanic-Serving Institutions in the Midwest: Ideal versus Current Identity." *Journal of Higher Education* 90 (4): 513–538.

Greenfield, Laura. 2019. *Radical Writing Center Praxis: A Paradigm for Ethical Political Engagement.* Logan: Utah State University Press.

Grimm, Nancy. 1999. *Good Intentions: Writing Center Work for Postmodern Times.* Portsmouth, NH: Boynton Cook.

Handbook for Academic and Library Leadership. 2020. Tucson, AZ: Pima Community College.

Handbook for Academic, Library, and Counseling Leadership. 2017. Tucson, AZ: Pima Community College.

Higher Learning Commission. 2013. "Public Disclosure Notice on Pima County Community College." April 6. https://bloximages.chicago2.vip.townnews.com/tucson.com/content/tncms/assets/v3/editorial/d/73/d739072a-a796-11e2-8697-0019bb2963f4/516efb386e941.pdf.pdf.

Hogan, Katie. 2005. "Superserviceable Feminism." *Minnesota Review* 63–64: 95–111.

Inoue, Asao B., and Open Textbook Library, Distributor. 2015. *Antiracist Writing Assessment Ecologies: Teaching and Assessing Writing for a Socially Just Future.* Perspectives on Writing. Fort Collins, CO: Parlor Press.

Institutional Research. 2018. "Headcount and Annualized Full-Time Student Equivalent (FTSE) Trend Report." October 12. Tucson, AZ: Pima Community College. https://pima.edu/about-pima/reports-data/student-reports/docs-enrollment/2018-enrollment-trend-report-ok-243.pdf.

Kezar, Adrianna, and Cecile Sam. 2013. "Institutionalizing Equitable Policies and Practices for Contingent Faculty." *Journal of Higher Education* 84 (1): 56–87.

North, Stephen M. 1994. "Revisiting 'The Idea of a Writing Center.'" *Writing Center Journal* 15 (1): 7–19.

North, Stephen M. 1984. "The Idea of a Writing Center." *College English* 46 (5): 433–446. National Council of Teachers of English Stable. http://www.jstor.org/stable/377047.

Rhoades, Gary. 1998. *Managed Professionals: Unionized Faculty and Restructuring Academic Labor.* Albany: State University of New York Press. EBSCOhost, search.ebscohost.com/login.aspx?direct=true&db=nlebk&AN=7929&site=ehost-live.

Saldana, Johnny. 2016. *The Coding Manual for Qualitative Researchers.* Los Angeles: Sage.

Strickland, Donna. 2010. "The Invisible Work of the Not-Quite-Administrator, or, Superserviceable Rhetoric and Composition." In *Over Ten Million Served: Gendered Service in Language and Literature Workplaces,* edited by Michelle A. Massé and Katie J. Hogan, 73–89. Albany: State University of New York Press.

11
WEIGHING DOWN THE BODY
Quantifying the Nature of Antiracist Work

Patti Poblete

While the need for antiracist work in writing program administration—or, indeed, in any and every field—has always existed, there's no denying that the urgency for it has come into the spotlight in the past few years. As we articulate the nature of labor, particularly the invisible and the emotional, it is imperative that we also account for how institutionalized racism compounds and intensifies that work.

Emotional labor has become shorthand for experiencing emotions in the course of one's work, which is true in its way but tends to elide the actual work. One of the originating concepts of emotional labor is inextricably linked with its maintenance, "the effort, planning, and control needed to express organizationally desired emotion during interpersonal transactions" (Morris and Feldman 1996, 987). That is, the work itself is ensuring that one only displays culturally acceptable emotions at appropriate times when in contact with others. In the case of administration, it seems the most, and perhaps only, permissible feeling is a "stiff upper lip." If you're reading this, you probably already know: keeping a stiff upper lip is *exhausting*.

The same exhortation extends into the province of racism as experienced by Black, Indigenous, and people of color (BIPOC). There is a consistent allure to the belief that racism only occurs in the most overt ways—burning crosses, vicious slurs, physical assaults. Racism, however, is much more subtle than that, as psychologists such as Derald Wing Sue and Madonna G. Constantine (2007, 136) have worked to establish: "Racial microaggressions are brief, everyday exchanges that send denigrating messages to people of color because they belong to a racial minority group." Microaggressions are things like being praised for speaking excellent English, constantly being spoken over during meetings, or perpetually being subjected to the myth of the meritocracy.

https://doi.org/10.7330/9781646423644.c011

Being scolded for being "too sensitive" when trying to raise the issue typifies the things against which antiracism must work.

To be clear, doing antiracist work is not limited to diversifying a curriculum or coordinating workshops on white privilege. It's beyond reconsideration of retention plans, beyond the provision of #OwnVoices mentorship, beyond allocation of funding. (Though can anything really be beyond funding?) As Staci M. Perryman-Clark and Collin Lamont Craig (2019, 8) observed in *Black Perspectives in Writing Program Administration*, BIPOC faculty and administrators are often "leveraged by the university for [their] de facto diversity perspective." Note that "perspective" is a keyword in that statement, wherein someone's personal viewpoint is considered and called upon as fulfillment of a task, regardless of whether that is made explicit.

THE ONLY ONE IN THE ROOM

Imagine: It's the start-of-term colloquium, and faculty had been pre-assigned to "conversation groups" focused on a variety of university functions. When it was time to break into pseudo-committees, one young woman walked across the hall to join the fundraising table. She was the last one to arrive and didn't spot an open seat right away. As she stood there, the others looked at her, confused. Someone said, in apparent kindness, "Oh, no, this isn't the diversity group. They're at that table over there."

In fall of 2018, the National Center for Education Statistics surveyed 1.5 million college and university faculty (ranging from professor to lecturer). Seventy-five percent of that count were identified as white. Six percent were Black, 6 percent were Hispanic, and 12 percent were Asian or Pacific Islander. The number of faculty identified as American/Indian was less than 1 percent—for statistical purposes, that figure was rounded down to zero.

What does it feel like to be the only BIPOC in the room? What does it feel like when everybody else knows you're the only BIPOC in the room?

In her memoir, *Minor Feelings: An Asian American Reckoning*, Cathy Park Hong (2020, 183) shared her reluctance to speak as if her experience as an Asian American could act as a fair representation of her perceived race: "I feared the weight of my experiences—as East Asian, professional class, cis female, atheist, contrarian—tipped the scales of a racial group that remains so nonspecific that I wondered if there was any shared language between us." Being the only one brings the weight of representation with it, as well as the suspicion that you're only a token. Race is a constructed normalizing concept, so stereotypes lump everybody of a particular ethnicity together for reasons purely cosmetic. Just as "the only one" is seen to satisfy the diversity quota, it's often easy to think there must be one way to fight discrimination. One seminar, one piece of legislation, one president, and then we don't have to worry about it ever again. Antiracist work, however, is not a simple one-size-fits-all, just as BIPOC aren't all alike. The only thing BIPOC have in common, in fact, is that racism's effects have always included some measure of pain.

(Perhaps I should clarify: being primarily Filipina means I have a specific set of experiences that folks from other ethnic groups can't fully understand, just as I can't grok the full damage visited upon others. Further, it means that my experiences with racism fluctuate depending on context, so my uses of "we" and "our" do as well. Racism is institutional, but its avenues are diverse.)

Racism, being institutionalized, perpetuates trauma. In an interview with *Essence*, Joy DeGruy (2009), author of *Post Traumatic Slave Syndrome*, stated: "Our ancestors learned to adapt to living in a hostile environment and we normalized our injury. And because they didn't get free therapy after slavery, these behaviors were passed through the generations." Children of refugees who learn to comply with authority figures. Girls who endure the relentless machismo of their male counterparts. Boys who know to never, ever talk back to a cop.

Bearing centuries of trauma is likely to become a personal investment, a thing we're doing because it's important and it needs to be done. Caring about something translates to putting effort into it, though. As Heather M. Robinson points out (chapter 8, this volume), when it comes to working against inequity, those who suffer from it are often doing the most to ameliorate it, as intrinsic motivation has been shown "to be exploited by institutions to extract uncompensated labor." Or, as author Miya Tokumitsu put it, "If you make passion a job requirement, you can't complain about your workload" (quoted in Lam 2015). We care about antiracist work so much we'd be doing it for free . . . right?

TWICE AS GOOD FOR HALF AS MUCH

Two problems arise immediately when we consider quantifying antiracist work. First, there's the peril of ubiquity. Angela Mitchell and Jan Rieman (chapter 9, this volume) found that the omnipresence of email trivialized this peril, in its "kind of *tiresome* familiarity, in its mix of formality and informality, its apparent urgency, and user response expectations." That description similarly articulates how people can get used to calls for diversity. It is vital to the mission and it's the attention to the unvoiced. The wait between immediate consequences and their arc bending toward justice is long. If everybody's doing it, then we can rest easy because *someone else* is taking care of the issue.

Further, because administration doesn't *thingify*, if I can cadge Ryan J. Dippre's (chapter 6, this volume) invocation of ethnomethodology, then it's difficult to offer proof. As Dippre took measure of his hours, he realized that "much of my time is treated, bureaucratically, as nonexistent." An administrator's log was the only evidence of his mentoring, his inquiries, and his overtures. When we work to change the campus climate, that doesn't mean it rains.

This is particularly evident in our second problem: that no matter their perceived delineation, some things can't be quantified. In the face of a program functioning as expected, Brooke Anderson (chapter 10, this volume) found the lack of data for program growth stymied her efforts to create an administrative position. Her performance of some of the associated tasks failed to bear fruit; further, "because the position included no authority, my implementation efforts were met with unexpected resistance." If the argument boils down to *likely better*, often the response will be, *if it ain't broke . . .*

A common way to counter this attitude is metonymy—seminars, book circles, mentors, clubs. Behold antiracism! And thingification, in its thingness, can make ownable the actual thing. If we convert our antiracist labor into a thing, a product, a *deliverable*, that labor also becomes transferrable. The idea for an open forum becomes a recommendation from the committee chair. A reading list excising colonial texts becomes a department's curriculum revision. A photo of a BIPOC instructor is featured prominently on the university's front page. It's theater. Theater done with the best of intentions, perhaps, but still performed rather than enacted.

For BIPOC administrators, enacting antiracism means not only delving into their community trauma but also enduring the endless teachable moments and sharing personal experiences—all to account for the personal experiences of others. Even if we're all doing the work, some of us are hurt *more*. How do you thingify obligation? How do you thingify pain?

WHERE YOUR MOUTH IS

In the wake of George Floyd's death in May 2020, the fervor of resultant protests sparked a conflagration of organizational antiracist statements. Their subsequent commitment to their promises varied. Bath and

Body Works ("Fight against Racism and Inequality" n.d.), for example, included action plans with items such as "purposeful listening," "enhancing training," and "holding ourselves accountable." BabyCenter (Robinson 2020), a website for expectant parents, compiled a list of suggested names that paid tribute to boys and men who had been murdered in the name of public safety. Penzey's Spices spent $92,000 supporting the impeachment of then president Donald Trump (Heil 2019). In contrast, companies like Energy Transfer ("Corporate Responsibility" n.d.) generated public statements about "respecting all people and all cultures," which boils down to, *We don't like racism either, so don't @ us.*

Similarly, colleges and universities buffed up their diversity and inclusion statements. Sometimes they made their commitments specific and personal, such as Vanderbilt University's chief diversity officer André L. Churchwell (2021), who highlighted how heartbroken he was. Others worked on generating awareness on their campus, such as Drake University's creation of an Equity and Inclusion newsletter (Lain n.d.). Many began to work double-time to make vagaries in their strategic planning robust—for example, Louisiana State University generated a "Diversity and Inclusion Roadmap" (n.d.). If any institutions didn't already have a division, program, or committee specifically devoted to fighting racism, they certainly do now. (Though how many of us have served on diversity taskforces that don't actually have any tasks?)

The Council of Writing Program Administrators quickly released its "Statement on Racial Injustice and Systemic Racism" (2020). The statement itself was as expected: condemnation of racism, recognition of the educational system being intertwined with racism, and a promise to hold itself accountable. While the document itself adheres to the genre conventions, the organization also began developing several projects to raise awareness and encourage action. Writing Program Administrators–Graduate Organization (2020), the council's graduate student arm, compiled a statement explicitly detailing what antiracist assessment might look like.

While the initiatives of most of these organizations are commendable—articulating specifics rather than scattering goodwill—it's the evidence of follow-through that's needed. If antiracism is a goal of a program, if equity is a mission for an institution, then they should be assessed. If a diversity and inclusion statement is a checklist, then that should be evident upon the statement's completion.

Collecting and categorizing data are foundational to assessment. Not only do they help the assessor ensure that benchmarks are being met, but Lilian W. Mina (chapter 7, this volume) considers ways data collection can act as a prototype. If gaining outside support is needed, then the stuff of assessment "substantially enhances the visibility of writing program administrator (WPA) work at three intersecting tiers: visibility as better understanding of the curriculum goals, visibility as making pedagogical changes to achieve those goals, and visibility as conceptualizing assessment as research." Antiracist objectives can be recognized; therefore, they can be enumerated.

That countability, however, can also backfire, providing ways to neutralize attempts at antiracist work. Perryman-Clark (Perryman-Clark and Craig 2019, 4), for example, once put forward the possibility of making diversity and inclusion part of the curriculum, but her colleagues found her suggestions "too prescriptive and not feasible for programmatic assessment." Antiracism was deemed too rich for their blood. Certainly, that logic is sound in its own way: if racism is systemic, that means antiracism requires that the system itself be revised and, in many cases, wholly replaced. Why bother replacing the entire water distribution system if you can just give people bottled water instead?

Bree Newsome (2021) tweeted, "Capitalist logic says minimum wage hurts small businesses because the original capitalist model for starting a small business was to kidnap people & force them & all of their descendants to work for free for generations." Putting aside an implied equivalence of universities and businesses (that is a different rant for a different collection), the core of Newsome's (2021) observation translates thus: if universities are fundamentally dependent on what has been invisible labor, then it's against their interests to perceive it. They can't afford to make historic buildings accessible. They can't afford to pay all the adjuncts a living wage. They can't afford to recognize that to foster equity, the lowest bid won't and will never cut it.

Universities cannot function if they do not strive to "increase worker productivity while suppressing working-class living standards as a means to increase the rate of exploitation of labor" (Chacón and Davis 2019, preface). Writing programs are often sustainable only if their teachers don't get benefits. In a job market that is inexorably thinning, those with the least are expected to be content with the least. In curricula, the "great books" have ossified. In the writing classroom, students are taught that out there in the real world, the only pathway to success is to pass.

The work we do is not invisible; our work has been disappeared.

Universities are functionally and fundamentally racist. "'Institutional racism' and 'structural racism' are redundant," Ibram X. Kendi (2019, 18) wrote. "Racism itself is institutional, structural, and systemic." The system is built to break us. What's left but to burn it all down?

WHAT HAPPENS WHEN WE'RE DONE?

It was the second year of my graduate work, and our literary criticism seminar was a lively one. We'd fallen into a debate about which school of thought was our favorite and therefore the best. In the midst of lively banter about feminism, the sole male student in the room interrupted: "But what happens when feminism is done?" When has it completed its mission, when has it fulfilled its purpose? What happens when discrimination is no longer part of our lives?

In *Freedom Is a Constant Struggle* (2016, 34), Angela Yvonne Davis noted, "There are very important structural elements of racism and it's often those structural elements that aren't taken into consideration when there is discussion about ending racism or challenging racism." This is the contradiction that lies inherent in striving to be an antiracist WPA: the things we administer and administer through were never equitable in the first place. And someone's experience with racism isn't solely their own because it comes weighted with the experiences of all those who came before. If we are to truly examine what it means to do antiracist work, we must also find some way to consider the magnitude of history.

Because we function in a matryoshka of institutions that were molded through racist practices, the result of our work—our work in itself—is racist in some way. If we're going to make a stand about being antiracist, we need to do it intentionally. If we're striving to make antiracist work legible to those who haven't begun that work themselves, we should set concrete goals and assess for them. But if we accept that antiracism is needed in *all* our practices, then what exactly are we assessing?

What do I have to do to make you see me?

REFERENCES

@BreeNewsome. 2021. "Capitalist logic says minimum wage hurts small businesses because the original capitalist model for starting a small business was to kidnap people & force them & all of their descendants to work for free for generations." Twitter, February 25, 7:45 a.m. twitter.com/BreeNewsome/status/1364934536820310017.

Chacón, Justin Akers, and Mike Davis. 2019. *No One Is Illegal*. Chicago: Haymarket Books.

Churchwell, André L. n.d. "Statement from Vice Chancellor for Equity, Diversity and Inclusion André L. Churchwell Regarding the Death of George Floyd." Vanderbilt University, May 31. www.vanderbilt.edu/diversity/may-31-statement-from-andre-churchwell/.

"Corporate Responsibility." n.d. Energy Transfer. energytransfer.com/corporate-responsibility/.

Davis, Angela Yvonne. 2016. *Freedom Is a Constant Struggle: Ferguson, Palestine, and the Foundations of a Movement*. Chicago: Haymarket Books.

DeGruy, Joy. 2009. "Breaking the Chains." *Essence*, December 16. www.essence.com/news/breaking-the-chains/.

"Diversity and Inclusion Roadmap." n.d. Louisiana State University. https://www.lsu.edu/together/docs/roadmap-to-diversity.pdf.

"Fight against Racism and Inequality." n.d. Bath and Body Works. www.bathandbodyworks.com/m/our-fight-against-racism-and-inequality.html.

Heil, Emily. 2019. "A Spice Company Spent More Money on Impeachment Ads on Facebook than Anyone Not Named Trump." *Washington Post*, October 9. www.washingtonpost.com/news/food/wp/2019/10/09/a-spice-company-spent-more-money-on-impeachment-ads-on-facebook-than-anyone-not-named-trump/.

Hong, Cathy Park. 2020. *Minor Feelings: An Asian American Reckoning*. New York: One World.

Kendi, Ibram X. 2019. *How to Be an Antiracist*. New York: One World.

Lain, Erin. 2020. "Equity and Inclusion Update from Erin Lain." Drake University. www.drake.edu/diversity/initiatives/newsletter/fall2020/.

Lam, Bourree. 2015. "Why 'Do What You Love' Is Pernicious Advice." *The Atlantic*, August 7. theatlantic.com/business/archive/2015/08/do-what-you-love-work-myth-culture/399599/.

Morris, Andrew J., and Daniel C. Feldman. 1996. "The Dimensions, Antecedents, and Consequences of Emotional Labor." *Academy of Management Review* 21 (4): 986–1010.

National Center for Education Statistics. 2018. "Race/Ethnicity of College Faculty." Institute of Education Scientists. nces.ed.gov/fastfacts/display.asp?id=61.

Perryman-Clark, Staci M., and Collin Lamont Craig. 2019. *Black Perspectives in Writing Program Administration: From the Margins to the Center*. Urbana, IL: National Council of Teachers of English.

Robinson, Lucy. 2020. "Racial Justice Baby Names." BabyCenter, August 26. www.babycenter.com/baby-names/racial-justice-baby-names_40007468.

"Statement on Racial Injustice and Systemic Racism." 2020. Council of Writing Program Administrators, June 16. wpacouncil.org/aws/CWPA/pt/sd/news_article/321287/_PARENT/layout_details/false.

Sue, Derald Wing, and Madonna G. Constantine. 2007. "Racial Microaggressions as Instigators of Difficult Dialogues on Race: Implications for Student Affairs Educators and Students." *College Student Affairs Journal* 26 (2): 136–143.

Writing Program Administrators–Graduate Organization. 2020. "WPA-GO Statement on Antiracist Assessment." Council of Writing Program Administrators, July 17. wpacouncil.org/aws/CWPA/pt/sd/news_article/313021/_PARENT/layout_details/false.

PART 3

Advocating in and through Complex Institutional Contexts

12
INSTITUTIONAL MATTERS
The (In)Visibility of Localized WPA Labor

Michael Neal, Katelyn Stark, Amy Cicchino,
Michael Healy, and Kamila Albert

Contexts for college writing are not generalizable: the ways writing is framed, conducted, and delivered look different across institutions. Therefore, regardless of the type of writing program, writing program administrators (WPAs) must strategically adapt to local contexts, administrative roles and tasks, and institutional populations (Wooten, Babb, and Ray 2018; Fulford 2011) as they move into different administrative positions. This transition may be particularly challenging for new WPAs just finishing graduate school where they have been immersed in their particular institutional context for a long period of time. Since many graduate programs that produce WPAs are located in research or resource-rich institutions that serve traditional, privileged student populations, these recent graduates are often under-prepared for the challenges they will face at other institutional types.

To address this challenge, we suggest that graduate students interested in WPA positions would benefit from an investigation of various institutional types. During a semester-long course on WPA work, we participated in multiple, small-scale, targeted research projects during which each graduate student in the class interviewed four WPAs in various administrative positions at different institutional types and reported their findings of what made each institutional context unique. With more than a dozen graduate students enrolled in the class, this approach to the course provided a limited window into over fifty institutions. This interview-based approach to the class content increases the visibility of writing programs in diverse, institutional contexts and complements the local experience graduate students receive at their home institutions.

We acknowledge that this type of interview-based research looks different from the other chapters in this collection that consist of autoethnographic deep dives into a single location of WPA labor. These single-site research projects provide a richness of detail that we greatly admire; however, the purpose and scope of our research was quite different. Instead of investigating one site in great detail, our goal was to become more aware of the vast array of other institutional contexts of WPA labor. Instead of our analysis uncovering the nuances and invisible spaces of a single site, we found it beneficial to hear from a multitude of WPA voices to increase our appreciation of the highly contextualized nature of their labor, especially focusing on how WPAs adjusted to their current institutional contexts.

Since an increasing number of academics entering the field pursue WPA work as a primary professional identity (Elder, Schoen, and Skinnell 2014; Rose 2012; Charlton et al. 2011), graduate education in rhetoric and composition should be responsive to these emerging professional identities through its curriculum, mentoring, and ongoing professional development. Even though the field is showing slow movement toward fuller representation in its scholarship (Perryman-Clark and Craig 2019; Green 2016), research and resource-rich institutions are overrepresented in our publications, at conferences, and in our national organizations. Therefore, we argue that small-scale research within the context of graduate education in rhetoric and composition works toward the goal of increasing the visibility of various institutional types—institutions where WPAs may likely reside and work once they complete their graduate training. Establishing habits of seeing and studying other institutional programs in graduate school may produce WPAs who are more attuned to the wide range of institutional contexts in which we labor.

Many writing programs at graduate institutions use an apprenticeship model of WPA preparation. Cristyn L. Elder, Megan Schoen, and Ryan Skinnell (2014, 18–19) note that 81.5 percent of surveyed graduate students link their WPA preparation to local apprenticeship. In this practical training, graduate writing program administrators (gWPAs) assist in a variety of tasks: they facilitate teacher/tutor preparation or professional development, manage scheduling, and attend to issues such as plagiarism and grade appeals. However, the limitations of the apprenticeship model are twofold. First, as increasing numbers of graduate students desire this type of training (Phillips, Shovlin, and Titus 2016; Elder, Schoen, and Skinnell 2014;), the supply cannot meet the demand. Second, this apprenticeship model is employed in institutional contexts that often do not reflect the positions the gWPAs will fill following graduation. Certainly, gWPAs can further develop their administrative preparation by participating in annual conferences, publishing in WPA-related journals, and joining gWPA organizations, such as the Writing Program Administrators–Graduate Organization (WPA-GO). However, even in cross-institutional professional organizations, the voices and experiences of universities with graduate programs are often privileged. A gWPA might see and hear about other institutional contexts, but they do not get a range of diverse institutional perspectives.

We found that a graduate course on writing program administration in which students conduct interviews and site-based studies can help develop the mind-set of an administrator-researcher as well as increase the visibility of a more diverse range of people, programs, and institutions. This research invites graduate students to investigate and think more critically about how various institutional types shape WPA work in contexts they might encounter beyond graduate school. The research shared in this chapter is the result of an Institutional Review Board–approved research project embedded in a WPA graduate course called Designing Writing. Each student in the course researched various programs through website analysis and semi-structured interviews with WPAs working in various programs (e.g., college composition, writing centers, writing across the curriculum, writing majors/minors) and in various institutional types (e.g., region, size, public/private, mission, student population). The researchers developed institutionally specific questions through the examination of each writing program before conducting interviews with the WPAs about how local contexts shape their program and how the WPAs adjusted to their institutional contexts. The first portion of the interviews collected demographic information about the WPAs, their program, and their institution. The demographic questions were followed up by questions in key areas the graduate student researchers identified as essential to seeing the local context of each program. Knowing that the interviews would need to vary, the team identified the following touchstones to guide the interviews, knowing that follow-up questions and customized research questions would be necessary to supplement the general questions:

Curriculum
- What and how many courses, workshops, or other meetings do you offer each semester on average?
- How many people participate or attend on average?
- What do they cover? Describe their content. Who makes decisions about the curriculum or content?
- How is the relative success of the courses, workshops, or meetings assessed?

- What changes have occurred, and what changes do you imagine going forward?

Personnel and Professional Development
- Who works with/for the program, and what is their relationship to one another?
- What qualifications are they required to have? What training and/or support do they receive?
- How (not how much) are they compensated (e.g., credit, tuition remission, salary, health benefits)?

Material Conditions
- Describe the physical (e.g., rooms, offices, size, furniture) and/or virtual (e.g., platform, interface) spaces for this work.
- How do people interact in these spaces?
- How have these spaces changed over time at your institution, and how would you imagine them changing in the future?

Collaborations/Partnerships
- With whom does your program collaborate or partner?
- Describe the purpose and relationship with those individuals or programs.
- How have these partnerships evolved over time, and how would you imagine them changing in the future?

General Admin/Conclusion
- Is there anything that makes your program or institution unique?
- How did you learn to adjust to your specific institutional context?

We implemented semi-structured interviews so the general arch of questions would be comparable across our reports, but the semi-structured nature of the interviews also provided a desired flexibility to allow for variations unique to the institution, program, or WPA. Semi-structured interviews allowed the interviewee to guide the direction of the session. Therefore, the profiles below include what the WPAs thought was most important. In one instance, a WPA might talk about the demographics and career goals of the students, while in another case they might talk more about negotiating racialized or gendered identities. Aside from learning about diverse institutional contexts, engaging in this project gave each of the researchers an opportunity to practice methods they could later use to make their administrative work visible to stakeholders, including how to talk about WPA work to colleagues in the field, how to identify and respond to local constraints, and how to develop a WPA-focused research project.

The following seven profiles represent a wide range of institutional types we researched and reported on within the semester-long course: respectively, a comprehensive public university; a public Indigenous-serving institution; a military college; a private Hispanic-serving institution; a community college; a private historically Black college and university; and a private liberal arts institution. Of course, this is by no means a comprehensive list of all institutional types, but these selections reflect the project's intention of investigating a range of contexts in which a WPA's professional labor may function differently than in their home institutions—in many cases, their home institutions were large research universities. The individual graduate students and instructor conducted the interviews and wrote initial profiles before we shared our findings, developed a structure for reporting out these results, and collaboratively revised and edited the profiles for consistency in coverage, tone, and depth. The most challenging component of writing up each of these profiles was condensing them into such short summaries. However, we decided for the purpose of this publication that it was better to show a wider range of institutional types than to develop a smaller number in more depth because it better supports our purpose. We also believe these profiles demonstrate that small-scale research projects can be productive and manageable despite other responsibilities and commitments, which in and of itself is a lesson in WPA labor.

PROFILE 1: FIRST-YEAR COMPOSITION DIRECTOR AT A COMPREHENSIVE PUBLIC UNIVERSITY

Type of Institution: Small regional public university

Region: Midwestern US

Student Population: Fewer than 5,000 students

The Writing Program: This composition program is home to approximately twenty adjunct instructors and four tenured faculty in the English department who teach first-year composition (FYC), argumentative writing, technical writing, and science writing.

The WPA: Hired as composition director after finishing his doctorate at a midsize research institution.

Local Culture

At this small regional campus, composition courses are taught primarily by adjuncts, some of whom teach up to eight to nine classes across multiple institutions. The new composition director was brought onboard to "jump-start" the program's curriculum and "bring everybody up to speed" on emerging pedagogies in the field. This WPA introduced a writing-about-writing curriculum and needed to prepare instructors. Because he was no longer working primarily with teaching assistants (TAs), as he did as a gWPA at his degree-granting institution, this new WPA needed to employ faculty development that fit the constraints of this small regional campus.

Contextual Needs and Challenges

To begin professional development, this WPA drew on his grant-writing experience to secure funding for a three-day colloquium, which provided the instructors with foundational knowledge of the new textbook and ways to incorporate these theories into the writing classroom. Beyond this paid three-day workshop, however, instructors did not have the time to attend additional professional development events, as they were teaching at multiple institutions and lacked the physical space—such as individual offices—to hold regular on-campus hours.

He needed to find alternate ways to provide support for his staff. Before his arrival, instructors were already using a shared learning-management system as a collaborative pedagogical resource that worked across space and time constraints. He found that even a resource as simple as email worked to provide professional development for these decentralized instructors.

This WPA sent out weekly emails that included what the program was doing, which events were coming up, and what was happening in the WPA's own classroom. Through this approach, the English department was receiving weekly encouragement, updates, and resources. While not a cutting-edge technology, email offered adjunct instructors the opportunity to asynchronously converse with the WPA as their schedules allowed, and this often led to progressive conversations.

Implications

This WPA felt prepared by his graduate institution to develop and implement curricula but had limited understanding of the challenges of administering a program with a majority of adjunct faculty. The nature of the small regional campus required him to use different strategies to establish community and provide professional development. This particular case causes us to consider how many apprenticeship models for WPA training involve direct work with adjunct faculty. Graduate students may be better informed about labor issues for TAs than for adjunct labor. While labor issues related to these populations may overlap, they are not identical and should not be treated as such. Therefore, hearing from the WPA in this context was valuable because it illuminated labor and relational issues in a different way than the graduate students may have seen in their graduate institutions.

PROFILE 2: SOLO COMPOSITIONIST FYC DIRECTOR AT AN INDIGENOUS-SERVING UNIVERSITY

Type of Institution: Indigenous-serving remote university
Region: Pacific US
Student Population: Approximately 18,000
The Writing Program: This first-year composition program supports two courses with rhetorical approaches to academic writing.
The WPA: White woman, recent graduate, and gWPA from a predominantly white institution (PWI) program. A solo compositionist, she was hired to bring a cohesive vision to the curriculum.

Local Culture

This institution has a rich Indigenous culture and is "legitimately and consciously, on a day-to-day basis, student-centered." It supports a "nontraditional student population" composed of Indigenous peoples, former/current military, and returning students.

Contextual Needs and Challenges

While the WPA was hired for her disciplinary expertise, she did not want to ignore or colonize local knowledge. Through the act of listening, she came to see opportunities for overlap among Indigenous epistemologies, community needs, and disciplinary best practices. The WPA had to "understand an entire cultural context and history and, to some degree, an entire language." She spent years listening to understand how to "tal[k] with and for and next to some of the conditions happening [t]here and some of the sovereignty movements."

Originally, FYC was taught by contingent faculty who rarely met and delivered radically different versions of composition. In listening, the

WPA heard that these faculty wanted "to feel connected, not untethered floating in the ocean." Seeing an opportunity to align that need with her charge to create curricular vision, they began monthly cohort meetings. As a community, they "chose a very firm set of outcomes" with a "theme," "a set of assignments," and protocols for programmatic assessment. In creating a community—which the faculty wanted—the WPA worked with, not against, the local context: listening to community-driven values, hearing needs, guiding with disciplinary resources, and adopting a communal process of curriculum design.

Community and institutional stakeholders also wanted the program to be "meaningfully connected to the community." This led the WPA to spend "an awful lot of time managing . . . ecologies"—including writing fellows, assessment and retention protocols, early college and dual enrollment, a learning community initiative, a first-year writing symposium, and a writing in the disciplines (WID) program—in addition to managing a high faculty turnover rate (due to the remote location).

Implications

In adapting disciplinary knowledge gained from her PhD program, this WPA manages her expertise with her positionality as a non-Indigenous outsider. She negotiates many communities, both disciplinarily and institutional, relying on listening to connect those communities. Since so many WPAs are white and graduated from PWIs, this presents serious challenges for outsiders to immediately find administrative positions in institutions with a different mission, student population, and faculty than their previous experiences. In considering this interview, the class was able to see how easily new, white WPAs can become de facto "Comp-Bosses" (Sledd 1991), even despite their explicit values and best efforts to work against this hierarchical relationship. While many WPAs or graduate students preparing to become WPAs are committed to developing antiracist and decolonizing writing programs, the challenges associated with being non-native at an Indigenous-serving institution are real and often difficult to overcome, which became clear in this interview.

PROFILE 3: WRITING CENTER DIRECTOR AT A MILITARY COLLEGE
    Type of Institution: Small public military college
    Region: Southern US
    Student Population: Approximately 1,700, primarily white male students
    The Writing Program: This program is a writing center located outside

the English department. Faculty, professional, and cadet tutors offer face-to-face, non-directive, writer-centered sessions. Tutoring cannot violate the "work for grade" policy.

The WPA: A feminist, civilian WPA was hired to "revitalize and reinvigorate the writing center's identity and ethos." She has a double appointment in the English department and the writing center.

Local Culture

Military culture at this institution is everywhere: embodied by the uniforms students and faculty wear, rhetorically heard in terms used, and felt in the constraints on services such as the writing center. The WPA acknowledges that military culture often conflicts with her disciplinary knowledge and personal values.

Contextual Needs and Challenges

Cadets operate on a strict daily schedule, which means tutors are limited in the number of hours they can work and must receive time off for physical training, guard duty, and post-wide activities. When military procedures conflict with writing theory or common writing classroom practices, procedures win out. While the institutional rules and procedures rarely align with this feminist WPA's beliefs, responding to the constraints has prompted collaborations: "We have started spending our Sunday hours in the library . . . to meet cadets where they are. Particularly for [first-year students], the library is safe." The library also hosts digital resources, which has helped this WPA develop an ePortfolio assessment program and a career services collaboration that support cadets in developing professional digital presences.

The largest obstacle for this WPA is an institutional policy called "work for grade," which states that students must be the sole writers/thinkers of their work—an epistemological stance opposed by many in the discipline who see writing as inherently collaborative and social (Bruffee 1984). The regulation handbook for the institution states, "Cadets receiving assistance must indicate that their work is not solely their own by writing 'HELP RECEIVED' conspicuously on the document." As the WPA explains, "We have to make sure that whatever help we give is not in any way perceived as violating 'work for grade' and goes by the honor code."

Implications

While the military culture is a constant constraint in how she can teach and how tutors can help students, this WPA uses her unique identity as a feminist civilian to leverage moments of misalignment to collaborate and create safe spaces for students. In contrast to the previous profile, this example provides a more optimistic view of how an outsider to a particular institutional culture can leverage her outsider status to function in a way that is possible only because of that positionality. While a military culture may not reflect the approaches and values of the WPA's training and home institution, she demonstrates the careful negotiation and compromises that allow her to implement her values into this program. Knowing which battles to fight and which not to fight—pun intended—was an important insight the graduate students observed through this case study.

PROFILE 4: WRITING CENTER AND WID PROGRAM AT A PRIVATE HISPANIC-SERVING INSTITUTION

Type of Institution: Private research Hispanic-serving institution (HSI)
Region: Southeastern US
Student Population: Around 18,000 total, 6,000 undergraduates (largely residential)
The Writing Program: Writing and communication department houses a composition program, writing minor, master's program, writing center, and writing fellows program.
The WPA: Writing and communication center director

Local Culture

This private research HSI is known for its health, education, and business programs. The culture of writing is expanding as a result of a recent writing-focused Quality Enhancement Plan (QEP), which is a component of the regional accrediting process. The WPA recognizes that the QEP presents an opportunity to update and refocus the university's writing model and encourages collaboration with faculty across disciplines to reconceptualize writing as a situated, local practice. The QEP offers students general writing assistance, provides discipline-specific writing workshops, and expands the writing fellows program. The QEP team includes faculty from sixteen graduate and undergraduate programs, writing faculty coordinators, graduate assistants, and cross-disciplinary undergraduate writing fellows.

Contextual Needs and Challenges

Based on prior administrative experiences and institutional context, this WPA knew the writing across the curriculum (WAC) program had a negative reputation on his campus and needed an entirely new vision. The former WAC model communicated a reductive writing policy (including minimum word requirements), which resulted in little faculty buy-in or administrative support over the years. To update this program, the WPA changed to a writing in the disciplines (WID) model of writing-enriched classes and transferred the oversight of writing to individual departments and colleges. The QEP allowed the director to remove the prescriptive WAC model from the catalog and replace it with this new, discipline-empowering approach to WID.

At this institution, the writing-based QEP has prompted collaboration with graduate and undergraduate programs across the university. Now, writing fellows are placed in writing-enriched classes, and faculty can participate in discipline-specific support programs. The WPA is responsible for organizing workshops on topics such as providing feedback, scaffolding assignments, leading peer reviews, designing multimodal presentations, and working with writing fellows. Graduate assistants from the disciplines work alongside writing faculty coordinators to implement the writing QEP through staff training, semester workshops, and marketing.

Implications

The director's previous experiences provide unique insights into the local institutional context that allowed him to implement these wide-scale changes, which is no small task for a WPA. Not all WPAs have that experience. Nevertheless, this WPA noted the importance of identifying common interests, distributing ownership across disciplines, and fostering a culture that embraces fluidity and variation. This model is particularly important as part of graduate education in WPA work because, again, we see the importance of finding allies and common cause when coming into a new institutional context. His understanding that local values will vary allowed this WPA to assemble a team with local stakeholders, which was made possible through the distribution of authority and worked in this particular context. While this might not be the case in each local context, it becomes an interesting model to consider for future WPA work. This WPA's experience with the WAC program's history shaped decisions and choices to partner with faculty across disciplines. This case offers an example for graduate students who move on to professionally administer programs that require a new vision and encourages them to consider the localized manner in which that vision takes shape.

PROFILE 5: PROFESSIONAL WRITING SPECIALIZATION AT A MID-ATLANTIC COMMUNITY COLLEGE

Type of Institution: Public two-year community college

Region: Mid-Atlantic, suburban US

Student Population: Around 50,000, exclusively undergraduate, mixed traditional/nontraditional

The Writing Program: English department with a professional writing certificate that can be added to an AA or an AS. Courses for this certificate are primarily offered online.

The WPA: A longtime faculty member and prior assistant dean of first-year writing who went back to earn a PhD in order to revise and revitalize the Professional Writing Certificate

Local Culture

This institution features a Professional Writing Certificate, founded in 1980, that is being revised to better serve student needs. The WPA described the unique role the writing program plays, since it primarily serves students with bachelor's degrees at an associate degree–granting institution who pursue the certificate for government and industry career advancement. Most of the students in this program work professionally and have a wealth of life experience; however, they particularly need rhetorical education and genre awareness as professional writers.

Contextual Needs and Challenges

The thirty-one-hour certificate curriculum includes five core classes, electives related to each student's field, and a capstone course. Since the credit requirement is burdensome for many students, the writing program is reducing the requirements to reflect national norms. The program is staffed each semester by about ten instructors who have at least a master's degree and eighteen hours of coursework in English. Ideally, instructors have industry experience or have taken a course in professional writing pedagogy. Since the program is small, it does not yet have a coherent community, and there are no opportunities for professional development.

Implications

The WPA returned to graduate school for a PhD specifically to administer and develop the Professional Writing Certificate. She also drew on prior WPA experience as the assistant dean of the first-year writing program. While the initial move from a four-year to a two-year context required many adjustments, developing and chairing the certificate program was professionally engaging and beneficial. Many new WPAs in two-year colleges face similar adjustment periods in this new context.

This case study was significant for the graduate students in this class because while two-year colleges continue to play an important role in delivering college writing, graduate students often lack background, training, and experience in these settings. While not all two-year colleges serve identical populations, WPAs in two-year institutions are often some of the most innovative administrators in writing studies. They have led the way in developing online education, establishing partnerships and collaboration with secondary education, and accommodating the needs of nontraditional students. According to Columbia University's Community College Research Center, in 2019, approximately one-third of undergraduate students in America attended a community college. Community colleges also serve a diverse population of students: "In the 2018 academic year, 55% of Hispanic undergraduates were enrolled at community colleges, compared with 44% of Black undergraduates, 45% of Asian undergraduates, and 41% of White undergraduates" ("Community College Faqs" n.d.). While many other institutional types struggle to remain viable in the context of twenty-first-century higher education, two-year colleges continue to deliver writing curricula to large numbers of students. In conducting this interview, the graduate students saw an example of the way a WPA at a two-year college promoted an innovative and attractive writing certificate. At the same time, they saw some of the challenges she faced in adapting to institutional values and structures.

PROFILE 6: COMPREHENSIVE WRITING PROGRAM DIRECTOR AT A HISTORICALLY BLACK COLLEGE OR UNIVERSITY (HBCU)

Type of Institution: Small private women's HBCU

Region: Southeastern US, metropolitan city

Student Population: More than 2,000 undergraduate students

The Writing Program: This comprehensive writing program is situated alongside the English department and the first-year writing program, but it remains a separate entity that provides writing support to various communities on campus. The program includes the writing center, the first-year writing portfolio, and writing consultants for faculty and students.

The WPA: A tenured African American female with fewer than two years' experience at this HBCU but with previous WPA experience at a large state PWI and as a gWPA at another PWI.

Local Culture

In the comprehensive writing program, writing is scaffolded throughout the curriculum. First-year students submit a writing portfolio from their first-year composition courses and a general education course called African Diaspora Worldwide (ADW). These portfolios are assessed by a cross-disciplinary faculty, who evaluate and recommend workshops hosted by the writing center. Sophomores and juniors take writing-intensive courses in the disciplines, and many seniors write papers in capstone courses.

Contextual Needs and Challenges

This WPA teaches only one course, but she offers about a dozen writing workshops each semester to students and faculty. Student workshops often support the portfolio (e.g., developing an argument, integrating sources), while others are on professional topics (e.g., writing personal statements, abstracts, and résumés). The faculty workshops are geared toward an interdisciplinary audience and function much like a WAC program, covering topics such as integrating low-stakes writing assignments in larger classes, applying strategies for response and grading, and offering a range of high- and low-stakes writing assignments.

Implications

For this WPA, the community, collaboration, and philosophy of education are integrated and vital to her program: "[This institution] is a Black feminist space in every way. My adjustment was to be like a fish who was finally in water [laughter]. . . . My education and work experience [have] been in PWIs and oftentimes as the only one, right?" Part of being in this feminist collaborative institution is that the WPA exercises an important voice in the conversations across the campus. She described monthly college-wide faculty meetings at which they discuss and make curricular decisions collectively. She ended the interview with a narrative about how the provost invited her to share her vision of comprehensive writing at the first college-wide faculty meeting of the year, a gesture that publicly affirmed her voice and has allowed her to become deeply connected to the institution after only two years.

This case was interesting for the graduate students in the class because the experiences of this WPA were different from those of most others in the study. While most WPAs we interviewed initially struggled with new institutional contexts, this WPA immediately connected to the values, structure, and people in her new context. The value in conducting so many interviews with such a wide range of people and institutional types is that we quickly discovered that each experience was unique. While graduate students can certainly learn from the experiences of WPAs, they cannot assume that they will have a particular experience when entering a new context, only that their experience will also be unique to them.

PROFILE 7: WRITING AT A MIDWESTERN LIBERAL ARTS UNIVERSITY

Type of Institution: Private four-year Jesuit liberal arts university
Region: Midwestern US
Student Population: More than 8,000, majority full-time undergraduates
The Writing Program: First-year composition, a core curricular writing requirement, a master's program, and a writing center.
The WPAs: No formal WPA. Hiring and staffing decisions are made by the assistant department chair. This profile features two faculty: (1) a junior faculty member involved in teaching composition and supporting other faculty writing in the disciplines, and (2) a long-serving writing center director who sees the center as a natural extension of the Jesuit mission.

Local Culture

This institution is heavily influenced by its theological identity, which "direct[s the education toward] the intellectual, social, spiritual, physical, and recreational aspects of students' lives and to the promotion of justice." Both faculty members echoed the ways the local Jesuit context intersected with their work. The writing center director explained that the Jesuit characteristic of *cura personalis*—care for the whole person—allows the writing center to be a nurturing and supportive space "where students can come, and they get one-on-one, affectionate, and empathetic collaboration." The junior faculty member highlighted her collaborative research with undergraduates as "the best teaching relationships that I have because they come to you and say, 'I want to learn some stuff about the stuff that you do.'" They both mentioned how the Jesuit mission helps encourage these one-on-one, caring, and productive relationships.

Contextual Needs and Challenges

Because the faculty at this liberal arts institution associate WPA work with the Comp-Boss narrative (Sledd 1991), they purposefully eschew a formal administrative structure. According to the assistant professor, "We have a composition committee, which is our four rhetoric and composition specialists. But we don't have a writing program director, we don't have any kind of placement, and we don't do any kind of assessment"; plus, "it's even weird to call it a writing program because I don't think of it as a writing program." This is a common refrain heard at many liberal arts institutions.

Implications

In adjusting to the university context, the writing center director stated that "you become part of your institution over time; it influences you, and with any luck you influence it." He was drawn to the university due to the small size, the opportunity for one-on-one work, and the care and compassion that were interwoven with the academics and service of the university—noting that it was normal for professors to be accessible, available, and ready to help. The junior faculty member echoed this sentiment, even while acknowledging some difficulty adjusting since she had never previously been part of a private, Catholic, or Jesuit school. Graduate students who have been trained in places with clearly identifiable writing programs and WPAs may be surprised to find that many institutions do not have clear programs or administrators. As is true in this case, they may not want such a program or position because they see teaching writing as a shared commitment. Writing can thrive in these environments; yet the traditional authority, structure, and funding may look radically different in these institutions. Graduates entering this environment without an awareness of these non-programs may have to figure out how to function in a very different organizational structure.

CONCLUSION

As each of these profiles indicates, WPAs are often thrust into institutional contexts that are quite different from their graduate institutions. Therefore, we suggest that one way to better prepare aspiring WPAs for work in a variety of institutional types is to explicitly study a range of writing programs. These cases and many more were developed in a graduate class where part of the content became sharing the results with the rest of the class and reflecting on how institutional type matters to WPA work. To the extent that WPAs' preparation occurs solely through apprenticeships in their graduate institutions, other institutional contexts remain invisible, implicitly suggesting that all writing programs function the same way. Conducting case studies of writing programs in other institutions not only expands gWPAs' knowledge base and awareness, it also prepares them to engage in the kind of research that intellectualizes administration and makes administrative labor visible within the field at large.

The profiles we include here support what the field already knows: that no two institutional contexts are exactly alike. But we believe that investigating *how* these institutions are unique and how various WPAs negotiate local contexts different from their prior experiences increases the visibility of various writing programs and helps develop a healthy mind-set regarding working in diverse contexts. In conducting the interviews, the graduate students got a glimpse of the messiness and even the failure of being a WPA that is often not reflected in WPA scholarship. The literature that addresses challenges presents them in retrospect, often resulting in a success narrative. Importantly, some of the WPAs interviewed for this project are no longer at the same institutions, sometimes because of the immovable realities of their local contexts. Many WPA jobs end in isolation, frustration, and failure. While we celebrate the energy, creativity, and successes of WPAs, not all situations work out. This is an important insight for graduate students who aspire to WPA positions, especially immediately after receiving their degrees. The assumption many aspiring WPAs make is that if they are knowledgeable and capable and they work hard, they will thrive and build a healthy writing program. However, institutional constraints often thwart even the best-intended WPA, and this has implications for both the WPAs and the institutions.

Inquiring about and thinking locally across diverse institutional contexts compels us to see implicit biases we might have about writing programs at graduate institutions based on their disproportionate visibility (e.g., TA training programs, funding for professional development such as conference travel and workshops, faculty mentorship programs). Even the questions created for the interview protocol provided a framework to more clearly see local contexts. Several of the graduate students who conducted the study are now in or applying for WPA positions, and this research made them more keenly aware of institutional contexts and what to look for when interviewing and considering jobs. By intentionally attending to local contexts and engaging with conversations through WPA-focused, interview-based research, aspiring WPAs can be better equipped to see a range of possibilities and to better appreciate the various contexts—such as students, instructors, structures, missions, outcomes—in which writing is taught.

REFERENCES

Bruffee, Kenneth A. 1984. "Collaborative Learning and the 'Conversation of Mankind.'" *College English* 46 (7): 635–652.

Charlton, Colin, Jonikka Charlton, Tarez Samra Graban, Kathleen J. Ryan, and Amy Ferdinandt Stolley. 2011. *GenAdmin: Theorizing WPA Identities in the Twenty-First Century.* Clemson, SC: Parlor Press.

"Community College Faqs." n.d. Community College Research Center, Teachers College, Columbia University, New York, NY. https://ccrc.tc.columbia.edu/Community-College-FAQs.html.

Elder, Cristyn L., Megan Schoen, and Ryan Skinnell. 2014. "Strengthening Graduate Student Preparation for WPA Work." *WPA: Writing Program Administration* 37 (2): 13–35.

Fulford, Collie. 2011. "Hit the Ground Listening: An Ethnographic Approach to New WPA Learning." *WPA: Writing Program Administration* 35 (1): 159–162.

Green, David F. 2016. "Expanding the Dialogue on Writing Assessment at HBCUs: Foundational Assessment Concepts and Legacies of Historically Black Colleges and Universities." *College English* 79 (2): 152–173.

Perryman-Clark, Staci, and Collin Lamont Craig, eds. 2019. *Black Perspectives in Writing Program Administration: From the Margins to the Center.* Urbana, IL: Conference on College Composition and Communication and National Council of Teachers of English.

Phillips, Talinn, Paul Shovlin, and Megan L. Titus. 2016. "(Re)Identifying the gWPA Experience." *WPA: Writing Program Administration* 40 (1): 67–89.

Rose, Shirley. 2012. "Review: The WPA Within: WPA Identities and Implications for Graduate Education in Rhetoric and Composition." *College English* 75 (2): 218–230.

Sledd, James. 1991. "Why the Wyoming Resolution Had to Be Emasculated: A History and a Quixoticism." *Journal of Advanced Composition* 11: 269–281.

Wooten, Courtney, Jacob Babb, and Brian Ray. 2018. *WPAs in Transition: Navigating Educational Leadership Positions.* Logan: Utah State University Press.

13
LABOR AND LONELINESS OF THE MULTILINGUAL WPA

Greer Murphy and Troy Mikanovich

> *The Puritan wanted to work in a calling; we are forced to do so. (Weber 2003 [1905], 181)*

> *When the L2 metaphor is used as a way of explaining the difficulty of learning to write in the disciplines for native English speakers, there is no language left to explain the experience of second language writers, who are literally learning a second language in addition to various disciplinary languages. (Matsuda and Jablonski 2000)*

As Hilary Bradbury-Huang (2010) observes of action research, which has clear parallels to methodologies that inform our chapter, working to generate and analyze data simultaneously is not for the faint of heart. As a multilingual writing program administrator (WPA) turned curriculum designer[1] (Murphy) and writing consultant turned instructor (Mikanovich), we had inhabited multilayered roles before and knew what we were getting into as we collected, analyzed, and gave voice to people, positions, and places that bear such striking similarities to our own professional contexts. Or so we thought.

Halfway through collecting data and interviewing colleagues for this project, one of us (Murphy) moved across the country to take another job at another institution. In some respects, this shifted the impetus behind our project. For the first time in both of our professional existences, neither of us *technically* had direct ties to multilingual writing program administration (mWPA). In other respects, as our work remains largely "international" in character, not much has changed. One of us (Mikanovich) still teaches in the program that inspired what we report here, and faculty development–adjacent work still offers the other (Murphy) opportunities to advocate for diverse learners and pedagogies.

We remain motivated by the same overarching questions: how did *we* make sense of mWPA labor while one of us (Murphy) was in the position of doing it? How do colleagues in similar positions make sense of *their* labor? What do these stories suggest about visibility, sustainability, and the future of mWPA labor in writing studies? In the university at large?

THE METHODS

In attempting to address such questions, we sought colleagues whose voices and institution types were underrepresented in current WPA scholarship. Long-standing disciplinary differences and structures separating multilingual experts from "traditional" writing program administrators (Matsuda 1999; Atkinson and Ramanathan 1995) made specialists difficult to identify. More than one potential interviewee cited a lack of grounding in writing studies ("I only do ESL [English as a second language]," "only one of my program's learning outcomes relates to writing") as a reason for not joining the study.

Once we found colleagues willing to share their experiences (primarily through snowball convenience sampling and reaching out to whoever was willing to speak with us),[2] we asked how academic background and perceptions of fulfillment informed what they did and how they did it (from LaFrance and Nicolas 2012; LaFrance 2019). We focused on uncovering how boss texts (see Griffith and Smith 2014) such as job descriptions reflected (or not) on-the-ground realities of mWPAs' day-to-day working lives. After the interviews, we reviewed job descriptions and collected additional documents (workload calculations, performance review questions, HR classifications, title change documentation) we felt contributed to a fuller representation of who our mWPAs were professionally and the kinds of standpoint(s) they variously represented.

Beyond merely offering a broad view of the day-to-day labor—experiences and expectations, explicit and obscured—of these mWPAs, our brief institutional ethnography demonstrated the myriad ways their labor was relationally situated. Throughout interviews and data analysis, we were less concerned with standardizing research protocols than we were with guaranteeing that our inquiry remained open to the various expressions of our participants' labor *as they themselves expressed it*. We asked everyone essentially the same questions (focusing on how they viewed their role in the university and how they imagined others viewing it; a full list of questions can be found in appendix 13.A) and requested similar documentation from all three. But given how positions represented in this study are the products of unique institutional needs, it was never our expectation to make strict comparisons between participants. Further, it was not our goal to flatten the work of mWPAs, writ large, to a single set of comfortable archetypes.

Rather than embarking on this project with the goal of declaring monolithic edicts about the state of mWPA labor, we wanted to provide incisive glances into conditions that framed administrators' understanding of that labor. Instead of providing a comprehensive synthesis of these conditions, we aim to find relevance in their particulars. Bolstered and limited by the backgrounds of the mWPAs we interviewed, by differences in institutional context and standpoints within them, this chapter sketches a view of the *way things work*—the *way* work *works*—for a less-than-visible subset of the WPA population. In presenting their stories, we give voice to labor and laborers that remain underrepresented in traditional writing studies scholarship.

INTRODUCTION TO THE MWPAS

mWPA1[3] works at a small undergraduate liberal arts college in California. Part of a larger consortium of schools, her institution serves 1,300 students, with around two hundred from outside the United States. As assistant director of multilingual writing, mWPA1 works one-on-one with admitted students. She emphasized how her "concierge approach" complements larger structures of support, explaining that she is "the only person on campus who works *academically* with . . . multilingual writers." In addition to coaching students, mWPA1 helps admissions evaluate international applications, collaborates with faculty, and, as of the time of writing, had plans to teach a freshman composition seminar.

This last role was a particular point of pride for mWPA1; with an MA in linguistics and experience teaching high school, undergraduate, and adult-school ESL, the seminar marks her first time in the college writing classroom since she accepted the mWPA job. In addition to benefiting from supervisor support, she attributed this opportunity to her unique position(ing) in the college: "I don't have a PhD, and I get to teach at [a school like this]. I love that idea."

Like mWPA1, mWPA2 is the first person in her role. Her college has five undergraduate specialists supporting approximately five hundred undergraduate learners; mWPA2 is the lone English-language learning specialist serving 100–125 graduate students. She holds faculty rank and reports directly to the vice provost of graduate studies. Since her school does not grant tenure and organizes students into individualized programs rather than departments, the relative prestige of this rank is counterbalanced by a sense of institutional rootlessness: "The tricky part with ELL [is] there's no rhyme or reason to where it's housed . . . if it's housed *anywhere*, you know what I mean?" By her own report, mWPA2 repeatedly finds herself compelled to clarify misunderstandings about her role. Students see her as "the beyond"—a go-to source of guidance for anything and everything—yet she wishes that more faculty recognized her expertise as academic and "legitimate."

Similarly, mWPA3 is (or at least, at the time of writing, was) an inaugural mWPA. As assistant writing center director at a research-intensive, graduate-only institution in California, she restructured what had begun years earlier as a two-course, concurrent-enrollment English for Academic Purposes program. In a matter of weeks, mWPA3 launched, then quickly relaunched, nine intensive pre-matriculation courses. The first of three written job descriptions (ca. January 2016) allocated what amounted to a full-time teaching load to the position, accounting for no program oversight or curriculum development. The fact that mWPA3's institution offered no degrees in writing studies, applied linguistics, or Teaching English to Speakers of Other Languages meant she was the only formally trained multilingual specialist attached to the program. While this gave mWPA3 a clear mandate within the university, it also limited how well others on campus understood (or indeed, knew about) her role: "Oh, we hired this person to 'take care of international students' . . . would have been [my] broad headline [for] most people on campus."

NAVIGATING RULING RELATIONS AND STANDPOINT

> *One of the faculty members decided to send all his students to me. Domestic included. (mWPA1)*

> *So this is the thing that's really crazy—I don't have a department. (mWPA2)*

> *I'm in the spaces where a lot of people aren't. (mWPA3)*

One challenge to understanding the labor conditions of mWPA work in higher education is the extent to which conditions are (or are not) unique products of local context. Although writing studies has a clear, growing interest in the shared experiences of its members across imagined, monolithic academe, a dominant canon of scholarship (e.g., LaFrance 2019; Brewer and di Gennaro 2018; Enos and Borrowman 2008; McGee and Handa 2005) emphasizes that broader trends are subordinate to the effects an institution's leadership (and its faculty, student, and staff stakeholders) can have on the profession. With a focus on case studies and ethnography, the format much of our scholarship takes suggests that overarching reflections on WPA labor must grapple with the preponderance of personal data, not the other way around.

Nowhere is the importance of context more important than in determining *ruling relations* that govern professional work. Such challenges are far from inevitable; even when present, they do not necessarily indicate dysfunction. In the broader context of traditional WPA work, the kinds of "theoretical conflicts" (Gale 1990) that result from otherwise well-meaning interpretations of department or disciplinary goals do not go away. And relative to a field that already situates itself as "between" (McGlaun 2007), the ability to successfully navigate ruling relations becomes increasingly destabilized the further the lines of communication and authority extend across administrative channels (Lamonica 2008).

Each multilingual specialist in our study assessed and navigated the cultures of their institutions, with varying degrees of success. mWPA1 alluded to an idiosyncrasy in the way her school served diverse populations ("there are many specific issues that come with being at a small liberal arts college [and] working with multilingual students . . . it's a different feel") but embraced her role as a connecting thread ("to smooth things out . . . they needed [me] to take the reins on international students"). She was cognizant of the power dynamics encoded in HR classification ("if anybody can take this away from me, it's faculty") but said she felt recognized by her colleagues ("faculty has always seen me as doing a really good service . . . everybody [has] really nice things to say"). Though she has presented at national conferences, mWPA1 talked of deriving greatest satisfaction from working one-on-one with students; of the three mWPAs, she seemed to maintain the strongest ties with others on her campus. While she made passing references to a lack of visibility in some of the labor she provides for the institution ("if anything, they were worried I'm too busy"), she remains eager to do more work.

Whereas mWPA2 acknowledged her between-ness as a multilingual specialist, she did not seem to fully accept it. Where appropriate, she sought to impose limits. Her self-described role as change agent ("[there's this] culture shift I'm trying to work on") at times clashed with a quest for recognition and legitimacy. For mWPA2, the way through this potential minefield meant aligning herself with broader institutional goals such as "this big push on diversity, . . . inclusion, and globalization." She proposed a co-curriculum that would have involved expanding work into more of an adviser role, which "really kind of fulfills those things, too." Even when it meant doing more than anticipated, choosing between investing more labor into what she already felt was a two-person job versus passing up opportunities to engage with colleagues and gain recognition from supervisors was a tradeoff mWPA2 was willing to make.

Such "voluntary" over-investment took its toll at times ("I do feel very frazzled ... pulled in a lot of directions"), but at the time we spoke with mWPA2, her professional energies did not seem exhausted. mWPA3 spoke frankly about how burnout and misaligned expectations were a major (though not the only) reason behind her decision to begin exploring job markets again after a year in the position.

Extending from ruling relations, one can see how mWPAs construct professional identities and understand how those identities enter into varying degrees of alignment with the norms, values, expectations, and constraints of their respective universities. As a conceptual category, *standpoint*—the subjective histories and social and professional locations of laborers, as well as the way those elements depend on the buy-in of peers, bosses, and others—complicates the more universalist assumption that "realities are neutral or just waiting in some pure form to be uncovered ... unadulterated" (LaFrance 2019, 37; see also DeVault and Gross 2012). Moreover, because a person's standpoint can be neither entirely personal nor fully objective, the way mWPAs must navigate the ruling relations they are faced with cannot be strategized in the abstract. As the experiences of these mWPAs demonstrate, the prospect of being fully a part of the university is coupled with the threat of having your position defined for you—imagined as a different position entirely—with your expertise "spilling" over semi-voluntarily into the realms of yeoman's work, such as personal counseling, advising, and enrollment.

NEGOTIATING THE JOB DESCRIPTION AS BOSS TEXT

> *"Coordinator" was bugging me; once I had the title change, I felt better about the job. (mWPA1)*
>
> *They call it "adviser." I feel like my hands are in so much more of it than just advising. (mWPA2)*
>
> *It never spoke to what became the reality of what I did. (mWPA3)*

Due to the liminality (Phillips, Shovlin, and Titus 2014) of mWPAs' roles, *boss texts* (Griffith and Smith 2014) associated with their work are useful sites for understanding how issues of authority and accountability are encoded—received and decoded, taken seriously or not—by administrators and faculty across reporting lines. Apart from whatever they say as final products, job descriptions are important for how they make manifest institutional between-ness, recording processes by which design becomes power and power is repackaged as *task* and *expectation*.

As anyone who has ever negotiated titles or fretted over how to word a line on a description can attest, an important limitation of such documentation is that documents *about* labor are not the same thing *as* labor. What Émile Durkheim wrote about contracts is true of the gulf between promises of professional documentation and practices of professional work.[4] Boss text analysis, then, must go beyond seeing documents[5] as mere *markers* of power relations to recognize how they "*enact* processes of evaluation and classification" (LaFrance 2019, 81, emphasis added). Such analysis must identify not only explicit terms of labor negotiation (hours, classifications, tasks, all of which can be compared from one job description to the next) but also aspects of power that benefit from going unsaid, often intentionally (institutional jargon, euphemisms, and "other duties as assigned").

For those who look to job description boss texts to understand labor and labor relations, such documents should not (cannot) be separated from the settings in which they evolved. Expanding on Alison L. Griffith and Dorothy E. Smith (2014), Michelle LaFrance (2019, 80) shows how a close reading of WPAs' boss texts highlights the importance of local context: "Even in positions that are ostensibly set up to reflect the value systems central to writing center studies, the institutional mechanisms that coordinate and review the local work of administrators often refuse or resist alignment with the field's values, catching writing center professionals between the ideals of their work as conceived by discussions in the field and the realities of their work in local settings." A further complicating factor for mWPAs is that within writing studies, multilingual expertise is often framed as a response to ad hoc conditions[6] rather than an indispensable, mainstream resource. This characterization contributes to isolating mWPAs further from traditional lines of reporting and institutional communication; for the three in our study, it was (part of) what rendered their labor less than visible.

Each of the mWPAs described a host of ways they negotiated (in material terms and with respect to how they each handled) discrepancies among what they *did*, what their job descriptions and titles *suggested* they did, and what their own properly executed visions of the job *would have required* them to do. Often, these negotiations seemed to unfold in similar ways. All three described processes of material bargaining that led to changing job descriptions or updating contracts. Whether in response to outside interventions or self-initiated lobbying, the mWPAs sought avenues by which perceived dissonance between the surface of boss texts (job descriptions, performance evaluations, HR classifications) and the substance of their labor could be mitigated.

mWPA1 recalled how a conversation about time spent on day-to-day work tasks, prompted by a co-worker at another institution, motivated her to request a title change from coordinator to assistant director. mWPA2 explained how being first in her position justified ongoing discussions about what should be expected: "They never had a role like this before . . . [but] the vice provost and I did have a good conversation about kind of tweaking the job description." Relative to senior administrators on her campus, mWPA3 framed efforts to revise her job description in the first year, then again in the second year, as an evolving process of "exploring their willingness to understand what . . . the program had become."

Despite similarities in *how* mWPAs negotiated job descriptions, their motivations for doing so reveal differences. For mWPA1, altering her boss text was more instinctual than deliberate. She expressed satisfaction at how her role incorporated projects others had asked for, commenting that once she realized she "really liked" doing something, she would get it "folded into" the job description to make sure she retained permission to do it. Some support mWPA1 reported providing (taking a student to get wisdom teeth removed, for instance) plays at the margins of this mandate, pointing to how mWPA1 leverages her outgoing personality and seems more than eager to keep expanding her role.[7]

In contrast, mWPA2 recognized that her work in some areas exceeded that of colleagues in equivalent positions ("I'm not sure other faculty meet with students as much as I do"). At the time of writing, she was endeavoring to convince supervisors that she should no longer spend time or energy executing responsibilities (counseling students on mental health, dating, other personal issues) outside the scope of stated job duties. Where mWPA1's motivation to negotiate boss text was so her position could retain work she had already started, mWPA2 tried to alert others to the kind of work she was not yet doing but that she *ought* to be allowed to do.

Like mWPA2, mWPA3 was not averse to proposing new initiatives or taking on projects with potential for collaboration, recognition, or allocation of more resources to her position or her program—at least not fully. mWPA3 mentioned that she had not counted on doing nearly as much curriculum design as was necessary in the first six months. But she embraced this part of the job, in part because she could ("f*** it—I have the skills") and in part out of professional intuition that if the program was to become "something I could be proud of," there were two options—"dig in or quit." mWPA3's choice to temporarily expand the scope of labor beyond what she deemed reasonable was informed by knowledge of what roles like hers needed, a desire to execute that vision, and a willingness to educate colleagues on "the position as I thought it should exist."

Boss text negotiations illuminate mWPA considerations that otherwise go unstated. An overabundance of responsibilities in an individual mWPA job description offers that person avenues to pick, choose, and make a position their own. mWPA1 shows how bargaining *personalizes* (with a caveat that similar extensions might not be sustainable in the long term). Boss text negotiations also signal (to faculty members, staff, and students) what responsibilities an individual has or is fulfilling. As mWPA2 explained, a change in job title would add duties *and* more explicitly mark her as a designated expert, "[giving] clarity for others . . . so I can do my job better." mWPA3 suggests a more abstract potential for the deployment of material deliberations. Her story also underscores how boss text conversations can alert institutions to the possibility of being unprepared to fully or fairly utilize an mWPA's position—even, perhaps especially, when it is a role they have just created or filled.

CONCLUSION: WHITHER THE LABOR OF THE MULTILINGUAL WPA?

The invisibility of mWPA labor differs from that of a traditional WPA in degree.

From the experiences of the three mWPAs profiled here, common underlying assumptions about labor emerged that have strong implications for the formation of future mWPAs' professional selves: that they are the only ones students can turn to, that being an mWPA is a calling, that being an mWPA is something that counts as Good Work regardless of whether an institution supports the labor and regardless of the material or emotional tolls taken on to do it. Not all mWPAs face identical pressures, and not every mWPA responds to pressure the same way—but no mWPA is an island. All must learn to navigate space between their expectations and those of others, strike what they hope will turn out to be a sustainable balance between *hyper*-visibility and *in*visibility, and do the work even if it feels as though no one else on campus knows or cares what that work is. In this regard, our findings point to multilingual writing program administrators and mainstream counterparts walking not too dissimilar paths.

But, does the invisibility of mWPA labor also differ in kind?

The prospect of quantifying WPA labor is complicated by the very contingencies that make it worthy of trying to quantify in the first place;

indeed, questions of whether mWPA labor can be distinguished in its own right have informed every aspect of this project. Facets of our mWPAs' working lives go beyond what previous literature documents. Emergent themes show mWPAs assuming responsibility to educate an even wider cross-section of colleagues, gate keeping with admissions to decide who gets in (in the case of F-1 visa holders, who pays full tuition), and working even harder than their mainstream counterparts to justify scholarly legitimacy in professional conference spaces as well as on home campuses. Our findings expand Paul Kei Matsuda and Jeff Jablonski's (2000) observation on how few words there are to distinguish challenges of learning to write versus being multilingual to program administrative contexts. Participants struggled to articulate with certainty how leading multilingual programs differed quantitatively or qualitatively from directing mainstream writing (no mWPA we interviewed had the experience of administering both program types). But that does not mean such differences do not exist.

Similar to the ways these experiences proved challenging for both us and participants to parse, we found ourselves straining the literature on which we relied. The few ethnographic treatments of multilingual writing programs that exist (e.g., Atkinson and Ramanathan 1995) focus on bigger schools and more established roles, limiting the extent to which they predict what our participants experienced. This literature scaffolds the visions of mWPA labor presented in this chapter but also frames them according to material conditions and ruling relations that threaten to become more the exception than the institutional rule. The project of quantifying and understanding mWPA labor both demands *and can facilitate* better understanding of the modern university as it exists outside canonical, research-intensive settings. If current institutional exigencies are any indication, such understandings will only become more, not less, essential over the long term.

APPENDIX 13.A

- Read through consent form with participant; answer any questions.
- In addition to asking participants if they consent to be interviewed, ask if they consent to be audio-recorded and to have their audio-recorded interviews transcribed using an outside transcription service.
- Check signature/initials.
- These questions are merely a starting point for engaging in conversation. Keeping discussion moving is more important than hitting any/all particular questions.

Potential Questions
- When/how did you come to hold your current position?
- Please tell us (briefly) about your background, preparation, and any special certification or qualifications for the position that you currently hold.
    » What interested/interests you about working with multilingual students?
    » What interested/interests you about working in a writing program?
- How well does your formal job description/title capture what you do?
    » Do you feel like it adequately signals to university constituents (students, staff, and faculty) what your role is on campus?
- What would you say your students think you do?
    » What misconceptions, if any, do they have about your position?
    » How many of these misconceptions stem from a lack of understanding about ML issues?
    » How many stem from a lack of understanding about your HR designation?
- What would you say that colleagues think you do?
    » What misconceptions, if any, do they have about your position?
    » How many of these misconceptions stem from a lack of understanding about ML issues?
    » How many stem from a lack of understanding about your HR designation?
    » Who are your colleagues? On campus? In the field?
- How engaged are you with colleagues outside of your institution?
    » Conferences?
    » Professional workshops?
    » Publication?
- What would you say that faculty/supervisors/other college or university constituents think you do?
    » What misconceptions, if any, do they have about your position?
    » How many of these misconceptions stem from a lack of understanding about ML issues?
    » How many stem from a lack of understanding about your HR designation?
- Have your title or job description changed in the time you have held your current position? If so, how?
    » What brought about these changes?
    » How have these changes impacted the way you feel about your job, your compensation, the way others perceive your role, your ability to do your job?
- How clearly recognized/acknowledge/mentioned (if at all) is _____** in your job description?
    » Scholarly engagement (research, publishing, conferences, etc.)

- » Campus engagement (committee work, program development/assessment, student advocacy)
  - » Teaching
- How clearly recognized/acknowledge/mentioned (if at all) is _____** in your <u>day-to-day work</u>?
  - » Scholarly engagement (research, publishing, conferences, etc.)
  - » Campus engagement (committee work, program development/assessment, student advocacy)
  - » Teaching
- How do you understand the importance of <u>multilingual</u> pedagogy on your campus? Do you think that others on your campus understand it similarly? How is (or isn't) this aspect of your work acknowledged?
- What does "advancement" or "professional development" mean to you?
  - » What do you think are the prospects for professional development or advancement in this position?
  - » In this line of work?
- What does "labor" mean to you?
- What aspects of your work, if any, are recognized/acknowledged/mentioned in your job description but take a far greater amount of time/labor/emotional labor than might be anticipated?
  - » How, if at all, do you keep track of your time/labor/emotional labor?
  - » What do you see as the benefits and/or drawbacks of tracking time/labor/emotional labor in this way?
  - » How, if at all, might you envision keeping track of your time/labor/emotional labor in the future?
- What's something you do as part of your job that goes unrecognized/unacknowledged, but if you stopped doing it, the entire building/program (so to speak) would go up in flames?

NOTES

1. A word about terminology: throughout the chapter we adopted the acronym mWPA (multilingual writing program administrator) to refer to administrators of writing programs that serve a multilingual, often but not necessarily always international, student population. While we are well aware that other scholars have qualified this term as WPA (see Adler-Kassner 2008) or adopted it into new terms like jWPA (see Dew and Horning 2007; Duffey 2007), gWPA (Helmbrecht and Kendall 2007), and GenAdmin (see Charlton et al. 2011), to the best of our knowledge we are the first to coin the particular designation of mWPA.

2. In total, we approached six potential interviewees about participating in this project; of the six, three ended up saying yes and agreeing to be interviewed. After reviewing their job descriptions, we interviewed each mWPA once for a total of sixty to ninety minutes; these interviews took place in person (mWPA1) or on Skype

(mWPA2, mWPA3), were audio-recorded, and were transcribed on Rev.com. We reserved the option to contact the mWPAs for follow-up emails and inquiries; the only mWPA we interviewed twice was mWPA3.

3. Although we clarified to mWPAs we interviewed that participation would not be kept fully confidential, as a matter of professional courtesy we have decided not to use their names.

4. "The contract is not sufficient by itself, but . . . only possible because of the regulation of contracts, which is of social origin" (Durkheim 1984 [1893], 162).

5. Documents such as job descriptions, professional evaluations, HR classifications, job ad postings, and others. For our study, we requested job descriptions, annotated time allocations relative to lists of each mWPA's stated job duties, questions from/outlines of performance evaluations, and any other professional documentation the mWPA considered relevant. In instances where mWPAs were not able or did not wish to provide specific documentation, we discussed these boss texts with them extensively during interviews.

6. See Cox (2014), who in problematizing this point of view refers to it as a "felt need."

7. mWPA1 noted, not without trepidation, that her college was considering creating a new position of international student counselor, possibly to overlap with the one-on-one support she provides for multilingual students. mWPA1 hinted that she was comfortable with the idea, insofar as it didn't push her out of the role she'd assumed as "counselor": "I don't mind . . . the more the merrier is how I look at it."

REFERENCES

Adler-Kassner, Linda. 2008. *The Activist WPA: Changing Stories about Writing and Writers.* Logan: Utah State University Press.

Atkinson, Dwight, and Vai Ramanathan. 1995. "Cultures of Writing: An Ethnographic Comparison of L1 and L2 University Writing/Language Programs." *TESOL Quarterly* 29 (3): 539–568.

Bradbury-Huang, Hilary. 2010. "What Is Good Action Research? Why the Resurgent Interest?" *Action Research* 81 (1): 93–109.

Brewer, Meaghan, and Kristen di Gennaro. 2018. "Naming What We Feel: Hierarchical Microaggressions and the Relationship between Composition and English Studies." *Composition Studies* 46 (2): 215–236.

Charlton, Colin, Jonikka Charlton, Tarez Samra Graban, Kathleen J. Ryan, and Amy Ferdinandt Stolley. 2011. *GenAdmin: Theorizing WPA Identities in the Twenty-First Century.* Anderson, SC: Parlor Press.

Cox, Michelle M. 2014. "In Response to Today's 'Felt Need': WAC, Faculty Development, and Second Language Writers." In *WAC and Second Language Writers: Research toward Linguistically and Culturally Inclusive Programs and Practices,* edited by Terry M. Zawacki and Michelle M. Cox, 299–326. Fort Collins, CO: Parlor Press.

DeVault, Marjorie L., and Glenda Gross. 2012. "Feminist Qualitative Interviewing: Experience, Talk, and Knowledge." In *Handbook of Feminist Research: Theory and Praxis,* edited by Sharlene Nagy Hesse-Biber, 206–237. Thousand Oaks, CA: Sage.

Dew, Deborah Frank, and Alice Horning, eds. 2007. *Untenured Faculty as Writing Program Administrators: Institutional Practices and Politics.* West Lafayette, IN: Parlor Press.

Duffey, Suellyn. 2007. "Defining Junior." In *Untenured Faculty as Writing Program Administrators: Institutional Practices and Politics,* edited by Deborah Frank Dew and Alice Horning, 58–71. West Lafayette, IN: Parlor Press.

Durkheim, Émile. 1984 [1893]. *The Division of Labor in Society.* Translated by W. D. Halls. New York: Free Press.

Enos, Theresa, and Shane Borrowman, eds. 2008. *The Promise and Perils of WPA Work.* Lauer Series in Rhetoric and Composition. West Lafayette, IN: Parlor Press.

Gale, Irene. 1990. "Conflicting Paradigms: Theoretical and Administrative Tensions in Writing Program Administration." *Writing Program Administration* 14 (1): 41–50.

Griffith, Alison L., and Dorothy E. Smith. 2014. *Under New Public Management: Institutional Ethnographies of Changing Front-Line Work.* Toronto: University of Toronto Press.

Helmbrecht, Brenda M., and Connie Kendall. 2007. "Graduate Students Hearing Voices: (Mis)Recognition and (Re)Definition of the jWPA Identity." In *Untenured Faculty as Writing Program Administrators: Institutional Practices and Politics,* edited by Deborah Frank Dew and Alice Horning, 172–188. West Lafayette, IN: Parlor Press.

LaFrance, Michelle. 2019. *Institutional Ethnography: A Theory of Practice for Writing Studies Researchers.* Logan: Utah State University Press.

LaFrance, Michelle, and Melissa Nicolas. 2012. "Institutional Ethnography as Materialist Framework for Writing Program Research and the Faculty-Staff Work Standpoints Project." *College Composition and Communication* 64 (1): 130–150.

Lamonica, Claire C. 2008. "Neither Fish nor Fowl: The Promise and Peril of Directing a Program on an Administrative Line." In *The Promise and Perils of Writing Program Administration,* edited by Theresa Enos and Shane Borrowman, 146–152. Lauer Series in Rhetoric and Composition. West Lafayette, IN: Parlor Press.

Matsuda, Paul Kei. 1999. "Composition Studies and ESL Writing: A Disciplinary Division of Labor." *College Composition and Communication* 50 (4): 699–721.

Matsuda, Paul Kei, and Jeffrey Jablonski. 2000. "Beyond the L2 Metaphor: Towards a Mutually Transformative Model of ESL/WAC Collaboration." *Academic Writing: Interdisciplinary Perspectives across the Curriculum.* http://wac.colostate.edu/aw/articles/matsuda_jablonski2000.htm.

McGee, Sharon James, and Carolyn Handa, eds. 2005. *Discord and Direction: The Postmodern Writing Program Administrator.* Logan: Utah State University Press.

McGlaun, Sandee K. 2007. "Administering Writing Programs in the 'Betweens': A jWPA Narrative." In *Untenured Faculty as Writing Program Administrators: Institutional Practices and Politics,* edited by Debra Frank Dew and Alice Horning, 219–248. West Lafayette, IN: Parlor Press.

Phillips, Talinn, Paul Shovlin, and Megan Titus. 2014. "Thinking Liminally: Exploring the (Com)Promising Positions of the Liminal WPA." *WPA: Writing Program Administration* 38 (1): 42–64.

Weber, Max. 2003 [1905]. *The Protestant Ethic and the Spirit of Capitalism.* Translated by Talcott Parsons. Mineola, NY: Dover.

14
CONCEPTUALIZING TIME IN HYBRID AND ONLINE WRITING INSTRUCTION AND PROGRAM ADMINISTRATION

Jennifer M. Cunningham, Natalie Stillman-Webb, Lyra Hilliard, and Mary K. Stewart

In 2007, Jonikka Charlton and Shirley K. Rose (2009) surveyed the Council of Writing Program Administrators (CWPA) to determine changes in writing program administrator (WPA) demographics over the previous twenty years. Comparing their findings to Linda H. Peterson's (1987) survey results, they found that WPAs now include more women who hold degrees in rhetoric and composition than in literature and who are more likely to be non-tenure track or not yet tenured. The authors of this chapter, all women with a variety of administrative positions at four institutions, represent these shifts as well as an additional, important shift in WPA responsibilities: online writing instruction (OWI). These OWI responsibilities, which include developing online and hybrid writing classes and providing support for instructors who teach them, are growing in relevance to WPA work.

WPAs and those in WPA-like roles who are responsible for online and hybrid writing classes face an additional set of often invisible labor conditions that range from designing and piloting online classes to developing and implementing robust teacher training and mentoring programs (Hewett and Ehmann 2004; Breuch 2015). The invisibility of this labor parallels the invisible labor of teaching online courses, which composition scholars have been discussing for years (e.g., Blair and Monske 2003). In this chapter, we explore those parallels through interviews with seventeen online and hybrid instructors from four institutions. Our goal is to make more visible the work of online and hybrid instruction as well as the way accessibility is an important aspect of OWI, with particular attention to how instructors discuss the concept of time and how that informs writing program administration.

TIME IN ONLINE WRITING INSTRUCTION

Teaching online can be much more demanding in terms of time needed to plan, organize, and deliver course content when compared to teaching face-to-face classes (Stevens 2013; Worley and Tesdell 2009). Wanda L. Worley and Lee S. Tesdell (2009) report on results of a two-semester study, finding that instructors spent approximately 20 percent more time per student in an online class. Similarly, Lee A. Freeman (2015) surveyed sixty-eight instructors from three universities, reporting that over 50 percent of instructors shouldered the time-intensive task of developing more than 90 percent of their course content within their learning management systems (LMS). Freeman (2015) also found that while less time is needed to create and organize an online course as it is taught in subsequent terms, certain factors such as facilitating discussion forums and providing feedback to weekly writing assignments remain time-consuming.

In her recent study that included interviews with fifteen first-year writing instructors teaching both face-to-face and hybrid or online courses, Lauren E. Salisbury (2018, 14) found that "very few instructors felt confident and satisfied with their online course design, regardless of whether they taught online-only, hybrid, or web-mediated face-to-face course sections." The instructors pointed to time as one factor that limited their ability to engage in design work.

Researchers continue to discuss the ways instructors require time, training, and support when developing and delivering online and hybrid courses. This chapter contributes by reporting on seventeen instructors' views of time and discussing the implications for hybrid and online WPA work.

PARTICIPANTS

We interviewed instructors who teach hybrid or online composition classes at four public universities in the United States. The four institutions in our study differ in size, from 7,000 to 30,000 students, and vary in diversity, with 14 percent to 43 percent of students identifying as minorities. Interviews were conducted through video chat, and all interviewees were asked the same IRB-approved sixteen questions (see appendix 14.A). Seventeen instructors volunteered to participate: twelve women and five men with teaching experience ranging from 1.5 to 30 years and online teaching experience ranging from 1 to 20 years. Table 14.1 provides further self-reported information for each participant—including pseudonym, institution, and teaching experience—and is organized by training followed by total years teaching.

Table 14.1. Instructor demographics

Instructor	Delivery Format	Position	Formal Training or Support	Total Years Teaching	Years Teaching Hybrid or Online
Adele	Hybrid	Lecturer	Yes, formal training	15	3
Cameron	Hybrid	Senior lecturer	Yes, formal training	10	6
Elizabeth	Hybrid	Lecturer	Yes, formal training	7-ish	1.5
Sheba	Hybrid	Graduate student instructor (PhD)	Yes, formal training	4.5	1
April	Hybrid	Lecturer	Yes, formal training	1.5	1.5
Nicole	Hybrid	Graduate student instructor (MA)	Yes, formal training	1.5	1.5
Olivia	Online	Graduate student instructor (MA)	Semester-long pedagogy class	2	2
Hannah	Online	Associate professor	Learning community	18	10
Kate	Online	Assistant professor	Learning community	18	5–6
Bryan	Online	Assistant professor	Learning community	Not reported	1
Julia	Online	Adjunct instructor	Week-long colloquium	8	Not reported
Joan	Online	Professor	No formal training; learning community	23	3–4
Filip	Online	Assistant professor	No formal training	30	20
Michael	Online	Associate professor	No formal training	25	22
Sonya	Online	Professor	No formal training	>25	10
Katherine	Online	Assistant professor	No formal training	11	2
Mike	Hybrid	Adjunct instructor	Not discussed	Not reported	Not reported

METHODS

We asked participants seven background questions and nine questions related to the Community of Inquiry Framework (Garrison, Anderson, and Archer 1999). The concept of time occurred consistently and organically. We asked one question relating to time—what is your typical week like as an online/hybrid instructor—yet found that instructors brought up their use of time throughout their responses to the other questions. Applying content analysis and a grounded theory approach to analyze the ways these instructors described their conceptualization of time online, we each read all seventeen transcripts, taking note of the ways instructors discussed their time. During open coding, we identified excerpts from the raw data that included the concept of time and determined potential themes through shared research memos.

After discussing the research memos as a group, two authors further examined the raw data for emerging patterns, which were then used to identify the themes presented in this chapter. A third author ultimately identified the excerpts presented in the next section by compiling lists of excerpts and sorting them according to theme.

FINDINGS

Although no interview questions asked directly about the concept of time, it permeated the ways instructors talked about different aspects of their hybrid and online courses. When we asked instructors to describe their typical week or their course design, they often framed their answers around the notion of time, discussing three identifiable patterns related to the concept: (1) saving/managing time, (2) time needed for training, and (3) time spent designing and delivering the course.

Saving/Managing Time

Time was an important factor in instructors' decisions to teach online. More than half of the seventeen instructors named schedule flexibility as the reason they chose to teach online. Just two instructors noted that they made the decision for pedagogical reasons; two mentioned their interest in and experience with using technology; and four discussed wanting to experiment with a modality that is a growing trend.

The importance of a flexible schedule for online instructors has been determined in previous, non-writing-specific studies, in which faculty members indicated that schedule flexibility was the most important element in their decision to teach online (Wright 2014), as well as in their satisfaction with online teaching (Wasilik and Bolliger 2009). Of the instructors who emphasized schedule flexibility, several noted the benefit of saving hours that would have been spent commuting to campus. One instructor, Kate, also noted the ability to have the on-campus schedule she wanted: "One of the reasons why I have to teach online is

I teach a five/five and I live an hour from campus. And so, in order to have a three-day week schedule I have to teach online, and it was just what was needed." This idea of teaching online to reduce time spent driving was echoed by Nicole: "It was my own schedule, actually. I absolutely understand where the students are coming from. I live in [town] and commute two and a half hours to [town]. I'm only there on campus two to three days a week."

In addition to saving commuting time, several instructors mentioned the need for flexibility to take care of family responsibilities. Some referenced both commuting and childcare as reasons for teaching online. One graduate student instructor, for instance, stated: "I live about 45 minutes from campus. Then, I had a baby also this year. I just thought, 'It's going to be way more doable to graduate on time if I can teach online.'" Filip discussed balancing the needs of family by teaching online courses during the semesters he spends abroad: "This coming fall, all of my classes will be online because my family lives in [another country], so I will be with them. Then I physically come here in the spring to work, to teach courses at [institution]. So that helps me do my research, do my classes, and keep in touch with the university." Like Filip, Sheba—a graduate student who teaches hybrid courses—also mentioned her need for more flexible time for research spent off campus: "Being a PhD student, there's a lot of research that I have to do on my own time. Having less time to be physically at school and more time to do research and then do just different online activities, that's always been appealing to me."

Time to address physical limitations also emerged. One instructor discussed the flexibility necessary to teach while addressing a health concern: "I had moved out of state and I was having some health problems. . . . So I was really fortunate to just tell the [omitted] department and they worked with me."

Finally, instructors talked about their decision to teach online emerging out of a desire to support their students' needs for time flexibility. Michael, who has substantial online teaching experience, expressed a desire to support students who are unable to attend face-to-face courses: "I felt like, okay, if this is something that is of value to people, particularly people who wouldn't otherwise be able to attend college or receive this kind of instruction, I am all for it."

These instructors' perspectives parallel students' priorities in deciding to enroll in online courses. For example, in Angela Eaton's 2002 and 2010 surveys of technical communication students, 95 percent and 90 percent, respectively, responded that their reason for choosing distance education was that "distance education courses fit into my schedule better than traditional courses" (Eaton 2013, 139). Just as online courses make university education accessible for student populations, including those in remote rural locations (Gos 2015), or for individuals with physical disabilities (Oswal and Meloncon 2017), online teaching may enable employment for instructors who face some of the same circumstances.

Time Needed for Training

Among the seventeen interviewees, twelve discussed formal training offered by their institutions, while five mentioned that they had no formal training opportunities. Of the twelve instructors who received some sort of formal training, eight—all of whom were teaching at the same institution—discussed continuing support offered during the semester, such as learning communities.

Nicole indicated that she spent a lot of time learning how to teach a hybrid course, including a summer course with modules, a professional development day, and meetings: "We have, typically, a summer to complete all of those modules to work through lesson planning, learning how there are different affordances when you're teaching online versus when you're having those face-to-face classes and then how you bridge that divide with those time lapses and trying to connect all of the content together in meaningful ways. You have, typically, a summer to complete all of that. Then, we come together and have a professional development day separate from the typical face-to-face [one]. There's just an added cushion there of training."

Likewise, Sheba, who teaches at the same institution as Nicole, discussed the ongoing training and support but also considered the fact that instructors were not compensated for the time required to complete mandatory training:

> We have monthly meetings. . . . There's always what they call a professional development day where all of the [course] instructors come together to discuss different strategies. We have workshops. Then, there's a separate one just for [hybrid] as well. I feel like there's a nice, smaller, [hybrid] community within the larger community. . . . It's been great. I really enjoyed the program . . . [but] no [it's not paid]. It's just I guess they want us to all be—so we can be on the same page and everything, but it's not an extra [payment]. It's just a one-day workshop thing that we have discussing ideas.

Other instructors described participating in an initial workshop rather than an ongoing professional development program. For example, at

Julia's institution, instructors participated in a week-long training colloquium "to become eligible for teaching" online courses.

Speaking of her experience at an institution different from that of the previous instructors, Kate estimated that she received six hours of training prior to teaching online, which was not enough for her to feel prepared for this new modality: "I think online teachers need a lot more support than we're given. You know, the quick little training things, I literally had to sit through I think three two-hour training seminars and then it was, 'okay, go play.' And it's like, wait a minute. Hold on. I've been teaching one way for almost 20 years, and I have lots of questions, and I am freaked out, and I really care about my students, and I want to do well by them."

Other instructors, like Joan at the fourth institution, discussed limited training opportunities in the past and noted that while training is more readily available now, scheduling conflicts restricted her ability to participate: "Now it's much more present in our department, the online teaching circle and things like that. So that is a good excuse [to attend], but I can never find time to go there because there's always a schedule conflict."

These interviews suggest that when provided with robust training that includes a semester-long course along with ongoing support, instructors feel more confident and prepared. These findings corroborate online and hybrid learning scholars' calls for training in accessible and effective course design and facilitation (Breuch 2015; Griffin and Minter 2013) and provide empirical evidence to support the argument that more training means more confident and prepared instructors. The instructors in this study are also aware of the amount of time required for training and for developing and delivering their courses—time for which they are not compensated. Beyond designing the course, as Karl B. Stevens (2013) points out, more time is still needed to facilitate discussions, create digital content, and assess both low- and high-stakes assignments than is typical for face-to-face classes.

Time Spent Designing and Delivering the Course

When discussing their typical week, course design, and interactions with students, instructors without prompting returned to the notion of time, with two overarching themes emerging: (1) facilitating student-student interaction through discussions and (2) responding to students via essay feedback and emails. Two instructors discussed the importance of setting boundaries or working within time constraints in an effort to manage their time related to responding to students. Filip emphasized the importance of setting boundaries to mitigate the temptation to be available during every waking hour:

> I'm always available, like I always have to respond. And after this many years, I'm pretty clear anymore that I'm not available from A to B, and Saturday and Sunday, no. That kind of thing I have to do, otherwise it takes over your life because you're always responding. And it's not that you're always spending three hours in front of the machine, but I'm spending 20 minutes here or 30 minutes here . . . now I take a couple, three hours during the middle of the day when the kids are gone. I can work that way, I can respond, and then I know at night, I know I will have some other time. So the flexibility of it is great, but it's a double-edged sword.

Setting boundaries and managing time are equally important but can be difficult for instructors with heavier teaching loads or multiple places of employment. Speaking for many part-time instructors, Mike discussed the importance of time in an effort to manage multiple job responsibilities: "I have another full-time job. I kind of do this on the side. Especially when I'm teaching an online class, I'm always reading and working on that class when I'm not doing anything else basically. It kind of happens around the edges of my life, morning and night. Sometimes, it's 4:30 a.m. if I'm going through papers just because I'm more of a morning person than a night person. It's kind of early morning things, late at night, that kind of battle."

Facilitating the course "around the edges" of his life was also described by Michael, a tenured professor. He noted that in addition to being available for questions sixteen hours a day through Skype and conducting individual twenty- to thirty-minute video conferences with students, he works about seven-and-a-half hours a week facilitating his course: "I usually work on the classes at night, between maybe 9:30 and 11:00 each night, checking in, catching up on things. . . . So that kind of goes from Monday to Thursday that way, and then on Sunday, I catch up on whatever has happened on Friday and Saturday, and it goes that way from week to week." These instructors discuss structuring their days and weeks around online availability, their teaching time described not in terms of traditional, predetermined "contact hours" but as frequently intermittent and negotiated around other employment, family time, and student needs.

In addition to describing their work hours in general, the instructors in this study specifically described time spent monitoring discussion forums or providing feedback to students. Fourteen of the seventeen instructors discussed monitoring and/or participating in discussion forums. Some instructors were highly involved in discussions, while others were intentionally uninvolved. Some instructors offered individual feedback to students in the forums, like Julia: "Some weeks, I'll respond to every student. Some weeks, I will write students private notes. Sometimes, I will only respond to maybe half the students." Filip further commented that the student-instructor interaction in online discussions is indicative of the individual nature of online learning: "Daily, I look at the interactions that have been created and try to respond to the interactions and manage the work. I mean, that online moment is so individual, even though you are part of the class, right? And I can try and structure and say, 'You have to have X number of interactions across peers, etc., etc.,' but it's really just me and the other person doing the interaction." These instructors characterize the discussion forum as a space for individualized student-teacher interactions and suggest that these online forums are particularly time-consuming to facilitate because the space invites one-to-one interaction despite its public (and ostensibly one-to-many) nature.

Providing feedback on writing is a pedagogical activity that instructors in all modes practice as an essential part of teaching composition. As such, it is not surprising that all seventeen instructors discussed providing feedback as an important but time-intensive part of instruction, varyingly describing feedback on weekly writing, rough drafts, and final drafts. Julia explained that she spends at least twelve hours each week grading assignments and providing feedback, which is possible in part because of her teaching load: "On Mondays, usually 9:00 a.m. to 4:00 p.m. Then, Tuesdays it's split. I usually do 8:00 a.m. to 10:00 a.m. Then, I do 3:00 p.m. to 5:00 p.m. or 6:00 p.m., usually. That's probably reproduced on Thursdays and Fridays as well . . . I've been teaching different preps, so I'm not getting an onrush of forty-five papers . . . I'm getting fifteen, if I'm lucky [and the rough drafts] only have to be 75 percent of full-length . . . for a six-page, I'm only responding to maybe four pages of it." Julia, like many of the other instructors, also described providing feedback on students' rough drafts as part of the writing process. Conceptualizing feedback as happening across time, Julia described a time line rather than specific feedback or commenting strategies: "They hand in a rough draft. They do peer review. I give pretty intensive feedback on those drafts. Then, the next class period is a revision workshop where they go through a series of revision activities I assign. Then about a week later, they hand in their final drafts. . . . Pretty much every paper they write goes through that process. I'm pretty hands-on with the feedback."

These interviews suggest that online and hybrid courses might be more time-intensive than traditional face-to-face courses. Based on these self-reported data, instructors estimate that they spend about fifteen hours each week per class to deliver and facilitate their hybrid and online courses. If an instructor teaches three courses in a semester, we can estimate that instructors are spending at least forty-five hours per week (excluding time spent for training and course development). This estimation is comparable to that of Joseph Cavanaugh (2005), who found that time spent teaching online was double the amount of time spent teaching face-to-face—a direct correlation with the number of students and time needed to communicate with them. This suggests a need, at the very least, to maintain lower caps in these courses.

CONCLUSIONS AND IMPLICATIONS FOR WPA WORK

WPAs face an additional set of labor conditions related to providing faculty training and support for teaching online writing classes. Our research indicates that some instructors make this choice because of the flexibility afforded, while others want to create flexibility for their students and still others have pedagogical reasons. A greater number of instructors teaching online means that WPAs are charged with creating opportunities to train and support faculty—often without the ability to compensate them. Like Salisbury (2018), we found that many instructors continue to feel under-prepared and insecure about teaching online, despite the calls for training in OWI scholarship (Breuch 2015). When discussing their typical week, their course design, and the ways they interact with students, instructors consistently returned to the notion of time, mentioning facilitating discussions and providing feedback as time-intensive activities. They further implied that for hybrid and online writing instructors in particular, "feedback" equals "teaching."

WPAs, who often set course schedules, need to ensure that they have instructors who are prepared and knowledgeable about OWI. Teaching writing online requires knowledge, experience, and skills specific to composition theory, which is why the responsibility of OWI training and support often falls to WPAs rather than to distance learning or teacher resource centers within institutions. Although our sample size is small, one-third of the instructors interviewed indicated that they did not receive formal training; while several instructors did receive formal training, a few of them indicated that it was insufficient. The participants also recognized the obstacle presented by providing sufficient training and support without compensating faculty for their time. While Isis

Artze-Vega and colleagues (2013, 175) suggest offering graduate courses that focus on faculty development in OWI, resulting in graduate students who "become effective scholars, writing program administrators, and university or college citizens," this suggestion overlooks contingent faculty. Mahli Mechenbier (2015) addresses this concern, pointing out that many online and hybrid courses are taught by contingent faculty and that WPAs in particular are responsible for providing conscientious access to training and support for those faculty. Given this consideration and our instructor participants' emphasis on schedule flexibility, we recommend offering online/hybrid training that is flexible—for example, offering self-paced content—more than one schedule option for any required synchronous meeting and/or video conferencing options or archived recordings alongside any face-to-face workshops.

Discussions of instructor time in online teaching have often related to labor issues, part-time instructors, and the affordances (time saving) and drawbacks (autonomy) of using course shells. While Keri Dutkiewicz, LuAnne Holder, and Wayne D. Sneath (2013), for example, discuss pre-designed materials or online course shells as a means of saving time, few of our interviewees teach at institutions that provide or encourage pre-designed courses, so these instructors have performed the labor of course design themselves. Furthermore, even after instructors develop their courses, OWI remains time-consuming to facilitate. Freeman (2015) specifically points to discussion forum facilitation and feedback in his argument that online and hybrid courses remain more time-consuming than face-to-face classes, even when taught in subsequent terms. Given this challenge, we suggest that WPAs can support online and hybrid instructors by providing sound pedagogical techniques that are effective and efficient, such as creating learning communities and virtual spaces where instructors can share materials they have developed and successful strategies they have pioneered. Such administrative actions can help reduce the time individual instructors spend on course design and facilitation while maintaining quality writing instruction.

APPENDIX 14.A: INSTRUCTOR INTERVIEW QUESTIONS

Background Questions
1. What is your position at your institution? How long have you been teaching there?
2. How long have you been teaching overall? How long have you been teaching online/blended classes?

3. Did you receive any kind of training or guidance when you began teaching online/blended classes?
4. Have you taught **blended or online** courses before?
5. Why did you **choose** to teach this course online/blended?
6. What is your **typical week** like as an online/blended instructor?
7. Number of sections you are currently teaching? Number of students in each section? LMS you use?

Teaching Presence
1. Tell me a little bit about your **course design**.
2. How do you instruct students in writing or help them improve their writing?
3. What kinds of writing feedback do you give students?

Social Presence
1. What kinds of activities do you assign that require student-student interaction? How often do these activities occur?
2. To what extent do you interact with the students individually or during their collaborative activities?
3. What is the **purpose of asking students to interact** with each other? Why do it?

Cognitive Presence
1. How would you describe what your students are **learning** in this course?
2. How do you, as the **instructor**, support student learning in the course?
3. How do you expect your students to support their **classmates'** learning in the course?

REFERENCES

Artze-Vega, Isis, Melody Bowdon, Kimberly Emmons, Michele Eodice, Susan K. Hess, Claire Coleman Lamonica, and Gerald Nelms. 2013. "Privileging Pedagogy: Composition, Rhetoric, and Faculty Development." *College Composition and Communication* 65 (1): 162–184.

Blair, Kristine L., and Elizabeth A. Monske. 2003. "Cui Bono? Revisiting the Promises and Perils of Online Learning." *Computers and Composition* 20 (4): 441–453.

Breuch, Lee-Ann Kastman. 2015. "Faculty Preparation for OWI." In *Foundational Practices of Online Writing Instruction*, edited by Beth L. Hewett and Kevin Eric DePew, 349–387. Anderson, SC: Parlor Press.

Cavanaugh, Joseph. 2005. "Teaching Online: A Time Comparison." *Online Journal of Distance Learning Administration* 8 (1): 1–11.

Charlton, Jonikka, and Shirley K. Rose. 2009. "Twenty More Years in the WPA's Progress." *Journal of the Council of Writing Program Administrators* 33 (1): 114–145.

Dutkiewicz, Keri, LuAnne Holder, and Wayne D. Sneath. 2013. "Creativity and Consistency in Online Courses: Finding the Appropriate Balance." In *Online Education 2.0: Evolving, Adapting, and Reinventing Online Technical Communication*, edited by Kelli Cargile Cook and Keith Grant Davie, 45–72. Amityville, NY: Baywood.

Eaton, Angela. 2013. "Students in the Online Technical Communication Classroom: The Next Decade." In *Online Education 2.0: Evolving, Adapting, and Reinventing Online Technical Communication*, edited by Kelli Cargile Cook and Keith Grant Davie, 133–158. Amityville, NY: Baywood.

Freeman, Lee A. 2015. "Instructor Time Requirements to Develop and Teach Online Courses." *Online Journal of Distance Learning Administration* 18 (1): n.p. https://ojdla.com/archive/spring181/freeman181.pdf.

Garrison, D. Randy, Terry Anderson, and Walter Archer. 1999. "Critical Inquiry in a Text-Based Environment: Computer Conferencing in Higher Education." *The Internet and Higher Education* 2 (2–3): 87–105.

Gos, Michael. 2015. "Nontraditional Student Access to OWI." In *Foundational Practices of Online Writing Instruction*, edited by Beth L. Hewett and Kevin Eric DePew, 309–348. Fort Collins, CO: WAC Clearinghouse and Parlor Press.

Griffin, June, and Deborah Minter. 2013. "The Rise of the Online Writing Classroom: Reflecting on the Material Conditions of College Composition Teaching." *College Composition and Communication* 65 (1): 140–161.

Hewett, Beth L., and Christa Ehmann. 2004. *Preparing Educators for Online Writing Instruction: Principles and Processes*. Urbana, IL: National Council of Teachers of English.

Mechenbier, Mahli. 2015. "Contingent Faculty and OWI." In *Foundational Practices of Online Writing Instruction*, edited by Beth L. Hewett and Kevin Eric DePew, 227–249. Fort Collins, CO: WAC Clearinghouse and Parlor Press.

Oswal, Sushil K., and Lisa Meloncon. 2017. "Saying No to the Checklist: Shifting from an Ideology of Normalcy to an Ideology of Inclusion in Online Writing Instruction." *WPA: Writing Program Administration* 40 (3): 61–77.

Peterson, Linda H. 1987. "The WPA's Progress: A Survey, Story, and Commentary on the Career Patterns of Writing Program Administrators." *WPA: Writing Program Administration* 10 (3): 11–18.

Salisbury, Lauren E. 2018. "Just a Tool: Instructors' Attitudes and Use of Course Management Systems for Online Writing Instruction." *Computers and Composition* 48 (1): 1–17.

Stevens, Karl B. 2013. "Contributing Factors to a Successful Online Course Development Process." *Journal of Continuing Higher Education* 61 (1): 2–11.

Wasilik, Oksana, and Doris U. Bolliger. 2009. "Faculty Satisfaction in the Online Environment: An Institutional Study." *Internet and Higher Education* 12: 173–178.

Worley, Wanda L., and Lee S. Tesdell. 2009. "Instructor Time and Effort in Online and Face-to-Face Teaching: Lessons Learned." *IEEE Transactions on Professional Communication* 52: 138–151.

Wright, James M. 2014. "Planning to Meet the Expanding Volume of Online Learners: An Examination of Faculty Motivation to Teach Online." *Educational Planning* 21 (4): 35–49.

15
COMMUNITY COLLEGE WPAS CREATING CHANGE THROUGH ADVOCACY

Lizbett Tinoco

For decades, two-year college scholars in writing studies and writing program administration have vocalized the fact that very little scholarship focuses on writing program administrators' (WPAs) work at two-year colleges. Why is this significant? It is significant because according to the American Association of Community Colleges (2019), there are 1,051 two-year colleges, which teach 41 percent of the nation's undergraduate student population. According to the Two-Year College English Association (TYCA) (2004), two-year colleges teach an estimated 70 percent of all developmental composition courses in higher education, and the majority of those courses are taught by adjunct faculty. In addition, a report by the National Center for Education Statistics (NCES) (2008) claims that two-thirds of faculty at community colleges are employed part-time. According to the NCES (2008), "The primary activity of almost 90 percent of faculty at community colleges is teaching," and only 3 percent of those faculty report administrative duties as their main activity. Since community colleges are so diverse and only a small portion of community college faculty report their administrative duties, it is difficult to describe the role of a community college writing program administrator. More recently, however, scholars working in two-year colleges have broadened our understanding of what it means to be a WPA at a two-year college.

To date, there is only one book, by Heather Ostman (2013), that focuses solely on writing program administration at community colleges. Ostman argues that "the WPA does not necessarily fit into a single, defined academic role" (101). Furthermore, Mark Blaauw-Hara and Cheri Lemieux Spiegel (2018, 247) share their experiences as community college WPAs and their transition into the larger WPA community to emphasize that "what it means to be a community college WPA is still largely unexamined." More than likely, someone in a two-year college is performing WPA work, but that work looks different than a WPA position at a four-year university.

WPA scholarship at two-year colleges has faced challenges, especially when it comes to defining a writing program and a writing program administrator. Decades ago, Helon Howell Raines (1990) received survey responses from 236 two-year college faculty, only to conclude that she could not create a cohesive definition of community college writing programs. In addition, Jeffrey Klausman (2008, 239) argues that two-year colleges that have no WPA "have [only] a collection of writing classes, not a program." Furthermore, Carolyn Calhoon-Dillahunt (2011, 124) claims that "part of the problem CWPA [Council of Writing Program Administrators], as an organization, may have gaining traction in the two-year college is that, while two-year college English faculty generally agree that their primary job is to teach writing, they, too, may not see these sequences of composition courses as a 'program,' and many see themselves primarily as teachers, so may not identify with the title of 'administrator.'" Blaauw-Hara and Spiegel (2018, 246) also draw attention to this idea: "WPA work at the community college is often further complicated by the fact that it is frequently not called writing program administration at all. WPAs are frequently department chairs, associate deans, or coordinators." The titles associated with WPA work at two-year colleges are very institution-specific.

In 2009, Tim N. Taylor (2009, 127) replicated Raines's (1990) study, but Taylor only received twenty-one survey responses—a fraction of the responses garnered by Raines. Only three of the respondents identified having a designated WPA. Like Taylor, I, too, replicated a similar study to the one conducted by Raines to gain a better understanding of WPA work at two-year colleges and to address Victoria Holmsten's (2002, 430) point that "the written record of the WPA in the community college appears to be virtually non-existent." In this chapter, I'd like to contribute to the efforts of this collection by illustrating the ways data-driven information regarding the work of two-year college WPAs can function as a powerful tool for others performing this type of work. Drawing on a mixed-methods approach conducted to collect data about community college WPAs across the country, I aim to provide visibility to work that is often underrepresented and unaccounted for—specifically, various forms of advocacy. The purpose of this chapter is not only to illustrate the labor performed by two-year-college WPAs but also to advocate for the need for more data-driven research performed with and alongside WPAs at two-year colleges.

ADVOCACY AND WRITING PROGRAM ADMINISTRATION

The term *advocacy* encompasses a broad range of activities that affect social change. If WPA work is much more than managerial work, then WPAs enact various forms of advocacy in the workplace. From the data collected in this study, WPAs, I argue, foster advocacy since they must account for their students, faculty, and communities. To do this, they negotiate, mediate, and organize to change practices and policies, which often leads to significant reforms within their programs and institutions and at the state level. In essence, effective advocacy is about persuasion, and a lot can be learned from the experiences and various forms of advocacy enacted by the community college WPAs described in this chapter.

STUDY DESIGN

To explore the work of community college WPAs, I used a qualitative approach to collect data.[1] This approach allowed me to collect data that provided a more complete story of WPAs' institutional contexts and the work they perform. First, a survey enabled participants to respond to open-ended and demographic survey questions. The one-on-one interviews gave participants the opportunity to share their experiences through their own voices.

The survey contained a total of twenty-two questions, which asked participants to respond to multiple choice, open-ended, and demographic questions. A brief sample of questions in the survey included: (1) What is your job title? (2) Please describe your job responsibilities as the writing program administrator. (3) What resources do you draw from to support your work? (4) Do you get course release time for directing the writing program?

Participants had the option to respond to as many questions as they liked and could opt out at any time. As a result, I received some surveys with partial responses.

The survey was distributed to the WPA listserv and the TYCA listserv during the summer months of 2016. Because WPAs are busy year-round, I distributed the survey during a time when I hoped WPAs would have more time to complete it. Although I recognize that there are limitations to only sending the survey to two listservs, these two were chosen because they are the primary professional and disciplinary listservs for writing program administrators and writing faculty at two-year colleges.

A total of fifteen community college WPAs provided their contact information in the survey and stated that they were interested in the interview phase of the study. I contacted each of them but only received responses from nine. I conducted thirty- to forty-five-minute semi-structured interviews with each of the nine community college WPAs. The interview questions were based on major themes that presented themselves during the coding and analysis of the survey data. Because participants were located in community colleges across the country, the interviews were conducted through video conferencing or by telephone.

RESULTS

As mentioned, respondents had the ability to skip questions they did not want to answer; as a result, here are some general demographics acquired from the survey. Twenty-four respondents identified as female and six identified as male. Forty respondents identified their age. The range of ages varied from thirty-one to sixty-five years, with the majority—nine respondents—indicating that they were between thirty-one and thirty-five years of age. In terms of ethnicity, a total of thirty-one participants responded. Twenty-eight identified as white, two identified as American Indian or Alaska Native, and one preferred not to answer.

Other demographic questions related to educational background were also included. Twenty-two respondents identified as having a doctorate, sixteen selected MA/MS, and three selected "none of the above." Of the three who selected "none of the above," two stated that they had MFAs and one had earned a MEd. Respondents were also asked to identify the discipline or field of study their highest degree was in, and a total of forty-five responded. Twenty-one identified rhetoric and composition as their field of study. Nine respondents identified literature and four identified creative writing as their main areas of study. Eleven respondents did not identify with the choices provided and listed degrees in cinema studies; Teaching English to Speakers of Other Languges; English education; new media studies; cultural studies; speech, reading, and education; and film studies.

In addition, participants were asked to provide general demographics of their community college contexts. Nine participants identified their community college as having 1,000–5,000 students. Ten respondents reported 11,000–15,000 students, and ten other respondents responded with 16,000–20,000. Two responses reported that enrollment at their institutions was over 31,000. Participants were also asked to describe their institution. Twenty-five respondents identified their community college as urban, fifteen as rural, seven as Hispanic-serving colleges, zero as historically Black colleges, and one as a tribal college. Other respondents also described their community colleges as suburban or statewide multi-campuses.

In addition, participants were asked if their department referred to its writing courses as a writing program. There were forty responses to this question: twenty-five replied no and fifteen replied yes. This is significant because, as Klausman (2008, 239) argues, "A program . . . is characterized by an explicitly expressed coherent curriculum with integrated faculty and assessment . . . lacking that, we have only classes loosely related by too-often unspoken and, most likely, conflicting assumptions about aims, means, and purposes."

Furthermore, participants were asked to identify their job title. A total of forty-three respondents responded to this question. Seventeen respondents gave more than one answer. The majority of respondents identified as professors, while only four selected writing program administrator. Sixteen participants did not identify with the answer choices but provided a wide range of responses: adjunct faculty coordinator, developmental program coordinator, academic program coordinator, composition coordinator, writing center director, instructor with writing program coordination duties, English department coordinator, writing center coordinator and English department coordinator, assistant department chair, assistant dean of composition, and faculty (there are no faculty ranks at the institution). These data collected show the many titles community college WPAs use.

Although various major themes were uncovered in the data, for the purpose of this chapter, I focus on the fact that many of the community college WPAs described their work as a form of advocacy. In the context of this study, advocacy can best be described by the ways community college WPAs engage with departmental and institutional constraints through the process of negotiation, mediation, and collaboration to effect change. The concepts of mediating and negotiating are closely associated with advocacy, which is what many of the participants in this study describe as doing when attempting to develop their position, outlining their job descriptions and negotiating compensation, and developing stronger support for adjunct faculty. Each community college WPA who was interviewed gave perspective to the ways they engaged in advocacy within their specific contexts.

Scholars such as Jeffrey Andelora (2008) and Patrick Sullivan (2015) have called for instructors at community colleges to view themselves as "teacher-scholar-activists." In addition, Sullivan (2015, 327) urges two-year college WPAs to "deliberately frame [their] professional identity, in part, as activists." For example, many of the community college WPAs interviewed in this study had been performing various degrees of advocacy on their campuses, and a large number of them are also involved in research and publishing scholarship, which is instituting change at the professional level. Although advocacy can take on many forms, WPAs described this work as "championing," "building trust," and "fighting." For example, one participant, Julia,[2] stated, "The WPA position is something I've always been championing, you know, I'm a champion from behind the scenes and also directly when I was chair."

One form of advocacy extracted from the data was self-advocacy. Many times, WPAs at community colleges engage in self-advocacy when attempting to establish a WPA position or something similar at their institutions. One of the most prominent ways self-advocacy manifests itself is pushing for and negotiating to establish a WPA position. For example, John advocated for the position for many years; he stated, "I advocated for it; about ten years after I got here, it finally became a reality. It became a reality because I advocated for it and I happened to have a good relationship with our vice president. I advocated for it and, you know, I wrote about basically arguing the importance of coherence in a writing program to student success. I think that was a little bit persuasive." Another participant, Michelle, described going to her administration to get support for the WPA position: "At least for us since we have scholarship, it doesn't necessarily totally change the administrators' [minds], but it's a lot easier to say 'look. These other places have these WPAs.' That was what we were able to say. It was like 'look. Everybody else in our system has one, we don't have one.' We have one of the biggest writing programs in the state." To advocate for their WPA position, these two-year college writing faculty needed to draw on scholarship and the fact that other two-year colleges had developed a WPA position. Participants used their connections, such as other administrators on their campus, in support of the position, while some used their connections at the state level. Knowing the importance of the work they are doing, community college writing faculty used many of the professional resources available to them to advocate for and develop a WPA position.

Community college WPAs also engaged in self-advocacy by making sure their job responsibilities were clearly outlined and that they received compensation for their work. For example, Diana described, "I sat down with the vice president of the school and the chair at the time and the incoming chair because we just switched chairs as well. I sat down with them and the previous WPA and we went over everything in the job description to make sure it was clear. To make sure that it was outlined properly. To make sure that the time that was designated for each role was very clear. All that. My job description was pretty clear. We fine-tuned it some more." Another participant, Elizabeth, explained that throughout her time as WPA she was able to slowly but surely get her workload down: "It started at nine credits of release for the year, and then it went up to twelve, and then by the time I handed over the position it was at fifteen. I was able to argue twice for additional release time." Most WPAs in this study were compensated through course reassignment time, but some had an additional contract with compensation for their WPA work. However, these types of negotiations are often not discussed in WPA scholarship. What is at stake when WPA work is not clearly defined, according to Susan H. McLeod (2007, 9), is that the lack of definition leaves a space for others to provide one: "Without a clear definition of the work, WPAs sometimes find themselves in positions that others define for them in unrealistic ways." Community college WPAs should encourage each other to share what these negotiation processes are like so others can draw from the strategies to advocate for themselves. However, negotiation takes time and can vary from context to context, and there are community college writing faculty in precarious positions that make this negotiation process difficult.

In addition to self-advocacy, many community college WPAs also performed what I'm referring to as peer advocacy, in particular for adjunct faculty. In many ways, community college WPAs wanted to ensure inclusion and connections between different people in their writing programs. To advocate for adjuncts, many of the community college WPAs noted the importance of understanding the roles and perspectives of adjunct faculty. Diana described, "One of the things I had to do was create an environment where part-time faculty would come and would feel connected and valued enough to stay even though the tangible benefits in terms of pay were really not so great." To do this, participants described the importance of listening. Anne described, "I spent a year kind of doing a Hillary Clinton–style listening tour." She mentioned listening and speaking to as many adjuncts as she could to understand how to better support them.

One way a community college WPA, Julia, created environments that were welcoming for adjuncts was to establish collaboration across all faculty in her department. Julia explains how she started a peer partnership program: "We paired all of our new adjuncts with full-time members, and again, it's completely voluntary and they are peer mentoring back and forth. We didn't want it to be 'let the full-timers show you how to do your job.' We wanted it to be a connection. You know, how where we create cohorts for our students, we're creating cohorts with our new adjuncts. It's informative instead of evaluative, so it's been really beneficial to both the full-time [faculty] and the adjuncts who participated."

In addition to mentoring support for adjuncts, some WPAs are also advocating for adjuncts to participate in local and national professional development. Julia mentioned encouraging part-time faculty to lead professional development workshops at the departmental level: "I think we paid one adjunct member [a] $1,000 stipend to kind of be my co-leader in a couple of the roundtable workshops, and that was amazing. It was really nice for adjuncts to have another adjunct who has been in the trenches for a while talking to them about jumping through the hoops as an adjunct, as opposed to me talking about it who hadn't been an adjunct for twenty something years."

Some participants described their commitment to create space for and include part-time faculty in national conference presentations. Michelle described, "We have some [adjuncts] that we're trying to work with to get in a part of Cs [Conference on College Composition and Communication], which we've done this year, to have them join our presentation." Advocating for adjuncts in the workplace to receive professional development support benefits the entire writing program. Peer advocacy enriched the outcomes of collaborative work between faculty and contributed to community building within programs.

IMPLICATIONS

Gregory R. Glau (2002) discusses the importance of institutional data for writing program administrators to advocate for their programs. However, it's also important for community college WPAs to have data to advocate for their own work. During the data collection for this study, especially the interview portion, a number of community college WPAs mentioned the importance of data for making a case to their institution's administration about keeping a WPA position or creating one. For example, one participant commented, "I think the fact that there isn't literature that we can draw from to make the case to the deans or to admin for this position results in not being able to even have a discussion with administration about the position because there's not a lot of literature that we can draw from." In addition, a few months after I completed the interviews, a participant emailed me asking if I could share preliminary results on the number of community colleges with WPAs so she could make a case to the vice president for funding for the following year. Without these data, WPAs are often in precarious positions when their jobs and additional compensation for this work are on the line.

Simply put, there is a need for quantitative data on community college WPAs. The issue, however, is, how do we collect these data? How do we reach a larger audience of community college WPAs?

Many of the community college WPAs who participated in this study are already part of disciplinary conversations about WPA work. For the majority of participants in this study, using scholarship and the knowledge of colleagues from other community colleges gave them more credibility among administrators and colleagues in their institutions. It's important to know how community college WPAs advocate for themselves and others in various situations by presenting their stories to better prepare and inform other community college WPAs. Having more documentation, such as examples of contracts, can help future community college WPAs advocate for their positions and assert their professional authority within their institutions. The CWPA Labor Resource Center is a useful resource with a repository of materials WPAs can draw from; however, how can we promote and make this resource better known among two-year college WPAs?

CONCLUSION

The community college WPAs in this study found ways to frame their advocacy efforts so they could make significant differences at their institutions. As Blaauw-Hara and Spiegel (2018, 253) describe, "We began to realize WPA could be a role of vision and activism, not just one of basic managerial management." This study has uncovered that community college WPAs are working within their institutional contexts to get things done and create change. They are advocating for the importance of a writing program administrator, making sure their job responsibilities are clearly outlined so they are not overworked without appropriate compensation, and coming up with innovative ways to support adjuncts in local and national professional development—all while building community within their programs. Advocacy and activism can take many forms. Often, advocacy work is not very visible and can take on a much quieter role in higher education, especially because those who challenge existing structures and cultures within institutions can be subject to professional risks—yet these community college WPAs are enacting various forms of advocacy on a daily basis. I'd encourage more WPA scholars to take up and extend research on community college writing programs and with community college WPAs.

NOTES

1. The study was approved by the Institutional Review Board at the University of Texas at El Paso.
2. Pseudonyms were used for all participants.

REFERENCES

American Association of Community Colleges. 2019. "Fast Facts." https://www.aacc.nche.edu/research-trends/fast-facts/.

Andelora, Jeffrey. 2008. "Forging a National Identity: TYCA and the Two-Year College Teacher-Scholar." *Teaching English in the Two-Year College* 34 (4): 350–362.

Blaauw-Hara, Mark, and Cheri Lemieux Spiegel. 2018. "Connection, Community, and Identity: Writing Programs and WPAs at the Community College." In *WPAs in Transition: Navigating Educational Leadership Positions*, edited by Courtney Adams Wooten, Jacob Babb, and Brian Ray, 245–259. Logan: Utah State University Press.

Calhoon-Dillahunt, Carolyn. 2011. "Writing Programs without Administrators: Frameworks for Successful Writing Programs in the Two-Year College." *Writing Program Administration Journal* 35 (1): 118–134.

Glau, Gregory R. 2002. "Hard Work and Hard Data: Using Statistics to Help Your Program." In *The Writing Program Administrator's Resource: A Guide to Reflective Instructional Practices*, edited by Stuart C. Brown and Theresa Enos, 291–302. New York: Routledge.

Holmsten, Victoria. 2002. "This Site under Construction: Negotiating Space for WPA Work in the Community College." In *The Writing Program Administrator's Resource: A Guide to Reflective Instructional Practices*, edited by Stuart C. Brown and Theresa Enos, 429–438. New York: Routledge.

Klausman, Jeffrey. 2008. "Mapping the Terrain: The Two-Year College Writing Program Administrator." *Teaching English in the Two-Year College* 35 (3): 238–251.

McLeod, Susan H. 2007. *Writing Program Administration*. West Lafayette, IN: Parlor Press.

National Center for Education Statistics. 2008. "Community College." In *The Condition of Education*. https://nces.ed.gov/programs/coe/analysis/2008-sa02f.asp.

Ostman, Heather. 2013. *Writing Program Administration and the Community College*. Anderson, SC: Parlor Press.

Raines, Helon Howell. 1990. "Is There a Writing Program in This College? Two Hundred and Thirty-Six Two-Year Schools Respond." *College Composition and Communication* 41 (2): 151–165.

Sullivan, Patrick. 2015. "The Two-Year College Teacher-Scholar-Activist." *Teaching English in the Two-Year College* 42 (4): 327–350.

Taylor, Tim N. 2009. "Writing Program Administration at the Two-Year College: Ghosts in the Machine." *WPA: Writing Program Administration* 32 (3): 120–139.

Two-Year College English Association. 2004. "Guidelines for the Academic Preparation of English Faculty at Two-Year Colleges." Urbana, IL: National Council of Teachers of English.

16
HEAVY LIFTING
How WPAs Broker Knowledge Transfer for Faculty

Lisa Tremain

CONSIDERING TRANSFER AS A THEORETICAL FRAME FOR WPA LEADERSHIP

For our programs to thrive, writing program administrators (WPAs) must make choices.[1] One paramount decision of WPA labor concerns how to design opportunities and spaces for professional development for program faculty—often our contingent or graduate colleagues, some of whom don't have scholarly background in writing studies. How, then, do WPAs strategically facilitate program-wide exposure to and experimentation with exigent research from the field of writing studies? Elizabeth Wardle (2013, par. 1) describes this aspect of WPA labor as moving "macro-level knowledge and resolutions from the field . . . [to] inform the micro-level of individual composition classes."

In this chapter, I investigate how three WPAs planned for and designed macro- to micro-professional development opportunities for program faculty. I extend the scholarship on transfer to suggest that as *programs* and *instructors* take up exigent theories from the field, they are—like students—engaged in uptake and transfer of learning, and WPAs are consistently and recursively the folks who facilitate this transfer. What does (or can) this look like? What choices can WPAs make to draw on the work that's happening in the field and facilitate its conscious uptake in their programs? What are the constraints, catalysts, and/or ecological factors of doing this work?

The data I collected for this project, which consisted of three extended interviews with current WPAs, capture two ideas. First, WPAs can design opportunities for writing program faculty to explicitly take up and transform research from the field in their local programs. Second, WPAs can utilize theories of *kairos* to broker transfer, in this case David N. Perkins and Gavriel Salomon's (2012) theory of detect-elect-connect, as a framework for professional development design. A consideration of the conditions that allow or restrict WPAs to act as brokers of transfer can help the field better understand *how* teaching faculty take up and transform theories and research from the scholarly field.

This investigation makes the labor and knowledge of WPAs visible in distinct ways that are not generally recognized by those outside our field but which sit alongside some of the more institutional understandings of the WPA as an administrator. Specifically, this research considers how WPAs move knowledge from the scholarship and the field into their programs. In other words, as WPAs, we are always thinking about how to productively change and develop our programs and the instructors in them. When we do, we are facilitating instructor uptake and learning. This chapter makes visible the labor of WPAs as they create opportunities for such uptake. By explicitly viewing the WPA as a broker and facilitator of knowledge, we make visible the various (sometimes conflicting) elements that support or constrain such facilitation. Drawing on Wardle (2013), this chapter applies the concept of kairos to show how WPAs situate instructor uptake in ecologies bigger than the program itself and offers a framework for knowledge transfer that helps operationalize this aspect of WPA labor.

KAIROS AND DETECT-ELECT-CONNECT AS FRAMEWORKS FOR PROFESSIONAL KNOWLEDGE MAKING

In 2013, Wardle described some "intractable problems" of WPA work as she facilitated experimentation with writing-about-writing approaches in her program at the University of Central Florida. One of the purposes of her narrative was to argue that WPAs might recognize and strategize from moments of kairos to "leverage our field's knowledge and narrative to work with our good teaching faculty and make changes" (par. 41). Wardle's framing of kairos emphasizes an important element of (not always visible) WPA work: to look for moments where institutional moves, educational policy, programmatic and student needs, and faculty labor conditions converge in a way that might support strategic programmatic change. But these factors can also conscribe the "intractable problems" WPAs regularly deal with as they work to make the changes. Wardle draws on Carolyn Miller's definition of kairos as a "critical occasion for decision or action" to suggest that by recognizing kairotic moments, WPAs can better strategize how teaching faculty might creatively engage in both uptake of the field's knowledge and the transformation of it into their classrooms and curriculum (par. 21).

When WPAs use moments of kairos to move the field's knowledge into their programs, this is an iterative act of knowledge transformation, a place where new learning (from the field) is applied and where prior knowledge (e.g., about writing and the teaching of writing) might be adapted or adjusted. In other words, the movement from macro to micro is an act of *transfer*. It is a process in which knowledge is transformed across situations and, in this case, where *instructor* learning can take place. However, as a process, knowledge transfer is neither predictable nor prescriptive; it always occurs in relationship to specific contextual factors, including (at least) social dynamics, knowledge mediation, intersectional identities, representation, orientations to collective knowledge, dispositions and attitudes toward learning and change, epistemological concerns, local contexts and constraints, and material conditions. Transfer is, to say the least, a highly complex phenomenon.

In addition, for knowledge transfer to occur, new knowledge (including situational knowledge) comes into contact with prior knowledge, which is affirmed, renegotiated, or possibly abandoned. Transfer happens in all learning situations, whether implicitly or explicitly. Perkins and Solomon's (2012) framework of detect-elect-connect is a useful structure for studying the complexities of this process. Perkins and Solomon argue that much of the research on learning transfer maintains a focus on what they've called the connect moment, the observable space where new knowledge merges with prior knowledge and is applied in context. The study of how learners connect their prior knowledge and use it anew across situations makes empirical sense in transfer research, since it shows when transfer occurred, what transferred, and what didn't. But Perkins and Salomon ask us to widen our perspectives of transfer to consider elements of learning that happen prior to the connect moment; that is, we need to also consider where and in what ways learners *detect* opportunities to transfer knowledge and *elect* whether or how to pursue them. Perkins and Salomon argue that these elements of transfer are as important as the actual moment of *connection*.

Instructors in writing programs, for example, when exposed to emergent research from the field, engage in the cognitive processes of detect and elect before any negotiation of their prior knowledge in relation to new knowledge. The steps of detect and elect, then, expose some of the complexity of transfer, including that dispositional orientations are also at work across these occasions—such as motivation, evaluation, efficacy, and task value (Driscoll and Wells 2012). In the case of instructors working (often contingently) in a postsecondary institution, these orientations link to things such as working conditions, program structure, entrenchment or fluidity of curricular approach, and professional development designs. While writing programs and professional development structures, much like writing, never offer an ideology-free zone, the detect-elect-connect framework offers WPAs distinct clues for how transfer might function in professional development models. Specifically, WPAs can draw knowledge from the field into the writing program by creating spaces for instructional faculty to explicitly detect connections between new and prior knowledge about teaching and writing and then work with them in community or individually to elect how (or whether) to pursue these connections.

In the remainder of this chapter, I share findings from interview data with three WPAs that illuminate how kairos and Perkins and Salomon's detect-elect-connect framework work as a heuristic WPAs might use as they consider professional development designs—including what, when, and how new knowledge is introduced into the writing program.

INTERVIEW ACCOUNTS OF WPA WORK AND FACILITATING PROFESSIONAL DEVELOPMENT

The methods for this chapter include data from three extended interviews of WPAs. The interview questions were designed to capture the extent to which scholarship and research from the field was integrated into these programs through professional development models. I conducted these interviews, each at least seventy-five minutes in length, using a semi-structured interview format. Because the interviews were semi-structured, interview conversations allowed participants to raise relevant issues related to (mostly invisible) WPA labor, such as shaping their programs, structuring leadership opportunities, everyday management, and responding to institutional shifts. Each participant was asked the same questions, but the order of the questions differed across interviews, and I used additional probing questions to explore participants' responses. Because interview questions asked participants to describe the institutional and programmatic shapes of their programs, as well as their WPA assignments and experience, I designed the study to *not* anonymize participants. Therefore, these participants were aware in advance that they would not be anonymized in the reporting; to account for such transparency, each participant was invited to review, edit, and amend the planned reporting of data that concerned their interview.

The interviews were transcribed and then segmented in two different sets (full responses and then noun-verb clauses) to allow me to explore qualitative codes both in and out of context. Both sets of segments were subsequently explored through open and then selective coding processes. Open coding was employed to help reveal initial patterns and rich points across interview data without determining preconceived categories. Open coding helped me to define some of the codes that were used subsequently in selective coding analysis, and segmenting allowed me to test and refine codes and definitions through additional rounds of coding. This coding approach was useful in this application, as it allowed me to examine data from two angles. First, I was able to consider the WPA participants' responses to questions in the context of more complete descriptions of their programs and their orientations to WPA work. Second, by isolating noun-verb clauses, I could consider more generally how these WPAs rhetorically described their work (e.g., what verbs were common or distinct across interview transcripts).

These methods ultimately led me to examine language use in context, which resulted in the development of final codes and subcodes within initial categories. Selective coding was applied through codes and subcodes within specific dimensions—such as leadership, teaching, and professional development but also kairos, detect-elect-connect, and community. Codes under "leadership," for example, included verbs such as meet, facilitate, lead, and design. Subcodes under the code "meet" included online, informal, professional development, and ad hoc. Although numeric reporting using counting and percentages of coded data is often used as a final step in qualitative work, that process did not make much sense here, as the total number of participants (3) was small, and the examining of the codes in context pointed more directly to explorations of the research questions.

What follows, then, is both a reporting and an analysis of the interview data, particularly in regard to how each WPA thought about or facilitated professional development, how and whether scholarly research from the field was taken up through professional development, and what factors constrained or facilitated these processes. The next section examines trends from across interviews with the three WPAs: Darci Thoune from the University of Wisconsin at La Crosse (UWL), Andrew Hollinger from the University of Texas Rio Grande Valley (UTRGV), and Kaitlin Clinnin from the University of Nevada at Las Vegas (UNLV).

USING KAIROS AND DETECT-ELECT-CONNECT TO CONCEPTUALIZE PROFESSIONAL KNOWLEDGE TRANSFER AND WRITING PROGRAM PROFESSIONAL DEVELOPMENT

Kairos and Leadership

Across interviews, recognizing moments of kairos was essential for these WPAs to facilitate moving research and work from the field into the program; such movement occurred in informal and formal professional development designs. I extend Wardle's (2013) conceptualization of how macro-level knowledge from the field transforms into the micro-level of the program by suggesting that scholarly knowledge from the field is taken up at macro- and micro-levels *inside* the program itself. What I'm calling *micro-kairos*, for example, such as when instructors demonstrate interest in the same ideas and then connect them to the scholarship through collaborative engagement, was reported across all three interviews. Micro-kairos as part of WPA leadership appeared when Darci, for example, discussed the importance of "hallway conversations" with teaching faculty and her belief in being both visible and available as a WPA so that faculty can individually bring ideas to her for low-risk brainstorming and feedback. Andrew stressed the value of ad hoc "workshopping" that faculty in his program engaged in through informal settings. This work trickled into his program's formal professional development design through opt-in meetings every two to three weeks that were meant to mimic a professional "conference style." For these WPAs, recognizing moments of micro-kairos can help them, as Darci noted, "build consensus from the margins."

However, macro-kairos (or what it means to recognize and leverage moments for critical curricular or programmatic shifts) was also present—and highly different for each WPA. This difference had to do with each program's readiness to take up scholarship and research from the field—as well as with how such readiness functioned in proportion to the positionality of the WPA, educational policies, faculty labor conditions, and shifting program structures. In Darci's program, for example, receiving tenure allowed her to more strongly advocate—both in and outside the program—for more deeply theoretical and pedagogical orientations to writing studies. She said, "I felt like I could be bolder. Tenure gave me courage."

But in Andrew's and Kaitlin's programs, other circumstances—an institutional merge, the lack of a shared vision across the program—slowed opportunities for professional development and program transformation. For Kaitlin and Andrew, macro-kairos revealed some "intractable problems" that stalled the pace at which programmatic or curricular changes could happen. For Andrew, locating macro-kairos, for example, was highly nuanced. Before becoming the WPA at UTRGV, Andrew was a longtime lecturer (he recently completed his third year in the non-tenure-track WPA position). At the time of our interview, UTRGV had recently merged two separate institutions in the UT system. (It is now the second-largest Hispanic-serving institution in the United States.)

Andrew described handling constant administrative adjustments resulting from the UTRGV merge as "waking up each day and your clothes don't fit from the day before." He was managing and leading a program that had recently doubled in size, and he was doing that work without long-term job security. He realized that "as both contingent faculty *and* a WPA, I am the program's first cheerleader. Some of that is tricky in how I lean into some of these overly austere measures that loom over our program." In Andrew's case, the institutional merge and his WPA positionality occluded some of the opportunities related to macro-kairos.

Macro-kairos in Kaitlin's work as WPA revealed institutional and programmatic structures that made it difficult to facilitate necessary change. During our interview, Kaitlin had just finished her second year as UNLV's first WPA with a writing studies background. A lack of full-time teaching faculty positions at UNLV challenged Kaitlin's ability to co-construct and reshape the program's curriculum in response to writing studies scholarship. Kaitlin noted, "I feel like I need to be more directive at this point about informing people about what's out there. What does it mean to have a writing class? What can it be? How can we bring what we learn here and adjust it for our own context?" However, by engaging various stakeholders—including administrators—through direct questions that aimed to establish a shared vision for the program, she used the macro-kairotic moment to think about leadership through collaboration and a shared road mapping of its future.

Darci's, Andrew's, and Kaitlin's experiences are illuminative of how moments of micro- and macro-kairos are inseparable from the unsteady pace and conditions of WPA work. They also emphasize the importance of strategizing among and across various campus identities and units. These frames for understanding WPA labor also inform the discrete, everyday labor of WPAs to facilitate knowledge transfer related to teaching, learning, and writing.

Using Kairos to Engage the "Detect" Moment for Professional Knowledge Transfer

As they worked within their highly specific programmatic and institutional contexts, each WPA used moments of kairos to think about (if not create) informal and formal designs in which teaching faculty would engage the moment of detect. That is, these WPAs considered designs that would provide instructors with access to emerging knowledge from the field, spaces where programmatic and instructor prior knowledge about writing might necessarily be renegotiated.

When WPAs introduce new information about teaching or writing into the program, instructors tacitly or explicitly consider it in relation to their current knowledge. For a program to stay current with the field, which is recursively responsive to research about writing and writers, the faculty in that program must detect the ways their existing prior knowledge about and dispositions toward teaching and writing can be reimagined or adapted in relation to new knowledge. (I discuss how this process can be unsettling for some faculty in the subsequent section.) In Darci's program, for example, the composition committee developed a college writing symposium each year to share knowledge about teaching and writing development across the campus; this event promoted professional knowledge transfer within *and* outside the program. This committee's work in Darci's program reveals one way it valued emerging scholarship and new knowledge. Darci noted that these symposiums "bleed back into the program in interesting ways." WPA visibility, individual mentoring, and creating space for faculty members to professionally collaborate allowed knowledge from the field to be locally re- and co-constructed.

In Andrew's case, many (but not all) UTRGV faculty adopted a writing-about-writing (WAW) approach to teaching. As faculty shared their WAW experimentations with each other, unexpected transfer opportunities to detect and reimagine prior knowledge about teaching writing happened through a type of positive contagion. Andrew estimated that at least "a third of the faculty are working to live the lives of scholarship" by attending conferences and participating in faculty development opportunities. He engaged these faculty to actively share and workshop ideas across the broader program—by promoting not a "specific line of assignments and assessment but more of a philosophy and attitude with which you approach curriculum." His emphasis on philosophy and attitude reflected some of the broader ecological factors that inform a detect-elect-connect transfer framework. While knowledge propagation tends to drive questions in transfer research, community dynamics are also essential elements of transfer, including collective orientations to knowledge making and dispositions toward learning and change.

For Kaitlin, while vision building with the community was the first priority, she also considered small-scale approaches that would integrate the field's scholarship into the writing program. At the time of our interview, Kaitlin was designing a paid opportunity for instructors to participate in a reading group in which they would study and discuss scholarship together, starting with threshold concepts from writing studies articulated in *Naming What We Know* (Adler-Kassner and Wardle

2015). She was also developing an anchor syllabus that grounded the curriculum in the field's disciplinarity, a text she planned to share with new and potential instructors to the program. An additional and perhaps amorphous detect opportunity for Kaitlin concerned how to shape conversations about the broad mission of the program, which needed to be revised. Kaitlin looked forward to such moments of macro-kairos: "When I've been here for five years, I'm hoping that the vision can be clearer to everyone who is part of this community so that I won't have to be doing so much of the actual leading, and we'll be focusing on maintaining and empowering other folks."

Moving toward Elect: Program Culture and WPA Philosophy

What happens after WPAs have leveraged moments of micro- and macro-kairos to introduce scholarly knowledge into their programs? What do the elect and connect steps look like for individual teaching faculty and the broader community? Because the elect step in this framework concerns how and whether individuals choose to pursue new knowledge that can disrupt (often entrenched) prior knowledge and also because detect-elect-connect is highly bound up in social dynamics and enculturation, WPAs must also consider the structures and spaces they create for (sometimes uncomfortable) transformations of knowledge and teaching. Program design moves such as these count as one of the myriad ways WPA labor is invisible; yet responsive teaching, collaborative learning, and collective visioning are crucial for writing program health and ultimately students' writing development.

Co-constructed and collaborative work in any writing program is both iterative and complex. When I asked Darci to talk more about the transformation of her program and how they moved toward embracing some of the research-informed changes happening in the discipline, she discussed the importance of developing connections over time: "A lot of this work is slow. This is my advice to new WPAs. You're going to want to do work in the program that is really awesome. And it will be awesome, but it's never going to be fast. Not if you respect people's feelings, not if you care about the people you work with, not if you really want to create a community of people who trust you and believe that you're good at your job." As findings across the interview data revealed, having a sense of what the program was ready for correlated with the ability to facilitate programmatic or instructional changes. These WPAs were highly attuned and sensitive to both their community members' needs and the health of the program community in a more general sense.

Like Darci, Andrew considered faculty knowledge and teaching practices relative to the program's readiness for change: "Being the WPA gives me this broad overview, and I ask the teaching faculty about what they need. Although I might be the principal architect of our [professional development], I'm not the sole architect. The teaching faculty demonstrate and participate in ways that are meaningful and interesting to them." Andrew also recognized that the UTRGV merge was an opportunity to draw on teaching evaluation data across newly combined programs as a way to set goals for faculty development: "Our data suggested that we could be doing better in our classrooms, so our focus for PD [has been] about that. Having this theme allows us various potential garden paths." These garden paths—where individual faculty select, define, and then represent knowledge of teaching and writing—are always grounded in the broader shape of the writing program (i.e., the garden itself) and are always backdropped by the leadership philosophy of the WPA.

Kaitlin noticed some of the discomfort faculty felt about making curricular and pedagogical changes. Because the program had not previously been led by a WPA who was also a writing studies scholar, most of the faculty were teaching writing in ways that did not reflect the currency of the field. Meanwhile, at the time of our interview, first-year writing at UNLV was predominantly taught by graduate students and part-time lecturers. A lack of full-time teaching positions at UNLV challenged Kaitlin's initial plan to co-construct and reshape the curriculum in response to new practices and theories in the field. Constant shifts in the faculty body each summer prevented collaborative long-term programmatic work. However, like Darci and Andrew, Kaitlin's goal to develop shared understandings of what writing is, what it does, and what it can be in the program guided her leadership approach and inspired her to expand her list of collaborators to include administrators, staff, and the graduate program: "My goal is really to think about the writing program as a community that includes administrators, instructors, and students. We're creating a community of teaching, of writing, and [of] teaching writing. As leaders, how do we facilitate that? For me, it's 'what is our common vision? What is our common purpose?'"

POSSIBILITIES FOR FACILITATING PROFESSIONAL KNOWLEDGE TRANSFER IN THE WRITING PROGRAM

An important theme across the interviews shared in this chapter was the emphasis on the program as a *community*. Each WPA emphasized developing a shared vision with faculty, and they each valued co-constructing professional development agendas with those faculty. The emphasis on community here could easily be linked back to the administrative trope of establishing "buy-in," but we can ground this trope by reorienting to collective, adaptive learning. As Étienne Wenger (1998) has theorized, all learning is fundamentally social and contextual, and it occurs in and across communities of practice. Participation in community must always be flexible; it necessarily engages individuals' intersectional identities, influences, knowledge, dispositions, and interpretations and helps shape the collective knowledge the community enacts, for better or for worse. The WPAs interviewed in this chapter were highly aware of developing and maintaining a sense of community around shared knowledge.

In our writing program communities, when/if theories and research from the field are explored formally or informally—and later, when/if they are applied to curriculum and classrooms—they are necessarily taken up and transformed in highly specific ways. The data analyzed in this chapter showed how these WPAs explicitly used kairos to think more consciously about learning for all community members, not only for students, and how this learning informs professional development designs and opportunities.

Some questions WPAs might ask themselves or that might be asked in subsequent research on WPA labor, then, are:

- How do WPAs recognize moments of macro- and micro-kairos to broker scholarly knowledge from the field into programmatic or individual instructional practice?
- How do WPAs create spaces where instructional faculty engage in the detect phenomenon, or that moment where new knowledge is introduced and integrated with prior knowledge?
- How do WPAs recognize the synergies between the powerful shaping forces of institutional and program culture and research exigencies?
- How do WPAs model or make visible curricular risk taking, knowledge sharing, and experimentations that might occur for instructors in the elect step? How can we productively learn from what happens in the elect step?
- How can this kind of WPA labor be made visible in ways that speak back to or fit into institutional structures? How can the labor of WPAs as leaders of professional development be recognized in ways that might facilitate institutional change?

Without engaging questions such as these, we don't yet have a rich picture of the "heavy lifting" WPAs do in their programs to support uptake of knowledge from the field. This chapter brings into focus three examples of how WPAs labored to move emerging scholarly exigencies into the on-the-ground work of the program. These examples make visible the ways WPA labor includes taking on the role of broker and facilitator of knowledge. We need to know more about how WPAs work to move the macro to the micro (e.g., how theory moves into practice), including exploring moments of first exposure to and ongoing application of emerging research and scholarship for writing instructors. We also haven't yet investigated how and why faculty choose among, prioritize, adapt, and apply ideas from the scholarship or how broader ecologies shape and impact instructor uptake—including material, labor, programmatic, institutional, cultural, and personal conditions. This project attempts to chip away at these gaps by making visible the ways WPAs make choices to facilitate scholarly uptake; the frameworks of kairos and detect-elect-connect can help sharpen this picture.

While we cannot predict the specifics of powerful scholarly turns in the field, we can anticipate that these turns will occur. This chapter makes visible the ways WPAs labor to bring writing studies scholarship to our individual writing programs and institutional contexts and how part of WPA labor includes thinking deeply about and facilitating teaching and learning, what Seth Kahn, in the foreword to this collection, has argued should be treated "with the same intellectual weight and scholarly respect as other subjects in our field." It also suggests conceptual frameworks WPAs can consider when creating designs for scholarly uptake for the faculty in those frameworks. Such consideration must include an understanding of the broad ecological elements that impact and interact with these processes. The concept of kairos and the transfer framework of detect-elect-connect can inform the decisions WPAs make about professional development designs, including what, how, and when faculty and other community members engage as learners and how emerging knowledge from the field can create re-visionings of teaching, learning, and the program. This kind of administrative labor spirals back out to the scholarly field and facilitates new understandings of the teaching of writing, the labor of WPAs, and the learning we must continue to do together.

NOTE

1. I extend exponential gratitude to Darci Thoune, Andrew Hollinger, and Kaitlin Clinnin for their time and honest reflections on WPA work for this chapter. Thank you for sharing your insights on what it means to lead your writing programs.

REFERENCES

Adler-Kassner, Linda, and Elizabeth Wardle, eds. 2015. *Naming What We Know*. Logan: Utah State University Press.

Driscoll, Dana Lynn, and Jennifer Wells. 2012. "Beyond Knowledge and Skills: Writing Transfer and the Role of Student Dispositions." *Composition Forum* 26: 1–15.

Perkins, David N. 2010. "Foreword." In *Threshold Concepts and Transformational Learning*, edited by Jan H. F. Meyer, Ray Land, and Caroline Baille, ix–x. Rotterdam, Netherlands: Sense Publishers.

Perkins, David N., and Gavriel Salomon. 2012. "Knowledge to Go: A Motivational and Dispositional View of Transfer." *Educational Psychologist* 47 (3): 248–258.

Wardle, Elizabeth. 2013. "Intractable Writing Program Problems, *Kairos*, and Writing about Writing: A Profile of the University of Central Florida's First-Year Composition Program." *Composition Forum* 27: 1–16.

Wenger, Étienne. 1998. *Communities of Practice: Learning, Meaning, and Identity*. Cambridge: Cambridge University Press.

17
BUILDING AN ANTIRACIST WAC PROGRAM

Genevieve García de Müeller and Ana Cortés Lagos

EPILOGUE: A WARNING

Antiracism work is not a set of static strategies. Antiracism, in our context, is a dedication to actively dismantle white supremacy in academia. This work is constantly evolving, locally relevant, and contingent on the situation; and it strategically de-centers whiteness. Although below we outline strategies we have used and find valuable in our antiracist work at Syracuse University (SU), we do not argue that these strategies are inherently antiracist. History has taught us that any tool can be used or co-opted by white supremacists to inflict violence on marginalized folks—even tools developed by marginalized people. So, it is imperative to note that antiracism, like writing, is a lifelong endeavor and must be embedded in every aspect of academic and pedagogical pursuits. It is emotional and physical labor. We start with this warning to make it clear that as soon as the term *antiracism* is appropriated by white supremacists, as *diversity* and *inclusion* were (Ahmed 2007; Kerschbaum 2014; Kynard 2015), we will resist this and change course if needed.

With that being said, the intention of our work here is to clearly define what an antiracist approach to writing across the curriculum (WAC) looks like, to describe how we strategized to gain support for our program, and to offer tools for building a program like the one we have. We do this by weaving the story of our program with a theoretical foundation. We used a method of reflective storytelling by weaving together a series of conversations between us: Genevieve García de Müeller, director of WAC, and Ana Cortés Lagos, assistant director of WAC. Through these conversations, we reflected on how we experienced the process of creating a WAC program from our specific roles and positions in the institution. We started by asking each other about our understanding of WAC, antiracist pedagogies, and our projections for a WAC program at

SU. These first conversations were recorded and transcribed. We then used them as a starting point to identify common threads across both conversations, and we marked salient themes. These themes and fragments were the foundation of a longer and deeper reflection about our experience and practice.

WHY ANTIRACIST WAC IS NECESSARY

The theoretical framework of our program is embedded in resisting racism, resisting white supremacy, and resisting marginalization in our classrooms. This chapter is our first attempt at building our story as an emerging antiracist WAC program. Using this as our exigence allows us to ask critical questions about our system and start constructing the effort and labor it takes to sustain what we're building at SU. Antiracist WAC is an important and necessary step toward addressing the whiteness of writing studies (Tanner 2019; Grinage 2019) and doing what Carmen Kynard (2018, 523) calls us to do, which is to "constantly name the structural violence of our institutions (our local settings, colleges, nation, and our field)."

Certainly, we acknowledge that at the basis of both antiracist pedagogies and WAC movements is the belief that the university should be a space for transformative work. Moreover, antiracist pedagogical movements in writing seek to acknowledge student linguistic power by recognizing their language tools in engaging in academia, while WAC encourages institutions to support students' participation in transforming the university. The critical race turn in WAC that we propose here works from these shared transformative values as well as the work of other scholars in the field to advance the conversation from one about how to best teach academic language standards across the curriculum to one about how to challenge and transform academic languages across the curriculum. This move is necessary for higher education pedagogies to effectively include diverse students instead of simply assimilating them into the culture of predominantly white academia by effacing their own ethnic, social, racial, and linguistic identities (Piller and Takahashi 2011).

In the introduction to the *Across the Disciplines* special issue "Anti-Racist Activism: Teaching Rhetoric and Writing," Vershawn A. Young and Frankie Condon (2013, 2) write, "Our specific claim in this regard is that we, that is, those interested in a just and egalitarian society, need to renew our commitment to intelligently and publicly deliberate race and to counteract the effects of racism." In this call to action, Young and Condon articulate the environment of "a death of racism" on college campuses in a post-Obama era, paying particular attention to how uncomfortable discussions of race can be for many students. This special issue was pre-Trumpism yet in many ways signaled the growing intensity of racism denial, rising incidences of hate crimes on college campuses, and overt racism on social media. Most folks of color working at universities prior to the 2016 election can attest to the fact that racism in academia didn't start with Donald Trump. It would be remiss to suggest otherwise. Trumpism has, however, led to more explicit white supremacist violence on campus (Gomez and Huber 2019; Best 2020) and in the country as a whole. A recent report from the Center for the Study of Hate and Extremism stated: "Newly released Federal Bureau of Investigation (FBI) annual hate crime totals for 2019 hit their highest level in over a decade on a small overall increase of almost three percent. The 7,314 hate crime 'incidents' or events tabulated from voluntarily collected complaint reports submitted by 15,588 agencies across the country represent the third consecutive year of an elevated plateau of over 7,100, increasingly violent, criminal incidents" (Levin 2020, 1). This increasing violence has led to a crisis on campuses, with ill-prepared faculty members unable to address race, much less combat racism and white supremacy.

In his chair's address at the Conference on College Composition and Communication, Asao B. Inoue (2019) asked that we consider how to teach against racism. One strategy to combat white supremacy is to explicitly discuss white privilege in classes. In their study on this topic, Su L. Boatright-Horowitz, Marisa Marraccini, and Yvette Harps-Logan (2012, 905) found that "White students showed relatively high levels of agreement that learning about White privilege made them uncomfortable, as if they were the 'bad guys.'" They also noted that when white students were asked about their experiences with learning about white privilege, they "began responding to [a] questionnaire with a negative attitude, refusing to answer" (907). Student pushback can be difficult. At the same time, focusing antiracist interventions on students often means asking students of color to engage in conversations about race that are redundant and even burdensome. So instead of promoting discussions around white privilege, our WAC program focuses on training faculty to design and implement racially just teaching and assessment practices, thereby challenging and transforming conceptions of pedagogy, writing, and language. With the conversation between WAC and antiracist pedagogy in mind, in this chapter we use storytelling to narrate our process of creating the Antiracist Writing across the Curriculum program at Syracuse

University and discuss the challenges and limitations we have found along the way. Thus, following Delia Lerner's (2001) practical principles for implementing reading and writing pedagogies, we show how we reconciled our goals and ideas about what is necessary with the real constraints to doing antiracist WAC work, finding our way to what is possible.

We understand the process of writing this chapter to be more than simply a way of reporting our experience and findings. The collaborative and reflective process involved in critical narrative inquiry (Clandinin 2006; Valeras 2010) is also part of developing and working through the challenges of doing innovative, antiracist WAC work. Critical narrative inquiry, as we're using it, is a method of building a story and a model for how faculty and graduate students can become what Juan C. Guerra (2014) calls "literacy insurgents." In this specific project, we use storytelling and the analysis of those narratives to reflect on our experiences and identify elements on which to build a project moving forward. The term *critical* emphasizes this programmatic aspect of our approach to our own narratives. Our purpose is to undo the workings of white supremacy on academic spaces and discourses. In the following, we create the story of our antiracist WAC strategies and practices. We show how we navigated upper administration, dealt with a lack of infrastructure, considered the role of research—particularly its limitations—and ultimately made peace with this work as a long-term struggle. We start by defining our approach to antiracist WAC and providing a short history of WAC at SU.

DEFINING ANTIRACIST WAC

Antiracist WAC includes the following foundational concepts:

1. Academia is constructed on white supremacist views on language and meaning.
2. Academic white supremacist views on language and meaning marginalize minoritized students and faculty.
3. WAC pedagogies should be a site to dismantle this white supremacy and mitigate this harm.

We delineate between traditional WAC and antiracist WAC in table 17.1.

Despite many years of writing curricula initiatives, SU's Writing across the Curriculum program officially began in 2018 as a series of workshops for faculty across campus who were invited to be in the first cohort of writing fellows. The initial workshops focused on defining WAC, writing to learn strategies, assessment tools, and student-centered assignments. With the hiring of García de Müeller in 2018, the program shifted to a

Table 17.1. Traditional WAC vs. antiracist WAC strategies

Traditional WAC	Antiracist WAC
Makes language conventions explicit and teaches them	Interrogates language conventions and encourages them to be influenced by students and diverse linguistic practices
Describes the languages of the disciplines and their values to better understand them	Interrogates values and conceptions around writing and the power dynamics that sustain them
Describes the genres of the disciplines so students can learn how to (re)produce them	Questions why we teach certain genres and whether there are some we turn to out of habit more than purpose Finds genres that foster student agency
Communicates rubrics and standards to make assessment criteria transparent	Challenges traditional assessment methods; introduces contract grading Shares responsibility with students for creating standards Creates opportunities for non-vertical evaluation (such as peer or self-evaluation)

focus on antiracism and anti-assimilationist practices. Antiracist WAC focuses on interrogating writing, access, and equity and facilitates hard conversations about race, racism, and language in the disciplines. The program is committed to supporting the teaching and learning of writing in all disciplines across campus. Our goal is to help and support instructors in developing strategies to teach writing in disciplinary courses, generating ideas for using writing as a tool for learning, designing writing-intensive courses, revising syllabi to integrate writing more purposefully into teaching, and implementing culturally inclusive antiracist writing practices. The Writing across the Curriculum program at Syracuse University supports faculty in developing antiracist writing instruction and assessment practices. Our program challenges the traditional notion of WAC as an assimilationist process by using WAC as a way to subvert academic discourse that upholds white supremacist ideologies of language. Our work builds on theories that support multilingual writers and promote antiracist assessment strategies, as we see such work as an integral part of writing across the curriculum.

WAC takes place through both the department and its writing center. It consists of a range of programs that include the WAC Faculty Fellows Initiative, the writing center, the Reimagining Student Writing symposium and workshop series, and the developing CNY (Central New York) Humanities Corridor Antiracist Writing across Curriculum Working Group. SU WAC works in articulation with these other writing initiatives in place, but they are not necessarily part of the WAC program. Despite there being a robust writing program, a vertical curriculum (Thaiss et

Table 17.2. Topics addressed in antiracist WAC workshops

Topic Description	Objectives
Antiracist composition pedagogy	Writing pedagogy that de-centers whiteness and combats persistent racism
Genres in the disciplines	Identifies the main genres written by students in fellows' courses and discusses their purpose Interrogates assumptions and expectations surrounding students' learning of academic genres
Conceptions about writing (Villalón and Mateos 2009)	Interrogates potentially racist or reproductive ideas about writing and language Discusses pathways for students to challenge and transform academic languages across the curriculum
Antiracist writing assessment ecologies	Acknowledges how historically, writing assessment has been couched in white supremacy Provides methods to combat racist and assimilationist models of assessment

al. 2016), writing-intensive courses, and a writing center at SU, there has not been, to date, a coordinated antiracist WAC initiative that spans all parts of the department. This has been one of our major challenges. How do you make a point, in an institution that has an extensive writing curriculum in place, that there is still room for WAC? How do you communicate that antiracist WAC in particular is essential and not the same as or a little necessary add-on to everything else?

Antiracist WAC is not a "quick fix" but an initiative that requires sustained conversations among faculty that extend beyond a single workshop or consultation; therefore, our WAC fellows are in our program for one year. They complete a series of workshops that cover the topics below. In table 17.2, we outline the topics and definitions.

After the workshops, the fellows revise their syllabi and assessment tools. The WAC team provides feedback in one-on-one sessions. During the following semester(s), when the fellows are teaching the courses, the WAC team completes observations and reports on faculty progress. The fellowship concludes with the fellows giving a presentation about their new courses at our annual Reimagining Student Writing symposium. During every step, faculty self-reflect, challenge their notions, and think of ways to start conversations in their own departments.

All of the former explains the plans and principles that guided our work, as well as the steps we took to implement this WAC initiative, but not everything always went as smoothly. In the following section, we explain some challenges we faced and the possible solutions we came to as we reconciled our ideals with our institutional and material reality.

OUR STORY

When we started working on Syracuse's WAC initiative, we had a great deal of enthusiasm. We had dreams for what a WAC program could allow us to do in terms of research, community building, inclusion, and transformative social justice work. In the long term, all of these goals may be achieved. WAC programs require commitments, strategic alliances, funding lines, and people power that are not always in place at the moment we are called to do the work. As we soon learned and as WAC literature has already pointed out (Cox, Galin, and Melzer 2018), a lot needs to happen for a wide-reaching, sustainable WAC program to be put in place. Some structures need to be bent, others need to be created, and much resistance needs to be overcome.

Syracuse University has a troubling history of institutional racism and student-led antiracist activism. In response to its fraught history and repeated racist incidents, the university has implemented a campus-wide course for students and offered multiple diversity training opportunities for faculty members. Yet issues remain and events continue to occur. In 2019, a series of hateful events fueled the emergence of a BIPOC-led (Black, Indigenous, and students of color) student movement called #NotAgainSU, which organized multiple actions on campus including rallies, sit-ins, occupations, and colloquia. While these events came after the hiring of Genevieve and her antiracist approach to transformative writing pedagogies, they gave us a new sense of urgency, served as a confirmation that we were moving in the right direction, and made us part of a coalition of voices that was too loud for anyone to ignore. Further, our expertise allowed us to approach this problem by providing some much-needed concrete and practical (albeit partial) solutions. Thus, our WAC program at Syracuse began to get stronger by paying attention to and collecting information about what was going on around us on campus, what were the needs and issues raised by students, where was the institution failing to provide articulate answers, and which faculty seemed dedicated both to naming the violence against our students and to systemic changes. When we first integrated antiracism as a central element in our WAC fellows workshop series, we realized just how deep this need was.

Our conversations with faculty showed us that faculty members are often disoriented when confronting issues of racism in and outside their classrooms and that they struggle to make connections between antiracism and their own pedagogical practice. During a workshop, one of the things we did was ask our fellows a question. We looked at data from a study showing that the students who failed writing courses were predominantly Black, and we asked the question: why? Why do you think that's happening? Genevieve remembers there was an awkward pause at first, but we began to really think about the reasons. That opened up some honest conversations with faculty members. One in particular said he had gone to so many diversity training programs, and afterward he felt as though he didn't know what to do. It felt so huge to him, like such a massive problem.

Through our workshop series, we discovered that while conversations about race were reaching faculty, creating a good deal of guilt and shame (Grzanka, Frantell, and Fassinger 2020), they were perhaps not very effective in providing them with concrete tools or strategies to make effective change in their classrooms. So, our workshops were geared toward that goal: identifying problematic conceptions regarding race—especially as it relates to language, writing, writing expectations, and requirements—and then finding specific strategies to address those issues and start working toward improvement. Hence, the goal entails doing something productive with that feeling of guilt instead of allowing white guilt to be the center of the experience. We prompted ideas about writing through conversations, genre analysis, personal reflections on course materials (such as syllabi and assignments), and small-scale surveys. These instances of small-scale research carried out collaboratively between professors in the disciplines and writing experts allowed us to illustrate how certain decisions about writing and language may have marginalizing or racist effects, even when their authors claim to have no racist intentions. This experiential understanding of our context progressed in parallel to our development of a method to gather more systematic data on writing, language, and racism through a campus-wide survey. For this, we used the European Writing Survey (EUWRIT) for professors (Chitez, Kruse, and Castelló 2015), which we modified slightly by adding explicit items about racism. We also conducted a systematic analysis of conceptions of writing in WAC fellow syllabi. Though we are still combing through those data and will publish them at a later date, our early findings from these studies show that despite Syracuse's solid writing curriculum, there is still a lot of work to be done regarding the creation of shared values and ideas around language, writing, and antiracist pedagogies across campus.

Surely, WAC cannot solve all of our systemic racism problems, but it is a great entryway because in academia, conceptions and attitudes about writing and language tend to work very closely with mechanisms that marginalize, exclude, or other certain groups and identities (Lillis 2001; Zavala and Córdova 2010). When we reinforce a language standard with no other reason than "this is how it is done here" or we penalize a student's writing because "the style is not right," the message is that the only way to be in academia is to speak, sound, and act a certain way. If so, diversity and inclusion is a fiction. Why invite someone in if we are not interested in what they have to contribute? So, our work is about challenging those conventions. In this sense, asking what about the language of academia is necessary for making disciplinary knowledge and what about it is simply there to reproduce the ways of doing of those who have always been here is a necessary step toward an antiracist (self-)awareness.

Finally, another way we generate and collect information about the WAC program is through assessment. Currently, the WAC Faculty Fellows Initiative is assessed in three ways: feedback and evaluations solicited from the WAC fellows, observations of WAC fellows teaching, and an analysis of the revisions WAC fellows have made to their course materials. This holistic approach has served us well over the last several years. It has taught us that fellows seek different things from a WAC intervention and that not only writing-intensive courses can benefit from WAC, as this reflection by a science faculty member explains: "Writing has always been an integral part of the learning process, but I have struggled with how to best implement writing in my classes, especially those with large student enrollment. Through the Writing across the Curriculum program I have explored new ways to use informal writing exercises to support student learning and encourage metacognition. I am especially interested in the potential benefits of writing to learn for students from historically underrepresented groups in science." We have also been reassured in our conviction about the value of encouraging fellows in new directions. As one WAC fellow who taught biology stated: "Through the WAC program, I have been encouraged to explore new, exciting avenues—ones, for example, in which the students interact with primary sources and adopt creative writing strategies to place themselves within the historical period we are studying. I am especially in favor of assignments that give students agency in their writing voice while steeping them in the subject matter of the course." The diversity of voices and insights has also made us reflect about a complex balance between the value of this diversity and the need for a certain degree of cohesion and coherence in the principles and orientation that emanate from the work we do. This is part of the ongoing work we do.

CONCLUSION

There are always institutional challenges to doing this kind of work. It requires the support of faculty and upper administration; WAC work can very easily become driven by one charismatic figure and die soon after they step down; and it is difficult to communicate a set of shared principles and values across a university campus, that is, across disciplines that already have their own values and beliefs about writing and writing pedagogies (Cox, Galin, and Melzer 2018; Townsend 2008). Our answer is twofold. First, WAC must fundamentally be an antiracist practice. Second, to achieve this, WAC programs must build a network of faculty literacy insurgents and work to dismantle white supremacist underpinnings of academia in institutions. Universities are committed to antiracist efforts that make them look good but are not willing to transform academia so that material inclusion and diversity can take place and space. University governance will give a department funds for a WAC hire but not for a WAC team. They will create curricular space for a course or two but not plan for a revision of campus-wide curricular designs. They make resources available so that students can learn academic discourse, but they will not move to challenge academic discourse so the languages of a diverse student body gain prominence in knowledge-making practices. This is, we believe, what an antiracist WAC program can promote: an overt conversation about our level of commitment to dismantling the predominance of white discourse across the university campus.

This is a change of terms that should prompt us to face the depth of the question about what it means to teach writing in a way that is transformative, not simply reproductive and assimilationist. This is definitely a whole new set of challenges. We do not know what antiracist disciplinary languages will or should look like, but we take it to be a good sign, as it helps level the ground for our students—making their input as valuable as ours in figuring it out.

REFERENCES

Ahmed, Sara. 2007. "The Language of Diversity." *Ethnic and Racial Studies* 30 (2): 235–256.
Best, Christiana. 2020. "Hate Crimes on College Campuses and in Higher Education Spaces." *Journal of Blacks in Higher Education (Online)*. https://libezproxy-syr-edu.libezproxy2.syr.edu/login?url=https://www-proquest-com.libezproxy2.syr.edu/scholarly-journals/hate-crimes-on-college-campuses-higher-education/docview/2334829298/se-2?accountid=14214.
Boatright-Horowitz, Su L., Marisa Marraccini, and Yvette Harps-Logan. 2012. "Teaching Antiracism: College Students' Emotional and Cognitive Reactions to Learning about White Privilege." *Journal of Black Studies* 43 (8): 893–911.
Chitez, Madalina, Otto Kruse, and Montserrat Castelló. 2015. *The European Writing Survey (EUWRIT): Background, Structure, Implementation, and Some Results*. ZHAW Digital Collection, Papers in Applied Linguistics series 9. https://digitalcollection.zhaw.ch/bitstream/11475/1016/1/407433819.pdf.

Clandinin, D. Jean. 2006. "Narrative Inquiry: A Methodology for Studying Lived Experience." *Research Studies in Music Education* 27 (1): 44–54.
Cox, Michelle, Jeffrey Galin, and Dan Melzer. 2018. "Building Sustainable WAC Programs: A Whole Systems Approach." *WAC Journal* 29: 64–87.
Gomez, Valerie, and Lindsay Pérez Huber. 2019. "Examining Racist Nativist Microaggressions on DACAmented College Students in the Trump Era." *California Journal of Politics and Policy* 11 (2): 1–16.
Grinage, Justin. 2019. "Reopening Racial Wounds: Whiteness, Melancholia, and Affect in the English Classroom." *English Education* 51 (2): 126–150.
Grzanka, Patrick R., Keri A. Frantell, and Ruth E. Fassinger. 2020. "The White Racial Affect Scale (WRAS): A Measure of White Guilt, Shame, and Negation." *Counseling Psychologist* 48 (1): 47–77.
Guerra, Juan C. 2014. "Enacting Institutional Change: The Work of Literacy Insurgents in the Academy and Beyond." *JAC* 34 (1–2): 71–95.
Inoue, Asao B. 2019. "How Do We Language So People Stop Killing Each Other, or What Do We Do about White Language Supremacy." *College Composition and Communication* 71 (2): 352–369.
Kerschbaum, Stephanie L. 2014. *Toward a New Rhetoric of Difference*. Urbana, IL: National Council of Teachers of English.
Kynard, Carmen. 2018. "Stayin' Woke: Race-Radical Literacies in the Makings of a Higher Education." *College Composition and Communication* 69 (3): 519–529.
Kynard, Carmen. 2015. "Teaching while Black: Witnessing and Countering Disciplinary Whiteness, Racial Violence, and University Race-Management." In *Best of the Journals in Rhetoric and Composition 2013*, edited by Steven Parks, Brian Bailie, Romeo García, Adela Licons, Kate Navickas, and David Blakesley, 291–316. Anderson, SC: Parlor Press.
Lerner, Delia. 2001. *Leer y Escribir en la Escuela: Lo Real, lo Posible y lo Necesario*. Mexico City: Fondo de Cultura Económica.
Levin, Brian. 2020. *Report to the Nation: Illustrated Almanac—Preview Edition, with the Latest FBI/DHS Data*. Santa Barbara: Center for the Study of Hate and Extremism, California State University. https://libezproxy-syr-edu.libezproxy2.syr.edu/login?url=https://www.proquest-com.libezproxy2.syr.edu/scholarly-journals/race-is-most-frequent-motivation-hate-crimes-on/docview/2395051408/se-2?accountid=14214.
Lillis, Theresa M. 2001. *Student Writing: Access, Regulation, Desire*. London: Routledge.
Piller, Ingrid, and Kimie Takahashi. 2011. "Linguistic Diversity and Social Inclusion." *International Journal of Bilingual Education and Bilingualism* 14 (4): 371–381.
Tanner, Samuel Jaye. 2019. "Whiteness Is a White Problem: Whiteness in English Education." *English Education* 51 (2): 182–199.
Thaiss, Chris, Sarah Perrault, Katharine Rodger, Eric Schroeder, and Carl Whithaus. 2016. "Part of the Fabric of the University: From First Year through Graduate School and across the Disciplines." In *A Minefield of Dreams: Triumphs and Travails of Independent Writing Programs*, edited by Justin Everett and Cristina Hanganu-Bresch, 149–176. Logan: Utah State University Press.
Townsend, Martha. 2008. "WAC Program Vulnerability and What to Do about It: An Update and Brief Bibliographic Essay." *WAC Journal* 19: 45–61.
Valeras, A. 2010. "We Don't Have a Box: Understanding Hidden Disability Identity Utilizing Narrative Research Methodology." *Disability Studies Quarterly* 30 (3–4). https://dsq-sds.org/article/view/1267/1297.
Villalón, Ruth, and Mar Mateos. 2009. "Concepciones del Alumnado de Secundaria y Universidad sobre la Escritura Académica." *Infancia y Aprendizaje* 32 (2): 219–232.
Young, Vershawn A., and Frankie Condon. 2013. "Anti-Racist Activism: Teaching Rhetoric and Writing." Special issue. *Across the Disciplines* 10 (3): 1–5.
Zavala, Virginia, and Gavina Córdova. 2010. *Decir y Callar: Lenguaje, Equidad y Poder en la Universidad Peruana*. Lima: Fondo Editorial de la Pontificia Universidad Católica del Perú.

18
MAKING RESEARCH METHODS VISIBLE THROUGH THE ALTERNATIVE TABLE OF CONTENTS

Caleb Lee González

The title of this collection—*Making Administrative Work Visible: Data-Driven Advocacy for Understanding the Labor of Writing Program Administration*—generates space to explore both how and what it means to understand the work and labor of writing program administration through employed research methodologies. In her chapter in *The Writing Program Administrator as Researcher,* Muriel Harris (1999, 1) explains that "writing program administrators engage in wide-ranging types of research to produce knowledge about various facets of their institution. To do so, they draw on a variety of research methodologies, using those appropriate to the institution and the type of knowledge needed." The methodological range of articles published in *WPA Journal* in the seven years following Harris's (1999) observation demonstrates the validity of her claim about the scope of research methodologies employed by writing program administrators (WPAs). By scoping fourteen research methodologies in the *WPA Journal,* I found that scholars employed qualitative, quantitative, and mixed methodological approaches that, in turn, guide my examination of the research activities undertaken in the studies in this collection. Undertaking a similar scoping of the chapters in *Making Administrative Work Visible* and creating an alternative table of contents to examine its research methods provides a way for graduate students and instructors to engage in generative and insightful discussions about WPA research that render visible the research work of writing program administration.

The editors of this collection point out that writing programs are often some of the largest academic programs on college and university campuses (introduction, this volume). Given that writing programs are situated to meet a wide range of audiences, taking up the collection

https://doi.org/10.7330/9781646423644.c018

through its research methods can promote questions of how research advances the objectives and goals writing programs have developed for their students and their institutions at large. For example, we are enriched by Genevieve García de Müeller and Ana Cortés Lagos's (chapter 17) discussion of the work involved in building an antiracist WAC program. A representation of the research methods that inform that work—narrative/storytelling/self-reflection and WAC program analysis—provides a model for more insight from programs that seek to make visible the work of building antiracism within the fabric of their writing program. In short, making our research methods visible is an opportunity for emerging WPA research and researchers to build on and from the scholarship through their research activity. It is also an opportunity to ask questions about how WPA research is taken up and what opportunities exist for conducting research, especially as the call for innovative research practices that address challenges of writing program administration continues to rise.

Moreover, an alternative table of contents that organizes chapters by their research methods provides a lens for instructors teaching and graduate students taking classes in writing program administration and research methods to see the work of making administrative research visible. This chapter provides those who teach and enroll in research methods and writing program–related graduate courses with another way to examine how WPA administrators align their research with their topics of study and modes of inquiry. It provides an opportunity to understand how the authors in the collection engage topics that are salient in WPA work, including the ways their research activity is conversant with WPA scholarship and challenges the historical underpinnings of what has "counted" as research.

METHODS MAPPING THROUGH SCOPING STUDIES

Scoping the research activity of a discipline in this manner is characteristic of social research methodology. Social researchers Hilary Arksey and Lisa O'Malley (2005, 21) define scoping studies as aiming "to map rapidly the key concepts underpinning a research area and the main sources and types of evidence available and can be undertaken as stand-alone projects in their own right, especially where an area is complex or has not been reviewed comprehensively before." According to the authors, scoping studies can be used to examine the activity, more broadly, of research in a discipline. It can be used as one method among many to review literature alongside "systematic" and "traditional" review methods. Arksey and

O'Malley (21) add that one of the reasons scoping studies might be undertaken is "to examine the extent, range, and nature of research activity: this type of rapid review might not describe research findings in any detail but is a useful way of mapping fields of study where it is difficult to visualize the range of material that might be available."

I began to scope the methods of the *WPA Journal* with a mapping assignment for a graduate-level research methods course I took in 2021 with Professor Christa Teston. The objective was "to gain practice with identifying how the discipline responds to moments of critical importance by selecting specific research questions, methods, methodologies, analytic frameworks, and the articulation of resultant implications" (Teston 2021). To get a sense of which methods were present in three writing studies journals (including the *WPA Journal*), I coded and mapped the methods in a randomized sample, including seventeen articles from issues of the *WPA Journal* between fall 2006 and spring 2011. Table 18.1 illustrates the scope of methods deployed in that randomized sample of *WPA Journal* articles from fall 2006 (seven articles), spring 2007 (four articles), spring 2010 (four articles), and spring 2011 (two articles). It's not lost on me that during this period, the Council of Writing Program Administrators advanced questions about WPA work as it relates to preparing graduate students in the most relevant ways to find WPA positions that "fit well" with their strengths, goals, and research experience and that demonstrate the relevance of writing program administration to faculty work in the twenty-first century (Call for Proposals 2007 WPA Conference).

In 2022, scholars in rhetoric and composition, like the editors of this collection, continue to question the ways the work of research is defined and the ways editorial practices secure "acceptable" ways of conducting research activity. For example, what does it mean to hold antiracism as a core practice in the publishing industry and in the ways we conduct research? In the first episode of the *Funky Dope Podcast*, hosted by rhetoric and composition scholar Dr. Iris Ruiz (2022), Dr. Raúl Sánchez (former co-chair of the National Council of Teachers of English CCCC Latinx Caucus) discussed his experience as a Latinx scholar in the field. Sánchez referenced the heuristic on antiracist and editorial practices (see Cagle et al. 2022). He explained that "antiracism in publishing means opening up the field of academic publishing, the various arenas of academic publishing (journals, press etc.) to a variety of perspectives, sources of knowledge, that may have in the past been considered for one reason or another outside the pale of academic thought and academic study. It's long past time to move beyond that and to accept and to

Table 18.1. *WPA Journal* research methods scoping sample

Methods	Number of Items
Theoretical	5
Observations	4
Focus groups	3
Follow-up groups	2
Interviews (hour-long and group)	3
Surveys	9
Analysis of teaching materials	5
Program analysis	2
Analysis of grant proposals	1
Cross-comparative analysis	1
Textual analysis of scholarship and WPA statements	2
Discourse analysis	1
Polls	2

celebrate the fact that knowledge comes in a variety of forms and from a variety of places."

Thinking about knowledge and the variety of forms in which it comes, as Sánchez proposes, what does it mean to question the recurring methods that have defined the way the field establishes the "validity" of its research? What does it mean to accept and celebrate the variety of forms and future opportunities that can exist in WPA research methods? And how is work implicated in these questions and rendered visible within graduate studies in writing program administration? The alternative table of contents in this collection emerges from these questions.

The title of this edited collection implicates the activity of making administrative work visible. It seems crucial to also make visible the research activity that spans conversations about data-informed advocacy, especially as the work that occurs in higher education continues to be shaped by changing social, political, and economic contexts. Graduate students and researchers alike gain both an understanding of the conversations in the field and how those conversations are methodologically produced for institutional advocacy and programmatic practices. I find this to be increasingly beneficial for graduate students and the advancement of a field that has confronted institutional beliefs and even behaviors that have viewed WPA work as not intellectually rigorous. To study the variety of research methods used in making administrative work visible is to counter the very notion that administrative work cannot and should not be studied. Furthermore, by making research methods visible in the examination of WPA labor creates opportunities for advancing research. Moreover, it is equally crucial that graduate students in writing program administration continue to gauge their questions through research. We know that research is a way to document the concerns that exist in the field (Teston 2021) and, in this specific collection, to document the concerns of administrative work. Thinking about what it means to make visible our research activity through WPA research, three additional questions come to mind: (1) What does it mean to extend crucial conversations related to the work and labor of the discipline as more research opportunities are identified? (2) What are the implications of making our research activity visible for ourselves, our institutions, and a discipline that seeks to further engage data-informed advocacy? (3) What does it mean to make our research methods visible to those who will continue to examine the visibility of administrative work and seek to address educational challenges?

"SCOPING" THE QUESTIONS AND COURSE OBJECTIVES OF GRADUATE-LEVEL WPA AND RESEARCH METHODS COURSES

There are a variety of ways that graduate courses in research methods and writing program administration study research methods. This is to say that no two research methods classes are composed and designed the same way. However, there are questions and topics related to methods that shape the learning frameworks—or ways to enter conversations about writing program administration and research methods in rhetoric and composition—for graduate students. I completed several Google searches for both WPA and research methods course syllabi. My searches included these phrases: writing program administration course syllabus and research methods rhetoric composition syllabus. I can identify questions directly related to methodologies—a system of methods—that serve as the frameworks for the courses at large. For example, a seminar in writing program administration taught by Professor Bradley Dilger (2016) states as one of its key questions: what roles should assessment, research, and data-driven decision-making play in contemporary WPA work? A research methods course in rhetoric and composition taught by Professor Maureen Daly Goggin (2006) takes up these questions: What is the relationship between research problems and research design? What are the limitations of various research and scholarly methods? Between these courses, it's clear that graduate students are asked to evaluate the role of research in two crucial activities involved in WPA work: assessment and decision-making. They are also asked to identify relationships within and limitations of research activity. It is my hope that this collection and its alterative table of contents can move such conversations forward.

Scoping the course objectives of research methods and WPA graduate courses provides another reason for studying WPA scholarship through a methodological lens. In the same Google searches that resulted in six course syllabi taught by Professors Ashanka Kumari (2020), Bruce Bowles Jr. (2018), Michelle LaFrance (2015), Rebecca Lorimer Leonard (n.d.), Nancy Bou Ayash (2019), and Maureen Daly Goggin (2006), I identified a few trends that reveal how instructors and graduate students examine research methodologies. An additional two syllabi do not have instructors listed but are from these universities: the University of Nevada at Las Vegas and Northern Arizona University.

I aimed to find the widest range of colleges and universities, including minority-serving institutions (MSIs) and those with various Carnegie rankings in research activity. Recognizing that what I found should be wider in its contextual scope of institutions (e.g., predominantly Black institutions, historically Black colleges and universities, Asian American Native American Pacific Islander–serving institutions, tribal colleges and universities), I find it relevant to examine WPA and research methods course objectives in graduate programs that differ in context to better understand what trends emerge across institutions. We know that instructors and graduate students in the field approach the study of WPA work from different situations, both in their programs and their institutions. Many courses are at doctoral/very high research activity (R1) and predominantly white institutions (PWIs). However, some of the courses below are at Hispanic-serving institutions (HSIs), emerging Hispanic-serving institutions (EHSIs), flagship colleges and universities, land-grant colleges and universities, and R2 doctoral/high research activity institutions.

Objectives include:

- Conduct extensive research on various issues relating to writing program administration (Bowles 2018)
- Become familiar with a range of methodological options in the fields of rhetoric, composition, and literacy (visiting some others as well) (Lorimer Leonard n.d.)
- Become more familiar with the major empirical methodologies and fields of inquiry important in language and rhetoric research (Bou Ayash 2019)
- Become aware of the methodological, theoretical, and rhetorical assumptions that underlie empirical research in language and rhetoric (Bou Ayash 2019)

- Gain a better sense of the development of empirical research in language and rhetoric (Bou Ayash 2019)
- Identify key conversations and trends in methods and methodologies for writing studies (Kumari 2020)
- Develop an understanding of current research methodologies and methods for use in the study of dynamic sites of writing (LaFrance 2015)
- Practice "thinking like" a writing studies researcher by exploring the methodologies and methods posed by our core texts, responding in writing to the central questions raised, and applying those questions in a shared, research-based project (LaFrance 2015)
- Strengthen your ability to evaluate research and identify areas of intervention (Lorimer Leonard n.d.)
- Evaluate and reflect critically on methodological practices and concepts used in research designs in rhetoric, writing, and digital media studies (Introduction to Research Methods n.d.)
- Evaluate the strengths and weaknesses of rhetorical methods (Rhetorical Critical Research Methods n.d.)
- Develop strategies for using and incorporating specific method/ologies in your own research (Kumari 2020)
- Become a critical reader of research and a scholar in the field (Goggin 2006)
- Closely read, with more understanding and critical evaluation, empirical research publications in language and rhetoric (Bou Ayash 2019)

What stands out is the kind of work involved in scoping the research methodologies of the field. A trend includes familiarizing students with methodologies, identifying conversations through those trends, evaluating those methodologies, and becoming critical and close readers of research. Moreover, the action verbs implicate a kind of activity that is rooted in critical thinking and studying the ties between languaging WPA work through research activity. For example, Lisa Tremain's use of qualitative methods in examining how WPAs make use of kairos is significant because kairos may be utilized in different ways at different institutions with different contextual realities. In this respect, her use of qualitative methods matters as Tremain studies how WPAs maximize how timing impacts their roles. Readers gain specific examples of kairos that WPAs can utilize within their own practices. Furthermore, regarding Tremain's use of methods, readers can increase their understanding of studying kairos in WPA work which include the larger complex networks that may or may not be in their control though inevitably tied to the work we do. To study kairos through various qualitative approaches shows the complex networks that shape WPA work. In this sense, it is also my hope that this chapter of *Making Administrative Work Visible* can not only advance the questions that frame conversations of research methods in WPA work but also provide a space to engage the work that course objectives implicate.

There is a particular connection between a collection like this and what graduate-level courses in WPA work and research methods ask students to do and be: critical and close readers. Such action verbs set high stakes for the future of the research involved in writing program administration. By mapping the methodologies of the field and those in this collection, the work—mapping and evaluating methodologies—graduate students are often asked to do becomes a way to better understand the conversations the authors in the collection bring forth.

The editors of the collection mention an important question related to research methods: what would it look like to rethink "acceptable" research methods and processes for WPA work (introduction, this volume)? The significance of the question arises at a time when the field continues to ask crucial questions about location and what it suggests about a sense of belonging, whose ways of knowing are invited and whose are not (Perryman-Clark 2021). Through a methodological lens in our reading, there can be room to ask questions related to research methods and their implications for access and equity in the work of WPA research. This also requires asking questions about how we language WPA work, including the language that is produced from our research that can have implications for writing programs and their material working conditions. For example, Lizbett Tinoco's and Lisa Tremain's chapters show through coding methods that this practice of language is significant to WPA labor advocacy. It's significant because researchers can see what it means for WPA labor to be tied to the ways in which we language the conditions of our work and the work of others in our programs and departments. Language—through our research practices—reveals how we understand WPA work in addition to how we advocate both for and through our work. As a current graduate student, I hope this part of the collection can aid me in reading closely and critically the research activity involved in making administrative work visible.

ALTERNATIVE TABLE OF CONTENTS OF RESEARCH METHODS IN *MAKING ADMINISTRATIVE WORK VISIBLE*

Informed by my scoping studies work in a research methods course, the alternative table of contents offered below is organized by four major methodological frameworks often identified in graduate-level courses: quantitative, qualitative, mixed methods, and theoretical. This structure provides instructors with a way to identify the chapters in the collection for their course needs and purposes. The alternative table of contents might list a chapter more than once, as it can be used for different research methods purposes. Furthermore, it includes methods students can familiarize themselves with—ones that carry a history in the field. The outline also includes research methods that have specifically emerged from making WPA work visible. For example, Ryan J. Dippre's year-long record-keeping project provides an opportunity to discuss hour tracking as a quantitative method. The table of contents therefore intends to provide space for both generative and insightful conversations that take up questions of the role research plays in WPA work.

Because instructors might also organize their courses through topics or themes related to WPA research methods, the alternate table of contents identifies the specific methods used in each chapter. Moreover, it is informed by research method trends in the *WPA Journal* to demonstrate the ways authors in the collection draw on, build from, and chart new ways for rethinking the research activity in WPA work.

ALTERNATE TABLE OF CONTENTS
Data Collection Methods

The alternate table of contents serves as a teaching tool for a graduate-level WPA or for research methods courses. Chapters are organized here based on the degree to which they illustrate a particular method.

Quantitative Data Collection Methods

Descriptive/document analysis
- Robinson, "Making Administration's Exchange Value Visible"

Big data/data analytics
- Gladstein, "Revising the Terminology and Frames around WPA Work to Uncover Networks of Sites of Writing Administration"

Topic modeling algorithms
- Johnson, "Teacher, Manager, Developer, Advocate: Representations of Work in WPA"

Corpus analysis
- Johnson, "Teacher, Manager, Developer, Advocate: Representations of Work in WPA"

Hour tracking
- Dippre, "Trading Time: Communicating Grand Strategy to Stakeholders through Hour Tracking"

Qualitative Data Collection Methods

Surveys
- Gladstein, "Revising the Terminology and Frames around WPA Work to Uncover Networks of Sites of Writing Administration"

Interviews
- Murphy and Mikanovich, "Labor and Loneliness of the Multilingual WPA"
- Mina, "Theorizing Programmatic Assessment as a Site of Visibility of WPA Intellectual Work"
- Cunningham, Stillman-Webb, Hilliard, and Stewart, "Conceptualizing Time in Hybrid and Online Writing Instruction and Program Administration"

Literature review
- Carter-Tod, "Nothing New: Systemic Invisibility, Epistemological Exclusion, and Faculty and Administrators of Color"

Coding
- Gladstein, "Revising the Terminology and Frames around WPA Work to Uncover Networks of Sites of Writing Administration"
- Dippre, "Trading Time: Communicating Grand Strategy to Stakeholders through Hour Tracking"
- Anderson, "Opportunity Lost: Failing to Make Administrative Work Visible"

Ethnomethodology
- Dippre, "Trading Time: Communicating Grand Strategy to Stakeholders through Hour Tracking"

Narrative/storytelling/self-reflection
- Emmons and Schaffer, "The Value of Mentoring in Writing Program Administration"
- Costello and Navickas, "Naming What We Feel: Self-Dialogue as a Strategy for Negotiating Emotional Labor in WPA Work"
- García de Müeller and Cortés Lagos, "Building an Antiracist WAC Program"

Case study
- Neal, Stark, Cicchino, Healy, and Albert, "Institutional Matters: The (In)Visibility of Localized WPA Labor"

Mixed Method Approaches

Explanatory sequential design
- Mitchell and Rieman, "Invisible Labor: Tracking Email Practices in WPA Work"

Survey & Semi-Structured Interviews
- Tinoco," Community College WPAs Creating Change Through Advocacy"

Open-Coding & Semi-Structured Interviews
- Tremain, "Heavy Lifting: How WPAs Broker Knowledge Transfer for Faculty"

Research Methodological Scoping & Syllabi Review
- González, "Making Research Methods Visible Through the Alternative Table of Contents"

Theoretical Framework Methods

Antiracism
- Carter-Tod, "Nothing New: Systemic Invisibility, Epistemological Exclusion, and Faculty and Administrators of Color"
- Poblete, "Weighing down the Body: Quantifying the Nature of Antiracist Work"
- García de Müeller and Cortés Lagos, "Building an Antiracist WAC Program"

Thingification
- Dippre, "Trading Time: Communicating Grand Strategy to Stakeholders through Hour Tracking"

Marxist theory
- Robinson, "Making Administration's Exchange Value Visible"

REFERENCES

Arksey, Hilary, and Lisa O'Malley. 2005. "Scoping Studies: Towards a Methodological Framework." *International Journal of Social Research Methodology* 8 (1): 19–32. doi: 10.1080/1364557032000119616.

Bou Ayash, Nancy. 2019. Research Methods in Language and Rhetoric [Syllabus]. Department of English, University of Washington, Seattle.
Bowles, Bruce, Jr. 2018. Writing Program Administration (Independent Study) [Syllabus]. English Department, Texas A&M University Central Texas, Killeen.
Cagle, Lauren E., Michelle F. Eble, Laura Gonzales, Meredith A. Johnson, Nathan R. Johnson, Natasha N. Jones, Liz Lane, Temptaous Mckoy, Kristen R. Moore, Ricky Reynoso, Emma J. Rose, GPat Patterson, Fernando Sánchez, Ann Shivers-McNair, Michele Simmons, Erica M. Stone, Jason Tham, Rebecca Walton, and Miriam F. Williams. 2021. "Anti-Racist Scholarly Reviewing Practices: A Heuristic for Editors, Reviewers, and Authors." tinyurl.com/reviewheuristic.
Call for Proposals 2007 WPA Conference. 2006. "Preparing Ourselves and Our Programs: Readiness, Relevance, Relationships in Tempe, AZ." *Council of Writing Program Administrators Past Conferences.* https://wpacouncil.org/aws/CWPA/pt/sp/past-conferences.
Dilger, Bradley. 2016. Seminar in Writing Program Administration [Syllabus]. Department of English, Purdue University, West Lafayette, IN.
Goggin, Maureen Daly. 2006. Research Methods: Rhetoric and Composition [Syllabus]. Department of English, Arizona State University, Tempe.
Harris, Muriel. 1999. "Diverse Research Methodologies at Work for Diverse Audiences: Shaping the Writing Center to the Institution." In *The Writing Program Administrator as Researcher: Inquiry in Action and Reflection*, edited by Shirley K. Rose and Irwin Weiser, 1–17. Portsmouth, NH: Boynton/Cook.
Introduction to Research Methods in Rhetoric and Composition [Syllabus]. n.d. Department of English, Northern Arizona University, Flagstaff.
Kumari, Ashanka. 2020. Methods and Methodologies in Writing Studies [Syllabus]. Department of English, Texas A&M University, Commerce.
LaFrance, Michelle. 2015. Research Methods in Rhetoric and Writing [Syllabus]. Department of English, George Mason University, Fairfax, VA.
Lorimer Leonard, Rebecca. n.d. Introduction to Research on Writing [Syllabus]. Department of English, University of Massachusetts, Amherst.
Perryman-Clark, Staci M. 2021. "The Promises and Perils of Higher Education: Our Discipline's Commitment to Diversity, Equity, and Linguistic Justice." CCCC National Council of Teachers of English. https://cccc.ncte.org/cccc/call-2022.
Rhetorical Critical Research Methods [Syllabus]. n.d. Department of English, University of Nevada at Las Vegas.
Ruiz, Iris D. (host). 2022. "The *Funky Dope Podcast* Episode 1: Dr. Raúl Sánchez" [audio podcast episode]. January 11. In *PodBean.* https://www.podbean.com/media/share/pb-g354f-1178197?utm_campaign=i_share_ep&utm_medium=dlink&utm_source=i_share.
Teston, Christa. 2021. Research Methods [Syllabus]. Department of English, The Ohio State University, Columbus.

AFTERWORD

Rita Malenczyk

During my entire career as a writing program administrator (WPA)—twenty-five years at this writing—I've worked on the same campus, Eastern Connecticut State University, which is part of a four-campus system governed by a contract between the Board of Regents and our faculty union, CSU-AAUP. As a union member, I have a very particular view about how faculty work in general and WPA work in particular is valued, a view that might be uncommon at best and skewed at worst. For example, on our campus, promotion and tenure (P&T) processes are very clearly spelled out in our union contract as well as by the University Senate, which has issued a bill that lists in exhaustive fashion the kinds of things that count for promotion and tenure under each of the four categories in our contract: teaching and other load credit activity, creative and scholarly activity, service to the department and the university, and other professional activity. Having chaired my department's tenure and promotion committee several times and the University Promotion and Tenure Committee once, I can say with some certainty that the guidelines in the senate bill are taken very seriously, in part because not doing so can lead to a grievance. However, the extent to which they are followed, for whatever reason, might restore some people's faith in faculty and administrators' ability to do the right thing.

This is true except perhaps in the case of writing program administration, which falls under the first category; it's the "other load credit activity" in "teaching and other load credit activity." Because I receive reassigned time as WPA, my administrative activities fall into that category; they are most emphatically not "service," as they are on some campuses (see, for example, Robinson, chapter 8, this volume). However, it's up to WPAs and other faculty members with reassigned time to articulate what they do with that time. This could be an unfortunate situation if the committees and administrators involved in the P&T process find the articulation unconvincing; I, however, have a description of duties contained in my department's bylaws that I always included in my review, tenure, and promotion materials and which almost certainly lent my work an aura of legitimacy it may not have had if I'd had to rely solely on my own record keeping. The description of duties was fairly skeletal, though, so I did have to amplify by adding the particulars of WPA work I did. Since I'm now a tenured full professor, my description of my work obviously went over well with those at the different stages of the promotion and tenure process. In other words, I managed to make my work visible—despite the occasional suggestion by one disgruntled member of my department that I "get all this free time." (Let's not even go there.)

My experience of how WPA work is valued on a campus is therefore not necessarily generalizable (though, I think, interesting). As I see it, there are three themes about visibility running through the chapters in this book:

- Making WPA work visible to stakeholders within the institution
- Making WPA work visible to the field
- Making WPA work visible to yourself

MAKING WPA WORK VISIBLE TO STAKEHOLDERS WITHIN THE INSTITUTION

Perhaps the most cited work in this collection is Melissa Ianetta's keynote address at the 2015 Council of Writing Program Administrators (CWPA) conference in Normal. In that address, Ianetta convincingly uses the CV as a way of showing how invisible WPA work is if said WPA follows the form of the academic vita rather than the form of the administrative vita. The administrative vita—which emphasizes administrative accomplishments right at the top, before publications and teaching—might better showcase the types of work WPAs actually spend most of their time doing: getting grants, developing programs and curricula, educating faculty about the teaching of writing, educating and supervising tutors; the list goes on (Ianetta 2015). However, while one could change the form of one's vita to fit one's work and emphasize what one wants to emphasize when, say, applying for jobs, it is still difficult to overcome reader bias when doing so: most readers have certain genre expectations that dominate their reading of CVs, so most people, then, play it safe and stick with the traditional academic form. Within institutions, it's perhaps even more difficult to move away from that form; for instance, many faculty who comprise university promotion and tenure committees have a bias against administrative work—sort of an "us versus them" thing. It's even more important, then, to represent one's work in a form they can relate to. Lilian Mina (chapter 7, this volume) shows in convincing detail how WPAs working with faculty might encourage relatedness outside of P&T procedures by joining and leading them in university-mandated efforts such as assessment; such efforts are important and meaningful for WPAs' relationships with both faculty and the rest of the institution. However, my own experience notwithstanding, matters of representation still complicate and even negatively affect the way WPA work is valued in high-stakes situations such as promotion and tenure decisions. In describing her experiences at CUNY, Heather M. Robinson (chapter 8, this volume) emphasizes these complications, showing how describing WPA work is still a fraught task, particularly when that work is considered "service."

MAKING WPA WORK VISIBLE TO THE FIELD

As chapters in this volume show, even our own field has some work to do. Kristine Johnson (chapter 2) demonstrates how *WPA: Writing Program Administration*, the journal of the CWPA, privileges some types of work over others, often rendering that "other" work invisible. This is particularly true when, as Jill Gladstein (chapter 3, this volume) describes, certain types of institutions—for example, small liberal arts colleges, community colleges—may not have a designated WPA doing the type of work described in the pages of the journal and the program of the annual CWPA conference. The National Census of Writing, which Gladstein largely developed and administered, revealed that sites of writing and writing administration do not necessarily correspond with those described in our dominant professional conversations. As Gladstein notes, "An institution may have a writing requirement or a set of elective writing courses, but nothing on the campus has the label 'program' or the resources associated with such an entity. In addition, several people who work in a writing center responded negatively to the [census] because they assumed we only wanted to inquire about curricular-based sites of writing, which they associated with the term *WPA*." The way the journal and the conference have wound up creating a space for some types of administrative work has, in the minds of many, excluded others, including writing center directors (though it could be argued that the International Writing Centers Association and the *Writing Center Journal* have if not a monopoly on representing such work, then at least a venue for doing so).

MAKING WPA WORK VISIBLE TO YOURSELF

In a hopeful turn, Kristi Murray Costello and Kate Navickas (chapter 5) describe how attending to the emotional aspects of WPA work through self-dialogue and other strategies can make that work visible to WPAs themselves and can also contribute to the field in a range of ways, for example, enriching graduate preparation for WPA work, helping institutions develop job descriptions for new hires "that name and support new hires in all dimensions of the work," and adding new dimensions to our disciplinary conversations—publications and conference presentations—about WPAs and what they do. Murray Costello and Navickas also note that such strategies, as well as being institutionally and disciplinarily beneficial, can help individual WPAs acknowledge and better handle the emotional labor that necessarily goes along with any part of the job.

So, where might we go from here? My own takeaway from this volume is that we still have a lot of work to do. Reading these chapters has shown me, as I suggested at the beginning of this afterword, how my own view of WPA work and how it is valued has been affected not only by the comparatively positive experience I've had at my own institution but also by the disciplinary conversations I've been privy to and contributed to as well. As president of the Council of Writing Program Administrators for two years, I was responsible for the programs of two national CWPA conferences, and I'm well aware of how my own biases of what constitutes WPA work were brought to bear on what was included in those programs and discussed in the rooms and halls of the conference venues.

Nevertheless, this volume has shown us a way forward. We can find data-driven ways of documenting the types of work WPAs do; we can develop strategies for documenting that work for others; we can find ways of articulating that work for ourselves. In doing so, we can bring greater depth and fairness to our professional publications and conversations and broaden the term *WPA* to include more of those who do the work of maintaining and developing the sites of writing (to use Gladstein's term) to which we have dedicated our time and—not to put too fine a point on it—our lives.

REFERENCE

Ianetta, Melissa. 2015. "Absence and Action: Making Visible WPA Work." *WPA: Writing Program Administration* 38 (2): 141–158.

INDEX

academia. *See* higher education
academic advising: gender/racial imbalance of advisors, 136; invisibility, 33, 140, 145; mentoring, 76; time tracking, 111*t*, 136, 137*t*; workload, 39, 138, 141, 146, 207, 208
academic career persistence, 27, 28, 30
academic discourse, 6, 10, 15, 58, 59, 91, 257, 262, 267*t*
"academic housework," 11, 12, 136, 138, 140, 141, 143
academic labor, 132, 133, 135
academic language conventions and standards, 17, 32, 116, 254, 256, 257*t*, 261, 263
academic scholarship. *See* scholarship
acceptable practices in research, 20, 35, 266, 271
accountability: advocacy, 5; boss texts, 208; email practices, 158; race and labor practices, 36; time and labor output, 10
accreditation, 128, 164, 194–95
Action Working Group of the Standing Committee against Racism and Bias in the Teaching of English, 36*n8*
action-research method, 92, 100–102, 203
activism, 5, 10, 14, 17–19, 50, 51*t*, 234, 238, 254, 259
Adams Wooten, Courtney, 97, 102
adjunct faculty: community colleges, 16, 230–31, 234; peer advocacy, 236–37; professional development, 237; writing programs, 189–91
Adler-Kassner, Linda, 7–8, 10, 50, 110, 120, 122, 123, 127, 130
administrative labor: community colleges, 230–31; email volume, 12–13, 154–56, 159–60, 190; faculty, 30, 34, 137*t*, 145, 166–67; first-year writing, 66, 67*f*; graduate students, 15, 102, 186–87, 266, 268; institutional contexts, 190, 193, 201, 208, 234; intellectual work, 11, 21; intrinsic motivation, 134–35; reappointment, tenure and promotion (RTP) committees, 27, 135–36, 139, 141–42;

reassigned time (adRT), 137–38; sites of writing, 66–68, 69*f*, 71; terminology, 74*n9*; time constraints, 96, 109, 116, 190, 223; use value, 11, 12, 134; visibility, 5–6, 13, 143–44, 267; workload, 13, 40, 236. *See also* writing program administration; writing program administrators (WPAs)
advising: gender/racial imbalance of advisors, 136; invisibility, 33, 39, 140, 145; mentoring, 76; multilingual writing program administrators (mWPAs), 207; time tracking, 111*t*, 136, 137*t*; workload, 39, 138, 141, 146, 208
advocacy work: antiracism, 18, 267; challenges, 4–6, 13, 14; community colleges, 231–35; detect-elect-connect, 17; grant writing, 44, 45*t*; job responsibilities, 74*n8*; mediation/negotiation, 234, 236; peer advocacy, 16, 236–37; research results, 237; scholarship, 7; scope of work, 44; self-advocacy, 6, 16, 235–36; social change, 232; tenure, 21; topic modeling, 41, 49–50, 51*t*, 52*f*; visibility, 238; *WPA Journal* topics, 43; writing program administrators (WPAs), 13, 32–33, 40–42, 53, 55, 237; writing center discipline coordinator (WCDC), 171–72
African Americans. *See* Black, Indigenous, and people of color (BIPOC)
African Diaspora Worldwide (ADW), 198
agency, activism, 7, 50, 51*t*, 55–56, 101, 257*t*
Ahmed, Sara, 91–93, 98, 167
algorithms. *See* topic modeling algorithms
American Association of Community Colleges, 230
American Indian/Alaska Native faculty, 28, 176, 233, 269
Andelora, Jeffrey, 234
Anderson, Brooke, 18, 178
Annals of Behavioral Medicine, 103*n2*
anonymity of research participants, 103*n3*; 131*n2*, 215*n3*, 239*n2*

282   INDEX

Anson, Chris M., 3
AntConc, 56n3
antiracism initiatives: advocacy, 5–6, 17–19, 176; assessments, 179–80; college campuses, 259; course material assessment, 261; critical narrative inquiry, 256; emotional labor, 253; European Writing Survey (EUWRIT), 260; feedback assessment, 261; institutional challenges, 261–62; interventions, 255; invisible labor, 6, 178; language conventions and standards, 257t; organizational commitment, 178–79; pedagogical changes, 18, 32–34, 203, 253–56, 258t; position statement, 36; reflective storytelling, 19; systemic institutional transformation, 22, 32–33; teaching observation, 261; theoretical framework method, 274; writing across the curriculum (WAC), 253–55, 256–57; writing programs, 192, 265
apprenticeships, 15, 186–87, 191, 201
Arbery, Ahmaud, 36n2
Arksey, Hilary, 265–66
Artze-Vega, Isis, 226–27
Asian/Pacific Islander faculty, 28, 176, 197, 269
assessment as research, 11, 124t, 127–28, 130, 180
assessment. See portfolio assessment; programmatic assessment
assigning classes, 43, 45
attendance, writing programs, 187
authorship in scholarship, 20–22
autoethnographic methods, 13, 162–63, 186
axial coding, 95, 98

Babb, Jacob, 102
baccalaureate degrees, 61t
Balester, Valerie, 74n1
Ballif, Michelle, 74n10
Bastian, Heather, 120
Bauer, Dale M., 133
Bawarshi, Anis, 74n10
Beersma, Bianca, 130
big agency, 55–56
big data/data analytics, first-year writing, 64, 65t, 66t, 67f; research participants, 60, 61t, sites of writing, 68, 69f, survey design, 61–64; 70f; 272
Bird, Sharon, 133, 145
Blaauw-Hara, Mark, 5, 230, 231, 238
Black, Indigenous, and people of color (BIPOC): activism, 259; emotional labor, 175; faculty, 14, 28, 176, 197–98; personal experiences, 178; racial microaggressions, 175–76; students, 28; stereotypes, 35; workshops, 260
Blei, David, 56n1
blended writing instruction. See online/hybrid writing instruction
Bloom, Lynn, 76, 86
Boatright-Horowitz, Su L., 255
Borrowman, Shane, 142
boss texts, 204, 205, 208–11, 215n5
Bou Ayash, Nancy, 269, 270
Bousquet, Marc, 40, 162
Bowles, Bruce, Jr., 269
Bradbury-Huang, Hilary, 203
Brooks, Rayshard, 36n2
Bruffee, Kenneth, 39–40, 44, 45, 50
Brumberger, Eva, 159
Buchanan, NiCole T., 34, 35
budgets, 33, 63, 100, 116, 142–47, 154
Bullock, Richard, 92

Cahill, Ann J., 29
calendars, time usage, 8, 80, 86
Calhoon-Dillahunt, Carolyn, 231
campuses: awareness of on-campus writing programs, 110; racial incidents, 32, 36n3; racism denial, 255
Carter-Tod, Sheila, 6–7, 19, 36n6, 273, 274
case studies research, 121, 197, 200–201, 206, 274
Caswell, Nicole, 74n1, 92, 93
categorical time tracking, 115–17
causes of emotional labor, 97–98
Cavanaugh, Joseph, 226
Central Office of the General Counsel, 148n2
Charlton, Jonikka, 74n1
Charmaz, Kathy, 95, 96
Churchwell, André L., 179
Cicchino, Amy, 14–15, 274
classroom assessment theory and practice, 129–30
Clinnin, Kaitlin, 244–46, 248, 251n1
coding, 81, 273; axial, 95, 98; email practices, 153; grounded theory, 95; hour tracking, 109, 111t, 114–17, 118n1, 226, 272, 273; interview responses, 243–44; in vivo, 167; journaling, 95, 96; numeric reporters, 244; selective, 16–17; survey responses, 65, 233; testing/refining, 244; time tracking, 111
coherence validation, topic modeling, 56n3
cohort meetings, 192, 236, 256
collaboration, 131n1; authorship, 78; engagement, 245; faculty, 192; first-year

Index   283

writing administrative responsibilities, 67; K-12 school writing programs, 110; knowledge transfer, 247; partnerships, 188; professional development, 129; programmatic assessment, 19, 121, 122, 124*t*, 130; writing research, 81
collective mentoring, 77–78, 81, 82*t*, 83, 247
colleges and universities: advocacy, 51; antiracism, 259; diversity and inclusion, 179, 253; email culture, 157–58; liberal arts, 199–200, 205; National Census of Writing (NCW), 60, 61*t*; organizational identity, 164; predominantly white institution (PWI), 191, 192; racial incidents, 36*n3*; systemic invisible labor, 180; writing program administrators, 189–81. *See also* community colleges; higher education
collocates, 42–43, 56*n3*
co-mentoring, 76
committee assignments/meetings, 33, 63, 81, 82*t*, 88, 111*t*, 137*t*, 145, 146
Committee on the Status of Women in the Profession, 148*n3*
commodification of labor. *See* exchange value
Community College Research Center, 197
community colleges: advocacy work, 13, 231–35; compensation, 234, 235; composition courses, 230; data-driven research, 231; diversity, 197, 230; enrollment, 197, 233; faculty, 230–31; institutional context, 164–66, 234; invisible labor, 18; lack of scholarship on writing programs, 230–31, 237; local context, 196–97; National Census of Writing (NCW), 61*t*; rural/suburban/urban, 233; statewide multi-campuses, 234; writing instruction, 36*n4*; writing program administrators (WPAs), 13, 230–31, 234, 237
community learning, 6, 44, 45*t*, 55, 140, 192, 249–50
Community of Inquiry Framework, 219–20
Comp-Boss narrative, 192, 199–200
compensation, 13; academic exchange value, 132, 133; administrative labor, 12, 141, 162, 165, 188; community colleges, 234; faculty, 33, 166, 235–36; reassigned time, 141; service labor, 162; uncompensated labor, 12, 30, 141, 177; women, 135
composition studies, 93; adjunct faculty, 187, 190; community colleges, 230; graduate students, 186; journaling, 102*n2*; mentoring, 85, 186; professional development, 40, 44, 186; research, 266, 268, 269; tutors, 166; women, 217; writing program administrators (WPAs), 8, 44, 233
concordance. *See* corpus analysis
Condon, Frankie, 93, 254, 255
Condon, William, 129
Conference on College Composition and Communication (CCCC), 36*n8*, 99, 155, 237, 255
conferences, professional development, 6, 34, 53*t*, 64, 72, 74*n8*, 148, 174, 186–87, 213
connect moment, learning transfer, 242
Constantine, Madonna G., 175
contingent faculty, 16, 111, 112, 142, 192, 227
contracts, 215*n4*
corpus analysis, 41, 42, 56*n3*, 272
Cortés Lagos, Ana. *See* Lagos, Ana Cortés
Costello, Kristi Murray, 9, 280
Council of Writing Program Administrators (CWPA): administrative labor, 139; antiracism, 31, 179; community colleges, 231; demographics survey, 217; intellectual work, 8, 10, 11, 39, 117, 133, 134; Labor Resource Center, 55, 238; linguistic diversity, 31; membership diversity, 62; mentoring, 76; sites of writing, 71; visibility, 120; writing program administrators (WPAs), 74*n1*, 142
course content and design: antiracism, 261; online/hybrid writing instruction (OWI), 218, 223–26, 227, 228; proposals, 81
course offerings sections, management function, 45, 47*t*, 48*f*, 187
cover letters, assessment, 121, 122, 123, 124*t*, 126, 130
covert racism, 6; covert racialized structures, 28. *See also* microaggressions
COVID-19 pandemic, 4, 19, 22, 117, 152
Cox, Michelle, 215*n6*
Craib, Ian, 93
Craig, Collin Lamont, 31, 32, 35, 74*n1*, 176
Crapo Kim, Ruthanne. *See* Kim, Ruthanne Crapo
creative writing, 233, 261
credit, dual, 50, 51*t*
critical narrative inquiry, 256
Croom, Natasha N., 30
cross-comparative analysis research method, 267*t*
Crowley, Sharon, 66
Cultural Historical Activity Theory, 160
cultural structures, 17, 29

culture of email, 157–58
Cunningham, Jennifer, M., 15–16, 18
CUNY Board of Trustees Bylaws, 147–48
curriculum development: design, 39, 44, 55, 63, 203; diversity and inclusion, 180, 261–62; first-year writing, 65*t*; goals, 121, 128, 130, 180; intersection of race and writing, 31; pedagogical changes, 249; policies, 88; professional development, 49*t*; Professional Writing Certificate, 196–97; programmatic assessment, 122, 124–26, 130, 245; race-based revisions, 33; rhetoric and composition studies, 186; risk taking, 250; shifts in authority, 17; sites of writing, 60, 62; structures, 11, 60; Teaching-for-Transfer (TFT), 121–22, 130; writing-about-writing, 190; writing across the curriculum (WAC), 19, 51, 73; writing program administrators (WPAs), 187–88, 190, 210, 248
curriculum vitae, 139, 142, 278
Curry, Barbara, 13, 163, 164, 173

Dancy, T. Elon, 29
data analysis: advocacy work, 14; appointments, 27; big data, 55–56; coding, 243–44; demographic survey questions, 233; email, 152–53; memo writing, 95; mentorship activities, 82; promotions, 27; tenure, 27; thingification, 113; topic modeling, 56*n4*; website content, 41
data collection: administrative documents, 135–36; advocacy work, 14, 237; autoethnographic methods, 13; community colleges, 231, 232; email records, 12, 80–81, 152–53; full responses, 243–44; interview questions, 243; mentoring, 80–81; multilingual WPAs, 15; programmatic assessment, 122; qualitative approach, 232–33; qualitative coding, 81; semi-structured interviews, 16, 187, 188; survey questions, 232–33; time-use diaries, 10, 136–38; topic modeling, 41–44; website analysis, 187
data-driven methods: community colleges, 231; inequity, 19; race considerations, 27
data-informed advocacy, 267
Davila, Bethany, 32
Davis, Angela Yvonne, 181
Davis, James Earl, 29
DeGruy, Joy, 177
demographics, 16, 60, 176, 187, 188, 219*t*, 232, 233
DePaola, Tom, 22

departments, colleges, organization, 140, 146–48, 165*f*, 166*f*, 167, 234
descriptive/document analysis, 272, routine responsibilities, 138–40, 146–48; time-use diaries, 136, 137*t*, 138, 145
detect-elect-connect, 17, 240–44, 246–48, 251
development function, topic modeling, 47, 49*t*, 50*f*, 51, 53, 55. *See also* professional development
developmental composition courses, 230
Dilger, Bradley, 268
Dippre, Ryan J., 10, 11, 19, 178, 272
directed self-placement process, 79
disciplinary narratives: advocacy, 7, 16, 18; antiracism, 258*t*; best practices, 192; coordinators, 166, 167, 169*f*, 170, 173; emotional labor, 91–94; professional development, 49*t*; racial bias, 35; scholarship, 5; status, 100–101; writing workshops, 194–95
discourse, academic community, 6, 10, 15, 58, 59, 91, 257, 262, 267*t*
discrimination, 29, 36*n1*, 177
discussion forums, hybrid/online writing instruction (OWI), 218, 223–25
distance education. *See* hybrid writing instruction; online writing instruction (OWI)
diverse logics and rhetoric, 34
diversity and inclusion: administrative labor, 5, 27, 28, 59, 207; advocacy, 177, 254; appropriation, 253; committee assignments, 33; curriculum, 180, 181; epistemological inclusion, 6, 34–35; faculty of color (FOC), 6, 7, 14, 28, 30, 176; higher education, 7, 179, 197, 207, 230–31, 236, 253; initiatives, 7; institutional contexts, 200; language standards, 8, 17, 31, 32, 59, 116, 254, 257*t*, 260, 263; mentoring, 9; performative speech acts, 167–68; professional organizations, 62; scholarship, 33; sites of writing, 20, 71, 27; students, 254; writer assessment, 31, 59–60
doctoral degrees/universities, 28, 61*t*, 233, 269
documentation, email, 81, 151, 157–59
Dotson, Kristie, 34, 35
dual credit, 50, 51*t*
Durkheim, Émile, 209, 215*n4*
Dutkiewicz, Keri, 227

Eaton, Angela, 221–22
Eble, Michelle F., 77, 86
ecologies. *See* writing programs

Index   285

economic labor, 33
education reforms in higher education, 79–80, 83, 84, 85
educational work, 39–40, 233
Edwards, Kirsten T., 29
Einarsdóttir, Þorgerður, 140
Elbow, Peter, 93, 94
Elder, Cristyn L., 32, 186
elect, 248; prior knowledge, 242, 243; step, 248, 250
elective writing coursework, 67–70
email practices, 87; coding, 153; data collection, 80–81, 152–54; documentation, 151, 158–59; emotional labor, 151; higher education, 160; invisible labor, 151; journaling, 153; management systems, 152–53; organization, 158–59; quantity/patterns, 12, 153–57, 159; racial microaggressions, 177–78; responsive workplaces, 159; taglines, 157–59; time usages, 156–57; workload, 159–60; writing program administrators (WPAs), 12–13, 155, 190
EmailAnalytics, 153, 156, 157
emerging scholarship, 242, 247, 251, 265
Emmons, Kimberly, 8–9
emotional labor: administrative labor, 12, 97; antiracism, 253; causes, 96–98, 100; collective/individual, 91, 93; cultural acceptability, 175; disciplinary narratives, 100, 101; email, 151; epistemological exclusion, 34; faculty, 67, 137t; graduate students, 102; institutional contexts, 91, 101; invisible, 29; journaling, 94–96; mentoring, 82, 87; navigation, 92; racial battle fatigue, 36nr; scholarship, 91; self-control, 93; self-dialogue, 92, 102, 103$n3$; shared, 91; stability, 93; writing program administrators (WPAs), 39, 58, 92–94, 99
empirical methodologies: language and rhetoric research, 269–70; programmatic assessment, 128, 129f
empowerment, writing program members, 78
Engels, Friedrich, 132, 133
English departments, 58, 79, 135–36, 165f, 166f
Enos, Theresa, 142
enrollment trends, 4, 164, 197
epistemological exclusion/inclusion, 6, 29, 33, 34, 35, 36$n7$, 242
e-portfolios, assessment, 126–27
equitable representation in scholarship, 20–22
ESL writing, 44, 45t, 55, 79, 233

ethical and rhetorical action, 50
ethnography, 204, 206
ethnomethodology, 109, 112, 178, 273; coding, 111; daily tactics, 115–17; hour tracking, 109, 111t, 272; hybrid/online writing instruction, 226; invisible labor, 118nr; program administration, 114, 115f
European Writing Survey (EUWRIT), 260
Evaluating the Intellectual Work of Writing Administration, 39, 53, 55, 134
evaluation metrics, administrative labor, 12, 142
event planning, 63
exam proctors, 140, 146
exchange value: administrative labor, 19, 59, 132–35, 139, 141, 145; intellectual work, 133, 134; invisible labor, 148nr; promotion, 133, 134; scholarship, 134; time-use diaries, 136–38, 148$n3$; visibility, 11, 12
exigent research, 240, 241
explanatory sequential design, 274; content, 153–54; methods, 152–53; quantity, 154–55; 274
explicit sites of writing, 63, 66, 67, 72
external representation of writing programs, 20
extrinsic motivation, 135

faculty: adjunct, 189; administrative labor, 135, 137t, 138, 141, 142, 145, 166–67; advising, 137; collaboration, 192, 247, 145; compensation, 135, 141, 166, 235–36; contingent, 16, 142; conversations on race, 259–60; curricular changes, 249; demographics, 176; leadership roles, 164–65; non-writing, 80; pedagogical changes, 249; professional development, 39, 44, 70, 190, 198, 240, 242, 249, 250, 251; promotion, 139; reappointments, 139; retention, 33; routine responsibilities, 80–81, 139–41, 146–47; scholarly uptake, 139, 145, 251; tenure, 138–39; time-use diaries, 132, 135–36; turnover rate, 192; use value, 230–31, 234; women, 148$n3$
faculty of color (FOC): appointments, 27; challenges, 29, 31–32; committee assignments, 30, 33; compensation, 33, 135; credibility, 34; discrimination, 29; diversity and inclusion, 28, 30, 176; epistemological exclusion, 29; exchange value, 133; higher education, 27; Hispanic students, 28; internalized stress, 30; invisible labor, 27, 29, 33; promotions, 27, 30, 34; race scholar-

ship, 34; research censorship, 29; sabbaticals, 30; scholarship, 29, 33, 34; tenure, 27, 30
feedback assessment, 225, 261
field scholarship, 59, 243, 245, 247, 248
First Seminars, 79
first-year writing: administrative labor, 66, 67f, 68, 73, 189–91; curriculum goals, 60, 125; electives, 67–68, 70; email practices, 154, 155; emotional labor, 67; English departments, 58; first-year seminars, 64, 65t, 189; four-year institutions, 66t; Indigenous-serving institutions, 191–92; intellectual work, 67; National Census of Writing (NCW), 64–66; portfolio assessment, 198; requirements, 65–66; self-identity, 64; sites of writing, 63; teaching and learning, 130; writing across the curriculum (WAC), 58, 67
flexibility of schedules, hybrid/online writing instruction, 220–22, 226, 227
Floyd, George, 36n2
focus/follow-up groups research method, 142, 267t
formal metrics evaluation, 12
formal professional development designs, 245
formal/structural mentoring, 81, 82t, 83
Foundations of College Writing program, 79
four-year institutions. *See* colleges and universities; higher education
Fralix, Brandon, 74n2
framework: implementation, 164; institutionalization, 164; kairos, 241–43; mobilization, 164; sites of writing, 71; theoretical, 163–64
Freedom Is a Constant Struggle, 181
Freeman, John, 151
Freeman, Lee A., 218
freewriting, 93
full-time faculty positions, 28, 79
Funky Dope Podcast, 266

Gaillet, Lynée Lewis, 77, 86
Gallagher, Chris W., 120, 121, 129, 130
García de Müeller, Genevieve, 17, 19, 30, 34, 36n5, 253, 256–57, 259, 260, 265
Garcia, Claire, 30
Garcia, Gina Ann, 164
Garfinkel, Harold, 10, 109, 113
GenAdmin, 214n1
gender equality initiatives, 136, 140, 233
general education reforms, 79–80, 83, 84, 85

Genres in the disciplines, 18, 258t
George, Diana, 92
Gillam, Alice, 134
Gladstein, Jill, 8, 65t, 74n1, 74n5, 74n7
Glaser, Barney G., 95
Glau, Gregory R., 237
Goggin, Maureen Daly, 41, 54, 55, 268, 269
Goldstone, Andrew, 56n2
González, Caleb, 18
Google Form surveys, 163
government bureau/legislatures, 44, 49
graduate students: academic ecologies, 15; administrative labor, 15, 102; advising, 33; community colleges, 197; English departments, 79; mentoring, 21, 33; pedagogical development, 79; professional development, 15, 84; professional identity, 186; research projects, 185; rhetoric and composition studies, 186; teaching assistants, 49t, 79
graduate student writing program administrators (gWPAs), 15, 214n1; administrative labor, 185–87, 266, 268; institutional contexts, 200–201; apprenticeships, 186–87; institutional contexts, 187; limitations, 186; professional development, 186–87; published articles, 186–87; scheduling, 186; site-based studies, 187; teacher/tutor preparation, 186; visibility, 187; Writing Program Administrators–Graduate Organization (WPA-GO), 187
grand strategies, program development, 110
grant proprosals analysis research method, 267t
grant writing, 34, 44, 45t, 63
Graziano, Leigh, 136, 143
Griffith, Alison L., 209
grounded theory approach, 16, 95
Grutsch McKinney, Jackie, 74n1, 92, 93
Guerra, Juan C., 256

Halasek, Kay, 136, 143, 148n1
Harper, Kimberly C., 32
Harps-Logan, Yvette, 255
Harris, Jeannette, 98
Harris, Muriel, 264
hate crimes, 255
HBCUs. *See* historically Black colleges and universitites
Healy, Michael, 14–15
Heijstra, Thamar M., 140
Hesse, Douglas, D., 7, 40, 41, 43, 44, 45, 51
hierarchies in scholarship, 21

higher education: advocacy, 51*t*; antiracism and institutional transformation, 22, 32–33, 36, 253; budgets, 33, 100, 116, 143, 146, 147, 154, 165; community colleges, 230; COVID-19, impact on, 4, 22; diversity and inclusion, 7, 30, 207; email use, 160; enrollment trends, 4; faculty of color (FOC), 27; general education reforms, 79–80, 83, 84, 85; importance of writing programs, 87; institutional merges, 245; labor issues, 5; neoliberalism policies, 162; racism, 32, 255; sites of writing, 59; social problems, 35; systemic racism, 14, 175, 263; white dominant discourse, 34; writing instruction, 36*n4*
Hilliard, Lyra, 15–16
hiring, 63
Hispanic faculty, 28, 176
Hispanic-serving institutions (HSIs), 19, 164–66, 194–95, 197, 233, 269
historically Black colleges and universities (HBCUs), 19, 197–99, 233, 269
Hogan, Katie J., 133, 134, 162
Holder, LuAnne, 227
Hollenbeck, John R., 130
Hollinger, Andrew, 244–49
Holmstein, Victoria, 231
Horner, Bruce, 74*n1*, 133, 134, 140, 144
hostile campus climates, racism, 29
hour tracking, 109, 111*t*, 272, 273; coding, 111; daily tactics, 115–17; hybrid/online writing instruction, 226; invisible labor, 118*n1*; program administration, 114, 115*f*. *See also* time tracking/time-use diaries
human resources classifications, 204, 207, 209, 215*n5*
Hunston, Susan, 56*n3*
hybrid writing instruction. *See* online/hybrid writing instruction (OWI)

Ianetta, Melissa, 63, 74*n6*, 120, 120, 142, 144
identity politics in scholarship, 31
implementation, system change operations, 164
implicit/inherent mentoring, 82*t*, 83
improvement in teaching and learning, 122
in vivo coding, 167
inclusion. *See* diversity and inclusion
indexing, topic modeling, 41
Indigenous-serving remote universities, 191–92
individual labor, 250; advocacy, 6; emotional labor, 93; hybrid/online writing instruction, 217; mentoring, 77–78, 85*t*, 86, 247; sites of writing, 60; professional development, 77, 82*t*, 83
individualized racism, 14
inequity, data-driven research, 19
informal professional development designs, 245
informal/unplanned mentoring, 81, 82*t*, 83
information use, teaching function, 44, 45*t*
Inoue, Asao B., 31, 255
institutional contexts: academic journals, 41; advocacy, 51*t*, 237; antiracism, 32–33, 261–62; apprenticeships, 186; community colleges, 196–97, 234; diversity, 28–29; emotional labor, 91, 101, 175; exchange value, 134; goals, 60, 136; graduate students, 200–201; merges, 245; multilingual writing programs, 15, 206–209; narratives, 94, 101; non-performative speech acts, 167–68; outsider status, 192, 194; programmatic changes, 14, 35, 62, 246–50; racism, 14, 175, 177; sites of writing, 59, 74*n11*; writing program administrators (WPAs), 94, 132, 134, 185, 187, 188, 181, 192, 204, 232
Institutional Review Board (IRB), 123, 187, 239*n1*
institutionalization framework, 13, 163, 164
institutionalized racism, 14, 175, 177
instructors: evaluation, 55, 141; hybrid/online writing, 223–23, 226, 227; knowledge transfer, 246–48; professional development, 9, 241, 242; teaching function, 44, 45*t*
intellectual work: academic journals, 41, 53; administrative labor, 11, 21, 39, 58, 67, 130; exchange value, 133, 134; mentoring, 82, 87; programmatic assessment, 127–28; scholarship, 21, 53*t*; sites of writing, 64, 72; time and labor output, 10
intellectual/programmatic development, 85*t*
interaction, time tracking, 113
interdisciplinary approach, sites of writing, 71
intersectional identities, 6, 31, 32, 242
interventions, antiracism, 255
interview data, 185; 267*t*, 273; full responses datasets, 243; institutional context, 187; multilingual writing program administrators (mWPAs), 212–14, 215*n2*; noun-verb data sets, 243–44; semi-structured, 16, 123–24, 187, 188, 233

288   INDEX

intrinsic motivation, exchange value, 134–35
invisible labor: administrative labor, 18, 27, 40, 112, 142–44, 172; antiracism, 178; community colleges, 18; email, 151; economic labor, 33; epistemological exclusion, 34; exchange value, 148*n1*; faculty of color (FOC), 6, 7, 27, 29, 33; mentoring, 81, 87; multilingual writing program administrators (mWPAs), 207, 209, 211–12; online writing instruction (OWI), 18; ontological labor, 29–30; programmatic assessment, 18; race-based scholarship, 31, 33; racial battle fatigue, 29, 33, 36*n1*; service labor, 162; systemic, 180; time and labor output, 10; time tracking, 10, 112
Iverson, Ellen R., 129

Jablonski, Jeffrey, 212
Jackson, Rebecca, 74*n1*, 92, 93
Jacquart, Melissa, 29
job descriptions: administrative labor, 51, 73, 142–43; community colleges, 230–31; department chair, 147–48; multilingual writing program administrator (mWPA), 204, 208–11, 215*n5*; self-identity, 64; writing center discipline coordinator (WCDC), 167
job responsibilities: community colleges, 230–31; first-year writing instruction, 66, 67*f*; hybrid/online writing instruction, 217; mentoring, 86, 88; multilingual writing program administrator (mWPA), 204, 210, 215*n7*; research, 74*n8*, 265; routine responsibilities, 139–41; sites of writing, 63; writing center discipline coordinator (WCDC), 167–68, 169*f*; writing program administrator (WPA), 40, 53*t*, 55, 79, 234, 235, 243, 246
Johnson, Kristine, 7
Jones, Martinque K., 34, 35
journal articles, scholarship, 20
Journal of Blacks in Higher Education, 36*n3*
journaling: benefits, 102*n1*; coding, 96; email practices, 153; emotional labor, 94–95; making plans, 96; memo writing, 96; mental health, 103*n2*; open coding, 95; pedagogy, 102*n1*; professional development, 102*n1*; reflecting on the process, 96–97, 99–101; self-advocacy, 6; self-dialogue, 93–95, 97–98; sorting journal entries, 95, 98, 100; staying with emotions, 95–96, 98, 100; themes, 100; trauma, 103*n2*; writing studies, 36*n5*
junior writing program administrators (jWPAs), 109, 214*n1*

K-12 schools: writing program collaboration, 110
Kahn, Seth, 22, 251
kairos: detect-elect-connect, 241–43; 251; instructor uptake, 240–41; knowledge transfer, 244–48; macro-kairos, 17, 244, 248, 250; micro-kairos, 17, 245, 250; qualitative methods, 270; racial unrest, 29
Kei Matsuda, Paul, 212
Kendi, Ibram X., 180
key terms in topic modeling, 7, 41, 121
Kezar, Adrianna, 164
Kim, Ruthanne Crapo, 29
Kirsch, Gesa, 94, 95
Klausman, Jeffrey, 231, 234
knowledge of mediation, 242
knowledge transfer, 125; collaboration, 247; connect moment, 242; detect moment, 246–48; dispositions and attitudes toward learning and change, 242; epistemological concerns, 242; exigent research, 240; field scholarship, 250–51, 266–67; instructional practices, 250; intersectional identities, 242; local context, 242; material conditions, 242; new knowledge, 247; orientations to collective, 242; prior knowledge, 247; professional development, 243, 250; representation, 242; social dynamics, 242; teaching function, 44, 45*t*; writing programs, 80, 240–41, 244–46; writing-about-writing (WAW), 247
knowledge transformation, 128, 241, 247, 248
knowledge value, 36*n7*
Kumari, Ashanka, 269
Kuvaeva, Alexandra, 136, 138
Kynard, Carmen, 18, 254

labor issues: accountability, 36; faculty of color (FOC), 27; first-year writing instructors, 60; higher education, 5; writing program administrators (WPAs), 191
labor logs: in vivo coding, 167; time usage, 163*f*; writing center discipline coordinator (WCDC), 168–71
labor resources, sites of writing, 74*n12*
LaFrance, Michelle, 209, 269
Lagos, Ana Cortés, 17, 19, 253, 265

Lancaster, Sonya, 120
Landmark Essays in Writing Program Administration, 74n6
language and rhetoric research, 269–70
language conventions and standards, 17, 31, 256, 257t, 260–61
Latent Dirichlet Allocation (LDA) algorithm: advocacy function, 49–50, 51t, 52f; collocates, 42, 43f; development function, 47, 49t, 50f; management function: 45, 47t, 48f; teaching function, 44, 45t, 46f; writing program administration topics, 51, 53t, 54f
Latinx students, 34, 165
Lauer, Claire, 159
leadership roles: English department, 165f, 166f; faculty, 164–65; program assessments, 121, 130; sites of writing, 72; writing program administrators (WPAs), 53t, 72, 244, 246, 249; writing tutors, 166–67
learning center faculty, 63, 66, 73
learning management system, 190, 218, 228
learning transfer, connect moment, 242
Lebduska, Lisa, 74n5
Leonard, Rebecca Lorimer, 269
Lerner, Delia, 256
liberal arts universities. *See* colleges and universities
literacy instruction, teaching function, 7, 44, 45t
literature review, 273
literature studies, 217, 233
Litt, Jacquelyn S., 133
local context. *See* institutional context
local racial unrest, 27, 29, 35
Loftus, Dennis, 13, 173
Lorenz, Taylor, 156
Lowery, Lillian M., 13, 173
Lutgendorf, Susan, 103n2

macro-aggressions, 36n1
macro-kairos, 17, 245, 248, 250
Mailstrom, 152–53, 155–56, 158
making plans, self-dialogue, 96
Malamud, Randy, 151, 158
Malenczyk, Rita, 62, 73n1
management function, 51, 53, 55; scope of work, 43; topic modeling, 41, 43, 45, 47t, 48f; *WPA Journal* articles, 43, 50
Manduca, Cathryn A., 129
mapping fields of study, 266
mapping key concepts in research work, 265–68
marginalized groups: classrooms, 254; epistemic exclusion, 34; faculty of color (FOC), 7; language conventions and standards, 256; oppressive norms and behaviors, 29; scholarship, 21
Marraccini, Marisa, 255
Martinez Alemán, Ana, 133
Marxist theoretical framework, 132–36, 274. *See also* exchange value
Master's degree, 61t, 233
material conditions. 17, 242
Matthew, Patricia, 30
McBeth, Mark, 128
McCormack, Tim, 128
McDade, Tony, 36n2
McDonald, James C., 74n1
McGee, Sharon, 74n11
McKinney, Jackie Grutsch. *See* Grutsch McKinney, Jackie
McLeod, Susan H., 74n1, 236
Mechenbier, Mahli, 227
meetings, writing center discipline coordinator (WCDC), 169f
membership, Council of Writing Program Administrators (CWPA): diversity, 62
memo writing, 95, 96
Memorandum of Evaluation (MOE), 139
mental health, journaling, 103n2
mentoring, 8, 63, 82t; administrative labor, 169t; benefits, 76, 86; collective, 77–78, 81–82; co-mentoring, 76; emotional labor, 82, 87; faculty, 29, 79, 137t, 145; gender/racial imbalance, 136; graduate students, 21, 33; individual labor, 77–78, 247; intellectual work, 82, 87; job responsibilities, 88; multidirectional relationships, 78, 86, 87; mutual discovery process, 77; one-on-one, 81; orientations, 80–81; professional development, 9, 76, 78, 88; program development, 77, 86; research, 80–81; responsibilities, 86; rhetoric and composition studies, 85, 186; social/interpersonal development, 85t; storytelling, 77, 88; students, 137; teaching labor, 141; time usage, 80–83, 86, 88; tutors, 163f, 167; undergraduate students, 33; value, 89; workshops, 80–81
Micciche, Laura R., 55–56, 91, 92, 93, 94, 158
microaggressions, 175–78
micro-kairos, 17, 245, 250
micro-professional development, 240
Mikanovich, Troy, 15
military colleges, writing programs, 192–94
Miller, Carolyn, 241
Miller-Cochran, Susan, 136, 143
Mina, Lilian W., 11, 18, 19; 179–80

minority-serving institutions, 61*t*
Minter, Debbie, 77
mission statements, 15
Mitchell, Angela, 12–13, 177
mixed methods approach, 231, 264, 271, 274
mobilization, system change preparation, 164
multidirectional mentoring, 78, 86, 87
multi-discipline writing programs, 194–95
multilingual writing program administrators (mWPAs), 205: action research, 203; anonymity of research participants, 215*n*3; boss texts, 204, 208–11; conflicts, 207; Cox, Michelle M., 215*n*6; curricular design, 210; diversity, 207; ethnography, 206; HR classifications, 204, 207, 209, 215*n*5; institutional contexts, 204–209; international application evaluation, 205; invisible labor, 207, 209, 211–12; job responsibilities, 204, 208–11, 215*n*7; performance reviews, 204, 209; research interviews, 204, 212–14, 215*n*2; ruling relations, 206–8; standpoint, 208; terminology, 214*n*1; title changes, 204; workload, 204
multiple-choice survey questions, 232
multi-site research projects, 186
Murphy, Greer, 15
mutual discovery process, 77
Mutual Information Score, 56*n*3

Napolitano, Frank, 136, 143
narrative/storytelling/self-reflection, 53*t*, 85, 265, 273
National Census of Writing (NCW), 8, 19, 36*n*4; collaboration, 74*n*2; first-year writing, 64–68, 70; revisions, 71; self-identity, 70; sites of writing, 68–70; survey questions, 60, 61*t*, 63, 64, 74*n*3, 74*n*4; terminology, 59–60, 62
National Center for Education Statistics (NCES), 28, 176, 230
national racial unrest, 27, 29, 35
Native American. *See* American Indian/Alaska Native faculty
Navickas, Kate, 9
Neal, Michael, 14–15
negotiation: advocacy, 234, 236
neoliberalism policies, higher education, 93, 162
networks of sites of writing. *See* sites of writing
new curriculum, 49*t*
new knowledge, 242, 243, 247, 248
Newsome, Bree, 180

non-native speakers of English, 79
non-performative speech acts, 167–68
non-tenure track positions, 21, 99, 100, 101, 162, 217
norming sessions, 123, 126
norms, racially oppressive, 29
not-for-profit private colleges, 60–61
noun-verb clauses, 244
numeric reporting, 244
NVivo coding, 163
Nyunt, Gudrun, 136, 138

O'Malley, Lisa, 265–66
O'Meara, KerryAnn, 136, 138
O'Neill, Peggy, 122, 123, 127, 130
objectives and goals, writing programs, 122, 265
objectivity, topic modeling, 41
observations research method, 267*t*
Office of Institutional Effectiveness (OIE), 122, 124*t*, 131*n*1
on-campus events attendance, 139, 146
one-on-one interviews, 16, 232
online/hybrid writing instruction (OWI), 15–16, 18, 55; curricular design, 218, 223–26, 227; discussion forums, 218, 223–25; mentoring, 217; schedule flexibility, 220–22, 226, 227; student-instructor interaction, 218, 224–26; study participants, 218, 219*t*; survey questions, 16, 218, 227–28; teaching function, 44, 45*t*; time management, 218, 220–23
ontological labor, 29, 31–32
open coding, 16–17, 95, 243–44, 274
open-ended survey questions, 16, 232
open-house receptions, 140, 146
oppressive racial norms, 29
optimal keywords, 41
orientations, 80–81, 242
origins of emotional labor, 96
Ostman, Heather, 230
outcomes statement, 49*t*
outreach, 169*f*, 171
outsider status, institutional contexts, 192, 194
overt systematic racialized structures, 28–29
ownership, scholarship, 20–22

Palmeri, Jason, 102
papers, teaching function, 44, 45*t*
Park Hong, Cathy, 176
part-time lecturers, 79
pastoral care, time-use diaries, 138
patterns, email use, 156

Index   291

pedagogical research, 34; administrative labor, 39; antiracism, 18; changes, 128, 130, 180, 249, 255; genre-based, 18; journaling, 102*n1*; programmatic assessment, 125–26, 130; race-based, 32; teaching function, 44, 45*t*; writing program development, 79, 80
peer advocacy, 16, 236–37
peer-review timelines, 20
Pennebaker, James W., 103*n2*
percentage distribution, topic modeling, 56*n4*
performance reviews, 33, 35, 81, 88, 142, 204, 209, 215*n5*
Perkins, David N., 17, 240, 242, 243
Perryman-Clark, Staci M., 31, 32, 35, 74*n1*, 176, 180
personal development: invisible labor, 30, 188, 221; mentoring, 76, 88; self-identity, 234
perspicuous settings, 112
Peterson, Linda H., 217
Pétursdóttir, Gyða M., 140
physical invisible labor, 29, 39, 188, 253
Pinkert, Laurie, 74*n12*
placement, management function, 45, 47*t*
Poblete, Patti, 13–14, 19
polls research method, 267*t*
portfolio assessment, 42, 43*f*, 49*t*; assessment specialist, 127; benchmarks, 142, 179; committees, 88; cover letters, 121; first-year students, 198; rubric, 123; student writing, 83, 193; topic modeling, 42
Portland Resolution, 5, 8, 39, 53, 55
position descriptions, 15
predominantly white institution (PWI), 191, 192, 197, 198
pre-tenured writing program administrators (WPAs), 21
primary texts, topic modeling, 41
prior knowledge, 242, 243, 247, 248
problems, management function, 45, 47*t*
process, reflection, teaching function, 44, 45*t*
productivity, qualitative research, 5
professional development: advocacy, 16, 237; administrative labor, 168–69, 188; collaboration, 129; conferences, 34; designs, 242, 245; detect-elect-connect, 240–41; faculty, 70, 190, 237, 240, 250; field research, 244; graduate students, 15, 84, 186; grant applications/proposals, 34; individual, 77, 82*t*, 83; institutional and program structures, 245; instructor training, 9, 16, 129, 222–23;

job responsibilities, 74*n8*; journaling, 102*n1*; knowledge transfer, 243, 250; mentoring, 76, 78, 86, 88; models, 243; online writing instruction (OWI), 16; rhetoric and composition studies, 186; self-reflection, 126; training materials, 80–81; *WPA Journal* articles, 53*t*
professional identity, writing program administrators (WPAs), 15, 186, 208
Professional Writing Certificate, 196–97
program administration: hour tracking, 114, 115*f*; intersectionality, 32; mentorship relationships, 78; sites of writing administration, 70–73
program analysis research method, 267*t*
program development, 63; budgets, 142; collective mentoring, 78; curricular design, 39, 44, 245; exigent research, 241; faculty development, 44; grand strategies, 110; historical progression, 42; materials, 15; mentoring, 77, 85*t*, 86; narrative coherence, 85; policies, 88; programmatic shifts, 245; purposes, 78; storytelling, 78; statements, 87; strategies, 110–11; topic modeling, 41, 43–44, 47, 49*t*, 50*f*; textual production, 44; values, 78; *WPA Journal* topics, 43; writing program administration, 41
programmatic assessment, 39, 44; challenges, 246; classroom assessment theory and practice, 130; collaboration, 19, 121, 122, 124*t*, 130; curricular goals, 120, 122, 125, 245; data-gathering methods, 122; empirical research, 128; interview questions, 122; invisible labor, 18; knowledge transformation, 248; leadership roles, 121, 130; networking, 120; pedagogical practices, 125–26, 130; qualitative approach, 15; reflective writing, 126; research model, 55, 127–28, 130; scholarship, 11; semi-structured interviews, 123–24; teaching and learning, 128, 250; Teaching-for-Transfer (TFT), 121–22; visibility, 121, 128; student learning outcomes (SLOs), 121, 130
promotions, 11, 12, 19, 21, 27, 34, 35, 133–35, 139–40
Public Library of Science (PLOS), 20–21
public relations advocacy, 44, 49, 45*t*
publications, scholarship, 73*n1*, 73*n2*, 186–87, 235, 266

qualitative data collection, 5, 122, 264; case studies, 121, 197, 200–201, 206, 274; coding, 16–17, 81, 98, 243–44,

273, 274; cover letter readers, 121; demographics, 16; email practices, 12, 152–53; ethnomethodology, 109, 111, 112, 115–17, 178, 273; hour tracking, 109, 111*t*, 114–17, 118*n1*, 226, 272; in vivo, 167; interviews, 185, 187, 212–14, 215*n*2, 243–44, 267*t*, 273; journaling, 95, 96; literature review, 19, 273; narrative/ storytelling/self-reflection, 53*t*, 85, 265, 273; numeric reporting, 244; program assessment, 11; semi-structured interviews, 16, 123–24, 187, 188, 233; surveys, 49*t*, 61–64, 65*t*, 66*t*, 74*n3*, 74*n4*, 219–20, 227–28, 231–33, 267*t*, 273, 274

Quality Enhancement Plan (QEP), 194–95

quantitative data collection, 5, 122, 237, 264; big data/data analytics, 60, 61*t*, 62–64, 65*t*, 66*t*, 67*f*, 68, 69*f*, 70*f*, 272; corpus analysis, 41, 42, 272; descriptive/document analysis, 136, 137*t*, 138–40, 145–48, 272; email practices, 12, 153–56; hour tracking, 109, 111*t*, 114–17, 118*n1*, 226, 272, 273; one-on-one interviews, 16; open-ended survey questions, 16; portfolio cover letters, 121; topic modeling, 7, 41–44, 45*t*, 46*f*, 47*t*, 48*f*, 49*t*, 50*f*, 51*t*, 52*f*, 53*t*, 54*f*, 56*n1*, 56*n2*, 56*n3*, 56*n4*, 272

Quiroz, Pamela, 32

R software, 42

race: invisible labor, 31; labor practices, 36; pedagogy, 32; scholarship, 6, 27, 30, 33, 335

racial battle fatigue, 29, 33, 36*n1*

racial bias: academic scholarship, 7; administrative labor, 136; disciplinary practices, 35; epistemological exclusion, 35; intersectional hierarchies, 6, 32; language use in writing programs, 31; mentoring, 136; racialized structures, 6, 28–29; student advising, 136

racial unrest, 27, 29, 35

racially-just teaching practices, 255–56

racism: denial, 255; higher education, 255; incidents on college campuses, 32, 36*n3*; institutionalized, 177; language used in writing programs, 31; microaggressions, 29, 34, 175–78; non-performative speech acts, 167–68; social media, 255; stereotypes, 177; systemic, 181; trauma, 177

Raines, Helon Howell, 231

Rand, Erin J., 91

randomness: scoping studies, 266; topic modeling, 56*n2*

Rao, Leena, 156

reading pedagogies, 44, 45*t*, 55, 256

reappointment, tenure and promotion (RTP): academic housework, 140; administrative labor, 11, 12, 136, 139, 141, 145; curriculum vitae, 142; exchange value, 134, 136, 141, 145; extrinsic motivation, 135; service labor, 139, 140; tenure, 138–39; use value, 139–40

reassignment, 141

recommendation letters, 140, 146

reflecting on the process, 17, 19, 96–97, 99, 100–101, 121, 126, 253

Regaignon, Dara Rossman, 65*t*, 74*n1*, 74*n5*, 74*n7*

Reid, E. Shelley, 139, 142

Reiff, Mary Jo, 74*n10*

Reimagining Student Writing symposium and workshop, 257, 258

reiterative reflective writing, 121

reorganization of academic departments, 165*f*, 166*f*, 167

reports, 87

representation of work, 41, 242

research methods: acceptable practices, 266, 271; analytical frame, 93; autoethnography, 13, 162–63; case studies, 273, 274; coding, 243–44, 273, 274; corpus analysis, 272; disciplinary practices, 18; ethnomethodology, 273; explanatory sequential design, 274; grounded theory, 95; hour tracking, 273; interviews, 185, 204, 214*n2*, 243, 273; literature review, 273; multi-site, 186; narrative/ storytelling/self-reflection, 77, 265, 273; semi-structured interviews, 274; scoping and syllabi review, 265, 267*t*, 274; single-site, 185–86; study participants, 94, 136–38, 215*n3*, 243; survey and semi-structured interviews, 273, 274; topic modeling, 53, 272; visibility, 265, 267; *WPA Journal* articles, 266. *See also* mixed methods approach; qualitative data collection; quantitative data collection; theoretical frameworks

research work, 49*t*; advocacy, 237; community colleges, 231; critical imagination, 94; cross-disciplines, 240; emerging scholarship, 251, 265; epistemic exclusion, 34; hybrid/online writing instruction, 218, 219*t*, 227–28; job responsibilities, 74*n8*; knowledge sources, 83, 266–67; National Census of Writing (NCW) survey questions, 60–61; programmatic assessment model, 127–29; race consid-

Index   293

eration, 35; strategic contemplation, 94; transparency, 243
revision process, 59–60
rhetoric and composition studies. *See* composition studies
Rieman, Jan, 12–13, 177
Ritter, Kelly, 74n6, 92
Roberts, Laura, 156
Robinson, Heather M., 10, 11, 12, 19, 144, 177
Rose, Shirley K., 74n1, 217
routine responsibilities, writing program administrators (WPAs), 139–42, 146–47
Royster, Jaqueline Jones, 95
rubrics, programmatic assessment, 49t, 82t, 123, 130, 257t
Ruiz, Iris, 31, 36n5, 266
ruling relations, 206–208
rural community colleges, 233
Rutz, Carol, 129

sabbaticals, faculty of color (FOC), 30
Salisbury, Lauren E., 218, 226
Salomon, Gavriel, 17, 240, 242, 243
Sam, Cecile, 164
Sánchez, Raúl, 266, 267
Saur, Elizabeth, 102
Schaffer, Martha Wilson, 8–9
schedule flexibility, classes, 40, 43, 45, 63, 109, 186, 220–22, 226, 227
Schoen, Megan, 186
scholarship: advocacy, 7; agency, 55; authorship, 20, 21, 22; book-length projects, 20; censorship, 29; chapters, 20; collaborative, 21; community colleges, 230–31, 237; curricular development, 11, 248, 249; diversity initiatives, 7, 18, 21, 27, 31, 33–35, 36, 59–60, 254; emerging research, 247, 251, 265; emotional labor, 91; equitable representation, 20–22; exchange value, 134; faculty of color (FOC), 6, 21, 29; field scholarship, 243–46; 250, 266; intellectual work, 21; journals, 36n5, 41, 42, 53, 266; mentoring, 76; ownership, 20, 21, 22; production, 51; program assessment, 11; single-author journal articles, 20; systemic change, 7; threshold concepts, 247; transfer research, 93, 241, 247; workshops, 194–95; writing programs, 4, 43, 235, 241
Schouten, Maartje E., 130
scope of work: advocacy, 44; management function, 43; teaching function, 43
scoping studies: mapping fields of study, 266; randomized samples, 266;

research methods, 265, 267t; *WPA Journal*, 266
scores data, 49t
search engines, topic modeling, 41
selective coding analysis, 16–17, 243–44
self-advocacy, 16, 235–36
self-care, neoliberal approach, 93, 102
self-dialogue, 9; emotional labor, 92, 94, 102, 103n3; journaling, 93–95; reflecting on the process, 96–97, 99–101; sorting, 95, 98, 100; staying with emotions, 93, 94–96, 98, 100
self-identify, 59, 60, 61, 62, 64, 70
self-reflection, storytelling, 92, 96–97, 126, 265, 273
semi-structured interviews, 11, 16, 123–24; 187, 188, 233, 274
service labor: annual institutional reporting system, 136; compensation, 162; exchange value, 133, 139; faculty, 137t, 139, 145; gender/racial imbalance, 136; hierarchies, 33; mentoring, 141; reappointment, 139–41, 135, 136; routine responsibilities, 139–41, 146; uncompensated, 141
service-based scholarships, 34
Settles, Isis H., 34, 35
Sevenker, Justin Ross, 120
shared learning management system, 190
Sinclair, Christine, 160
single-site research projects, 185–87
sites of writing: administrative responsibilities, 66, 67f, 70–73; administrative structures, 68, 69f; curricular structures, 60; ecology, 74n10; embedded/explicit, 63, 66, 67, 72; first-year composition, 63, 66t, 67–68; inclusion, 71, 72; intellectual work, 64; interdisciplinary approach, 71; job responsibilities, 63; labor resources, 74n12; leadership, 72; networks, 68–69, 70f; terminology, 59, 71, 72
Skinnell, Ryan, 186
small liberal arts colleges, 61t
small-group professional development, 82t, 83
Smith, Dorothy E., 209
Smith, William A., 36n1
Sneath, Wayne D., 227
social/interpersonal development, 85t
social media, 255
solo compositionist FYC director, 191–92
Solo Sites of Writing Administrator, 66, 73
sorting, self-dialogue, 95, 98, 100
Spiegel, Cheri Lemieux, 5, 230, 231, 238
staffing, 40, 45, 47t, 141

Stark, Katelyn, 14–15
Statement on Racial Injustice and Systemic Racism, 179
statewide multi-campuses, community colleges, 234
statistical analysis, *WPA Journal* articles, 42–43
staying with emotions, self-dialogue, 93, 95–96, 98, 100
Steinþórsdóttir, Finnborg S., 140
Stenberg, Shari, 77
stereotypes, 34, 177
Stevens, Karl B., 223
Stewart, Mary K., 15–16
Stillman-Webb, Natalie, 15–16
storytelling, 51; collaborative authorship, 78; critical narrative inquiry, 256; mentoring, 77, 86, 88; narratives, 53*t*, 265, 273; reflective, 8, 9, 17, 19, 253; self-dialogue, 94; self-reflection, 265, 273; theory making, 94; writing across curriculum (WAC), 255; writing faculty, 78, 79, 84
strategic change, program development, 241
strategic planning, 142
strategies, program development, 110–11
Strickland, Donna, 45, 162
structural racism, 18, 31, 254
students: advising, 137*t*, 140, 141, 146; advocacy, 6; community colleges, 233; diversity and inclusion, 254; interaction, 44, 45*t*, 140, 224–26; mentoring, 137, open-house receptions, 140, 146; placement, 63; schedule flexibility, 221; student learning outcomes (SLOs), 121, 130; writing instruction, 28, 80, 83, 121, 130, 198, 225
study participants: anonymity, 131*n*2, 215*n*3, 239*n*2; hybrid/online writing instruction, 218, 219*t*; survey questions, 232–33; time-use diaries, 136–38
suburban community colleges, 198, 234
Sue, Derald Wing, 175
Sullivan, Patrick, 234
support structures, writing programs, 33, 60, 62
survey: coding responses, 233; community colleges, 231; Community of Inquiry Framework, 219–20; data collection, 49*t*, 267*t*; demographics, 217, 232, 233; first-year writing, 64, 65*t*, 66*t*, hybrid/online writing instruction, 218, 227–28; listservs, 232; multiple-choice, 232; National Census of Writing (NCW), 60–64, 68, 74*n*3, 74*n*4; one-on-one interviews, 232; open-ended, 232; participants, 60, 61*t*, 232–33; self-identity, 61, 62; semi-structured interviews, 233, 273, 274; survey design, 61–64
systemic racism, 6, 28–29, 32–33, 181, 263
systemic review method, 265
Szymanski, Natalie, 136, 143

tactics, 110, 115–16
Taczak, Kara, 96
taglines, emails, 157–59
Taylor, Breonna, 36*n*2
Taylor, Tim N., 231
teacher-scholar-activists, 234
teaching function: mentoring, 141; online learning, 15–16; scope of work, 43; sites of writing, 71; topic modeling, 41, 43, 44, 45*t*, 46*f*, 53, 55; *WPA Journal* articles, 43–45
teaching materials analysis research method, 267*t*
teaching faculty, 40, 42, 51, 242, 244, 247; administrative labor, 186; community colleges, 230–31; co-mentoring, 76; epistemological hierarchies, 33; first-year composition, 60; graduate assistants, 84; language use, 17; pedagogical practices, 126; professional development, 49*t*, 110; racially-just, 255–56; schedules, 220–22, 227; student development, 80; teaching observation, 140, 141, 146, 261
Teaching-for-Transfer (TFT) curriculum, 121–22, 124–25, 126
tenure, 19, 35; advocacy, 21; curricular shifts, 17; data analysis, 27; exchange value, 133, 134; extrinsic motivation, 135; faculty of color (FOC), 27, 30; negotiation, 21; reappointment, tenure and promotion (RTP) committees, 135, 138–39; revision, 21; statistics, 27; use value labor, 139–40; women, 217; writing program administrative positions, 11, 12, 36*n*4, 245
terminology: administrative positions, 74*n*9; discourse community, 58; diversity, 59–60; first-year writing, 65*t*, 66, 71; multilingual writing program administrators (mWPAs), 214*n*1; National Census of Writing (NCW), 59–60, 62; revision process, 59–60; sites of writing, 71, 72; writing program administration, 8, 58
Tesdell, Lee S., 218
testing, management function, 45, 47*t*
Teston, Christa, 266

textual analysis of scholarship and WPA statements research method, 56*n3*, 267*t*
textual production, 44
theme identification, topic modeling, 41
theoretical frameworks, 132–34, 163–64, 254–56, 267*t*, 274
theory and practice, 44, 45*t*
thingification, 274; antiracism, 178; ethnomethodology, 109; grand strategies, 110–11; interaction, 113; time tracking, 10, 114, 115*f*, 117, 118
Thornberg, Robert, 95, 96
threshold concepts, 247
time tracking/time-use diaries, 5, 9–10, 19, 132, 143; assemblages of objects, 113; coding, 111; commitments, 111*t*; conflicts/constraints, 109; daily tactics, 115–17; data collection, 135–36; email, 156–57; exchange value, 136–38, 148*n3*; hour tracking, 109; hybrid/online writing instruction, 218, 220–23; instructor training, 16, 226, 227; interaction, 113; invisible work, 112; labor logs, 163*f*; mentoring, 80–83, 86, 88; program administration, 114, 115*f*, student-instructor interaction, 224–26; thingification, 109; writing center discipline coordinator (WCDC), 168–71; writing program director (WPD), 84
Tinoco, Lizbett, 16, 18, 271
title changes, multilingual writing program administrators (mWPAs), 204
tokenism, 29, 34
Tokumitsu, Miya, 177
topic modeling algorithms, 7, 272; advocacy function, 41, 49–50, 51*t*, 52*f*; collocates, 42–43; corpus analysis, 41, 42, 56*n3*, 272; development function, 43–44, 47, 49*t*, 50*f*, 51; introduction, 56*nr*; Latent Dirichlet Allocation (LDA) algorithm, 42–43; management function, 41, 43, 45, 47*t*, 48*f*, 51; percentage distribution, 56*n4*; randomness, 56*n2*; teaching function, 41, 43, 44, 45*t*, 46*f*, 51; word probability distribution, 43*f*; writing program administrators (WPAs), 51, 53*t*, 54*f*
tracking time, 9–10, 111*t*, 159
traditional academic language conventions, 257*t*
traditional review method, 265
training. *See* professional development
transfer equivalency policies, 142
transfer research, 93, 241, 247, 251
transformation of academic language, 254

transparency, research participants, 243
trauma, 94; journaling, 103*n2*; racism, 177
Tremain, Lisa, 16, 270, 271
tribal two-year colleges, 233
Trimbur, John, 142
T-score, 56*n3*
turnover rate, faculty, 192
tutors, 49*t*, 63, 69, 163*f*, 166–67
two-year colleges. *See* community colleges
Two-Year-College English Association (TYCA), 230
TYCA listserv, 232

Ullrich, Philip, 103*n2*
uncompensated labor. *See* compensation
undergraduate education, 33, 74*n4*, 79, 131*n1*, 197
Underwood, Ted, 56*n2*
universities. *See* colleges and universities; higher education
uptake: 240, 241; and transfer, 240; and learning, 241; instructor, 241, 250; of knowledge, 241; scholarly, 251
use value, administrative labor, 11, 12, 134, 139–40

Vidali, Amy, 74*n1*
visibility: activism, 20; administrative labor, 12–13, 15, 267; advocacy, 238; assessment as research, 127–28, 180; curricular goals, 124–25; email work, 159–60; exchange value, 11, 12; faculty of color (FOC), 29; graduate students, 187; intellectual work, 10, 128–30; mentoring, 80, 86, 87; methods and methodologies, 18, 265, 267; programmatic assessments, 121, 124; professional development, 55; use value, 11, 12; writing program administration, 3, 116, 128, 231, 247

Wang, Yong, 133
Wardle, Elizabeth, 240, 241, 242, 245, 246
website analysis, data collection, 41, 60, 74, 187
Weisser, Christian, 74*n10*
Wenger, Étienne, 250
WGA-GO Anti-Racist Assessment Task Force, 36*n8*
whiteness in academia: antiracism, 253, 258*t*, 262; dominant discourse, 18, 32, 34, 254, 255; faculty, 176; language standards, 256; predominantly white institutions, 269; scholarship, 7; student enrollment, 197; white guilt, 18, 260; white privilege, 6, 255

Willett, Gudrun, 129
Williams, E.A., 120
women in higher education, 30, 133, 135, 140, 148*n*3, 197–99, 217, 218
word frequency, topic modeling: advocacy function, 49–50, 51*t*, 52*f*; development function, 47, 49*t*, 50*t*; management function, 45, 47*t*, 48*f*; portfolio assessment, 43*f*; teaching function, 44, 45*f*, 46*f*; writing program administration, 51, 53*t*, 54*f*
workload: email labor, 152, 155, 157, 160; faculty, 135, 137*t*, 138, 141; invisible labor, 34, 135; mentoring, 146; reorganization, 165; time and labor output, 9–10; 204; writing program administrators (WPAs), 13, 204, 236
workshops: antiracism, 18, 176, 258*t*; discipline-specific writing, 194–95; faculty, 80–81; mentoring, 82, 176; professional development, 49*t*, 88; writing programs, 187
Worley, Wanda L., 218
WPA listserv, 12, 18, 155, 232
WPA: Writing Program Administration, 7, 32; advocacy function articles, 49–50, 51*t*, 52*f*; article topics, 18, 19, 43, 53; corpus analysis, 41, 42, 56*n*3, 272; development function articles, 47, 49*t*, 50*f*, 51; management function articles, 45, 47*t*, 48*f*, 50, 51; scoping studies, 266, 267*t*; teaching function articles, 44, 45*t*, 51; text generation, 41, 42
writing across the curriculum (WAC): administrative labor, 66, 73, 187; advocacy, 51*t*; antiracism, 19, 254, 258*t*; assessments, 261; challenges, 259; critical narrative inquiry, 256; diversity and inclusion, 255–56, 263; first-year writing, 58, 67; importance, 83; institutional structures, 259; language conventions and standards, 257*t*, 260–61; research methods, 265; survey questions, 64; teaching observation, 261; WAC Faculty Fellows Initiative, 257, 261; writing in the disciplines (WID), 194–95
writing center directors (WCDs), 27, 63, 69–70, 79; advocacy, 171–72; administrative labor, 73, 187; colleges and universities, 192, 197–200; emotional labor, 92–93, 99; invisible labor, 172; job responsibilities, 13, 66, 162, 167, 169*f*; National Census on Writing (NCW), 60; professional development, 49*t*, 168–69; time usage, 163*f*;

168–71; writing in the discipline (WID), 194–95
writing in the disciplines (WID), 22, 98, 192, 194–95, 199
writing instruction, 49*t*, 256; colleges and universities, 36*n*4; online writing instruction (OWI), 15–16; professional development, 129; student development, 80
writing program administration: advocacy, 4, 7, 13, 32–33, 235, 237; big agency, 55–56; budgets, 142, 172, 173, 246; co-mentoring, 76; community colleges, 230–31; Comp-Boss narrative, 199–200; demographics survey, 217; educational work, 39–40; emotional labor, 103*n*3; inclusion/exclusion, 59; intellectual work, 39, 58, 130; job responsibilities, 40, 42, 53*t*, 55; leadership, 53*t*, 72; managerial labor, 7, 39; pedagogical labor, 39, 128; portfolio assessment, 42; professional identity, 51; program development, 41, 122; publications, 73*n*1, 73*n*2; racism, 31, 32; scholarly inquiry, 43; sites of writing, 8, 59; social labor, 133; terminology, 8, 58; theory into practice, 251; topic modeling, 51, 53*t*, 54*f*; visibility, 3, 128, 228, 247. *See also* administrative labor
writing program administrators (WPAs), 240, 249, 265; accountability, 36; antiracism, 36, 192, 265; apprenticeships, 15, 186, 191; compensation, 188, 187, 233; curriculum vitae, 139, 142, 278; emotional labor, 9, 10, 12, 18, 93–98, 100; exchange value, 11, 12, 19, 132–35, 139, 141, 148*n1*, 148*n*3, 162; gender/race imbalance, 27, 28, 136; graduate students, 179, 187; interview data, 243–44; invisible labor, 18, 40, 112, 142; job responsibilities, 40, 51, 73, 141–43, 221, 230–31, 234–35, 243, 246; knowledge transfer, 251; leadership roles, 246; mentoring, 18, 77–78, 81, 88; performance reviews, 142; professional development, 11, 186, 188, 196–97, 241, 242, 249–50; scholarship, 235, 251; self-dialogue, 92, 97–98; self-identity, 59, 60, 234; tenure, 11, 12, 21, 36*n*4, 245; time-use, 19, 109, 132; women, 217. *See also* administrative labor; writing program administration
writing programs: campus awareness, 110; colleges and universities, 230–31, 234; curricular development, 187–88, 190; external/inclusive representation, 20;

first-year composition, 58, 79; general education reforms, 79–80, 83–85; hybrid/online writing instruction, 226–27; institutional contexts, 11, 62, 185–88, 191, 192, 200–201, 245, 246; narrative coherence, 85; objectives and goals, 265; programmatic assessment, 120, 192; purpose of, 78; sites of writing, 74*n10*; storying, 84; values, 78, 80; workshops, 187. *See also* first-year writing; writing across the curriculum (WAC); writing in the disciplines (WID)

writing-about-writing (WAW) approach, 190, 241, 247

Yancey, Kathleen Blake, 142
Young, Vershawn A., 254

Zahneis, Megan, 22
Ziker, John, 136

ABOUT THE AUTHORS

CONTRIBUTORS

Kamila Albert is a PhD candidate in rhetoric and composition. Kamila's research interests include multimodal composition, design thinking, and writing center studies. She has held administrative positions as the Florida State University reading-writing center assistant director and digital studio coordinator.

Brooke Anderson has been a full-time writing faculty member at Pima Community College in Tucson, Arizona, since 2007, where she also serves as the writing center discipline coordinator and the Faculty Senate Board of Governors representative. In 2019, she became a PhD candidate in higher education at the University of Arizona. Her research interests include equitable, antiracist assessment practices and pedagogy; shared governance and program administration; faculty working conditions; and self-care–oriented pedagogical approaches.

Sheila Carter-Tod is executive director of writing and associate professor of English at the University of Denver. She has chaired the NCTE's Racism and Bias Committee and held leadership roles on CCC's and CWPA's executive boards. She has published works in *College Composition and Communication, Enculturation, Composition Studies, Journal of the Council of Writing Program Administrators*, and others. Her research/teaching/service/outreach focuses on writing program administration, race and rhetorics, composition theory, and writing pedagogy.

Amy Cicchino is associate director of the Center for Teaching and Learning Excellence at Embry-Riddle Aeronautical University, Daytona Beach. She specializes in digital multimodal pedagogy and writing program administration. Her work has been featured in *ePortfolio as Curriculum, WPA: Writing Program Administration*, the *International Journal of ePortfolio*, and *Research in Online Literacy Education (ROLE)*. She received her PhD from Florida State University in 2019.

Ana Cortés Lagos is an ABD in writing studies, rhetoric, and composition at Syracuse University. She is also associate editor of the Latin American section of the WAC Clearinghouse International Exchange series. She has taught courses on academic writing, research writing, literacy education, and writing across the K–12 curriculum. Her research focuses on transnational writing studies traditions, the geopolitics of knowledge making, WAC, and WID. Her work has been published in *Calidad en la Educación, Latinx Writing and Rhetoric Studies, Lenguas Modernas, Onomázein*, and the *Transnational Literature Journal*.

Jennifer M. Cunningham is associate professor of English and the writing program coordinator at Kent State University. Her teaching and scholarship focus on connections among digital literacies, linguistics, and online pedagogies. With an emphasis on online writing instruction and digital African American Language, her work has been published in *Written Communication, Computers and Composition*, the *Journal of Response to Writing*, and *Online Learning*.

ABOUT THE AUTHORS

Ryan J. Dippre is assistant professor of English and director of college composition at the University of Maine. His research interests include writing program administration and lifespan writing research. He is co-chair of the *Writing through the Lifespan Collaboration*. His co-edited collection (with Talinn Phillips), *Approaches to Lifespan Writing Research: Steps toward an Actionable Coherence*, is available through the WAC Clearinghouse. He lives with his wife and son in Bangor, Maine.

Kimberly Emmons is Oviatt Professor and associate professor of English at Case Western Reserve University, where she serves as the director of composition. Her research focuses on medical rhetoric, especially contemporary linguistic and rhetorical constructions of (mental) health and illness. Her writing studies scholarship has appeared in *Composition Studies*, *College Composition and Communication*, and various edited collections.

Genevieve García de Müeller is senior research analyst at the Institute of Higher Education Policy in Washington, DC. Her work focuses on WAC, antiracism, WPA, and policy studies. Her publications have included the coauthored "Inviting Students to Determine for Themselves What It Means to Write across the Disciplines" and "Race, Silence, and Writing Program Administration: A Qualitative Study of U.S. College Writing Programs." In 2020, she received an AAUW American Publication Grant for her manuscript *Shifting Landscapes: The Deliberative Rhetoric of Citizenship in U.S. Immigration Policy*. Her antiracist WAC program received the 2021 CCCC Writing Program Certificate of Excellence Award.

Jill Gladstein is a full teaching professor at the University of California at San Diego, where she created and directs the Synthesis Program. She co-founded the Small Liberal Arts College–Writing Program Administrators consortium and, with her collaborator Dara Rossman Regaignon, wrote *Writing Program Administration at Small Liberal Arts College*. Jill serves as co-investigator with Brandon Fralix on *The National Census of Writing*, an open-access database on the sites of writing at two- and four-year colleges and universities in the United States.

Caleb Lee González is a PhD student in rhetoric, composition, and literacy at The Ohio State University, where he teaches first-year composition and professional writing. In addition to his teaching, he is also assistant coordinator of OSU's writing center and associate director of the 2020–2021 International Writing across the Curriculum (IWAC) Conference. He researches the ways writing programs at Hispanic-serving institutions and regional comprehensive universities are shaped by their institutional ecologies. As a committed teacher-scholar, his interests are motivated by antiracist programmatic practices of higher education that support and sustain inclusion, equity, and social justice.

Michael Healy is a PhD candidate in rhetoric and composition at Florida State University, where he has held an administrative position as the Digital Studio coordinator. Michael's research interests are at the intersections of the digital humanities, techne, and disciplinary historiography.

Lyra Hilliard is coordinator of the Undergraduate Teaching Assistant Program in the Department of English, the blended and online learning coordinator of the Academic Writing Program, and senior lecturer in the Department of English at the University of Maryland, College Park. Her research areas include critical pedagogy, peer mentoring, collaborative learning, and hybrid and online writing instruction.

Kristine Johnson is associate professor of English at Calvin University, where she directs the university rhetoric program and teaches courses in composition pedagogy, linguistics, and first-year writing. Her interests include writing program administration, undergraduate research, and teacher preparation; her work has appeared in *WPA: Writing Program Administration, College Composition and Communication, Pedagogy, Composition Studies,* and various edited collections.

Seth Kahn is professor of English at West Chester University of Pennsylvania, where he teaches courses in writing and rhetoric, serves as a faculty union leader, and writes about academic labor organizing. Recent publications include "United against Sexual Harassment: Building Alliances between Unions and Title IX and VII Victim Advocates," with Erin Hurt (2019), and "We Value Teaching Too Much to Keep Devaluing It" (2020).

Rita Malenczyk is professor of English and director of the writing program and the writing center at Eastern Connecticut State University. Her publications include *A Rhetoric for Writing Program Administrators* (Parlor Press, 2016) and *Composition, Rhetoric, and Disciplinarity* (co-edited with Susan Miller-Cochran, Elizabeth Wardle, and Kathleen Blake Yancey; Utah State University Press, 2018). She is past president of the Council of Writing Program Administrators.

Troy Mikanovich is graduate writing coach for the USC Annenberg School for Communication and a PhD candidate in religion and political science at Claremont Graduate University. He holds an MA in religion, ethics, and social theory from the Graduate Theological Union and a BA in astrophysics from the University of California at Berkeley.

Lilian W. Mina is associate professor and director of composition at Auburn University at Montgomery. She researches digital rhetoric with a focus on multimodal composing and writing teachers' use of digital technologies. Her research also focuses on the intersection between multimodality and transfer of writing knowledge and practice. She is also interested in WPA scholarship, especially (technology) professional development of writing teachers, program assessment, and curriculum development. Her work has appeared in multiple journals and edited collections.

Angela Mitchell has been a WPA in some form or other for most of her career and is currently director of first-year writing at the University of North Carolina at Charlotte. Her other research interests include work on transfer and placement issues for first-year writing, as well as exploring feminist administrative perspectives and approaches in WPA work.

Greer Murphy is director of academic honesty for policy and education at the University of Rochester and former director of the International Scholars Program at Claremont Graduate University. Her research interests include multilingual writers, writing, and writing program administration; policy process; and institutional development and change. She teaches and holds second-degree black belt rank in Kyokushin karate, a full-contact fighting style of martial arts.

Kristi Murray Costello is associate chair of writing studies and associate professor of rhetoric, composition, and writing studies at Old Dominion University. She is editor of the collection *The Things We Carry: Strategies for Recognizing and Negotiating Emotional Labor in Writing Program Administration,* alongside Courtney Adams Wooten, Jacob Babb, and Kate Navickas. Kristi lives in Norfolk, Virginia, with her partner, Liam, and their adorable dog, Rafa (pictures available upon request).

Kate Navickas is director of the writing centers and a teacher in the Knight Institute for Writing in the Disciplines at Cornell University. She is editor of (along with Courtney Adams Wooten, Jacob Babb, and Kristi Murray Costello) and a contributor to *The Things We Carry: Strategies for Recognizing and Negotiating Emotional Labor in Writing Program*

Administration. Kate lives in Cortland, New York, surviving central New York winters with her husband, Adam, Boston terrier Olive, and three cats.

Michael Neal is associate professor of English at Florida State University, where he explores the intersections among composition, digital technologies, and writing assessment. He is the author of *Writing Assessment and the Revolution in Digital Texts and Technologies* and is working on a project of digital composing case studies. Neal directs the Rhetoric and Composition Program and participates in university undergraduate research initiatives. He also facilitates workshops on writing assessment, ePortfolios, digital composing, and intellectual property.

Patti Poblete (poh-BLEH-teh) is a tenure-track assistant professor of English and writing program administrator at Henderson State University. Previously, she was assistant director of Iowa State University's writing center. Patti was assistant registrar at La Sierra University, where she gazed into the seeming abyss of university administration. She has been teaching at the college level for seventeen years. Her research focuses on pedagogy, cultural criticism, and institutional rhetoric. Yes, this is Patti from Twitter.

Jan Rieman is a teaching professor and former WPA in the Department of Writing, Rhetoric, and Digital Studies at the University of North Carolina at Charlotte. She teaches courses in first-year writing, the rhetoric of place, and composition pedagogy. Her research focuses on trauma-informed writing pedagogies and writing program assessment. She is co-editor of *Next Steps for/in Writing about Writing*.

Heather M. Robinson is professor of English at York College/CUNY. Her research explores feminist academic administration and people's translingual and diasporic language identities and writing in postcolonial and urban educational and community contexts. Her coauthored book, *Translingual Identities and Translingual Realities in the U.S. College Classroom*, was published by Routledge Press (2020). Her research has also appeared in, for example, the *Journal of Basic Writing, Administrative Theory and Practice*, and *Teaching American Speech*.

Martha Wilson Schaffer is instructor in the Department of English at Case Western Reserve University, where she serves as associate director of composition and teaches first-year writing, rhetoric, and linguistics. Her current research explores how writing teachers can help novice writers evaluate their own writing and potential for growth into future writing projects and writing selves.

Katelyn Stark is a PhD candidate in rhetoric and composition and former program assistant for the College Composition Program at Florida State University. She specializes in writing transfer and writing program administration. She has held administrative, research, and teaching roles in writing across the curriculum and graduate teaching assistant practicums.

Mary K. Stewart is associate professor and the general education writing coordinator at California State University at San Marcos, where she teaches first-year writing and graduate-level composition pedagogy. Her qualitative and quantitative research explores collaborative and interactive learning, blended and online writing instruction, composition pedagogy, and teaching with technology.

Natalie Stillman-Webb is professor-lecturer and coordinator of online writing instruction in the Department of Writing and Rhetoric Studies at the University of Utah. Her research interests include online instructional design, community-engaged learning, and writing in the disciplines.

Lizbett Tinoco is assistant professor of English at Texas A&M University at San Antonio. Her research focuses on writing program administration, two-year college writing studies, and antiracist writing assessment. Her publications appear in the *Journal of Writing Assessment, Composition Forum, Peer Review*, and edited collections.

Lisa Tremain is director of the first-year composition program and assistant professor of writing practices at Humboldt State University. Her research considers writing knowledge development and transfer through ecological perspectives. She is examining the intersections among instructor development and uptake, writing program design and assessment, and student and faculty labor. She most recently authored or coauthored chapters for *Composition Forum* and for the collections *Next Steps: New Directions for/in Writing about Writing* (2019) and *(Re)Considering What We Know: Learning Thresholds in Writing, Composition, Rhetoric, and Literacy* (2020).

EDITORS

Leigh Graziano is associate professor of English and director of the first-year writing program at Western Oregon University. Her research includes the visibility of WPA labor, WAW and antiracism, dual enrollment, and assessment. Her work has appeared in the edited collections *Using Reflection and Metacognition to Improve Student Learning: Across Disciplines, Across the Academy; The Dual Enrollment Kaleidoscope: Reconfiguring Perceptions of First-Year Writing and Composition Studies; Beyond the Frontier: Innovations in First Year Composition: Volume 3*; and in the journal *WPA: Writing Program Administration.*

Kay Halasek is professor of English at The Ohio State University. Kay's research spans a range of topics within rhetoric and writing studies: feminist historiography, teaching writing at scale, collaborative learning, writing program administration, portfolio assessment, and basic writing. Her work has appeared in *College English, Composition Studies, Computers and Composition, Pedagogy, Rhetoric Review, WPA Journal,* and *Written Communication.* She is co-editor (with Nels Highberg) of *Landmark Essays on Basic Writing* and is the author of *A Pedagogy of Possibility: Bakhtinian Perspectives on Composition Studies,* which received the CCCC Outstanding Book Award.

Remi Hudgins is a PhD student in rhetoric, composition, and literacy at The Ohio State University, where she teaches first-year composition classes. Her primary research interests include technical communication, composition pedagogy, and accessibility. Through her research, she hopes to make higher education more accessible for students and faculty.

Susan Miller-Cochran is professor of English and executive director of general education at the University of Arizona. She served as director of the writing program from 2015 to 2019. Before joining the faculty at the University of Arizona, she served as director of first-year writing at North Carolina State University and as English/ESL faculty at Mesa Community College in Arizona. Her work has appeared in journals such as *College Composition and Communication, Computers and Composition,* and *WPA: Writing Program Administration.* She is co-editor of *Composition, Rhetoric, and Disciplinarity* (Utah State University Press, 2018), *Rhetorically Rethinking Usability* (Hampton, 2009), and *Strategies for Teaching First-Year Composition* (NCTE, 2002). She is also coauthor of *An Insider's Guide to Academic Writing* (Macmillan, 2019), *The Cengage Guide to Research* (Cengage, 2017), and *Keys for Writers* (Cengage, 2016). She is past president of the Council of Writing Program Administrators.

Frank Napolitano is associate professor of English at Radford University, where he coordinated the Graduate Teaching Fellows Mentoring Program for ten years. His primary teaching and research interests are rhetoric and composition studies, graduate student mentoring, writing program administration, and medieval English literature, especially drama. His work has appeared in *WPA: Writing Program Administration, Studies in Philology, Early Theatre,* and *The Medieval Disability Sourcebook* (Punctum, 2019). Other research interests include writing across the curriculum, the history of rhetoric, and mindfulness in teaching.

Natalie Syzmanski has a BA from the University of Wisconsin at LaCrosse and an MA and a PhD in rhetoric and composition from Florida State University. She worked as the WPA at the University of Hawaii at West Oahu and is currently director of the College Writing Program at Buffalo State College. Her current research examines the invisible labor of WPAs across different institutional and professional contexts; the interconnected and interdependent ecological systems WPAs regularly navigate; and the nonlinear, unconventional tenure processes on GenAdmin WPAs. She teaches courses in the College Writing Program as well as upper-level courses in writing and rhetoric.

www.ingramcontent.com/pod-product-compliance
Lightning Source LLC
Chambersburg PA
CBHW020517080526
44583CB00013B/633